Ubiquity
Photography's Multitudes

The Lieven Gevaert Series is a major series of substantial and innovative books on photography. Launched in 2004, the Series takes into account the ubiquitous presence of photography within modern culture and, in particular, the visual arts. At the forefront of contemporary thinking on photography, the books offer new insights on the position of the photographic medium within art historical, theoretical, social and institutional contexts. The Series is produced by the Lieven Gevaert Research Centre for Photography, Art and Visual Culture (www.lievengevaertcentre.be) and covers four types of approaches: publication of outstanding monographic studies, proceedings of international conferences, book length projects with artists, translations and republications of classic material. The Lieven Gevaert Series is published by Leuven University Press, and distributed in North America by Cornell University Press.

Series editors
Alexander Streitberger
Hilde Van Gelder

Lieven Gevaert Series vol. 31

Ubiquity
Photography's Multitudes

Edited by Jacob W. Lewis and Kyle Parry

Leuven University Press

Table of Contents

Introduction: Ubiquity Has a History

Jacob W. Lewis and Kyle Parry

Among the most widespread orthodoxies about photography concerns the intensity of its reach.[1] The notion is both simple and all-encompassing. With the rise of smartphones and social media, the feedback loop of taking and sharing photographs has reached an omnipresent fever pitch. With more photographs produced every two minutes than were produced in the entire 19th century—although this comparison is likely outdated—the institution of photography has begun to pervade every dimension of social and political life.[2] Whereas cameras and photos once enjoyed only partial distribution, now they enjoy a total distribution. In sum, or so this line of thinking goes, photography has become ubiquitous. It is everywhere, and it always will be.

In 2016, having arrived by different paths, we found ourselves living and working in a city suffused with and indeed haunted by histories of photographic distribution: Rochester, New York. Situated on the ancestral and unceded territory of the O-non-dowa-gah, the adopted home of the most photographed American in the 19th century, Frederick Douglass (Stauffer et al., 2015), Rochester underwent a massive, photography-driven transformation in the early 20th century. (fig. 0.1) Once the largest flour-producing city in the United States, by 1901 it had become the largest image-producing one, as the Eastman Kodak company had managed to turn the otherwise time-consuming practice of composing and developing analog photographs into a full-fledged industrial operation, first with the Kodak No. 1 camera, launched in 1888, then with the Brownie camera, which debuted in 1900 and sold for the price of one U.S. dollar. Both the icons and the engines of their operation, the company's user-friendly cameras arrived at consumers' doors preloaded with roll film. When its operator had taken the allotted "snapshots"—in Kodak No. 1's case, one hundred exposures—the camera would be mailed back to Rochester along with the necessary payment, on the promise of being returned with both processed images and a newly loaded roll of film.

As Kodak users' home archives filled with these snapshots, Eastman Kodak's riches grew, and so, too, did the varieties of local educational and cultural institutions supported by George Eastman's philanthropy. At its height, Kodak employed over sixty thousand people in the

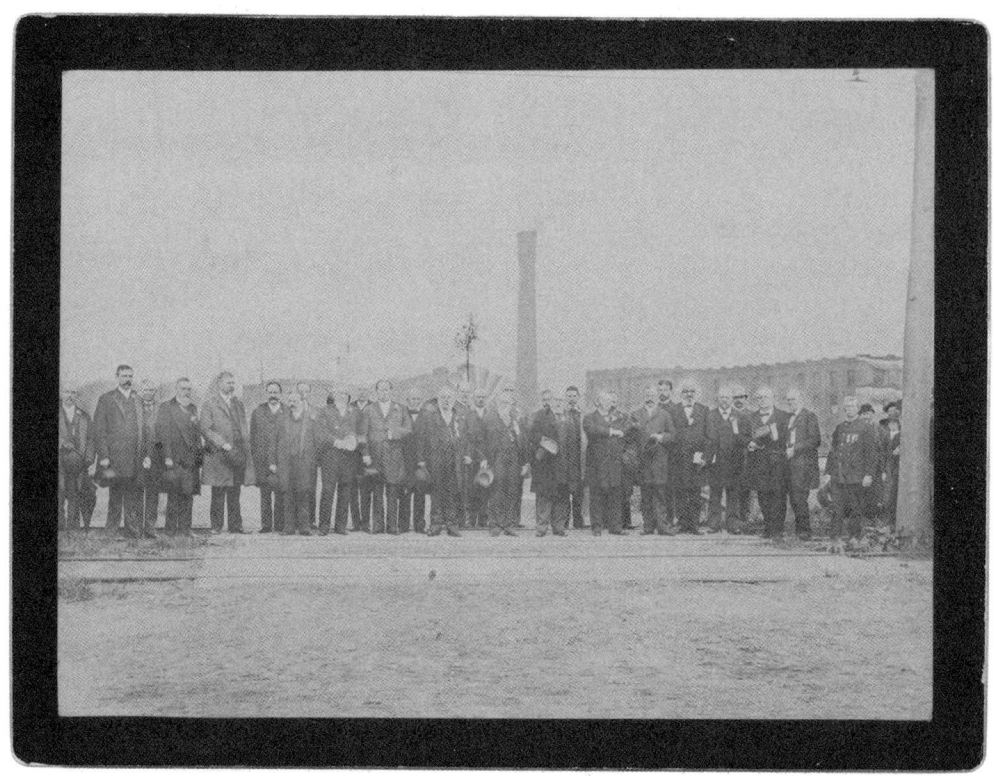

Rochester metropolitan area while also claiming over 80 percent of the United States' and half the world's market in photographic film (Viki, 2017). By 2012, however, having infamously failed to adapt to the rise of digital imaging, the company was forced to declare bankruptcy, leaving thousands of workers without jobs and the City of Rochester with only a critically weakened shell of its most essential and longest standing economic driver. Once the lifeblood of the "imaging capital of the world," Kodak has since faced such desperate straits as to seek to become a corporate welfare beneficiary indebted to President Trump, whose promotion of a $765 million plan for the corporation to pivot to pharmaceuticals in the wake of COVID-19 preceded a sudden halting of the arrangement in August 2020 due to "serious concerns" over recent executive stock deals (Robinson-Jacobs, 2020; Klebnikov, 2020).

Both outside observers and indirect beneficiaries of Kodak's and Rochester's past successes (we were both working at the University of Rochester, a major recipient of Eastman's philanthropy), we began to pursue the idea of a symposium that would make a theme of accumulation and abundance from photography's beginnings through to the digital present. The more we read and conversed, however, the

Figure 0.1

Souvenir photograph of guests, including Frederick Douglass, at President Harrison's visit to Kodak Park, Memorial Day, 1892, Frederick Douglass papers, A.D74, Rare Books, Special Collections, and Preservation, River Campus Libraries, University of Rochester. Courtesy of Rare Books, Special Collections, and Preservation, River Campus Libraries, University of Rochester.

See also Plate 1.

more our curiosities turned to the apogee of these themes: the notion that photography has become ubiquitous. For Jacob, as a historian of photography, it was especially striking how old this idea was, as numerous critics, historians, and theorists have, since the earliest days of the medium, identified the photographic image with a pervasive conquest of the world—from Charles Baudelaire and Paul Valéry to Susan Sontag and Christopher Pinney. For Kyle, as a media theorist, apart from the clearly consequential explosion of photography in the digital era, what stood out most was the universalizing nature of the claim, with little to no frameworks for digital photographic surfeit in circulation, and instead numerous unqualified assertions of photography's presence everywhere.

It was between these two initial observations that our inquiries into the history and theory of photographic ubiquity first took flight. Along one track, we would investigate whether and how one could trace a history of ubiquity purposely and emphatically decoupled from the digital-centrism that has come to mark discourses of pervasiveness. Along a second track, we would invite others to join and augment (and hopefully also trouble) that investigation through a symposium in Rochester comprised of papers addressing the insistent reality and enduring question of photography's multitudes. In 2018, thanks to support from the Humanities Center at the University of Rochester as well as the Arts Research Institute at the University of California, Santa Cruz, we were able to host ten participants from the United States, Canada, and the United Kingdom, as well as our keynote speaker, Ariella Aïsha Azoulay.

This anthology represents the convergence of these two investigative tracks. At its heart is a twofold argument. First, far from being a unique property of the digital era, photographic ubiquity is a historical construct that reaches back to the earliest days of the medium and is therefore open to theoretical revision or even outright rejection. Second, although most instantiations of the ubiquity thesis have tended to suffer from manifest shortcomings, including a false universalism and a flat overwriting of geographical and cultural difference, it remains essential to research and critique both mythologies and actual circumstances of photographic hyperabundance and hyperdistribution. At stake isn't just a much-needed addition to the history and theory of photography but also a sweeping revision of the terms through which questions of photographic presence and absence are conceived in the first place. This book asks what it means when artists and scholars consciously do not take for granted the event of photography's spread, and instead historicize these many *events* for their evident complexity, forgoing an identification of points on a timeline that too often reduce photography's spread to the terms of an abiding faith in technological progress.

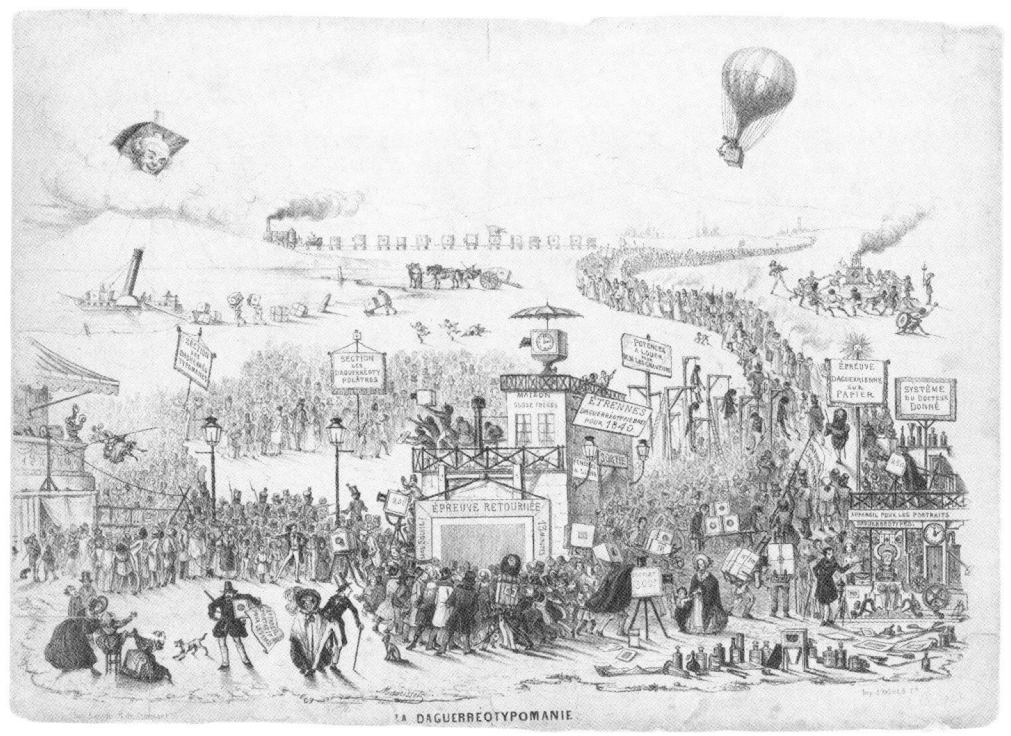

LA DAGUERREOTYPOMANIE.

From Simultaneous Invention to Conquest of Ubiquity

In late 1839, the caricaturist Théodore Maurisset responded to the release of details about Louis Daguerre's new invention, the daguerreotype, with a satirical image of the all-consuming reach of this novel instrument and its visual products, titled *Daguerreotypomania*. (fig. 0.2) In the lithograph, innervated crowds and queues assemble under banners pledging either irrational obsession (*Daguerreotypomanes*) or religious fealty (*Daguerreotypolâtres*) to the lauded inventor and his materials. In the foreground cluster various consumers hauling cameras, sitting for grueling portrait sessions, and gawking at oversized plates. In the center right, gallows for rent are provided for engravers whose profession is soon to be eclipsed by the advent of photographic illustration. Toward the horizon is a train whose interlinked cars are but giant cameras, placing photography together with that other modern marvel, the steam locomotive. With these details and so many more, Maurisset's image conveys not the culture surrounding a fad at one point in time but the expected impact of Daguerre's novel process. In short, rather than provide a description of photography's ubiquity, we see its anticipation,

Figure 0.2

Théodore Maurisset, *La Daguerreotypomanie (Daguerreotypomania)*, December 1839. Lithograph, 26 × 35.7 cm, J. Paul Getty Museum.

See also Plate 2.

furthermore delivered via a still novel medium (lithography) whose process conveyed reproductive fidelity (like photography) and was informed by the "larger picture of growth and proliferation" that emerged in 19th-century France (Farwell, 1977).

Maurisset's lithograph, according to Jan von Brevern, "makes clear that photography was not only a result of progress but one of its engines," showing that "the new kind of image photography produced was expected to have consequences in all social domains, be they artistic, economic, or epistemic." (Brevern, 2015: 72) While Daguerre's image was new, the ideas surrounding the chemistry and optics seemed already, historically, present everywhere. Responding to early notices of the "discovery," dozens of experimentalists and inventors across the world staked their own claims of priority to the invention, among them Hippolyte Bayard and William Henry Fox Talbot. In Brazil, artist and cartographer Antoine Hércules Florence even designated his own cognate process under the name *photographie* in 1832, before the term was even applied to the inventions of Daguerre and Talbot. Responding to the news of Daguerre's success across the Atlantic, Florence wrote to local newspapers to share his belief in simultaneous invention, and that a single idea can be shared at once, among many (Marien, 2015: 9).

While the invention phase indicated its own immanence, photography's discourse of universality generally belongs to academician and statesman François Arago, who successfully secured Daguerre's invention as a gift of the French state to the world. For Arago, the daguerreotype plate's unmatched power of visual exactitude confirmed Arago's ideas about the benefits of popularizing scientific knowledge, as well as the political necessity of expanded suffrage and representation for French citizens, as Theresa Levitt argues (Levitt, 2003). What made such scientific and political idealism possible was the simplicity of the operation: "There is not one of the different branch operations of the Daguerreotype that every body cannot perform, even without any knowledge of drawing or of chemistry, and even with as much success as Mr. Daguerre himself." (Arago, 2017: 236) Arago's faith in photography's utility and ease, however, belied the fact that the technical practice required an arsenal of costly materials, institutional access, as well as a certain operational knowledge that lay beyond Daguerre's published instructions. Nevertheless, reports in the robust print media landscape of the 19th century spread details of the process throughout the world. This networked world led far-flung amateurs such as Robert Cornelius in Philadelphia and William O'Shaughnessy in Calcutta to experiment with the process and expand its applications, the former pairing it with self-portraiture and the latter with telegraphy (Andreasson, 2014; Pinney, 2008: 104).

Just as Maurisset identified, commentators saw photography as part of a series of modern wonders, together with the electric telegraph and the steam locomotive, as technologies that shattered humanity's grasp of space and time and their presumed limits. In his 1872 study *L'Homme*, Catholic writer and critic Ernest Hello described how modern technologies large and small offered a glimpse of universals that were hitherto the province of philosophy and theology:

> The chemical match [...] certifies distinctly the universal presence of fire; photography certifies the universal presence of radiation. In a certain way, the electric telegraph delivering speech and steam power transporting man makes up for the desire for ubiquity to which man and his speech attest. (Hello, 1903: 197)[3]

In others' estimations, photography was set to reveal not only the ubiquity of visible and invisible energies but also an untapped infinitude of photographic applications for use by art and science. As Emily Doucet argues, the inchoate photographic discourse of early technical manuals and treatises often addressed the future of photography in terms of expansive frames of time and with a decidedly utopian rhetoric (Doucet, 2018).[4] Such idealism and faith in progress, however, also accompanied the increasing suspicion about photography's pervasiveness in the world of commerce. This is most notoriously explored in the art criticism of Charles Baudelaire, who in 1859, identified the love of photography with messianic materialism and blamed "the invasion of photography and the great industrial madness," if left unchecked, for the fated degeneration of art and of the faculty of imagination (Baudelaire, 1980: 89).

Pairing both utopian and critical modes in response to photography's increasing transformation of society and culture, photo-scientist Léon Vidal noted in 1886 that in the near future one will be able to practice photography "as one speaks prose." (Frizot, 1998: 237) In fact, Vidal's offhand prediction seemed to describe what was already in progress in Rochester. There, in 1888, entrepreneur George Eastman debuted the simplified Kodak camera, as well as its more innovative adjunct of in-house film processing for consumers. The vertical integration of Eastman Kodak's operations translated into advertisements for the company under the banner of "you press the button, we do the rest." Here, Arago's description of photography's effortlessness found its ultimate expression in the age of capital. Kodak enabled a democratization of the idea of photography, but by recasting it as a "black box" technology whose operators—shutterbugs, snapshooters, kodakers, and the like—understood the camera box's input and output but not the physical and chemical operations occurring within it, not to mention the labor that produced it and the environmental effects that result from it (Flusser, 2000: 16; Brunet, 2019). Kodak cameras, as well as the inexpensive Brownie developed for sale in 1900, helped bring about what Kris Belden-Adams names "the first revolution in photographic ubiquity," the events of which "freed the camera from being the tool of a few hobbyists and made photography ubiquitous, and even perhaps wasteful and indulgent." It is no surprise that online commentators and cultural scolds have resurrected the same critical reaction against the omnipresent selfie in the 21st century (Belden-Adams, 2018: 92).

In the late 19th century, Kodak was but one innovation among many in the field. Photography's input, output, and circulation expanded with the refinement and industrialization of such technical practices as photomechanical printing, stable dry gelatin film, instantaneous exposures, cinematography, and color processing. By its drastic mutation into the hybrid worlds of mass media and modernism, photography became an object of profound aesthetic, historical, and theoretical interest for the first time since its introduction, particularly during the interwar years in Europe.

Photography as a ubiquitous cultural force takes center stage in a few essays by Paul Valéry, whose views on technological media in the midst of its mass acculturation set a theoretical standard for subsequent discussions of modern visual culture, including the work of Walter Benjamin.[5] In Valéry's 1928 essay "The Conquest of Ubiquity"—to which this anthology's theme and title owe a significant debt—Valéry outlined the inevitable future of reproducible media and its apparatuses for a sense of its modern omnipresence: "Just as water, gas, and electricity are brought into our houses from far off to satisfy our needs in response to a minimal effort, so we shall be supplied with visual or auditory images." (Valéry, 1964) While Valéry's text promotes a sense of wonder about the ability to experience art and sensorial reality everywhere at once in the manner of public utilities, he also frames these relations in violent terms, from the imperial "conquest" of the essay's title to analogies like the following: "Just as we are accustomed, if not enslaved, to the various forms of energy that pour into our homes, we shall find it perfectly natural to receive the ultrarapid variations or oscillations that our sense organs gather in and integrate to form all we know." (Valéry, 1964) For Valéry, ubiquitous photography, as well as the cognates of cinema and recorded sound, were always to be experienced via the electrified, networked, and thus *tethered* apparatuses of modern space-time. His descriptions of the future of media barely differ from the dystopian aspects that pervade the worlds conjured in classic science fiction, not to mention the landscape of screens and speakers, as well as the inverse of cameras and microphones that conquer our attentions (and record our movements) in the present day.

While it was Vidal who identified the future of photographic practice in a manner of speaking prose, it was Valéry who articulated the impact that photography had on speech and the written word. In a lecture delivered to commemorate photography's centenary at the French Academy, he notes that the medium's development "has resulted in a kind of progressive eviction of the word by the image." (Valéry, 1980: 192–193) While Valéry welcomed this move as cleansing literature of poor prose, it was in the historical imaginary, however, that he argues for the lasting power of photography's reach: "The mere notion of photography, when we introduce it into meditation on the genesis of historical knowledge and its true value, suggests this simple question: *Could such and such a fact, as it is narrated, have been photographed?*" (Valéry, 1980: 195)

Here, photographic ubiquity is once again figured as pure potentiality—the "mere notion"—rather than a quantifiable actuality. Strangely, after Valéry nominated the era of technological reproduction in music and images as a "conquest of ubiquity," it is still nevertheless the *virtual* expansiveness of photography that defines both its past and its future. Ubiquity is an active imaginary, an abstraction, and not necessarily a threshold surpassed by quantity or spatial distribution. It is akin to what Siegfried Kracauer theorized as the "warehousing of nature" wrought by the "sheer accumulation" of miscellaneous studio portraits, snapshots, photo magazines, archival documents, and aerial views produced by photographic means (Kracauer, 1995: 59, 62). What both writers identify with the medium of their own moment is an understanding of photography's dramatic impact on historical consciousness, a claim that is unrecognizable without a belief in photography's total saturation in and through the world.

From Image-World to Everyware

The move to describe not just photography but nearly anything "in terms of multiplicity, excess, omnipresence, totality and networking" has long been a matter of people speaking to their experiences and impressions of the visible world or, in an explicitly theological vein, to their overriding beliefs about the invisible one (Azoulay, 2014: 64).[6] As much is evident in the English-language history of the term *ubiquity*, which is derived from the Latin *ubīque*, meaning "anywhere, everywhere, wherever."[7] What this history reveals is a longstanding dynamic of real or imagined phenomena to which a notion of being present everywhere seems like the necessary answer for certain communities at certain times.

In the earliest days, in an echo of the religious origins of the term "data," there is a theological (and, at the time, controversial) supposition among so-called "Ubiquitarians" that Christ manifests not only in the Eucharist but in all places.[8] Soon after the emergence of these Ubiquitarians, various writers, as if newly enabled to name something that had long been observed but not precisely named, refer to given people as "ubiquitarian." Like the Royalist commander Prince Rupert, for whom Sir Thomas Fairfax's army remains prepared lest "that ubiquitarian steale on them unawares" during the First English Civil War in 1644, some people manage to convey an impression of being everywhere at once (*Exact and Certaine Newes From the Siege at Yorke*, 1644: n.p). Subsequent variants on the ubiquity notion build on this more worldly use, not just around the presence of individuals but around a whole suite of modern phenomena. While those concerned with buying and selling speak of certain valued substances like saltpeter as "ubiquitarian" (Cressy, 2013: 15), those concerned with the arts invoke its "ubiquitory citizenship" as they defend the presence of foreign artists in England (Select Committee on Fine Arts, 1841: 585). Those faced with the fecundity of ants in a colonial context (in this case, Jamaica) describe them as "ubiquitaries" that "make Bridges of one another" to pass over "Hollows of Water" set around cupboards (Sloane, 1707: 223). Ubiquity even takes on a legal meaning, referring to the fact of "being, in the eyes of the law or for legal purposes, present in all places or not limited to one place." According to an 1841 Supreme Court decision, for instance, "The United States, in their sovereign capacity, have no particular place of domicile but possess, in contemplation of law, an ubiquity throughout the Union." (Curtis, 1855: 3) In other words, the law, too, maintains an awareness of the possibility of being everywhere, and the ability to name and codify that possibility is of use to none other than the sovereign state, a new kind of omnipresence that hovers between the holy and the secular, the abstract and the concrete.

As a collector of quotations in the vein of Walter Benjamin, and as someone equally concerned with the interplay of war, media, and capitalism, Susan Sontag might well have found these historical iterations of ubiquity quite suggestive. Indeed, for Sontag, what was an unexpected four-year period of writing about photography (culminating in the still influential 1977 book *On Photography*) began with an interest to address, as she puts it, "some of the problems, aesthetic and moral, posed by the omnipresence of photographed images." (Sontag, 1977: front matter)[9] Not one to shy from provocative and encompassing prose, Sontag crafts several characterizations of that omnipresence, doing so in a manner that could be mistaken for a response to the digital era. In one sense, the ubiquity of photography that had established itself by the 1970s was a matter of heightened accumulation; thanks to, among other things, the rise of instant photography and telecommunication, there are "a great many more images around, claiming our attention. This inventory started in 1839 and since then just about everything has been photographed, or so it seems." (3) In another sense, the recent pervasiveness of photography is a matter of the dramatically increased speed and extent of participation in the institution enabled by cheaper, easier, and faster cameras. "That age when taking photographs required a cumbersome and expensive contraption—the toy of the clever, the wealthy, and the obsessed—seems remote indeed from the era of sleek pocket cameras that invite anyone to take pictures," Sontag muses (7). "Like guns and cars," she goes on to say, "cameras are fantasy-machines whose use is addictive." (14) Photography "has become almost as widely practiced an amusement as sex and dancing." (8)

If there are hints of resignation or even bemusement in these characterizations of analog ubiquity, it is only a temporary suspension of the essays' radically suspicious approach to the profligate medium. For Sontag, in what comprises a significant departure from the white, male voices that had dominated theories of photography to this point, both the ubiquity of the photographic record and that record's "passivity"—the insidious ease and promiscuity and self-effacement of taking and sharing photographs—amount to photography's "message," which is nothing less than its fundamental "aggression." (7) Several decades before the horrifically banalized digital photographs of torture and sexual violence at Abu Ghraib that would come to occupy her attention in *Regarding the Pain of Others*, well before daily disaster selfies and viral deepfakes, Sontag finds in the profound pervasiveness of film-loaded cameras, printed photographs, and billowing image archives an entire "photographic enterprise" distinguished by "voraciousness," aggrandizement, and "willy-nilly" "antiquing" of what is real, persistently shifting between "degraded and glamorous realities," and perpetually beset by "confusions about truth and beauty."[10] In Sontag's aphoristic polemic, photographic ubiquity has managed to not only rend the real world in which the writer lives; it has also parasitically fostered a second, virtual one: an "image-world created by cameras" (178) that "bids to outlast us all" (109) and whose overall function is to sustain rampant consumerism, pervasive inequality, and the mere illusion of freedom. Although she is not alone in her attention to photographic ubiquity in this period—Roland Barthes's work influenced hers, and figures like Vilém Flusser and Jean Baudrillard would soon add their own visions of omnipresent media—by means of these concepts, Sontag manages to both naturalize and, as it were, de-neutralize ubiquity's existence and importance. To speak or work on photography is, after reading Sontag, to become increasingly subject to a perverse and pervasive force that exceeds any individual, community, or institutional capacities for control.

As the travails of criticism and scholarship persist, so do those of commerce and engineering. In 1975, Steven Sasson made a presentation to higher-ups at Kodak of what he called, in an unintentional send up of the company's prideful misreading of the future of the medium, "filmless photography." (Deutsch, 2008) The toaster-sized contraption he presented would become the first in a long line of attempts within and beyond the United States to woo businesses and consumers with "self-contained," and therefore portable, digital cameras. By the mid-1990s, just as the allures of cyberspace and instant messaging were beginning to take hold, it was possible but by no means common to forgo film in favor of digital formats, and this condition would more or less hold until the early 2000s, when DSLR and cheaper point-and-shoot cameras began to eclipse their slower rivals. But it was the abandonment of self-containment that ultimately set the digital image world alight.

In the first phase, starting with the Sharp J-SH04 (0.1 megapixels) in 2000 and the GSM-linked Nokia 7650 (0.3 megapixels) in 2002, cheap CCD- and CMOS-based cameras made their way into the mobile phones many people carried with them almost perpetually. By roughly 2006, nearly all mobile phones sported a cheap camera. Marked by a "more ubiquitous and lightweight presence" than their self-contained forebears, these early camera phones tended to enable "a kind of archive of a personal trajectory or viewpoint on the world, a collection of fragments of everyday life." (Okabe and Ito, 2006: 99) Although, as Chris Chesher writes, they did not manage to "displace the full technical or cultural functions of the film or digital camera," these image-ready phones nevertheless fostered a cross-national impression of intrusive omnipresence, such that "stories of regulatory reactions," including around fears of secret photographing of women in Saudi Arabia, "began appearing around the world." (Chesher, 2012: 105) Witnessing the advent of the phone-enabled "moblog" as well as Nokia's ultimately short lived, family-oriented "Lifeblog" (Gye, 2007: 283), at least one writer proclaimed the existence of a "Nokia moment" over and against the famous Kodak one (Palmer, 2005).

In 2007, Apple melded music and messaging by way of an iPhone that also boasted a 2.0 megapixel camera and associated app complete with shutter animation and sound effect. (fig. 0.3) Able to, as Chris Chesher puts it, "connect directly to the internet, and not to a tele-communications company's 'walled garden,'" and soon including "apps that used the camera in ways other than taking standard snaps," this new device further released the camera from the long-prevailing model of discrete and specialized production (Chesher, 2012: 106). By 2011, thanks in part to resolution and usability upgrades, the iPhone had become the most popular camera on the image-sharing platform Flickr. As smartphone technologies improved, and as new habits formed and new addictions took root, more and more people could perform "real-time digital transformations, translations and transmissions on mobile amateur images." (107) Over the subsequent decade, with access to the

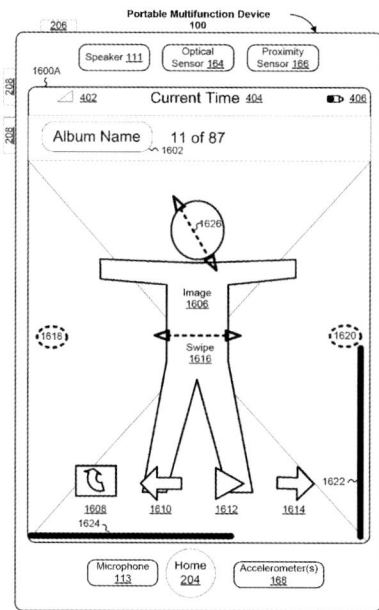

Figure 16A

Figure 0.3

From Steven P. Jobs et al., "Touch Screen Device, Method, and Graphical User Interface for Customizing Display of Category Icons." Patent filed September 5, 2007.

internet radically expanding, and with billions of smartphones entering purses and pockets (and, it should be noted, the global waste stream), a myriad of platforms further amplified this dramatic and widespread increase in vernacular communicative capacity. Starting in 2010, for instance, Instagram lured users into its galaxy of visual-verbal reference through nostalgic filters and easy captioning and commenting. (The app reached one billion users as of 2019 and, as of 2020, clocks more likes in two days than there are people on the planet.)[11] In 2011, Snapchat invited users to share ephemeral images well beyond the beautiful or the impressive. (As of 2020, users created over three billion snaps per day.)[12] And, as a final example, over the 2010s and into the early 2020s, the Chinese company Meitu introduced rapid photo-editing apps to its hundreds of millions of users, thus further accelerating an already perpetual planetary exercise of simultaneously algorithmic and user-driven image processing.

As phone-based photography proliferated, so did theories of ubiquity, so much so that, by the 2010s, assertions of the newfound omnipresence of photography had become a critical and journalistic commonplace. Within the necessarily partial history of the idea of photographic ubiquity that we have been tracing, this is the period of both amnesia and effluence—amnesia because of the gradual erasure of nearly two centuries of thinking through photography's multitudes, effluence because those multitudes had become so immanent and impactful as to warrant one critical project after another.

One strain of these projects echoes Arago and Valéry in its casting of ubiquity in terms of progress, habituation, and conquest. Typically, the overriding concern is a major shift ushered in by the hyperabundance of cameras and photographs in conjunction with the hyperconnectedness of photographing publics. "Now that cameras are ubiquitous, photographs of ordinary people are everywhere, too," reads a subheadline in *The Atlantic* (Eveleth, 2015). "Ubiquitous digital cameras," writes a contributor to BBC *News Magazine*, "turn events that in themselves would be a small story into a worldwide phenomenon." (de Castella, 2012) "Photography has become so ubiquitous and rapidly reproducible," proclaims a critic for *Seattle Weekly*, "that part of the magic of the image has been lost." (Flock, 2014) Alongside these journalistic accounts, other writers within this family speak in more theoretically complex terms of transformations wrought by the pervasiveness of cameras and images. For George Emeka Agbo, for instance, the ubiquitous "editing, circulation and interaction around the photograph in internet spaces" has "the tendency to transform the image into a strong political statement." Speaking of Nigerian political elites in particular, Agbo writes that "their appearances in photographs—and, of course, the circulation and conversations around those images—give a sense that they are under surveillance by the networked public." While not necessarily always visible or even effective, the "political critique that grows out of this visual culture is so strong that it creates tension among the elites who are denounced as they strive either to exonerate themselves or to forestall further attacks." (Agbo, 2019: 299)

A second strain of ubiquity-infused projects follows Sontag in reaching after more detailed and integrative accounts of disruptions and accelerations across art, society, politics, and visual culture. At the same time, unlike Sontag's approach, what is centrally at stake is a tension between the authenticity and inauthenticity of experience, subjectivity, and social interaction in the wake of the digitization of photography.[13] Fred Ritchin, for instance, invokes a longstanding perception of inauthenticity in describing the "multitudes of photographers now intensely staring not at the surrounding world […] but at their camera backs or cell phones searching for an image on the small screens, or summoning the past as an archival image on these same screens." Amid this "ubiquity of a billion cell phone cameras," he writes, the image has gained "primacy over the existence it is supposed to depict," thus "banish[ing] actual experience" and replacing it with "an unreality in which we hope to find a transcendent immortality, a higher, less finite, reality." (Ritchin, 2009: 21) In the eyes of Nathan Jurgenson, lines of thinking such as Ritchin's amount to a "popular fairy tale" in which the arrival of the "Internet, online social networking, and constant picture taking" replaces "real conversation and identity" with the "allure of the virtual—the simulated second life that uproots and disembodies the authentic self," and thus leaves only "digital posturing, empty interaction, and addictive connection." (Jurgenson, 2019: 61–62) In the language of Jurgenson's more optimistic corrective, in a context in which "digital connection" is indeed "fundamentally ubiquitous" (62), "the social photo"—whether it is highly filtered, rapidly produced, or otherwise—"is not just a reflection of yourself and your world but, at the same time, equally the creation of your self and your world. It is a primary way we now learn to recognize ourselves as selves, our reality as reality." (40)

Yet a third strain of inquiry into digital photographic ubiquity departs from this second one in its unqualified emphasis on domination over democratization. Speaking in broad terms, there is a split here in the source of that dominance, from political entities exercising sovereignty and violence to the distributed logics of capitalism. At least at one point in her work (see the interview in this volume for a discussion of her more recent work), Azoulay represents the former side of the equation. On the one hand, she writes, "[t]he increased number of cameras together with their increased potential presence all over enables the camera to operate, as it were, even when it is not physically present, by virtue of the doubt that exists with respect to its overt or covert presence, its capacities for inscription and surveillance." (Azoulay, 2015: 19) On the other hand, "[e]fforts made by various agents, usually state establishments, to control the content and accessibility of photographs, seek to obtain sovereignty over the event of photography and over the interpretive framework of its consequences. Yet the very conditions of photography as an encounter undermine the feasibility of such sovereignty." (231)

Such willingness to speak of the resistant potentials in photography (in however qualified of terms) seems effectively anathema to Jonathan Crary, for whom the contemporary world is constituted by "omnipresent conditions of social isolation, economic injustice, and compulsory self-interestedness." (Crary, 2013: 108) In the polemical sprint that is *24/7: Late Capitalism and the Ends of Sleep*, Crary makes sense of those omnipresent conditions by way of something relatively rare in the history of ubiquity discourses, which is to interweave accounts of not just one but multiple, overlapping forms of technical and medial ubiquity. At one level, in a familiar sense, technical devices like smartphones and televisions are ubiquitous, thus yielding "[i]ncalculable streams of images omnipresent 24/7." (48–49) At another level, though, there are both pervasive "electronic industries of temporal objects" (53) and the constant "opportunity for electronic transactions of all kinds." (75) Finally, at still another level (and in an echo of Michel Foucault's work), there is an "omnipresent field of operations and expectations to which one is exposed and in which individual optical activity is made the object of observation and management." (33) For Crary, one can hardly hope to resist this field of operations through yet more media, as both "[v]isual and auditory 'content' is most often ephemeral, interchangeable material that, in addition to its commodity status, circulates to habituate and validate one's immersion in the exigencies of twenty-first century capitalism." (52) In fact, or so Crary argues, it is *sleep* that is ultimately "a figure for a subjectivity on which power can operate with the least political resistance" and "a condition that finally cannot be instrumentalized or controlled externally—that evades or frustrates the demands of global consumer society." (24)[14]

Hardly distant from Azoulay and Crary, but closer to the work of Flusser and Baudrillard, one final strain de-emphasizes the agency of individuals and institutions in favor of the distributed dominance of machines, programs, and algorithms. In both their individual and their collaborative projects, for instance, Sarah Kember and Joanna Zylinksa take mediation as an "all-encompassing and indivisible" given, not just in human, cultural, and technical worlds but also across biological worlds (Kember and Zylinska, 2012: xv). In terms of ubiquitous photography, Zylinska asserts that photographs "function less as individual objects or as media content to be looked at and more as data flows to be dipped or cut into occasionally." One of the key implications of this new "photographic condition" is a persistent nonhuman dimension across the world of photography. (Zylinska, 2017: 74) This nonhuman dimension is evident in the ways mechanical and algorithmic agents shape photographic production. It is also evident in the manifold photographic practices, such as industrial and environmental monitoring, for which there is no human audience. While Kember parallels Zylinska in emphasizing these nonhuman operations, her own account of photographic ubiquity centers on the overt and largely commercial ambitions of ubiquitous computing or "ubicomp."[15] According to Kember's explicitly feminist approach, it is time to "think of ubiquitous photography as more than everywhere" and instead, using Adam Greenfield's term for computing integrated into all components of everyday life, to "rethink it in relation to the claims of 'everyware.'" (Kember, 2013: 67) Central in Kember's mind is the ongoing attempt to infuse human environments with so-called "ambient intelligence" and the role played by photographic systems thereby. Such systems, including face recognition technology, are increasingly used in the observation, analysis, and even manipulation of individual moods and actions. (fig. 0.4) Effectively "making mug shots of us all" (70), photography aids and abets an all-encompassing "reordering and instrumentalization of life in relation to technology and capital." (Kember, 2012: 334) What Allan Sekula once dubbed the "general, all-inclusive archive"—one that contains "both the traces of the visible bodies of heroes, leaders, moral exemplars, celebrities, and those of the poor, the diseased, the insane, the criminal, the nonwhite, the female, and all other embodiments of the unworthy"—can seem tame by comparison (Sekula, 1986: 10).

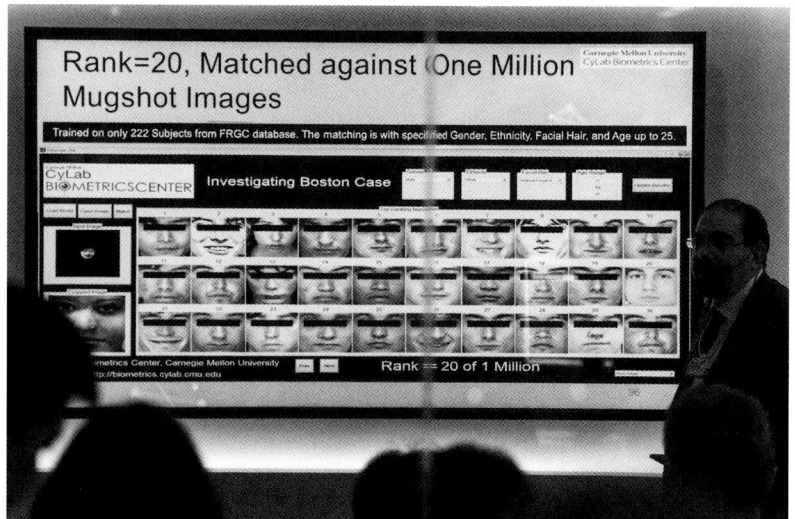

For Shoshana Zuboff, such critical warnings are far from hyperbole: in the new era of "surveillance capitalism," ubiquity has become a literal and explicit goal, and "the planning, investment, and invention necessary" to bring a "vision of ubiquity into reality are well underway." (Zuboff, 2019: 201) The ubiquity Zuboff speaks to far exceeds the fact of billowing digital archives of images in the cloud, or the supposed devolution in individual capacities to pay attention or remember because of constant visual stimuli. What is at issue is much larger and much more insidious, an ever-expanding "Big Other" that vacuums up information on human behaviors and vulnerabilities by means of the data so-called "smart" devices harvest and that, in turn, finds ways to act on that information to "coax, tune, and herd behavior toward profitable outcomes." (8) "Among high-tech leaders, within the specialist literature, and among expert professionals," Zuboff writes, "there appears to be universal agreement on the idea that *everything* will be connected, knowable, and actionable in the near future: ubiquity and its consequences in total information are an article of faith." (222) What this means is not just photographic ubiquity but surveillance ubiquity, computational ubiquity, search ubiquity, market ubiquity, and still other "ubiquities" naturalized, neutralized, and monetized. From data-gathering children's dolls to time-targeted notifications and ads, there are constant and persistent "habituation exercise[s] aimed at normalizing ubiquity in intimate spaces." (266) This is a "gradually accruing, smart, and muscular apparatus" over which no individual, government, or corporation can pretend to have full knowledge or control (201). The endgame isn't just ubiquity; it is "the comprehensive visibility, coordination, confluence, control, and harmonization of social processes in the pursuit of scale, scope, and action." (399) The vexing question is what can be done to defend freedom and democracy when this "new frontier of power" is both everywhere and nowhere at the same time. Maurisset's hallucinatory conflation of photography and industry is as relevant as ever.

The Chapters

The notion of photographic ubiquity is as pervasive as it is undertheorized.[16] Like this introduction, the chapters in this anthology respond to this paradox, sometimes in quite direct ways, other times through indirect, elegant, yet nevertheless essential means. What sutures them together are their invaluable endeavors to pin either the event, consciousness, or discourse to certain perceptions of photography's ubiquity and, in turn, to further describe and analyze the limits of such perceptions as part of photography's history. Thus, the chapters in this anthology attend in various ways to the question of when photography came to be "everywhere," with other historical priorities, whether they be technological, situational, or intellectual.

In the first chapter, "Early Photography's Presence," Jacob W. Lewis engages both photography's origins and its discursive formation to convey how public conception of photography was never consigned to its actual available examples. Instead, commentators chose to convey a virtual, if vague, future condition of possibility for Daguerre's process as well as its alternatives. Framing photography in the abstract was vital to its spread, but this abstraction also carried aspects of other modern signs of everywhereness, from utopian dreams and delusions to democratic acts and experiences. These signs tested the philosophical ideals of Saint-Simonianism, a 19th-century movement that promoted liberal and early socialist ideals, yet nevertheless helped engineer a powerful colonial and technocratic state in the French imperial context. While not yet a coherent medium—"photography, properly speaking"—the new technology's presence in these early decades is framed by a rhetoric of excess, an aspect that the caricaturist Théodore Maurisset realized in several illustrations.

Expanding the study of photography and its relations to power into the context of the 1893 Columbian World's Fair, Annie Rudd explores how the organizers' prohibitions and exertions of control over amateur photography rebounded with new amateurs envisioning their photographing of public space as individual acts of extraction and privilege. In her chapter "Photographic Privilege at the World's Columbian Exposition," Rudd details how mobile cameras equipped with instantaneous exposures enabled an event like the fair to have countless recorders and interpreters, whose resulting images told their own personal stories of visual conquest. Yet such techniques and narratives also opened the possibility of critique toward these demonstrations of an inalienable right to photograph that predominantly white, middle-class consumers practiced with corporate products such as the Kodak camera. Thus, Rudd shows that the familiar narrative of photography's democratization obstructs a more insidious truth: consumer photography necessarily extends photographic privilege into an imperial mode of being-in-the-world.

While a tacit right to extract views motivated early kodakers, Maura Coughlin explores how the Géniaux brothers, a pair of early documentary photographers active during Kodak's rise, figured the labor of extraction that was part of everyday life in their home region of Brittany. In "Material Ecologies in the Géniaux Brothers' Picture Archive of Brittany, ca. 1900," Coughlin adopts an ecocritical approach to delineate the taut connections between the shifting economic fortunes of the region and the visual culture of tourism that partly fueled the Géniaux brothers' work. Their photographs, while contributing to the nostalgic view of a premodern Brittany for metropolitan audiences, record not only the working class but also aspects of the rise and fall of industry, agriculture, and trade relative to the "cheap nature" of the region. In a set of interrelated examples, Coughlin analyzes how photography produces an ambivalent image of the encultured landscapes of the region's salt marshes, slate quarries, and hemp fields. Brittany, in their photographs of labor and material, becomes a site where rural culture is at once salvaged (in the crystalized photographic image) and destroyed (by modernization and economization). Furthermore, the photographs exhibit how the land's myriad resources already serve as emblems of transformation and destruction even in Belle Époque France—a marker of loss rendered ubiquitous in the age of capital and the climatological disasters that follow.

Following a related ecocritical view, Niharika Dinkar argues for the need to critique the anthropocentric definition of the medium to explore more expansive ways that light writing occurs beyond the human realm, as she details in her chapter "'Our Best Machines are Made of Sunlight': Photography and Technologies of Light." What if the photograph, as a recorded image of light that we deem ubiquitous in society or culture, makes up only a sliver of effects from a vast array of sensitive technologies that record not only visible sunlight but also chemical fire, electric filament, and invisible radiation? And what if, as Dinkar pushes us to ask, such materials and their illuminative effects cannot be sensed apart from their economic and geopolitical imbrications in history? Such is the case for her examples, from early photographic flash powder to the irradiant flash of atomic light inaugurated by nuclear warfare, whose own technology of light doubles as one of extinction and total destruction. As Dinkar proposes, light is continually weaponized by powers past and present; one cannot afford to believe the mythic exceptionalism of "honest sunshine" that governs photography's history.

Just as Dinkar's treatment of light expands our sense of the photographic condition of life, Joseph Moore interrogates similarly nonhuman aspects and actors to flesh out what else comprises this condition. In "Managing Time: Nonhuman Animal Labor in Photographic Images," Moore offers a statement detailing the creative process behind his body of artwork *Oversight/Rendered* and its relation to a history of animal life and photography. Moore connects the 19th-century photographer Étienne-Jules Marey, whose camera enabled a record of an animal's bodily movement in discrete phases using new instantaneous techniques, to the 20th-century Kodak corporation, whose manufacture of gelatin silver film necessitated the use of massive quantities of animal bodies and byproducts to increase Kodak's expanding consumer base. This ecocritical history of photography's labor links with today's "photographerless" internet protocol cameras and CCTV footage, from which the artist captures, automates, collects, selects, and finally prints in analog fashion the images of the animals that afford an essential labor toward the photographic condition, in life as well as in death.

An essential aim of the present book is to question the surface division between analog "mass" media and digital "ubiquity," the one quantifiably extended and the other immaterially present. Mette Sandbye addresses the trouble with such a notion directly in her chapter, "In 1973: Family Photography as Material, Affective History." Part of her inquiry is to examine how the digital turn has revised our understanding of the place of the family snapshot and photo album as texts embedded with data on social norms and cultural shifts. To redirect attention from the photograph as a memory object to the act of "doing" photography as part of everyday lived experience, Sandbye identifies the third wave of photographic ubiquity in terms of the multitudes of family snapshots produced by the 1970s. Her control group is vernacular photography produced in Denmark in the year 1973. What a synchronic study of typical photographs engenders is a description of codes, of affect and self-presentation, that can be named and organized into ad hoc binaries of gender, dress, pose, activity, environment, associated objects, and so on. Whether identified across a comprehensive archive or read within a single dynamic image (both of which have their rarity, as Sandbye indicates), these codes and their eventual breakdown in the act of analysis allow for a criticality otherwise lost in the context of the case-specific "particular" of the family photo album, or in the aggregate "universal" of today's social media platforms.

Shifting from Sandbye's concentration on Denmark in 1973 to Iran in 2009, Mohammadreza Mirzaei describes the synchronous and disparate views of the city of Tehran that became popular at a time of unrest. As outlined in his chapter "Where Is My Photo? A Study of the Representation of Tehran in the Work of Contemporary Iranian Photographers," the same moment that dramatic protests against election results spilled into city streets, there emerged a new direction in contemporary Iranian photography. In times of civil unrest, art styles and movements can enable a politics that is otherwise censored in online and public spaces to translate into aesthetic spaces instead, as Mirzaei suggests. In the empty urban spaces that featured so evocatively in the work of photographer Mehran Mohajer, whose work was on display during the protests, other artists adopted a similar strategy of "not seeing" as a deliberate political-aesthetic maneuver. In contrast to the citizen photography that circulated first among ordinary Iranians and then throughout international news media, photographers of Tehran's gallery scene demonstrate how the oblique, obstructed, evacuated, and depopulated city scene—in conjunction with titles and statements on depression and fear—became another kind of ubiquity: a commodity on the national art market.

The next two chapters address what it means to bring affect and politics into relation with the dramatic cultural saturation of technologies of recording and playback that are camera phones, social photo, and streaming video. In "Evidence of Feeling: Race, Police Violence, and the Limits of Documentation," Catherine Zuromskis describes the complexities of photographed police violence perpetrated against Black people in the United States, and how such shared events are complicated by the dispersion and flow of such images and videos through a variety of contexts: legal evidence, vernacular and social photography, social justice activism, and contemporary art. The affective mode that governs vernacular photography and streaming video undermines political agency for the makers and viewers of such content, particularly in a nation characterized by both digital prowess and racist violence. These conditions press Zuromskis to explore other kinds of responses, including recent critical aesthetic approaches that center photography's difficult relationship to futurity, taking us further away from the easy resolutions of liberalism that define much of documentary photography, whose classic proponents tended to approach visibility of—and exposure to—social injustice as an end in itself.

In "On Photographic Ubiquity in the Age of Online Self-Imaging," Derek Conrad Murray explores how the selfie and desire in online culture engender new subjectivities that distort and even challenge strains of cultural critique. Like Zuromskis, Murray situates the ideological backdrop for the selfie and its critical reception with that of waning liberalism in the United States, here in the context of how the ubiquity of "culture" in academic discourse and beyond has offered a poor substitute for politics. What, then, is the culture of the selfie, and where do we situate the sitter's psychology of desire in the making and sharing of self-representations? Within the ambivalent genre of the "influencer" selfie as practiced by women of historically marginalized groups, one is able to read a new romance, not only between the self and image but also between the self-image and the society that renders such self-fashioning into an all-consuming project. Even so, representational acts like the selfie are all the more impressive in their ability to instantiate selfhood, if also to give in to the flows of capital and spectacle.

With a work by the Turkish media artist and director Refik Anadol as her departure point, Kate Palmer Albers' chapter "Parafiction and the New Latent Image" redoubles Murray's emphasis on fashioning the self, but places it instead at the lively and uncertain intersection of computation and photography. The Anadol work, titled *WDCH Dreams*, finds its basis in forty-five terabytes of digitized visual and auditory media from the archives of Frank Gehry's famous Walt Disney Concert Hall in Los Angeles. Over ten nights in 2018, forty-two projectors cast a three-part, twelve-minute sequence onto the building, starting with "Memory"—the digitized materials read by Anadol's bespoke neural network—moving to "Consciousness"—the materials reconfigured into visualized data—and concluding with "Dream"—the neural network's mostly inscrutable and often uncanny productions of new images based on its interpretation of those data. For Albers, *WDCH Dreams* both raises crucial questions about "fictive archival engagements"—such as those explored by the artist Zoe Leonard and filmmaker Cathy Dunye—while also refusing to engage the uses and abuses of archives in history. At stake here is a more agential but also necessarily machinic means through which media-saturated publics can confront the critical and perceptual challenges of increasingly abundant visual data.

Likewise concerned with data and media abundance, Kyle Parry responds to the intuitive persuasiveness and deceptive universality of the widespread belief that photography has become ubiquitous in the digital era. An exercise in critical reconceptualization, Parry's chapter, "Dispersal and Denial: Photographic Ubiquity and the Microbial Analogy," follows Gilles Deleuze in finding conceptual resources in an "inexact" scientific concept, in this case Lourens Baas-Becking's microbial biogeographical aphorism that "everything," as in the totality of microbial life, "is everywhere, but the environment selects." On the one hand, analogous to the remarkable dispersal capacity of microbes, there is the extreme and seemingly unlimited spread and perpetuation of all manner of photographic forms. On the other, there are inevitable limits, whether political, social, technical, or material, to which photographic forms endure where, when, to what degree, and for whom. Acknowledging the inexact nature of this (and indeed any other) microbial analogy, Parry nevertheless suggests that attention to both the radical dispersal and inevitable denial of photographic forms means maintaining the best of the ubiquity concept while also evading its tendency toward universalization, naturalization, and erasure.

Attentive to the many imperfect conceptions of photography's spread, Michelle Henning's chapter, "That Liking Feeling: Mood, Emotion, and Social Media Photography," offers a way to subdue anxieties of digital omnipresence through a "thick description" of the everyday substance of social photo interaction. In the relations between hand and apparatus, or eye and screen, the practices involved in using social media harness the habitus of speech, gesture, affect, and anachronism, all of which tend to flow in and out of both digital landscapes and corporeal experience from moment to moment. For Henning, it is the singularity of the user/consumer/photographer's engagement with social media that complicates the litany of concerns surrounding digital ubiquity, routinely cast as either a "flood" of images or an information "overload." What binds the individual social photo user to digital culture are the larger complex modes of algorithmic metrics and data captures that pose at least one significant danger: the construction of a new physiognomy or behavioral pseudoscience, poised to take the social subject of the smartphone age and reduce them to a set of classifiable affective responses and definable cultural practices.

The book closes with an interview with Azoulay. Photography as a citizenry, the event of photography, potential history, imperial rights, worldly sovereignty—the conversation is a transit through many of the most vital and provocative concepts in Azoulay's evolving political ontology of photography. It is also a ranging exploration of questions of distribution and omnipresence as they pertain to photography, imperialism, capitalism, and modernity. For Azoulay, who refuses the smooth transitions of normative history, it is essential to maintain attention not just to the pervasiveness of this or that photographic device, but to the ubiquity of destruction in which photography emerged and upon which its most dominant logics of taking, opening, and extracting have been premised. How, Azoulay asks, can we "reconfigure the ontology of photography in a way that allows us to continue both to engage with it in order not to forget this mass destruction, and to transform it into the compass of repair?"

Notes

1. One source of inspiration for this collection is *Before and After Photography: Histories and Contexts*, edited by Jordan Bear and Kate Palmer Albers. Here, we echo that book's opening sentence as we call attention to a key "orthodoxy" in the study of photography, namely, ubiquity. The orthodoxy Bear and Albers cite is "a shared conviction that a single, authoritative account of the medium is both impossible and undesirable" (Albers and Bear, 2017: 1).

2. This often-quoted estimate originates from a post by Jonathan Good to the *1000 Memories* blog (Good, 2011).

3. Author's translation.

4. The editors are truly grateful for Emily's contribution to our 2018 symposium at the University of Rochester, the material for which resulted in a publication (Doucet, 2018).

5. Another significant cultural theorist indebted to Valéry is Walter Benjamin, whose essays on photography and film mostly posit their relation to traditional art and mass viewership, and not specifically as a sign of ubiquity (Benjamin, 2008).

6. Azoulay observes that "the pre-digital era saw frequent descriptions of cameras and photographs in terms of multiplicity, excess, omnipresence, totality and networking." She suggests that these visions of pre-digital ubiquity "must have suited their writers' world of experience" (Azoulay, 2014: 64).

7. This history of the term ubiquity is largely derived from the *Oxford English Dictionary*.

8. See entry on "Ubiquitarianism" in the *New Catholic Encyclopedia*.

9. Sontag's book ends with an anthology of fragments from the history of photography. It is labelled as an "homage to W.B."

10. The different references are as follows: enterprise, 3; voraciousness, 146; aggrandizement, 115; willy-nilly, antiquing, 79–80; degraded, 58; confusions, 112.

11. Salman Aslam, "Instagram by the Numbers: Stats, Demographics & Fun Facts," Omnicore, https://www.omnicoreagency.com/instagram-statistics (accessed July 15, 2020).

12. Janko Rottgers, "Snapchat Loses 3 Million Daily Users, but Beats Expectations in Q2 Earnings," *Variety*, August 7, 2018, https://variety.com/2018/digital/news/snap-posts-q2-revenue-beat-but-daily-users-down-for-first-time-1202898312.

13. Another example of this strain of ubiquity writing is the work of Martin Hand. For Hand, although there have been "previous perceptions" of cameras being everywhere, the now more profoundly "ubiquitous presence of the camera changes what can be, and is, seen, recorded, discussed and remembered, making the visualization of public and private life bound up with relations of power, expertise and authority" (Hand, 2012: 9).

14. In 2017, the CEO of the streaming platform Netflix, Reed Hastings, admitted to his company's ongoing battle with sleep: "You know, think about it, when you watch a show from Netflix and you get addicted to it, you stay up late at night. You really—we're competing with sleep, on the margin." The curators of the Netflix Twitter account saw in Hastings's admission a marketing opportunity, tweeting "Sleep is my greatest enemy" (Cox, 2017).

15. Mark Weiser coined the term "ubiquitous computing," suggesting that the "most profound technologies are those that disappear," weaving themselves "into the fabric of everyday life until they are indistinguishable from it" (Weiser, 1991: 94). For a variety of perspectives on ubiquitous computing, see a book that served as a precedent for this anthology: Ulrik Ekman, ed., *Throughout: Art and Culture Emerging with Ubiquitous Computing* (Cambridge, MA: MIT Press, 2012).

16. We derive this formulation from Jurgenson, who writes, "The photograph on social media is as underconceptualized as it is ubiquitous" (Jurgenson, 2019: 11).

Bibliography

George Emeka Agbo, "Challenging the Frivolities of Power: The Ubiquitous Camera and Nigerian Political Elites," *Africa*, 89, 2 (May 2019): 286–302.

Karin Andreasson, "Pictures from the Past: The First Ever Selfie, Taken in 1839," *The Guardian*, March 7, 2014, https://www.theguardian.com/artanddesign/picture/2014/mar/07/first-ever-selfie-1839-picture-from-the-past (accessed June 9, 2021).

François Arago, "Report," in *First Exposures: Writings from the Beginning of Photography*, ed. Steffen Siegel (Los Angeles: J. Paul Getty Museum, 2017), 230–240.

Ariella Azoulay, *Aïm Deüelle Lüski and Horizontal Photography* (Leuven: Leuven University Press, 2014).

Ariella Azoulay, *Civil Imagination: A Political Ontology of Photography* (New York: Zone Books, 2015).

Charles Baudelaire, "The Modern Public and Photography," in *Classic Essays on Photography*, ed. Alan Trachtenberg (New Haven: Leete's Island Books, 1980).

Kris Belden-Adams, "Locating the Selfie within Photography's History—and Beyond," in *Exploring the Selfie: Historical, Theoretical, and Analytic Approaches to Digital Self-Photography*, eds Julia Eckel, Jens Ruchatz, and Sabine Wirth (Cham: Palgrave Macmillan, 2018), 83–94.

Walter Benjamin, *The Work of Art in the Age of Its Technological Reproducibility, and Other Writings on Media*, eds Michael W. Jennings, Brigid Doherty, and Thomas Y. Levin (Cambridge, MA: Belknap Press, 2008).

François Brunet, *The Birth of the Idea of Photography*, trans. Shane B. Lillis (Toronto: RIC Books, 2019).

Chris Chesher, "Between Image and Information: The iPhone Camera in the History of Photography," in *Studying Mobile Media: Cultural Technologies, Mobile Communication, and the iPhone*, eds Larissa Hjorth, Jean Burgess, and Ingrid Richardson (London: Taylor & Francis Group, 2012), 98–117.

Peter Cox, "Amazon? HBO? Netflix thinks its real competitor is… sleep," April 17, 2017, https://www.vox.com/2017/4/17/15334122/netflix-sleep-competitor-amazon-hbo (accessed July 8, 2020).

Jonathan Crary, *24/7: Late Capitalism and the Ends of Sleep* (New York: Verso Books, 2013).

David Cressy, *Saltpeter: The Mother of Gunpowder* (Oxford: Oxford University Press, 2013).

B.R. Curtis, *Reports of Decisions in the Supreme Court of the United States with Notes, and a Digest, Vol. XIV* (Boston: Little, Brown and Company, 1855).

Tom de Castella, "Five Ways the Digital Camera Changed Us," BBC *News Magazine*, February 28, 2012, https://www.bbc.com/news/magazine-16483509 (accessed July 8, 2020).

Claudia H. Deutsch, "At Kodak, Some Old Things Are New Again," *New York Times*, May 2, 2008, https://www.nytimes.com/2008/05/02/technology/02kodak.html (accessed July 8, 2020).

Emily Doucet, "In History, the Future: Determinism in the Early History of Photography in France," *communcation +1*, 7, 1 (2018), https://scholarworks.umass.edu/cpo/vol7/iss1/4 (accessed July 1, 2020).

Ulrik Ekman, ed., *Throughout: Art and Culture Emerging with Ubiquitous Computing* (Cambridge, MA: MIT Press, 2012).

Rose Eveleth, "How Many Photographs of You Are Out There in the World?" *The Atlantic*, November 2, 2015, https://www.theatlantic.com/technology/archive/2015/11/how-many-photographs-of-you-are-out-there-in-the-world/413389 (accessed July 9, 2020).

Exact and Certaine Newes from the Siege at Yorke (London: Matthew Walbanke, 1644), n.p.

Beatrice Farwell, *The Cult of Images: Baudelaire and the 19th-Century Media Explosion*, exh. cat. (Santa Barbara: UCSB Art Museum, 1977).

T.S. Flock, "Photography Has Become So Ubiquitous and Rapidly Reproducible," *Seattle Weekly*, November 22, 2014, https://www.seattleweekly.com/news/photography-has-become-so-ubiquitous-and-rapidly-reproducible-what-with-smart-phones-and (accessed July 10, 2020).

Vilém Flusser, *Towards a Philosophy of Photography* (London: Reaktion Books, 2000).

Michel Frizot et al., *A New History of Photography* (Cologne: Könemann, 1998).

Jonathan Good, "How Many Photos Have Ever Been Taken?", *1000 Memories*, September 15, 2011. https://web.archive.org/web/20120410065516/http://blog.1000memories.com/94-number-of-photos-ever-taken-digital-and-analog-in-shoebox (accessed July 6, 2020).

Lisa Gye, "Picture This: The Impact of Mobile Camera Phones on Personal Photographic Practices," *Continuum*, 21, 2 (June 2007): 279–288.

Martin Hand, *Ubiquitous Photography* (Cambridge, MA: Polity Press, 2012).

Ernest Hello, *L'Homme: La Vie, La Science, L'Art*, 7th ed. (Paris: Perrin, 1903).

Nathan Jurgenson, *The Social Photo: On Photography and Social Media* (New York: Verso, 2019).

Sarah Kember, "Ubiquitous Photography," *Philosophy of Photography*, 3, 2 (2012): 331–348.

Sarah Kember, "Ambient Intelligent Photography," in *The Photographic Image in Digital Culture*, 2nd ed., ed. Martin Lister (Abingdon: Routledge, 2013).

Sarah Kember and Joanna Zylinska, *Life After New Media: Mediation as a Vital Process* (Cambridge, MA: MIT Press, 2012).

Sergei Klebnikov, "What's Happening to Kodak Stock? Shares Plunge Over 40% after Government Loan Is Held Up on Allegations of Wrongdoing," *Forbes*, August 10, 2020, https://www.forbes.com/sites/sergeikleb-nikov/2020/08/10/whats-happening-to-kodak-stock-shares-plunge-over-40-after-government-loan-is-held-up-on-allegations-of-wrongdoing/?sh=50e5074332bb (accessed June 9, 2020).

Siegfried Kracauer, "Photography," in *The Mass Ornament: Weimar Essays*, trans. Thomas Y. Levin (Cambridge, MA: Harvard University, 1995), 47–63.

Theresa Levitt, "Biot's Paper and Arago's Plates: Photographic Practice and the Transparency of Representation," *Isis*, 94, 3 (2003): 456–476.

Mary Warner Marien, *Photography: A Cultural History*, 4th ed. (Boston: Pearson, 2015).

Daisuke Okabe and Mizuko Ito, "Everyday Contexts of Camera Phone Use: Steps toward Technosocial Ethnographic Frameworks," in *Mobile Communication in Everyday Life: an Ethnographic View*, eds Joachim Höflich and Maren Hartmann (Berlin: Frank & Timme, 2006).

Daniel Palmer, "Mobile Exchanges," Paper presented at the Vital Signs conference, ACMI, Melbourne, September 8, 2005.

Christopher Pinney, *The Coming of Photography in India* (London: The British Library, 2008).

Fred Ritchin, *After Photography* (New York: W.W. Norton & Company, 2009).

Karen Robinson-Jacobs, "'Serious Concerns' Put Trump's Much-Hyped Pharmaceuticals Plan on Hold," *Forbes*, August 8, 2020. https://www.forbes.com/sites/karenrobin-sonjacobs/2020/08/08/trumps-much-hyped-plan-for-kod-ak-pharmaceuticals-put-on-hold/#13f69e5fcd1c (accessed August 11, 2020).

Janko Rottger, "Snapchat Loses 3 Million Daily Users, But Beats Expectations in Q2 Earnings," *Variety*, August 7, 2018. https://variety.com/2018/digital/news/snap-posts-q2-revenue-beat-but-daily-users-down-for-first-time-1202898312 (accessed June 9, 2021).

"Select Committee on Fine Arts" of the English House of Commons, published in *Blackwood's Edinburgh Magazine*, 50 (July–Dec 1841): 585–595.

Hans Sloane, *A voyage to the islands Madera, Barbados, Nieves, S. Christophers and Jamaica: with the natural history of the herbs and trees, four-footed beasts, fishes, birds, insects, reptiles, &c. of the last of those islands; to which is prefix'd an introduction, wherein is an account of the inhabitants, air, waters, diseases, trade, &c. of that place, with some relations concerning the neighbouring continent, and islands of America. Illustrated with figures of the things describ'd, which have not been heretofore engraved; in large copper-plates as big as the life, Vol. 2* (London: Printed by B.M. for the author, 1707).

Susan Sontag, *On Photography* (New York: Picador, 1977).

John Stauffer, Zoe Trodd, and Celeste-Marie Bernier, *Picturing Frederick Douglass: An Illustrated Biography of the Nineteenth Century's Most Photographed American* (New York: W.W. Norton & Company, Inc., 2015).

Paul Valéry, "The Conquest of Ubiquity," in *Aesthetics: Collected Works*, trans. Ralph Mannheim, vol. 13 (New York: Pantheon, 1964), 225–228.

Paul Valéry, "The Centenary of Photography," in *Classic Essays on Photography*, ed. Alan Trachtenberg (New Haven: Leete's Island Books, 1980), 191–198.

Tendayi Viki, "On the Fifth Anniversary of Kodak's Bankruptcy, How Can Large Companies Sustain Innovation?" *Forbes*, January 29, 2017, https://www.forbes.com/sites/tendayiviki/2017/01/19/on-the-fifth-anniversa-ry-of-kodaks-bankruptcy-how-can-large-companies-sus-tain-innovation/#34dcb69a6280 (accessed July 10, 2020).

Jan von Brevern, "The Eternal Child: On Expectations in the History of Photography," *Getty Research Journal*, 7 (2015): 67–80.

Mark Weiser, "The Computer for the 21st Century," *Scientific American* (September 1991): 94–104.

"Ubiquitarianism," *New Catholic Encyclopedia*, https://www.encyclopedia.com/religion/encyclopedias-alma-nacs-transcripts-and-maps/ubiquitarianism (accessed June 9, 2021).

"Ubiquity," *Oxford English Dictionary*, September 2021, Oxford University Press, https://www.oed.com/view/Entry/208517 (accessed September 9, 2021).

Shoshana Zuboff, *The Age of Surveillance Capitalism: The Fight for a Human Future at the New Frontier of Power* (New York: Public Affairs, 2019).

Joanna Zylinska, *Nonhuman Photography* (Cambridge, MA: MIT Press, 2017).

1. Early Photography's Presence

Jacob W. Lewis

The history of photography has long aimed to chart the discursive formation of its central object of study as an analytic unity, as medium or technology, framed as larger than the sum of its actual objects and procedures at a given moment in time. But since the 1970s, photography as such has been dutifully critiqued as an institutionally functional object of larger forces (Tagg, 1993). This includes corporations and small industry, the art market and art museum, and the state and its archive. The critical turn toward the study of "photographies" nevertheless occluded a more open analysis of photography's abstract unity. This unity, I argue, can be thought of not in terms of its identity but in terms of its presence.

An illuminating example of how photography as such came to be conceived immediately upon its introduction to the world is Théodore Maurisset's *Daguerreotypomania!* from 1839. (see fig. 0.2) A crucial bit of historical ephemera surrounding photography's origins, this satirical lithograph gave form to a variety of collective psychoses behind the rush to define Daguerre's new invention and its profligate cultural spread as a consequence of an ideological faith in progress, utopian idealism, and economic exploitation. Yet Maurisset's social panorama describes an imaginary rather than an actuality. In late 1839, most of the artist's audience, and plausibly even the artist himself, had yet to even see an object made by Daguerre's process. In this case, what remains is to interrogate the object of the disparate manias to which Maurisset's image points us, with his ambivalent register of both hopeful prognostication and outright critical refusal. All signs point to the delusion that photography was always already everywhere, amid other idealized demotic powers and more material expanses in the age of industry and capital. Early audiences understood photographic practice in relation to social traditions that came before, including professional organization, social emulation, and economic competition across 19th-century ideologies behind free-market capitalism and social utopianism. These early conceptions of practice and the discourses that shaped them needed photography to be a deferred object of thought. In short, photography's identity belonged to the future, but its contemporaneity was felt in quite specific, public terms.

To analyze further photography's identity as deferred to the future, this essay traces the importance of the *virtual*—the realm of the inchoate, the effective, the almost-as-described, the extant *in potentia*—to photography's early presence as an intelligible technology. Those academic scientists, amateur practitioners, hack journalists, and snobbish critics who helped define photography did so by expressing what the camera could potentially do that was neither measurable nor, in some cases, achievable in the moment. It is in early accounts and early images that the medium first expressed itself as, so to say, a virtual reality. One didn't need to handle a camera or be recorded by it to know the mania of *Daguerreotypomania!* was at least a cumulative affect, and, at most, a shared psychosis. The collective delusion of photography's omnipresence anticipates and, historically, continues to infuse contemporary notions of ubiquity in the digital domain. But that takes us too far from photography's start.

Arago's Utpianism

Photography's beginnings continue to clarify how the medium and its widespread applications have been historicized and intellectualized, so it follows that a return (again) to its contested origins is in order (Batchen, 1999; Sheehan and Zervigon, 2015; Siegel, 2017)—not with the inventor of photography, per se, but with the inventor of its discourse. That is, François Arago, the astronomer, scientist, statesman, and ardent Republican at a time of political repression under the July Monarchy regime. As a prominent member of the Académie des Sciences, Arago was responsible for the introduction of Daguerre's process as France's imperial gift to the world, recognizing its historic significance immediately, as well as utilizing it to promote his own political and cultural standing (McCauley, 1991; Levitt, 2003; Tresch, 2012).

In his framing of the many uses of the daguerreotype for archaeology, astronomy, biology, and the arts, Arago merits tremendous recognition as the preliminary architect of photography's expansive cultural imaginary. Delivering his report to the Académie on July 3, 1839, he was the first to further describe Daguerre's process to a curious public who, since January of that year, had read scant descriptions of the new visual technology. Not long after, Arago's speech was printed in the Académie's journal, as well as in a separate pamphlet, and the text outlines the technology's possible utilizations for the public good, the most specific of which was how daguerreotypy could be marshaled to complete the reproduction of ancient hieroglyphs of Egypt, a colonial project of science (and data extraction) that accompanied Napoleon's ill-fated North African and Middle Eastern campaigns at the close of the 18th century. Arago's discourse on the origins and future of photography is beholden to the history of modern France's imperial project, as Ariella Aïsha Azoulay identifies. The statesman's emphasis on archaeological documentation—in spite of Egypt's indigenous population, as well as their current occupation under Ottoman force—repurposes a desire to document into a "neutral procedure to be used by those who one the proper means for it, and regardless of the will of those from whom the objects have been expropriated." (Azoulay, 2019: 3–4)

Walter Benjamin, almost a century later, insists on the power that Arago's discourse must have played on the public's imagination at the time, and likewise accepts photography's right to record (and, by realization, the right to expropriate) as a given:

> The beautiful thing about this speech is the connections it makes with all aspects of human activity. The panorama it sketches is broad enough not only to make the dubious project of authenticating photography in terms of painting—which it does anyway—seem beside the point; more important, it offers an insight into the real scope of the invention. […] In a great arc Arago's speech spans the field of new technologies from astrophysics to philology: alongside the prospects for photographing the stars and planets we find the idea of establishing a photographic record of the Egyptian hieroglyphs. (Benjamin, 2008: 275)

While Arago in 1839 and Benjamin a century later never doubted the right to reproduce by photographic means, for both interlocutors of photography's history, it was the device's *potentiality* that provided the ground upon which (imperial) modernization forged violently ahead, and on which modernity took shape in increasingly visual and material ways. In the July report, Arago stresses not a determined future but an open field of potentiality—of things to come: "When observers apply a new instrument to the study of nature, what they have hoped for is always insignificant compared to the succession of discoveries which the instrument originates. In this manner, it is on *the unforeseen* [*imprévu*] that one must particularly count." (Arago, in Siegel, 2017: 238) In this sense, "the unforeseen" that Arago stresses as the boon of invention is what drives modern technologies and defines their logic of progress. Perhaps the unforeseen is that which complements that other generative, essential, *virtual* power of photography, such that the invention's many contributions, while not yet physically (ac)countable are at once conceptual and real.

Arago's expectations for the daguerreotype, even though denoted as an aspect of the unknown and unforeseen, nonetheless offer a skeletal reality for early photography, especially when the medium in its early years was consciously identified as "in its infancy," as Jan von Brevern has analyzed (Brevern, 2015). In one account of the new process by the critic Jules Janin, he writes, "here is an art very much in its infancy; it is indeed a wondrous preparation, but it is attended by so many difficulties of every kind as to be almost impossible to make use of." He continues, deploying a telling pharmaceutical analogy:

> It is at such a stage of experiment, if you will allow me the comparison, as characterizes drugs employed in medicine. Some drugs are simple, natural, and easy to use, so that any housewife may employ them: marshmallow, mullein, couch grass. On the other hand, other remedies very useful in medicine call for great skill in preparation, morphine, for example. Well, the Dagueréotype [*sic*], such as it is today, is like morphine; very few are skillful or wealthy enough to make use of it. It is now necessary to bring it to the condition of couch grass, within reach of all. (Janin, in Siegel, 2017: 209)

Janin's remarks are from reading and reviewing the process as it was in its introductory state amid Arago's overture to the Académie and to the public at large. The daguerreotype as both object and process, Janin notes, was something that had yet to transition from the possible to the real, despite his appreciation for its demonstration and debut. For the author, of course, it was a branch of medicine and (gendered) levels of expertise that begged consideration that the process may still yet achieve something greater, more democratic, more everyday, and "within reach of all." In short, Janin's analogy in 1839 suggests what he is describing is not a process debuting before the Académie, but photography qua an identifiable medium, one with the potential to become standardized, but also present everywhere and ubiquitous like a weed. Strangely, Janin's analogy of photography to couch grass—an invasive plant traditionally used in herbal remedies—cannot escape its pejorative character. While Europeans used *Elymus repens* for domestic remedies, in 19th-century agriculture and horticulture, couch grass was considered an obstructive weed (as it is figured today) that required various techniques and herbicides to curb its spread.

As Brevern writes, the following second generation of practitioners and observers "rarely imagined disappointments" in their discussion of the state of photography and its future. Along with articulating photography's historical forebears in lens-based technologies such as the camera obscura and chemical experiments with light-sensitive metals, "much more often, they stressed that photography's future applications were unforeseeable." (Brevern, 2015: 69) Thus, Arago's notion of "the unforeseen" found purchase with practitioners and critics who ventured away from discussions of actual process or technique in order to conceive of the practical field in larger, more conceptually coherent terms.

For photographers and other commentators in the 1850s, a bald utopian rhetoric became the norm (Doucet, 2018). To speak of photography was to speak of its future by describing its ever-present potential for various applications that had yet to manifest but were nonetheless anticipated, moving beyond "the unforeseen." Photographers of the 1850s saw techniques, practices, and their products exhibiting only the germ of ideality, technical perfection, or artistry. As the critic and novelist Francis Wey noted in 1851, public perception of photography was that it functioned as "a nascent thing" whose transitive power was that "*which promised.*" (Wey, 1851: 138) The greatest coherence of photography as a medium was seen to emerge in its virtual elements whose actual existence was either imagined or thought as bound to emerge through the force of progress. In lexical terms, photography in the 19th century had less to do with a distant concrete time, *le futur*, than with the active imagining of what was to come, *l'avenir*, an operative distinction that Jacques Derrida signals in remarks on language and reason (Derrida, 2005: 135).

Other examples of such futurity emerge in photography's second decade. In the wake of the 1855 Exposition Universelle and the dramatic expansion of photographic processes into the sphere of industry, a correspondent for the journal *Le Photographe* writes of this "novel art" and its prominence at the exhibition: "Photography proclaims itself a work of the future." (Latreille, 1855: 11) In another account, when faced with examples of improved techniques on display at the exhibition, the critic Louis Figuier saw photography as a tangled mix of the recent past, the actual present, and the inchoate future: "All these methods, these discoveries, which are so-to-say born yesterday, and of which many still only remain a germ, open a whole new world to photography. What will be their precise influence on the future of this art? No one can know it yet." (Figuier, 1859)

To remark on photography's current position in science and culture was inevitably to describe aspects that required development, such as its ease, permanence, cost effectiveness, reproducibility, instantaneity, and adaptability to industry—all of which were frequent frustrations and lacunae for many photographers and viewers (Lewis, 2012). These aspects, while still unintelligible or impractical, afforded signs of a more expansive, more precise, yet presently unknowable definition on the horizon. Photographic discourse was, in its first decades, mostly technical description paired with a strong sense of a virtual, unforeseen world of application, or a kind of science fiction avant la lettre.

In histories of photography, a position for the virtual is conspicuously lacking; that is, apart from instances in which photo media is incorporated into other associative and worn apparatuses that provide a "virtual reality," a term that first gained currency in early computer programming and data visualization. Yet the virtual is by no means special to these millennial technologies and the social relations that they reconfigure. In 19th-century photography, there existed a need to define photography, and with it to engage its virtual, conceptual elements that shaped the image of photography's future in a coherent array of techniques, uses, and objects. In this way, photographs, like traditional works of art, "are immersed in a virtuality," which Gilles Deleuze suggests "is not some confused determination but the completely determined structure formed by its genetic differential elements, its 'virtual' or 'embryonic' elements." (Deleuze, 1994: 209) These elements are conceived in terms of their ability to demonstrate potentiality, rather than the set of empirical characteristics perceptible in a given object.

Deleuze, whose early work engages with the "actual/virtual" axis of thought, still locates both concepts in reality. This maneuver constitutes his attempt to counter the prevalence of the real/possible axis in philosophy, which precludes the impossible as having a home in the "real." In effect, media theory necessitates an involvement with the virtual since mediated images offer presence where there is no traditionally sensible, tangible, physical one. Moreover, the virtual in media and in photography make gains in proximity to the project of representation, which was key to Arago's discourse—the (re)presentation of an absent presence, or a presence where there is no more but once was. There is another notion of presence, that, as the late Douglas Crimp wrote in relation to postmodernism, describes "the notion of a presence as a kind of increment to being there, a ghostly aspect of presence that is its excess, its supplement." (Crimp, 1980: 92) That is, photography in its debut had a virtual presence, a reality in excess, a supplement in its saturation—what Ernst Bloch would designate as the *Uberschuss* or "overshot" of utopian thought (Bloch, 1988). This excess first germinated in the pages of the Académie's *Comptes Rendus*, in news articles that parroted Arago's reports, and then in technical treatises, art criticism, the popular imagination, and finally the (ubiquitous) everywhere of photographic cultures to come, in particular the new amateur practice inaugurated by George Eastman and the Kodak camera in the late 19th century.

Nevertheless, photography's presence-as-excess was still founded on the relation between human subjects and the material objects. For one, Arago championed the daguerreotype plate as appropriate to envision photography's future precisely because of its representational power— what Edgar Allan Poe in 1840 identified as the daguerreotype plate's ability to withstand scrutiny to reveal "a more absolute truth, a more perfect identity of aspect with the thing represented." (Poe, in Trachtenberg, 1980: 38) An example of the exactitude and uncanny clarity of sight afforded by Daguerre's process can be found in the physicist Léon

Foucault's still life of grapes on the vine from the 1840s. (fig. 1.1) The mirrored daguerreotype surface, when paired with the aspect of a hyperreal natural specimen that dangles awkwardly before a clean backdrop, combine to demonstrate an account of the daguerreotype as an image of the world and, simultaneously, a thing of that same world represented therein. The irreconcilable figure of photography's representational power can be considered an aspect of not only the photograph's presence but also photography's presence.

Arago's position was in contradistinction to proponents of the main competitor to Daguerre's invention: the "photogenic drawing" and subsequent relative "calotype" process that William Henry Fox Talbot developed simultaneously in England. Arago's ideas about the power of resemblance and collective vision, as Theresa Levitt demonstrates, placed him in opposition to other academicians such as Jean-Baptiste Biot, who was drawn to Talbot's process not simply for its representational abilities, but for its potential development in sensitometry and the measurement of light-sensitive material (Levitt, 2003). Biot conceived of Talbot's work with silver salts on drawing paper as indicative of photography's power as a means to record light and to generate data for scientific purposes. Similarly, Biot's emphasis on photography's abstraction of light shares affinities with how in an 1839 description Talbot narrated his own process of mental abstraction that emerged from his first experiments with the camera lucida, and then later with his own photographic cameras:

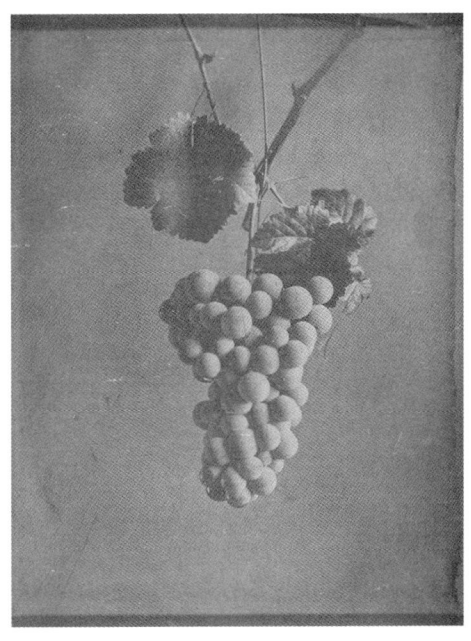

Figure 1.1

Léon Foucault, *Bunch of Grapes [Grappes de raisins]*, c. 1844. Daguerreotype, ¼ plate, 12×8.8 cm. Collection Société Française de Photographie.

See also Plate 3.

> The picture, divested of the ideas which accompany it, and considered only in its ultimate nature, is but a succession or variety of stronger lights thrown upon one part of the paper, and of deeper shadows on another. (Talbot, in Trachtenberg, 1980: 29)

Photography, in both its virtual and de facto forms, had to do with the choice of procedure and—to risk a technological deterministic claim here—the subject position that the chosen procedure instantiated (Crary, 1990). In contrast to Arago's emphasis on exactitude in representation, Biot located "the unforeseen" in the photographic object itself, which, with examination and measurement, would yield much more information beyond a first glance. Brevern characterizes the difference:

for Biot, who looked to photography for new scientific discoveries, expectations were of much higher relevance than for Arago, who viewed photography as a merely reproductive medium. For the latter, it was possible to expect all kinds of unforeseeable future applications of the new medium in general; but for the former, high expectations existed furthermore on the level of the single image. Every photograph was potentially able to reveal something hitherto unknown. (Brevern, 2015: 76)

The distinctions conjured by Arago and Biot also signal that photography was not only considered programmatic but also *programmable* (Flusser, 2000), residing in the control of both producers and observers—the latter privileged by Biot, and the former by Arago, both of whom took for granted both a right to reproduce and a right to look.

As is demonstrated by his politics and his utopian rhetoric, Arago was greatly influenced by the utopian socialism of Henri de Saint-Simon and industrialist Charles Fourier. Adherents to the movement of Saint-Simonianism, and its subsequent iteration in Fourierism, envisioned modern utopian society through theoretical writings, technological innovations, scientific management, and iconic images and architectural forms (Kerr, 2012). Fourier designed a new communal structure comparable to the palaces of old that he termed the phalanstery (*phalanstère*), referencing the Greek *phalanx*, an ancient military form, and the ascetic space of the medieval monastery. Within this serialized structure, labors and daily tasks would rotate regularly among members according to universal laws of social harmony, which "intensified affections and rivalries, spurring production." (Tresch, 237) Fourier's acolyte Victor Considerant published a detailed plan of Fourier's innovation after his mentor's death, showing "a societal palace dedicated to humanity" that envisioned a communal space where hundreds of families, separate from and at once dependent upon a larger economy and philanthropy, occupied various functional and living spaces that surrounded a central cultivated green space. Considerant's print carries the emboldened title *The Future* (*l'Avenir*), stressing the idealism and radical potentiality of the design for social reorganization. But its militaristic look is less akin to a palace; instead, it betrays similarity to soldiers' barracks, as if an architectural manifestation of a military term that earlier Saint-Simonian theorists reinvested with new meaning: the avant-garde.

In the centrist, juste-milieu political climate in which Charles Fourier's work was received, as well as that of François Arago, the reach of utopian socialism seemed not to extend beyond philosophy and experimentation shared by small social networks of the cultural elite. Those influenced by the movement's commitment to social reorganization, particularly the radicals Pierre-Joseph Proudhon, Karl Marx, and

Friedrich Engels, came to critique its lack of materialist analysis of economic and social conditions, its scant consideration of capitalism, and its role in class organization. Furthermore, the technocratic ideology that lay behind such imagined utopias was channeled into state-making ventures whose extremist outcomes were not community's salvation, but its violent destruction, in particular France's colonization of Algeria after the 1830 invasion of Ottoman-occupied territory. Rather than the *phalanstère*, the Saint-Simonians' most successful, lasting consequence was the institution of its ideas through the bureaucracy of colonial administration, to the benefit of France's economic empire and to the violent detriment of North Africa's Arab and indigenous populations (Abi-Mershed, 2010).

Maurisset's Realism

Utopia, whether considered mere fantasy or political danger, has always maintained ties to the genre of satire. One need only consider Thomas More's 16th-century *Utopia*, in which he describes an ideal society in the genre of a travel narrative, whose fiction also suggests its reading as a nascent satire of More's own political world (Kloeg, 2016: 210). If the utopian impulse at photography's inception lays embedded in the discourse of Arago, then the complementary actor that meets the challenge is the illustrator Théodore Maurisset.

A painter, lithographer, and caricaturist active in the middle of the 19th century, Maurisset, along with Honoré Daumier, counts among a few figures so central to the beginnings of photography who was never once known to make a photograph. His most widely known lithograph is *Daguerreotypomania!*, from late 1839, showing crowds stretched into the distance, waiting to catch a glimpse of Daguerre's new process and its explosion of cultural relevance. What Maurisset illustrates is the crowd, that demotic force that resists individual reason and adopts the "mania" of the mob. Their mania is for novelty, an ecstatic modernity, and material progress, akin to what Charles Baudelaire, in 1859, decried in his screed against photography's newfound public:

> An avenging God has heard the prayers of this multitude; Daguerre was his messiah. […] From that moment onwards, our loathsome society rushed, like Narcissus, to contemplate its trivial image on the metallic plate. A form of lunacy, an extraordinary fanaticism took hold of these new sun-worshippers. (Baudelaire, in Trachtenberg, 1980: 86–87)

While Baudelaire's heavily cited words describe a critical perspective on his present moment—and the marginal acceptance of photography in (or more specifically *near*) the Salon des Beaux-Arts of that year—Maurisset's earlier image conveys not the actual state of photography but its "expected impact" fated to unfold in society. Jan von Brevern indicates that Maurisset's image is not "a satirical comment on the immediate photographic craze" but "an image about the future" that saw Daguerre's novelty as a cult object, a "vehicle for the visual," and a robust engine of progress (Brevern, 2015: 72). Maurisset was likely as much influenced by the pages of the Académie's *Comptes Rendus* as he was by speculation and rumor directed at the process, and it remains very plausible that Maurisset himself had yet to see an example of a daguerreotype, much as how Baudelaire may have never viewed the photographic exhibition adjacent to the 1859 Salon in advance of writing his aforementioned critique. What Maurisset described at photography's inception was neither Arago's producers nor Biot's observers, but the future of photography as an object of visual consumption for the masses, whose spectacular presence for viewers is akin to the stage presence of the acrobat in transit on a tightrope on the print's far left. Photography is not only a presence but also a circus born of that presence, resembling pure excess.

Ten years later, Maurisset had the chance to depict once more the "vehicle for the visual" that was Daguerre's invention. In the early 1850s, the illustrator again portrayed photography's public in a promotional lithograph for the studio operator and lens manufacturer Pierre-Ambroise Richebourg. (fig. 1.2) No longer an image of expectation generating the madness of the crowd, photography's power now rests in the hands of able and trusted producers. The producer in question, Richebourg, is seen practicing his art perched upon a giant camera and lens that serves as both a stage and a rampart, enticing the crowd to the studio and protecting him from their unwieldy numbers. Satisfied customers and visual consumers in the foreground busy themselves with looking, scanning their gaze for something in oversize works, photomicrographs, reproductions of paintings, and stereoscopic series that litter the foreground before Richebourg's immobile giant camera. In one case, the exactitude and power of representation wielded by Richebourg deceives a loyal dog, whose gruff matron appears upset that her animal companion responds excitedly to her daguerreotyped representation and not her real, physical presence. On the left, behind the cashier's booth, laborers haul giant sacks of cash to the top of the ramparts (*forteresse*) whose caption identifies it as the business's strongbox, or safe (*coffre fort*). The desire for photography that Maurisset characterizes here, then, is the desire for the commodity and the value that undergirds it.

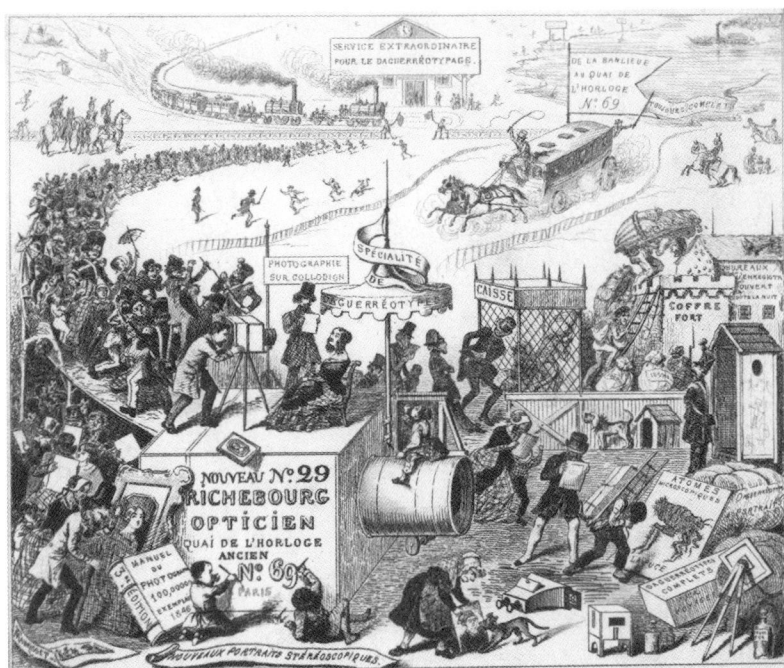

Figure 1.2

Théodore Maurisset, advertisement for the business of optician and daguerreotypist Pierre-Ambrose Richebourg on the Quai de la Horloge, Paris, ca. 1846. Lithograph, image: 10.2×12 cm; frame: 19.5×22 cm. George Eastman Museum, gift of Eastman Kodak Company, formerly collection Gabriel Cromer.

Maurisset's return to photography's public begs the question: are we faced with the same maniacal crowds that welcomed Daguerre as a modern "messiah"? The most dramatic change is that the earlier image's unruly mob is now fully policed by imperial grenadiers and artillery officers, and photography's public here forms standard lines that nonetheless stretch into the background. On the right, a guard stands at his post, surveilling the stream of people wending their way to the studio and the cashier's depot. On the left, another official tangles violently with a member of the public in line who grabs on to a bayonet; yet another military official counts himself among Richebourg's customers as a member of the public. Still others in full regalia patrol on horseback as incidental staffage filling out an imperial landscape. Maurisset's image likely dates to the years immediately prior to the Crimean War and Paris's 1855 Exposition Universelle, at which time Richebourg still prided himself as an early "primitive of photography," as the portraitist Nadar describes him in his memoir (Nadar, 2017: 180). Unlike many early photographers, Richebourg adapted to new markets, promoting not only his skill in daguerreotypy but also his use of the "new" collodion method introduced in 1851 (noted in Maurisset's advertisement). He continued to operate his studio and his work as a supplier of lenses into the early days of the Third Republic (McCauley, 1994: 359), seeing through not only photography's inception and industrialization but also its spread as a middle-class collectible in the form of portraits and instrument of imperial statehood in the form of expedition photography.

What, then, happened to the "unforeseen" in photography in its first decade? An advertisement is hardly the place to discover new futures of photography; rather, the commercial image can be a place where one finds not futures but the ideologically fraught desires that undergird a faith in progress toward some future. That said, Maurisset's image offers a further entrenched, materialist view of photography's economy that leaves the utopian idealism of the past behind for a kind of critical description if not pessimistic realism. The same elements from the earlier image are here—steamships, locomotives, carriages, banners, acrobats—but in the Richebourg image, the unruly crowd is hemmed in by desires economized, industrialized, and policed for the sake of modern wonder and the profits that follow. The economy of expectations that figured so wildly in *Daguerreotypomania!* are suddenly streamlined toward a recognition of industrial production, surplus value, and asset protection.

Still, I would argue that, in Maurisset's canny dystopia described in the space of a promotional print, photography nevertheless bears new details of the same "presence." This virtual presence, existing in supplement and in excess, is proximate to the late Douglas Crimp's deployment of the term to signify a governing force in postmodern art's critique of commodity culture (Crimp, 1980). The same presence, I argue, is an aspect of early photography's identity, or at least an identity of aspect (pace Poe), that asserts itself in early photography's perpetual shifts from virtual to actual, from utopian idealization to material realization. As Vered Maimon writes in her study of early photography *Singular Images, Failed Copies*, this is about photography's representational power transformed and harnessed by an even greater ubiquity, one that we cannot ignore:

> It is precisely by narrowing and standardizing photographic processes and thereby making them 'mimic' pictorial conventions of representation that photography came to be defined as a transparent medium of resemblance and representation. Yet this condition marks a shift in the discursive order of the photographic image, whose 'infancy' was marked by difference and repetition as a function of its inseparability from 'nature's hand.' That is, this new condition is not the logical outcome of the shift from the 'artist's hand' to 'nature's pencil' but precisely the opposite: the *historical* displacement of nature in favor of the 'second nature' of industrial capitalism. (Maimon, 2015: 149)

Bibliography

Osama Abi-Mershed, *Apostles of Modernity: Saint-Simonians and the Civilizing Mission in Algeria* (Stanford: Stanford University Press, 2010).

Geoffrey Batchen, *Burning with Desire: The Conception of Photography* (Cambridge, MA: MIT Press, 1999).

Walter Benjamin, "Little History of Photography," in *The Work of Art in the Age of Its Technological Reproducibility*, eds Michael W. Jennings, Brigid Doherty, and Thomas Y. Levin (Cambridge, MA: Belknap Press, 2008), 507–530.

Ernst Bloch, *The Utopian Function of Art and Literature: Selected Essays*, trans. Jack Zipes and Frank Mecklenburg (Cambridge, MA: MIT, 1988).

Jan von Brevern, "The Eternal Child: On Expectations in the History of Photography," *Getty Research Journal*, 7 (2015): 67–80.

Jonathan Crary, *Techniques of the Observer: On Vision and Modernity in the Nineteenth Century* (Cambridge, MA: MIT Press, 1990).

Douglas Crimp, "The Photographic Activity of Postmodernism," *October*, 15 (1980): 91–101.

Gilles Deleuze, *Difference and Repetition* (1968), trans. Paul Patton (New York: Columbia University Press, 1994).

Jacques Derrida, *Rogues: Two Essays on Reason*, trans. Pascale-Anne Brault and Michael Nass (Stanford: Stanford University Press, 2005).

See Emily Doucet, "In History, the Future: Determinism in the Early History of Photography in France," *communcation +1*, 7, 1 (2018), https://scholarworks.umass.edu/cpo/vol7/iss1/4 (accessed June 9, 2021).

Louis Figuier, "Exposition de photographie," *La Presse* (August 12, 1859).

Greg Kerr, "Utopia and Iconicity: Reading Saint-Simonian Texts," *Word & Image*, 28, 3 (2012): 317–330.

Julien Kloeg, "Utopianism and Its Discontents: A Conceptual History," in *Utopia 1516–2016: More's Eccentric Essay and Its Activist Aftermath*, eds Han van Ruler and Giulia Sissa (Amsterdam: Amsterdam University Press, 2016), 207–224.

Edouard de Latreille, "Revue de l'Exposition Universelle," *Le Photographe* (November 1, 1855): 11–13.

Theresa Levitt, "Biot's Paper and Arago's Plates: Photographic Practice and the Transparency of Representation," *Isis*, 94, 3 (2003): 456–476.

Jacob W. Lewis, "Charles Nègre in Pursuit of the Photographic," (PhD diss., Northwestern University, 2012).

Vered Maimon, *Singular Images, Failed Copies: William Henry Fox Talbot and the Early Photograph* (Minneapolis: University of Minnesota Press, 2015).

Anne McCauley, *Industrial Madness: Commercial Photography in Paris, 1848–1871* (New Haven: Yale University Press, 1994).

Anne McCauley, "François Arago and the Politics of the French Invention of Photography," in *Multiple Views: Logan Grant Essays on Photography, 1983–1989*, ed. Daniel Younger (Albuquerque: University of New Mexico Press, 1991), 43–69.

Nadar [Félix Tournachon], *Quand j'étais photographe*, ed. Caroline Larroche (Garches: Éditions À Propos, 2017).

Tanya Sheehan and Andrés Mario Zervigon, eds, *Photography and Its Origins* (New York: Routledge, 2015).

Steffan Siegel, ed. *First Exposures: Writings from the Beginning of Photography* (Los Angeles: The J. Paul Getty Museum, 2017).

John Tagg, *The Burden of Representation: Essays on Photographies and Histories* (Minneapolis: University of Minnesota Press, 1993).

Alan Trachtenberg, ed., *Classic Essays on Photography* (New Haven: Leete's Island Books, 1980).

John Tresch, *The Romantic Machine: Utopian Science and Technology after Napoleon* (Chicago: University of Chicago, 2012).

Francis Wey, "Des progrès et de l'avenir de la photographie," *La Lumière* 1, no. 35 (October 5, 1851): 138.

2. Photographic Privilege at the World's Columbian Exposition

Annie Rudd

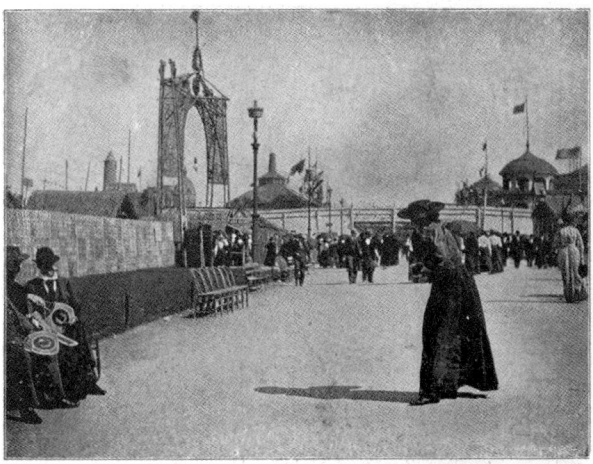

THE EVER-PRESENT "KODAK" FIEND.

Figure 2.1

"The Ever-Present 'Kodak' Fiend," from *Glimpses of the World's Fair: A Selection of Gems of the White City as Seen through a Camera* (Chicago: Laird & Lee, 1893), 160.

In *Glimpses of the World's Fair*, one of several photographically illustrated souvenir books that were published in commemoration of the 1893 World's Columbian Exposition in Chicago, the caption appended to one photograph draws attention to a figure within the frame that the reader is encouraged to regard as ubiquitous. (fig. 2.1) "The ever-present 'Kodak' fiend," the caption reads, referencing a woman dressed in black. Her back to the camera, this "fiend" is engrossed by a camera of her own. Her body hunches over it as she frames her shot, ostensibly a casually posed picture of two men who are seated on a bench at the left edge of the frame. In the background, crowds stroll through the Midway Plaisance. The ornate bamboo entry to the Java Village—an exhibition featuring "an exact reproduction of a village" found in West Java, sponsored by the Java Chicago Exhibition Syndicate, "a commercial enterprise with the object of introducing Java products in their pure state into America"—looms overhead in the distance (Java Chicago Exhibition

Syndicate, 1893: 1). If the reader of *Glimpses of the World's Fair* happens to flip back to the book's front matter, further evidence of the Kodak fiend's apparent omnipresence will be found. The book indicates, via a prominent credit line, that the photograph of this woman with her Kodak was captured by a photographer operating a Kodak No. 4 camera, as were the rest of the images in the book.

The closed loop of representation at work in this book—in which omnipresent Kodaks capture a world gathered for the leisurely visual consumption of ambling tourists—analogizes but also oversimplifies a broader shift underway in the United States in 1893. Affordable and easy-to-use Kodak cameras, like world's fairs themselves, depended on the wide acceptance among their target market of a logic of visual extraction. In other words, they hinged on the idea that the world was as spectacular as it was fungible: that it could be meaningfully captured for, and encapsulated in, a series of photogenic views. As Ariella Azoulay has contended, the flourishing of photography cannot be understood apart from the forcible assumption of imperial rights, and the World's Columbian Exposition, an event whose chief purpose was to celebrate the world that those rights created, might fairly be understood as an unparalleled spectacle of imperial extraction. Given Azoulay's provocation that we "[i]magine that the origins of photography […] go back to 1492," the Chicago exposition, which explicitly commemorated Columbus's 1492 colonization of the Americas, warrants attention for the ways in which its organizers and visitors framed the right to take photographs. (Azoulay, 2019: 2–3)

Coming just as the introduction of a spate of affordable cameras intended for use by nonprofessionals encouraged the mass adoption of snapshot photography as a hobby, this event was particularly ripe for extensive photographic documentation. Yet to regard the scene that *Glimpses of the World's Fair* presents as a neatly closed loop is to impose on that scene a degree of order and unanimity that was not, in practice, present. At the edges of the frame—of this particular image and of the aesthetic regime that it represents—uncertainty and anxiety about how the world is to be represented and who has the right to represent it abound. Studying these seams helps to clarify the dominant perspective that they surround, lending insight into what imperial views looked like at the fair, but also how those views were empowered and challenged in an age of expanding photographic abundance. This chapter explores how kodakers and other photographers present at the fair discussed, acclimated to, and practiced the newly widespread imperative to photograph in public. The semipublic spaces of fairs such as the 1893 Columbian Exposition, which framed the world as a consumable spectacle, functioned as a testing ground for the large-scale incursion of discreet and mobile cameras into public spaces. But the complications that individual photographers encountered in photographing the fair suggest that the shift toward a world characterized by the unabridged right to take photographs was partial and incremental rather than totalizing and immediate. While the marketing and pedagogical efforts of firms such as Eastman Kodak framed the world as a limitless font of photographic material, the representational capacities of amateur photographers were delimited in many unanticipated ways as they set about capturing the fair.

The trope of the Kodak fiend, pervasive in the popular journalism and visual culture of the 1890s, presents an image of snapshot photographers run amok at the world's fair and in the wider world, photographing whatever they pleased. In reality, however, photographic practices were significantly more circumscribed than this caricature suggests, hemmed in by tacit conventions that shaped how snapshot photography was practiced even in its infancy. A few decades later, Walter Benjamin would famously contend that film offered a kind of perceptual training that acclimated observers to the sensory experiences characteristic of modernity. Looking back to the 1890s with Benjamin's interpretation in mind, we might fruitfully read the framing of photographic practices in this pivotal decade—through the marketing of photographic equipment, characterizations of the photographer in popular journalism and the photographic trade press, and spectacular events such as world's fairs—as offering a kind of *representational* training. This training helped to code certain objects, gazes, and affects as appropriate material for photographic capture at a moment when photography's future seemed both immensely promising and highly indeterminate, given the mass adoption that was underway. Looking at the expansion of photography in the 1890s with attention to the frames and constraints that photographers encountered—and not just to the broadening of photographic opportunities that these new modes opened up—we move beyond a popular and rather hagiographic narrative that assigns Eastman Kodak credit for "democratizing" photography, for creating the conditions of photographic freedom.[1] As certain longstanding barriers to entry were diminished—namely, costly equipment and the need to develop substantial technical skill—subtler ideological forces continued to shape who photographed, what was photographed, and how photography was practiced.

Consumer photography's expansion into urban public spaces raised a number of questions, both existential and practical. How did new practitioners of photography, commentators in the photographic world, and corporate entities involved in popularization manage and exploit this new photographic profusion and address its possibilities and its dangers? What frames and controls served to delimit the scope of the photographable, making an infinity of photographic possibilities more controllable and graspable? What role did the particular event under discussion, the 1893 Chicago world's fair, play in this process, coming as it did at this decisive stage in the popularization of amateur photography? And, crucially, how did amateur photographers respond to prescriptions and proscriptions that were intended to structure photographic activity?

We can understand the ways of seeing privileged by the fair as an analogy for broader modes of visual acquisition and representation that people on the advantaged side of imperial relationships were encouraged to adopt in this period. The fair's organization and visual structure, as well as its official photographic record, privileged a view that was unmistakably imperial; in this way, imperial extraction was not only an event whose history the fair commemorated but also an ongoing practice of looking on which attending the fair was predicated. This imperial view positioned the world outside the individual photographic observer as a source of material ripe for capture. The fair's built environment, ordering, and optics encouraged visitors to treat their environs as a visual spectacle and a photogenic event, and these structures guided spectators toward extractive modes of engagement, treating physical spaces and humans alike as objects of visual consumption that were intended for unimpeded, one-way observation rather than sustained interaction or exchange.

While this training was certainly powerful, its power was not absolute or unabridged in practice. In fact, an irrepressible tension permeated the fair, appearing in the photographs that Kodak photographers took, but also materializing in the form of spirited arguments and invectives on the pages of photographic trade journals. Given the unimpeded, idealized view that visitors to the fair were promised, many amateur photographers were surprised to find that it was challenging or simply impossible to adopt this perspective in their own image-making. Instead, they met multiple limitations that constrained their photographic activity, demonstrating to them that, while this event celebrated and visualized imperial rights, access to what came to be known as "photographic privilege" was substantially constrained in practice.

Looking at the photographing of the World's Columbian Exposition in light of Azoulay's discussion of photography and imperial rights, it becomes possible to identify multiple registers of control in simultaneous operation. The pristine and uniform official image of the fair embodied the top-down control and restriction that the fair's administration sought to impose. To maintain the dominance of this official image, the fair's photography division, led by Charles Dudley Arnold, placed significant limitations on unofficial photographers' ability to photograph the fair, including a ban on tripods and a daily photographer's permit fee that was four times higher than the general admission fee to the fair itself.

But this top-down control helped amateur photographers to justify their own claims to imperial rights—and to characterize the claiming of these rights as a valiant battle against the dictatorial power of the fair's leadership. Amateur photographers who sought to photograph the world's fair coded their right to take photographs without restriction—including photographs of other people in public spaces—as a fundamentally liberatory, egalitarian act. In practice, the right that these amateur photographers sought was a right to go out and photographically "capture" the world. And despite invocations of collectivity and the commons in the photographic trade press, this right was far from universal: it was the province of those in positions of geographic, racial, and economic advantage. In this respect, the term "photographic privilege" was more apt than its proponents recognized. Moreover, as we shall see, despite amateur photographers' tendency to frame their demands as an opposition to the monopolistic dominance of the fair's organization, these photographers' conceptualization of photographic freedom in terms of the unabrogated right to take photographs was highly compatible with the nearly monopolistic dominance of another organization: Eastman Kodak itself.

World's Fairs and the Visual Logic of Extraction

The Chicago world's fair, like other expositions of the late 19th and early 20th centuries, was a colossal and heterogeneous affair. Running from May Day through late October 1893, it was attended by about twenty-seven million visitors; at the time, this was close to half of the United States' population.[2] While the fair, like others of the period, was typically framed as an opportunity for democratic education and international fellowship, bringing the world together, it was also intended to function as a triumphal display of modernity and technological advancement, and it served to consolidate ideologically a power relation that was also being expanded militarily in the 1890s: American imperial dominance. There were powerful economic incentives at work as well; the fair was regarded as a means to lend prestige to a given city and improve its financial circumstances. Ultimately, in 1890, Chicago was chosen by Congress as the site to host the fair after competing with New York City for the opportunity, and frenetic work began to plan and build the expansive site. At six hundred acres, the space of the fair was enormous, but given its claims to offer visitors the globe in miniature—one contemporary proclamation that "All the world is here!" was a popular refrain among fair visitors—such largesse was fitting, even if the condensed world that fair visitors experienced made fundamental alterations to the original (Putnam, 1894: n.p.).

The fair's official title, the World's Columbian Exposition, was a reference to what most descriptions of the fair referred to as Columbus's "discovery" of the Americas, and the fair was ostensibly a celebration of the four hundredth anniversary of this pivotal colonial event. The celebration of Columbus points to a central dialectic that colored the exhibition and others like it. Several decades later, and in a very different context, Frantz Fanon would write, "The colonial world is a Manichaean world." (Fanon, 2004: 6) Taking place in a metropole that was once a colony and reveling in its transformation from the latter to the former, the Chicago world's fair presented a particularly literal demonstration of Fanon's point. Incorporating a pervasive rhetoric of "civilization" that depended on the "primitive" as a necessary structuring Other, the central grounds of the fair were composed of two main regions that were carefully separated: the White City, consisting of stately buildings rendered in stark white, which were intended to produce an impressive and largely uniform ideal of Beaux Arts architecture, and the Midway Plaisance, which was presented, in ethnocentric terms, as the unruly underbelly of the fair, offering an international bazaar that gathered the world up for the consumption of a gaze that was interpellated as Western. If the White City sought to represent "civilization"—synonymous, in this context, with whiteness—at its pinnacle, then the Midway encouraged spectators to observe colonized people, as well as people of other nations that white American visitors would consider foreign. It presented what one commentator called a "novel and heterogeneous exhibition" of people of "many nations of each continent, civilized, semi-civilized, and barbarous," as well as their characteristic architecture, which ranged from "mosques and pagodas" to "huts of bark and straw that tell of yet ruder environment." (Bancroft, 1893: 836)

The fair claimed universality, and was presented as a comprehensive display of the world's accomplishments and its diversity. The official guidebook told visitors they should expect to see "the progress which the world has made in the arts, sciences, and industries," an experience that would be "a liberal education assured." (Flinn, 1893: 17) The World's Congress Auxiliary, a body that was organized as the ideological and intellectual heart of the fair, described its mission as assembling "a series of world-wide fraternities through whose efforts and influence the moral and intellectual forces of mankind may be dominant throughout the world." ("Preliminary Publication," 1893: n.p.) An illustrated souvenir book, *Martin's World's Fair Album-Atlas and Family Souvenir*, declared, more pithily and in blazing caps: "IT IS A COMPREHENSIVE PICTURE OF THE CIVILIZATION OF TO-DAY." (1893: n.p.) The illustrated Chicago publication *The Graphic* concurred, stating that the fair would be "a universal congress, which is no respecter of geographical boundary, race, color, party or sex." ("The Congress of All Nations," 1892: 1)

Despite these claims of universality, the fair presented the world for a particular kind of spectator. The perspective consistently emphasized was that of the affluent, white, American spectators who were assumed to be its chief visitors. This particular fair was wholly typical in its insistence on this point of view; world's fairs and ethnographic expositions have long been a subject of interest for visual culture scholars interested in the politics of display, because one of their constitutive functions was to neatly divide and present the world's people and objects in such a way that the world would be made legible to Western spectators. As Fatimah Tobing Rony has written, such events were both "site[s] of excess," where a seemingly limitless accumulation of cultural objects were made visible, and also "place[s] of spectacle where detail"—including details about the many ethnic groups being displayed—"was ordered, classified and rationalized." (Rony, 1992: 270) As Tony Bennett observed in *The Birth of the Museum*, expositions of this period "rendered the whole world metonymically present, subordinated to the dominating gaze of the white, bourgeois, and […] male eye of the metropolitan powers." (Bennett, 1995: 83) While these displays were ostensibly intended to educate, they depended on a loose interpretation of education, because the gaze that the fair catered to was one that tended to be both acquisitive and impatient.

The way of viewing the world that the fair emphasized was dependent on a willingness to accept a partial, selective, and authored visual representation as commensurate to reality, and to trust in the veracity of the display that was presented. In the context of the fair, this trust had a powerful naturalizing effect, reassuring visitors that the "dominating gaze" that the fair embodied and courted was the correct and default one. This way of seeing might productively be understood as extractive, because it was predicated on the capacity of imperial power to appropriate and restage the people and resources of the spaces it colonized, and to produce out of these subjects and objects its desired image of reality.

In this respect, world's fairs performed a function that was equally characteristic of photography itself. As Azoulay has argued, the medium of photography was "first institutionalized" on an "extractive principle" that privileged the right of "recognized members of imperial societies" to remove resources, visual and otherwise, from colonized communities, offering little in return. Through the process, those who claimed imperial rights authorized themselves to "enjoy the power of expropriating the rights of others, expropriation that photography not only made visible but perpetuated." (Azoulay, 2019: 147) This enjoyment of expropriation is at the crux of Azoulay's definition of imperial rights.

How was this enjoyment experienced and practiced among people in the metropole, who were the beneficiaries of these rights but were geographically sheltered from those they expropriated? Photography was central, particularly with its diffusion to larger and larger numbers of people who were the beneficiaries of imperialism. As this imaging practice was adopted by a critical mass of amateur practitioners in the West, spectators increasingly implemented and naturalized ways of seeing that privileged an unequal relationship between photographer and subject, observer and observed. While this was not a new dynamic in the 1890s, the growing popularity of photography as a hobby and the increasing ubiquity of cultural events and practices that encouraged unequal looking relations—such as world's fairs, as well as a vogue for travel photography among Western tourists—encouraged its normalization and expansion. With the increasingly widespread adoption of small-format cameras, one central feature of these newly extractive ways of seeing was the assumption among those wielding cameras of an unabrogated right to photograph, and the perception that any checks on one's ability to do so imperiled the freedom of the photographer in question. The selective, unidirectional nature of this "freedom" becomes particularly clear when we consider that its proponents were disinclined to ask questions about how free their own photographic subjects might have been.

Images and Events

The Chicago world's fair has been referred to by one historian as the "most photographed event of the nineteenth century." (Lewis, 2010: 12) If this statement is true—and it is difficult to establish with any degree of certainty whether it is—then its truthfulness has much to do with the elasticity of the term "event." In his brief book on the subject, Slavoj Žižek refers to the event "at its purest and most minimal" as something "out of joint" that "interrupts the usual flow of things." (Žižek, 2014: 2) The Chicago fair was, then, an ambiguous kind of event, both proximate to and distant from "real life": it was an attraction, something to visit and to write home about, and it initiated a festive, celebratory atmosphere, yet its lengthy duration meant that it was impossible to sustain a peak of dramatic intensity.

As a liminal event—one that was both exceptional and ongoing, and one that sought to reflect the world outside—the fair can be understood as both a pretext for a new array of photographic activity and an analogy for seismic shifts in the nature of photographic practice in the 1890s. The kinds of photography familiar to ordinary people before the Chicago world's fair had necessitated spatial and temporal isolation, producing a distinct kind of photographic event: they took place in the cloistered space of the studio, and they demanded an interaction between photographer and subject that took the subject out of context. Žižek refers to the event as "an appearance without solid being as its foundation"; this description has some analogy with Roland Barthes's characterization of the making of the photographic portrait in *Camera Lucida*. (Žižek, 2014: 2) Barthes describes this process as an event in which the person photographed creates an appearance for herself or himself, forming their physical corpus into an artificial, photogenic one—an appearance without solid being—in order to be photographically represented (Barthes, 1981: 10–11).

Together, these formulations leave us with an understanding of the event as something exceptional, disruptive, and out of step with normal experience, and they offer a heuristic for thinking about the distinctions between the event that studio portraiture entailed and the new representational possibilities that were opening for photographers as the fair took place. The expansion of snapshot photography in public spaces produced a different and more indeterminate kind of encounter. The subject could pose for the camera, but equally, the photographer could photograph subjects unawares, claiming the right to photograph another without consent. The photograph could take place in common space—always a possibility, but practiced far more frequently as cameras became more portable and copious in the 1880s and 1890s. The photograph did not have to take subjects out of the action in which they were embedded—the photograph could instead depict that action by freezing it at an interval in its unfolding. A common characteristic of amateur photographs made at the Chicago fair is the blurred appearance of photographs taken of subjects in motion. This blurring gives the appearance that the activity and movement occurring around the photographer could not be paused to meet the camera's demands; the frenetic activity of the fair instead needed to be captured as it unfolded. The blurred appearance of these photographs also speaks to the technological progression of instantaneous photography. By the 1890s, instantaneous photography had evolved from an experimental mode developed by technically skilled practitioners such as Marey and Muybridge to a widespread practice accessible to nearly any photographer, given that early Kodak cameras operated with rapid fixed exposure rates. Instantaneous photographic capture, an exceptional and tentative phenomenon in the 1870s, was, by the 1890s, virtually everywhere.

"The World is Mine"

Because they removed the necessary connection between the phenomenon of being photographed and the event of posing before the camera, hand cameras like Kodaks made it possible for amateur photographers to travel the world with their cameras and to extract photographic likenesses from unwitting or nonconsenting subjects. The marketing and consumer pedagogy efforts through which Eastman Kodak guided customers toward "appropriate" uses of photography helped to transform this possibility into a given, presenting the extractive potential of photography as a major selling point for prospective customers.

Advertisements for Eastman Kodak products that targeted fairgoers in 1893 demonstrate the framing of photography as a practice through which spectators in a position of imperial privilege can use cameras to represent the world on their terms, and in so doing, possess the world they have photographically captured. In this respect, these ads augured broader strategies of representation that Eastman Kodak advocated in its marketing in the years that followed. "Take a Kodak with you to the World's Fair," magazine advertisements implored readers in *Harper's* and *Scribner's*, presenting an illustration of two iterations of the Kodak Girl, the company's modern, adventuresome brand mascot. The ads emphasized the obvious appeal of roll film cameras compared with cameras using individual glass plates, still preferred by most professional photographers and "serious" amateurs at the time, although these cameras were unwieldy and heavy. These ads presented the work of photographing with a Kodak as a pleasure and a social activity, contrasted with the drudgery and heavy lifting associated with photography using glass plates. As in much of Eastman Kodak's advertising, the use of young, white women as the emblematic snapshot photographers drew on contemporaneous associations of this demographic with particular lifestyles and affective qualities—as living lives of pleasure and leisure that might be vigorous but did not demand hard work; as engaged in fun and eager to be modern. This was an image of modern womanhood that presented the woman as a commercial agent and a creator of her own images, but only with the guiding corporate hand of Kodak. Political agency, naturally, did not figure into this dynamic.

Other advertisements from Eastman Kodak established more explicit and practical links between the fair and the photographic activities of amateurs. One advertisement issued by Eastman Kodak in 1893 promoted "Kolumbus Kodaks"—a slightly forced alliteration, it has to be said—but more significantly, presented an appeal to memory that would become central to the company's advertising efforts writ large. "What's worth seeing is worth remembering," the ad stated. "There will be so much worth seeing and remembering at the World's Fair that you'll forget the best part of it. But you can faithfully preserve each scene if you'll just 'press the button.'" ("Kolumbus Kodaks," 1893: n.p.) Banal as this ad copy might appear, it introduces an idea that is highly questionable yet central to the logic of photographic ubiquity: "What's worth seeing is worth remembering." Suggesting that any conceivable view warrants photographic preservation and that mental memories are faulty, particularly when faced with the onslaught of memorable visions that one is bound to encounter at an event as avowedly spectacular as the world's fair, this ad casts the Kodak as the inevitable solution to a problem readers might not have known that they had: the problem of remembering each sight that one sees. The contention that any sight that appears before one's eyes is a potentially regrettable omission and a missed opportunity if it goes unphotographed powerfully establishes as a given the idea that nothing should exist beyond the camera's scope. Even as the fair itself presented a highly orchestrated and spectacular view, Kodak advertisements framed the snapshot photographer as an individual possessing the agency to personalize and appropriate that view, demonstrating through their photographic record a subjective encounter with it. The fair might be uniform, the advertisement suggested, but kodakers could nonetheless make it their own.

Further supporting this idea, Eastman Kodak ads targeting fairgoers also reassured readers that their materials could meet even the most exacting demands as far as a voluminous photographic record was concerned. They advertised film rolls containing up to 250 exposures, to obviate the need of changing the roll and disrupting the constant capture of potentially memorable sights, as well as the use of free darkrooms on site at the fair where users could change those rolls if they found they needed to exceed this upper limit. "We propose to leave nothing undone that will assist the Kodaker in getting a complete photographic record of the great fair," the ads stated.

The approach that these marketing materials adopted was consistent with Kodak's broader advertising strategies as they progressed into the early 20th century. In the years following the world's fair, advertising for Kodaks not only became less instrumental and more visually compelling than the text-heavy ads just discussed but also highly invested in the production and reiteration of a particular set of fantasies geared toward white, middle-class, and often female consumers. Travel was central to these fantasies in the first two decades of the 20th century, and many Eastman Kodak advertisements showed adventurous kodakers—usually women—viewing the world through the lens of their Kodaks. Even when they did not show "locals" being photographed by kodakers, these ads created a visual dynamic in which kodakers possessed forms of agency or social privilege that other figures in the ad, typically non-white people engaged in service labor, did not. For example, a 1905 ad in *Ladies' Home Journal* showed a delicate-looking white woman being pulled along on a rickshaw by a Japanese man while vacationing in what the caption calls "Fair Japan."[3] Another image, this one from 1912, showed the Kodak girl as a world traveler, with a Black railway porter lifting her well-traveled suitcase as she clutched her camera. (fig. 2.2) "The World is mine—" the ad read: "I own a KODAK." The overall impression that this advertisement leaves is that traveling with the Kodak will allow photographers to sublate the tension between a partial, personalized view and the kind of visual mastery that comes from a godlike view from above; after promising the reader that the Kodak is a way to possess "the world," the ad copy encourages users to "Take a Kodak with *you*, and picture, from your own viewpoint, not merely the places that interest you but also the companions who help to make your trip enjoyable." On one hand, the personal nature of the photographic record is emphasized: this is the Kodaker's subjective vision. On the other, the Kodak photographer is here positioned as a chronicler with unimpeded access not only to the world's places but to the people that populate them. The labor of people assisting kodakers with their travels tacitly began to include the work of being photographed by them. This tendency in early 20th-century Kodak advertisements signals the expansion of a notion originally presented in Kodak's 1893 advertising efforts, that kodakers could make their photographic records "their own" by supplementing snapshots of the expected tourist attractions with images demonstrating the photographer's personal encounter with the locale they were visiting. At this later stage, however, "locals" were expected to provide the Kodaker's album with this personal touch—and were framed in these advertisements as always available for photographic capture.

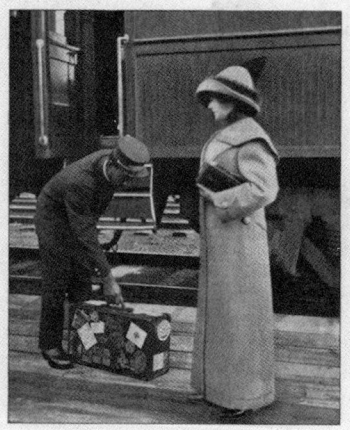

Figure 2.2

Kodak advertisement published in *Ladies' Home Journal*, 1912. Ellis Collection of Kodakiana, Duke University.

The Fair's Ideal Image

Taken together, these advertisements paint a picture of the Kodaker as a figure who, by virtue of possession of a camera, is granted access to an imperial view: one's surroundings, and the people who populate them, become a source of photographic material to be mined, and the photographer's viewpoint and access to desired photographic material, human or otherwise, is unobstructed. But in the run-up to the fair, many amateur photographers were frustrated—and in some cases downright angered—to learn that this idealized view did not align with the representational possibilities that they were afforded in practice. The fair was characterized by restrictions on which photographers could capture the fair as well as how they could capture it.

While Eastman Kodak's advertisements presented the fair as a bountiful and unconstrained source of material for photographs, the fair's organizational staff conceptualized a much more limited set of possibilities for most photographers who sought to capture this event. Charles Dudley Arnold, leader of the fair's photography division, which operated under the authority of the fair's Council of Administration, strongly believed that the photographic image of the fair should be tightly managed, generated through a uniform, carefully constructed repertoire of images that would represent the event advantageously rather than leaving its photographic representation open and indeterminate. Arnold was immensely troubled by the idea that images of the event could be polyphonic and unordered—limitless photographers photographing the fair, each capturing it from "their own viewpoint," was anathema to him—and his opposition to this approach led him to prescribe tight controls on photographic activity. But this attitude and this approach was so out of step with the increasingly heterogeneous photographic culture of the 1890s that it generated serious backlash.

Scholars including Julie K. Brown and Peter Bacon Hales have examined Arnold's role in the fair, and the fair's documentation in official imagery, in depth. Arnold, an architectural photographer who ran the fair's photography division and produced its photographic output, was chosen for this role largely because fair officials trusted him to create a pristine and respectable picture of the event, and he spent months photographing the construction of the fair and the finished product, ultimately generating several portfolios of oversize views using cameras that produced negatives of up to 20×24 inches. Hales writes that this imagery was supposed to possess a "monumental grandeur befitting the ambitions" of the fair organizers (Hales, 1984: 135). The agreements that Arnold made with the fair's governing body gave him full control over the photographic representation of the fair, dictating that newspapers, magazines, and the official fair guidebook would only be permitted to use photographs made by Arnold or personally approved by him. If the mediated visual representation of the fair is anything to go by, he was not liberal in permitting alternate approaches. Reproductions often added or subtracted incidental elements to create a more lifelike or more direct image, but the architectural details that his images emphasized tended to carry through in these images. As Brown has observed, "No real debate had taken place on the question of whether there should be a multiple photographic viewpoint because the Exposition's administrators had never had any intention of opening the field to competition […] The main purpose of the administrators was to ensure a controlled viewpoint." (Brown, 1994: 70) Arnold, who was paid a salary of $2,000 plus a 10 percent commission on the sale of prints, benefited materially from this arrangement.

The images generated by this arrangement tend to reflect in visual terms the desire for grandeur as well as the tight control that fair officials demanded. They largely emphasized the architectural features of the White City, and presented the pristinely white, grandiose buildings that populated this area of the fair from a distanced, detached view from above. The view was homogeneous and largely unpopulated by humans. When humans were featured, they were shown from a distance, existing as remote, incidental figures or else as set pieces intended to frame a given view in what appeared to be a carefully calibrated fashion. In some cases, they lent legibility to the images by metonymically representing the building's role in instances where it was unclear, as in an image where women are shown congregating around the Women's Building. Nothing is unruly or out of place in these images, and nothing is left to chance.

These images—highly legible and reproducible, because they appeared unrooted from a particular point of view—presented a godlike view from nowhere, offering a perspective sufficiently distanced that human subjects seen in the photographs never reciprocated the camera's gaze. In this respect, they mirrored the formal traits of another rapidly growing image genre in which photographs were called on to function as commodities: the picture postcard. In these images, the spectator surveying these images looks but is not looked at. The reproduction of highly similar views through print mass media—in the form of halftone photographs but also illustrations based on photographs—served to reinforce and reify these views, suggesting that while slight variations might be possible, the official visual record showed what needed to be shown. (figs. 2.3a and 2.3b)

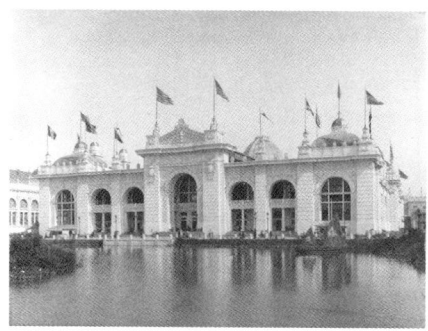

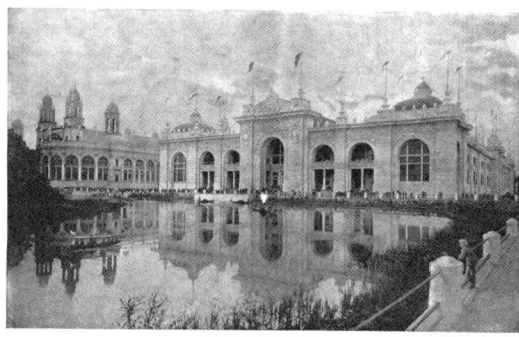

Figure 2.3a

C. D. Arnold, "Mines and Mining Building," 1893. University of Chicago Special Collections.

Figure 2.3b

Mines and Mining Building as illustrated in the *Youth's Companion* World's Fair Extra Number, May 4, 1893.

"Photographic Privilege": Controlling Photography at the Fair

The controlled view of the fair presented in its official imagery was supported by significant restrictions on all other photographers who sought to depict it. These restrictions seem to have been primarily aimed at restricting the work of professional photographers making images intended for public audiences, which would compete with Arnold's image of the fair. The fear that informed this control was a fear that other photographers' images would visibly and publicly undermine the fair's official image. But this top-down control over the photographic likeness of the fair could not have come at a more infelicitous time, given that in the early 1890s, legions of new people were beginning to think of themselves as photographers, and given that the public voice of amateur photographers in specialist journals and the popular press was stronger than ever.

In the months leading up to the fair, correspondents in journals dedicated to the photographic trade and to amateur photography began to speculate about, anticipate, and plan their photographic activity at the fair. One central subject of speculation was what the fair's organizers and commentators in the press began to refer to as the "photographic privilege" at the fair. Photographic privilege referred to the ability to photograph freely at the fair: to take photographs with the camera of one's choosing and to photograph what one pleased. After months of fervent speculation on the part of photographers both amateur and professional, the fair's administration announced that this privilege would not be granted. Restrictions on photographing the fair would include a ban on cameras that produced negatives larger than 4×5 inches, a ban on all tripods, and a daily photographer's permit fee of two dollars, which was substantially higher than the admission charge to the fair itself, which was fifty cents.

Critics of these restrictions described them as arbitrary and unreasonable at best, and dictatorial at worst.[4] While the restrictions were intended to discourage unsanctioned images of the fair from circulating in the press, criticisms of the fair's administrative decisions were not as easily censored as were photographs. Critiques of these policies quickly gathered steam, driven by publications ranging from *The American Amateur Photographer* to the *Scientific American*, among many others.[5] These publications' protests militated against what they described as undue restrictions on photographing at an event that, in critics' minds, seemed not only to warrant but to demand extensive and diverse photographic representation. These critics were united in their assumption that the fair was an event whose photogenic possibilities were unparalleled, and that anyone possessing a camera would be interested in capturing it.

Equally, the right to photograph at the fair was characterized as a cause that all photographers must want and support. *The American Amateur Photographer*, which had recently come under the editorship of Alfred Stieglitz, frequently reproduced excerpts from articles in a range of other specialist and general-interest publications to demonstrate these points. This effort gave readers the impression of unanimous opposition to restrictions on photographing the fair, suggesting that it was not merely correspondents in specialist publications like theirs that opposed this rule but all photographers, however skilled or unskilled they might be. In this way, the restrictions on fair photography helped to unite the motley array of amateur photographers then in existence, from technically skilled members of photographic societies and experimental photographic artists to kodakers.

This apparent chorus of voices presented the impression of widespread, grassroots opposition to these restrictions. "Every photographer, professional and amateur, whether he intends to visit the fair personally or not, should protest against the injustice of this narrow-minded scheme," asserted one commentator from the *Pacific Coast Photographer*, who also called the decision to license one firm the sole photographic privilege "absurd" and "ridiculous." ("Press Comments on World's Fair Photographic Privilege," 1892: 446) The *New Orleans Picayune* noted that restrictions on photography were "arousing a general and vigorous protest" from members of camera clubs nationwide, and noted gravely, "A monster petition is being signed." ("Press Comments on World's Fair Photographic Privilege," 1892: 446) Further afield, the *British Journal of Photography*, speaking a bit less brashly, asserted that the decision to restrict photographers at the fair "seems to us at present an unwise inhibition of the practice of photography in a direction altogether contrary to the spirit of the age." ("The Photographic Blunder at the World's Fair," 1892: 753)

This last point was one that many opponents of the photographic restrictions emphasized, and it was in this way that large numbers of amateur and professional photographers, as well as the Eastman Kodak Company itself, positioned the "photographic privilege" as an inalienable right, one whose suppression was an encroachment on photographers' freedom. In this way, these photographers recoded limitations on their ability to photograph as impositions of unfreedom, presupposing and helping to produce the norm of a context in which places and people were, by default, photographable. While the world's fair was not a truly public event—it took place in a semipublic space requiring an admission fee to enter—photographers who sought to operate in an unrestricted manner nonetheless argued passionately that rules limiting their ability to take pictures were contraventions of the public interest. One paper characterized restrictions on photography as "thoughtlessly unjust

to the public, for whose advancement the World's Fair is arranged."
("Press Comments on World's Fair Photographic Privilege," 1892: 446)
Another commentator observed, "There are some things practiced in
connection with the World's Fair as almost lead one to the belief that it
is a private enterprise, run for the few." ("Photography at the World's
Fair," 1893: 212) And another commentator, echoing a pervasive talking
point, mused, "Free America appears to be becoming the land of the
monopolist." ("The World's Fair Photographic Privilege—Comments
of the Press," 1892: 412)

In 1893, the charge of monopolistic activity held special significance
for American readers, given that 1890 had seen the United States pass
its first antitrust legislation with the Sherman Antitrust Act. With concern about monopolistic activity at a peak, this characterization lent
particular rhetorical force to the claim that the world's fair administration was defying the public interest and exerting unwarranted power.
But curiously absent in this discussion was any attention to the fact that
Eastman Kodak, whose cameras were central to the popularization of
amateur photography in this period, possessed a control of the market
for photographic equipment that was growing increasingly close to a
monopoly. The fact that discourses surrounding photography at the
fair painted the fair's administration as repressive allowed Eastman
Kodak to present their materials and their corporate identity as liber-
ators helping to encourage photographic freedom in an inhospitable
environment.[6] If amateur photographers saw any contradiction in the
framing of Eastman Kodak's products as tools that could be mobilized
against photographic monopolies, they did not express their reservations in the photography journals.

Discussions of photographic restriction and freedom at the fair
played out on multiple registers, and as they did, amateur photographers
developed an understanding of the right to take photographs as a fundamentally egalitarian capability. The fair organization *was* interested,
and materially invested, in restricting the visual likeness of the fair by
constraining photographers' activity. Yet the default assumptions that
these constrained photographers smuggled into their commentaries in
the press also reveal a growing assumption that photographers should
possess full agency over the domain they photograph.

This marks an important phase in the expansion of photography as
an imperial right, because the framing of photographing whatever one
wishes in public space as a right that should go unrestricted implicitly
negates rights that others, and particularly photographic subjects, might
have wished to claim: the right not to be photographed, the right to
collaborate with the photographer, the right to exert agency over photographic likeness. Needless to say, amateur photographers' discussions
tended not to countenance the fact that their unimpeded photographic

freedom might impinge on the rights of others. In rejecting the idea that photography should be a limited privilege subject to negotiation, these photographers may have been balking at a powerful institution aiming to control their photographic expression for financial gain, but they were also positioning a right that was, in practice, typically limited to those in a position of imperial privilege as a universal right whose curtailment was a threat to the public interest. The implicit agent and ideal subject of these rights was the photographer, not those who were photographed, and this dynamic perpetuated and dramatically expanded a tradition that predated the fair and stood at the crux of the linkage between photography and imperial rights: the refusal to consider the photograph's subject as an equal participant in the photographic encounter.

Conclusion: Undermining Imperial Views at the Fair

A common fixture of commentaries written by photographers at the fair was the complaint that the restrictions they faced on their photographic activity prevented them from seamlessly reproducing the idealized view from above that characterized much of the fair's official imagery. Yet in looking at these commentaries and at the images that unofficial photographers produced, it becomes possible to identify some new representational possibilities that are born from limitations on photographers' inability to replicate this view. In particular, these images break, by necessity, with the detached, godlike perspective that characterized official images of the fair.

This perspective is often absent or limited in the work of amateur photographers at the fair, because, in addition to asserting their control over photographic activity not only legally, through regulations restricting the photographic privilege, the fair's administration also reinforced it conceptually, through their exclusive command of certain views. One photographer, Fred Felix, reported that, when he climbed atop the colossal Administration Building to make a panoramic view of the entire fairgrounds from an elevation of 150 feet, a point "from which the view was imposing," he was apprehended by a member of the Columbian Guards, the semi-military police force in charge of overseeing the fair. The officer instructed Felix that Arnold, the official photographer, "was the only man who could take pictures there." (Felix, 1892: 410) In this way, the fair's organization claimed exclusive authority over dominant views of the whole grounds, denying Kodakers and other unofficial photographers these capacities.

This perspective possessed exclusively by the fair's controlling body was one that, much like the scopic regime that Nicholas Mirzoeff has termed "imperial visuality," was predicated on an increasingly vast distance between the gaze of imperial powers and the subjects they depicted, and on the attendant capacity of colonists to look in a surveillant, unreciprocated way (Mirzoeff, 2011). But instead of thinking of kodakers' inability to approximate this view as a limitation or privation, it is worthwhile to consider the generative potential of camera views that did not adopt this imperial viewpoint, whether they explicitly refused it or merely failed in their efforts to approximate it.

A photographic album from Jos. E. Hartman, one amateur photographer active at the fair, points us to a few representational possibilities generated through the denial or refusal of an imperial view. Hartman's photographic activity at the fair appears to have been limited to a single day—June 15, 1893—and it resulted in an album of cyanotype images, each accompanied by a handwritten caption in red ink.[7] (fig. 2.4 and 2.5) Hartman's decision to produce cyanotype positives of his own making, rather than ordering gelatin silver prints produced by Eastman Kodak's labs, demonstrates not only a pragmatic interest in cost-cutting but also an assertion of individual ownership of the production process.[8] Many amateur photographers' albums and snapshots of the fair hint at a thwarted interest in mimicking the grand views captured by Arnold, presenting the stately architecture of the White City from perspectives that are partially obstructed, with guardrails, balustrades, and errant shrubbery denying the spectator the impression of having total command over the view.[9] But Hartman's perspective is different. Presenting views from the level of the street, these images are decidedly situated, placing the spectator directly within the action taking place on the ground. At times, the images dramatize the spectator's smallness and inability to encompass the view, as in one photograph, ostensibly of the Administration Building, which is mostly blank foreground. In other images, we see fair visitors glancing at one another as they pass, adjusting their parasols, and craning their necks to look at the East Indian Palace and the Java Village. We also see performers dressed in an array of forms of native attire and laborers operating sedan chairs.

While the looking that we, like the photographer, engage in sometimes goes unnoticed, presenting a voyeuristic view of this common space and the people who fill it, that gaze is frequently reciprocated by subjects within the frame who look directly at the camera at the moment of exposure, as in an image of the Turkish Mosque. (fig. 2.4) The left side of the frame is dominated by a female passerby in a plaid skirt and unbuttoned jacket who appears to have just caught sight of the camera. Similarly, in a set of two photographs captioned "Sedan Chair Carriers," an undetected side view of men carrying a sedan is complemented, and its perspective undermined, by another shot that shows another group of carriers from the front as they look at and address the photographer directly, with one carrier raising his arm and appearing to call out to the photographer, as another figure—a white man in a suit and derby hat—strides across the picture's foreground. (fig.2.5) Rather than taking pleasure in viewing these subjects surreptitiously or observing them placed by the photographer into "characteristic" poses, the spectator looking at this photograph is hailed directly by the sedan chair carriers. Though they still appear within this image as representatives of a putatively "foreign" culture rendering a service to privileged fairgoers, the spontaneity of this image's capture and the photographer's inability to control or predetermine the reactions of his subjects means that, even though they are denied the capacity to deliberately pose themselves, they are able to reciprocate the photographer's gaze on their terms, and address him, and us, directly, substituting direct visual address and exchange for an appropriative view from above. These photographs do not radically depart from, or even explicitly challenge, the imperial logic at the heart of amateur photographers' efforts to depict the fair and the world unimpeded. What they succeed in doing is analogizing that logic: rendering it visible and therefore providing concrete grounds for its critique. Making visible the social relations that play out between those who Kodak as they go and those who are captured by the Kodak, and between those who must carry the sedan chair and those who are positioned to occupy it, these photographs demonstrate the disingenuousness of the idea, presented increasingly vocally in the 1890s, that the right to snap photographs unchallenged and without limits was a right anyone could conceivably exercise. By its very nature, these photographs tell us, not everyone could enjoy the photographic privilege.

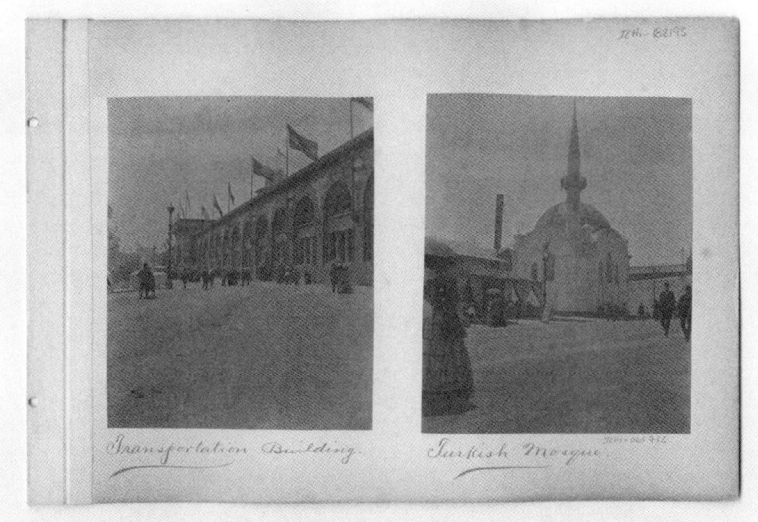

Figure 2.4

Page from an album of photographs, mostly cyanotypes, taken by Jos. E. Hartman at the Chicago World's Fair on June 15, 1893. Chicago History Museum.

See also Plate 4.

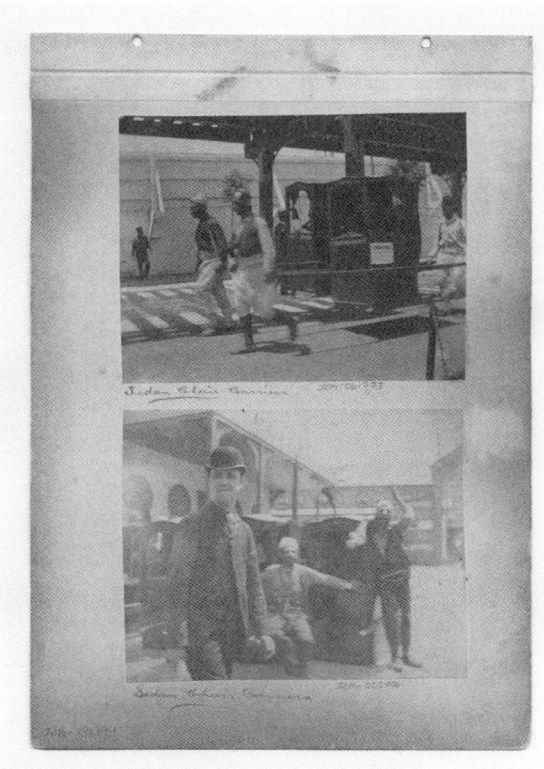

Figure 2.5

Page from an album of photographs, mostly cyanotypes, taken by Jos. E. Hartman at the Chicago World's Fair on June 15, 1893. Chicago History Museum.

See also Plate 5.

Notes

1. While it is common, this hagiographic narrative is not uncontested; Don Slater and John Tagg presented critical evaluations of the Kodak model in the 1980s.

2. The 1890 U.S. census estimated the country's population at sixty-three million. In his 1893 essay "The Significance of the Frontier in American History," first presented at the Chicago world's fair, Frederick Jackson Turner began his discussion with a gesture toward a bulletin released by the Superintendent of the Census in 1890, which stated that there could "hardly be said to be a frontier line" as of 1890 (1). For Turner, this statement signaled "the closing of a great historic movement"—and presented a troubling threat to the "expansive power" that he considered crucial to American identity (7). This anxiety among thinkers like Turner over the sudden lack of proximate space that Americans could colonize offered them a way to rationalize the United States' sharp turn toward imperial intervention at the end of the 19th century.

3. Space constraints prevent me from reproducing this striking image in the Figures section for this chapter, but it can be found online, as of 2020, from Duke University's Ellis Collection of Kodakiana at https:// repository.duke.edu/dc/eaa/K0431.

4. An untitled lead article in *The Photo-American* (1892: 266) for instance, asserted, "it does not seem right in this age of photography to prohibit the public at large from using a camera on the exposition grounds […] The camera is the note book of the modern traveler, and there seems to be no more justice in forbidding him to use it than there would be in interfering with the use of his pen or his field glass." The article concluded by encouraging readers to sign a petition being sent to the Ways and Means Committee of the World's Fair.

5. *The American Amateur Photographer* (1893a: 367) did not mince words in its critiques of the fair's administration: "A recent visit to the Fair grounds convinced us of the folly of the absurd restrictions enacted against the camera of the amateur and of the journalist," one article stated. "The incompetency of the [fair's] present Department of Photography is so notorious among all well-informed persons in Chicago, that it is invariably alluded to as a disgrace to the Exposition," the commentator added, noting that the department was run by "men totally unskilled in the science."

6. In the 1890s, Eastman Kodak's domestic sales grew at a rate of about 17.5 percent per year, amounting to 40 percent of all photographic sales in the United States by 1909. Christina Kotchemidova has observed that George Eastman's control over a number of crucial patents meant that the market for amateur cameras and film became "virtually a Kodak monopoly." (Kotchemidova, 2005: 4)

7. This album is in the collections of the Chicago History Museum, with the accession number G1983.222.

8. My thanks to Jacob Lewis for this insight.

9. This assertion is based on my examination of collections of amateur photographs of the fair held in repositories including the Chicago History Museum, the Chicago Public Library, the Newberry Library, and George Eastman House.

Bibliography

Ariella Aïsha Azoulay, *Potential History: Unlearning Imperialism* (London and New York: Verso, 2019).

Hubert Howe Bancroft, *The Book of the Fair* (Chicago and San Francisco: The Bancroft Company, 1893).

Roland Barthes, *Camera Lucida: Reflections on Photography*, trans. Richard Howard (New York: Hill and Wang, 1981).

Tony Bennett, *The Birth of the Museum: History, Theory, Politics* (London and New York: Routledge, 1995).

Julie K. Brown, *Contesting Images: Photography and the World's Columbian Exposition* (Tucson: University of Arizona Press, 1994).

Frantz Fanon, *The Wretched of the Earth*, trans. Richard Philcox (New York: Grove Press, 2004).

Fred Felix, "A Camera in the World's Fair Grounds," *The American Amateur Photographer*, 5, 9 (September 1892): 409–411.

John J. Flinn, *Official Guide to the World's Columbian Exposition* (Chicago: The Columbian Guide Company, 1893).

Peter Bacon Hales, *Silver Cities: Photographing American Urbanization, 1839–1939* (Philadelphia: Temple University Press, 1984).

Java Chicago Exhibition Syndicate, *The Java Village, Midway Plaisance, World's Columbian Exposition* (Chicago: Java Chicago Exhibition Syndicate, 1893).

"Kolumbus Kodaks," Eastman Kodak Company advertisement published in *The Century* 45 (1893), n.p.

Christina Kotchemidova, "Why We Say Cheese: Producing the Smile in Snapshot Photography," *Critical Studies in Media Communication*, 22, 1 (March 2005): 2–25.

Russell Lewis, *Historic Photos of the Chicago World's Fair* (Nashville: Turner Publishing Company, 2010).

Martin's World's Fair Album-Atlas and Family Souvenir (Chicago: National Book & Picture Co., 1893), n.p.

Nicholas Mirzoeff, *The Right to Look* (Durham, NC: Duke University Press, 2011).

"Photography at the World's Fair," *The American Amateur Photographer*, 5, 5 (May 1893): 212.

"Photography at the World's Fair," *The American Amateur Photographer*, 5, 8 (August 1893): 367–370.

"Preliminary Publication: The World's Congress Auxiliary of the World's Columbian Exposition of 1893," n.p. University of Chicago Special Collections.

"Press Comments on World's Fair Photographic Privilege," *The American Amateur Photographer*, 4, 10 (July 9, 1892): 446.

Frederic Ward Putnam, *Portrait Types of the Midway Plaisance* (St. Louis: N. D. Thompson Publishing Co., 1894).

"The Congress of All Nations," *The Graphic*, 7, extra (October 21, 1892): 1.

"The Photographic Blunder at the World's Fair," *The British Journal of Photography*, XXXIX, 1699 (November 25, 1892): 753.

The Vanishing City: A Photographic Encyclopedia of the World's Columbian Exposition (Chicago: Laird & Lee, 1893).

"The World's Fair Photographic Privilege—Comments of the Press," *The American Amateur Photographer*, 4, 9 (September 1892): 411–412.

Frederick Jackson Turner, *The Frontier in American History* (New York: Henry Holt and Company, 1921).

[Untitled lead article], *The Photo-American*, 3, 9 (July 1892): 266.

Slavoj Žižek, *Event* (London: Penguin, 2014).

3. Material Ecologies in the Géniaux Brothers' Picture Archive of Brittany, ca. 1900

Maura Coughlin[1]

Around 1900, brothers Paul (1873–1930) and Charles (1870–1931) Géniaux assembled a documentary archive of images, picturing both traditional and industrial forms of work, including the harvesting and processing of materials such as hemp fibers, salt, and slate in their native Brittany. In their realist approach to photography, the Géniaux brothers echoed established visual tropes of rural labor and locale, as they pictured the artisanal and industrial skills of extracting and processing natural resource materials. Using the tools of ecocriticism, I examine the ways that the Géniaux conceptualized material ecologies (a seemingly endless abundance of natural resources) and the extractive labors connected to them. Despite the ubiquitous proliferation of their photographs in the early 20th century, their collective projects have, until recently, been but a footnote in French photography.

Contemporaries of early 20th-century documentary photographers Lewis Hine, Jacob Riis, and Eugène Atget, the Géniaux brothers grew up as privileged bourgeois residents of the Breton city of Rennes. Their father was a military doctor, and their mother had income from several rental properties. As well-educated, bourgeois Bretons, they lived very different lives alongside their peasant subjects; they had multiple residences within France (in Brittany, Paris, and the south of France) and the privilege to travel and vacation. The peasant laborers they photographed only left home out of necessity to follow employment whether within Brittany, to Paris, or along the North Atlantic. Contradictory imbalances of power mark their engagement with many different communities throughout the region and their fascination with the particularities of working-class labor. Ariella Azoulay insightfully describes photography as a sample of relationships between people in which bonds of obligation and responsibility are generated between the subject photographed and the potential viewer (Azoulay, 2014). Taking Azoulay's insight to heart, and expanding this sense of responsibility to nonhuman life, the following ecocritical analysis of their works brings to the surface an entanglement of materials, places, and people. Furthermore, I suggest that the newly accessible digital archive of the Géniaux brothers' photographs offer 21st-century viewers a greater understanding of our social and ecological connections to "natural resources."

In Rennes in the early 1890s, the Géniaux brothers converted an old greenhouse in the garden of their family home to a shop for the photomechanical printing of their photographs. In 1893, they launched a journal devoted to literature and photography in Brittany titled *Bretagne Revue* (later renamed *Revue Pittoresque de Bretagne*) (Goujard, 2019: 68). Their photographs of Brittany had many material incarnations in a short succession: they sold them as souvenirs in sets, and many were later photomechanically reproduced in books as collotypes (Wright, 2004: 31; Boulouch, 2019: 46). Using printing technologies that had recently become widespread, the brothers accumulated an image base of rural peasant typologies; stock figures who stood for the labors, trades, traditions, and local communities of the region. Their sharp-focused gelatin silver prints had a detailed depth of field and a reproducible gray scale (which ranged from velvet blacks to crisp whites), resulting from shooting their subjects in natural light. A naturalistic, seemingly objective representation was at the heart of the Géniaux photographic practice, and this set them apart from many of their contemporaries whose themes may have been similar, but whose techniques tended toward a more graphic form of Pictorialism. The postcard explosion of the turn of the 20th century was timed perfectly for the Géniaux brothers' images to contribute to a flood of photographic images of Brittany that were consumed in France and parts beyond (Croix et al., 2012: 109). Charles, who is perhaps better known as a regionalist author, frequently reproduced their Brittany photographs in his later texts, using them as stock imagery to illustrate his nostalgic narratives. The title of his illustrated book, *The Old France That is Vanishing*, clearly articulates a lament for a traditional way of life that remained in Brittany but was rapidly retreating from the modern world (Boulouch, 2019: 46). Charles declared in this text that their "photographs will be like the living corollary of a study which has no other merit than to have been written from nature." (Géniaux, 1903: 209)

Charles gave up photography in preference for his career as a writer, according to an unpublished biography written by his widow Claire Géniaux (Prod'homme, 2014: 19).[2] Paul remained dedicated to photography; in the early 20th century, he started a project photographing Parisian street trades (in the same archival manner as the Brittany photographs) and in the 1920s turned to fashion photography in Paris. An exhibition in the Carnavalet Museum in Paris in 1984 put Paul Géniaux's Paris work in dialogue with the roughly contemporary street photographers Eugène Atget and Louis Vert for their shared interest in the popular traditions of markets and small merchants that were either surviving or dying out in Haussmannized Paris (Prod'homme, 2012 and 2014; Grossiord and Reynaud, 1984). Until quite recently, Paul Géniaux's Paris photographs were far better known than the brothers' Brittany archive. In the past decade, with several gifts of forgotten negatives and prints, the Musée de Bretagne in Rennes has greatly enlarged its photographic holdings and has contributed to the recovery of the history of the Géniaux brothers, as demonstrated in its 2019 retrospective exhibition of many formerly unknown photographs, curated by Laurence Prod'homme. Most recently, the images in the Musée de Bretagne database have been opened to the public domain and have begun a new circulation, this time as a freely reproducible digital cache of recovered regional memory. This essay is indebted to the current accessibility of these images.

Etudes Bretonnes: Representing Brittany

As rural types, the brothers' images of working Bretons are rooted in (and are conversant with) French realist and regional imagery at the turn of the century. The following overview of the visual representation of Breton culture in France illuminates the context of their images and the proliferation of their reproductions. As a photographic subject, Brittany had a great appeal to French audiences: even in 1900, it seemed to be a latecomer to modernity. This peninsular region was relatively isolated from France (with sea on three sides and marshland to the east); it had formally joined France in 1532, but remained relatively autonomous until the French Revolution. From the 1790s onward, travelers had described the people of Brittany as a remnant of a "pure" Celtic race, independent of France or any other culture. However, Brittany had always been networked with other coastal regions on the northeast Atlantic, whether by its connection to the British Isles in the low sea level of prehistoric times, sea trade with the Roman Empire, or its long maritime history in the medieval and early modern period. And yet the depopulated, rural landscape was viewed by many tourists as a relic region, existing in a suspended state of cultural ruin; its prehistoric past at once mysteriously distant and uncannily alive (Young, 2012: 139; Menzies, 2011: 21).

However, it is historically misguided to focus on Brittany as a space of primitivism in opposition to metropolitan France (Coughlin, 2013: 75–76). Seafaring Brittany, with its long coastline and many ports, was a participant in early modern Atlantic capitalism as it emerged; it had an age of great prosperity from both fishing and the production of textiles from the sixteenth to the eighteenth centuries. Early modern communities of coastal Europe repeatedly caused (and suffered) the depletion of fish stocks; these collapses, as anthropologist Charles Menzies argues, are entirely continuous with our present "globalized" world (Menzies, 2011: 20–21). As French fishing fleets exhausted wild food commons of the ocean, they moved ever westward to Iceland and Newfoundland. In the 16th century, on France's Atlantic coast, cod fishing and marine trade supported population growth and brought great wealth to ports such as Penmarc'h in the Bay of Audierne (Finistère) before the local fish stocks disappeared. Like the elaborate sculpture programs of the *enclos*, or parish church compounds in Finistère that were funded by merchants in Brittany's cloth trade, many other 16th-century churches and pilgrimage sites are testament to the region's past wealth, tied to its fishing and agricultural ecologies. By the 19th century, inland areas of Finistère had already deindustrialized following the collapse of the early modern textile industry. From the 1850s onward, there was a boom in industrial canned sardines from Brittany that traded on a global market: workers left impoverished villages on the interior of the peninsula to work in factories on the coast. Cod fishing had also become a global endeavor: boys from poor families in the interior were shipped off to work on the shores of Newfoundland, just as boys from coastal towns were sent for six-month journeys on cod boats (Coughlin, 2020). As these examples show, for many centuries, Brittany's economic fortunes had been tied to both global trade and planetary ecologies.

Before train lines opened up the provinces of France to mass tourism in the 1880s, many notable illustrated social panoramas (and travel texts) published on Brittany, including *Les Français Peints par eux-mêmes* (1840–1842), inventoried its climate, geography, and the effects of this local nature on the cultural character of the region and its inhabitants (Coughlin, 2003). In these volumes, peasant types were presented as markers of the landscape—like local landforms or indigenous plants, their festive costumes, labors, ways of speech, moral character, and their dwellings are described as timeless local features of the place. Some of the earliest popular photography in Brittany, such as the well-known album of 233 stereoscopic views from 1857 by Charles-Paul Furne and Henri Tournier, repeats imagery from these earlier visual mediums (Croix et al., 2012: 44; Jeaneau and Berthelom, 2006: 52; Prod'homme, 2014: 91). Early photographs of regional figures—as seen in early albumen prints mounted like cartes de visite—are posed to display their costume and physiognomies, but their labor is not the narrative (Jeaneau and Berthelom, 2006: 20). Photography historian Lucie Goujard explains that the French preference for images of working peasants in the later 19th century was influenced by the midcentury visual language of realist painting: French photographers cultivated "the naturalist paradox of photography," creating carefully posed scenes. In part, Goujard argues, this comes from the fact that some photographs made "after nature" were intended as studies for artists to copy (Goujard, 2009). Art historian Griselda Pollock concurs that, as the visual language of photography emerged, it was "heavily indebted to existing visual conventions and practices" but it also "offered a new kind of visuality when it restaged those poses and gestures in its own, emergent semiosis." (Pollock and Florence, 2001: 204) Salon painting, from the 1870s onward, had favored representations of Breton peasants in holiday costume, at times either anachronistic (using men's prerevolutionary costume) or unrealistic (e.g., women working in the fields in high lace festival *coiffes*). The Brittany that the Géniaux offered their public both partook of convention and, occasionally, broke with it.

In Belle Époque Brittany, amateur photo associations proliferated, especially in the cities of Nantes and Rennes. In an encyclopedic publication that draws from museum, regional, municipal, and private collections, Alain Croix, Didier Guyvarc'h, and Marc Rapilliard discuss this era in which the availability of cameras and gelatin silver print materials permitted amateur and professional photographers an unprecedented agency in selecting the particular aspects of Breton culture that they found picture-worthy (Croix et al., 2012: 101). Photographing a peasant performing a traditional task or *métier* was a commonplace in France by 1900, as the exhibition in Le Faouët, *100 Métiers Vus Par Les Artistes en Bretagne,* demonstrated (Bellec et al., 2017). Some of these compositions were made by artists such as André Dauchez, who used his photographs as studies for paintings and prints. In the early 1890s, Edmond Rudaux took photos in Brittany to translate both to engravings and for his book illustrations for Pierre Loti's wildly popular novel *An Iceland Fishermen* (Croix et al., 2012: 117). Charles Lhermitte (son of rustic painter Léon Lhermitte) filtered his Pictorialist images through the paintings of Millet, Corot, and Breton. Also notable are Gustave Gain's autochromes made around 1900 in Brittany. Lastly, there is the documentary work of Paul Gruyer, which most closely resembles that of the Géniaux brothers. Gruyer was among the earliest photographers to work directly with an author to produce book illustrations, as seen in his ambitions 1905 volume *La Bretagne*, a collaboration with regionalist writer Gustave Geffroy (Geoffroy, 1905; Croix et al., 2012: 107).

Much Belle Époque Breton photography repeats tropes of an archaic place lost in time: laundresses crouch at rustic *lavoirs* (washhouses), there are festive marriages, religious pardons, seaweed collectors at the shore, beggars, drunks, widows, witches, and peasant women selling their hair to nefarious wigmakers. And yet there are hints that a form of modernity is visible in Brittany: we occasionally see new trains, bridges, and modern clothing creeping into the compositions. Curator Laurence Prod'homme states that, in spite of the fact that many of their images seem nostalgic today (and indeed they repeated many of the tropes just mentioned), the Géniaux brothers were not interested in mythologizing Brittany as archaic or unwilling to modernize (Prod'homme, 2019: 77). Even as they did not escape conventions established in earlier visual culture, they often documented themes of rural life that the Pictorialists avoided, such as ruined landscapes, child labor, and routine work. The brothers were clearly aware of the continuing appeal of Breton imagery: their images both trade upon popular and academic images and (occasionally) resist them. Charles, for an egregious instance, exploited clichés of Brittany's exoticism and sold some of his stories abroad (illustrated with photographs) to journals such as the sensationalist *Wide World Magazine* in London, which ran his essay "Naia, the Witch of Rochefort," in 1899, and a tale of the predatory wig industry, "The Human Hair Harvest in Brittany," the following year (Géniaux, 1899; Géniaux, 1900). In cases like this, the Géniaux brothers' images were themselves extracted resources that circulated and perpetuated the ubiquitous image of Brittany as the exemplary case of old France being lost to modernity.

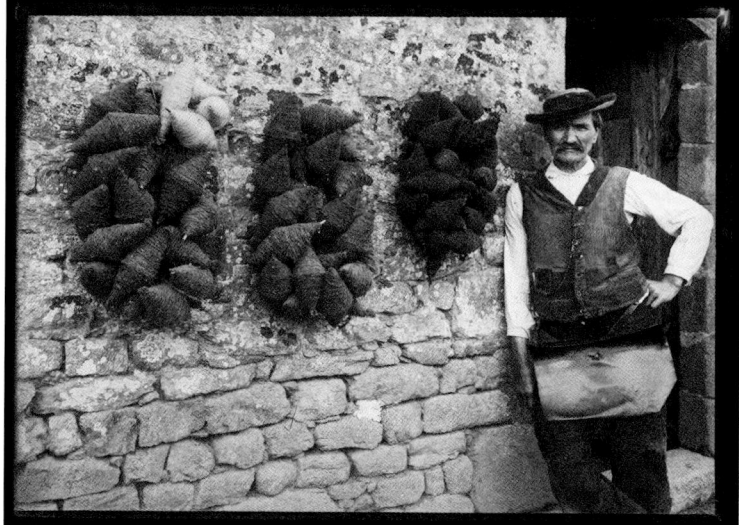

Figure 3.1

Charles Géniaux, *Tisserand et des fusées (Weaver and spools in Muzillac (Morbihan))*, ca. 1900–1903. Glass negative, Musée de Bretagne, Rennes.

The peasants photographed by the Géniaux were rarely named individuals; most of them would not have been in the habit of posing for a camera apart from wedding portraits or other formal occasions (Bourdieu et al., 2004). Yet most are aware of being photographed, and very few seem at ease. The brothers often photographed peasant subjects at work, performing skilled labor such as salt harvesting, spinning flax, or splitting slate. As the images were repurposed and relabeled on the way to mass reproduction, they lost much of the specific detail of their identities, locale, trade, and materials. For instance, Charles Géniaux's photograph *Weaver and Spools in Muzillac*, ca. 1900–1903, depicts an unnamed, older male weaver who stands beside three wreaths of drying skeins that hang on his stone workshop wall. (fig. 3.1) The vest he wears identifies him as a Breton; more importantly, it appears to be made of industrially woven cloth (likely wool and velvet) and is typical of clothing associated with local Breton identity at that time. Charles then used this photograph as an illustration of a chapter "Chez le Tisserand" ("At the Weaver's House") in his nostalgic book of 1903, *La Vielle France qui s'en va*. Among other exacting details about the relationships between weavers, their materials, and their customers, he notes that weavers work only for commissions and do not create work for a prospective market. A weaver, he tells us, must carefully gauge how much cloth will result from the spools of wool that he purchases from a farmer. Géniaux adds (without reference to the decline of the textile industry), "if we insist on the description of this manufacture, it is to emphasize the exceptional ingenuity of these modest weavers." (Géniaux, 1903: 86) When reproduced as a postcard in the series "Breton Customs and Costumes," with only the subtitle "A Weaver and Spools," the image of the weaver further lost personal and regional identity. Géniaux's text never reflects upon the divergence between its advocacy for the artisanal labor productive of a handmade or bespoke item and the industrialized material processes that made the image reproducible and widespread.

Many of the Géniaux brothers' photographs of Breton workers emphasize labor and routine gesture. The working body is a persistent motif of early 20th-century documentary photography, whether in the mills of Lewis Hine's images, the agricultural fields of the American South and West for Farm Security Administration photographers, or in the many typologies of German workers collected by August Sander. Annales school historian Lucienne Roubin describes peasant physical enculturation in peasant know-how as including both "familial" knowledge (secrets shared only among family members) and technical skills that were "corporative" (shared by those who practiced a *métier*) (Roubin, 1977). Applied to realist visual imagery, her work encourages a reading of working peasant bodies as enculturated by their daily realities and by the specificity of their corporeal demands and practices (Roubin, 1977: 97). Describing a photograph by Sander (ca. 1914) of German peasant men in suits, John Berger continues this line of thought, noting that the "characteristic physical rhythm which most peasants, both men and women acquire […] [is] related to the energy demanded by the amount of work which has to be done in a day, and is reflected in typical movements and stance." (Berger, 2009: 33) The imagery of the Géniaux brothers can be read as a collection of regionally specific labor typologies that articulate *corporatif* knowledge and of routine gestures that work to transform the matter of the natural world.

Cheap Nature

Photography historian and critic Michelle Henning proposes that we accept photography from the outset as an impure category, a congealing of nature and culture, of human and non-human, of material stuff and images and discourses, of a range of technologies, practices and effects. To treat it, in other words, as an *imbroglio* in the sense that Bruno Latour uses it: a tangled knot of human social practices and concepts and of the material, technical, chemical properties of things. (Henning, 2018: 6)

As Henning suggests, Latour's emphasis on entanglement is a productive starting point for examining the relationships, dependencies, and networks that are pictured in the Géniaux brothers' Brittany photographs. The growing field of ecomaterialist criticism is an interdisciplinary perspective drawn from the work of Latour, Alfred Gell, and Jane Bennett (among many others) to encourage thinking about relational networks of the human and more-than-human worlds and the ways that objects can afford action (Latour, 2005; Gell, 1998; Bennett, 2010). In addition to Latour's notion of entanglement discussed above, Donna Haraway extends the ecocritical vocabulary of inseparable relation further with her term "natureculture." This neologism effectively collapses previously opposed terms and recognizes their inseparability in ecological relationships that are both biophysically and socially formed (Haraway, 2008: 66). Feminist ecomaterialist Stacy Alaimo gives us the useful concept of "trans-corporeality […] material interchanges across human bodies, animal bodies, and the wider material world." (Alaimo, 2012: 476) And further, ecomaterialists Serenella Iovino and Serpil Oppermann summarize basic tenets of "new materialist" thought as

> a pronounced reaction against some radical trends of postmodern and post-structuralist thinking that allegedly 'dematerialized' the world into linguistic and social constructions. The new attention paid to matter has […] emphasized the need for recalling the concreteness of existential fields, with regard to both the bodily dimension and to non-binary object-subject relations. (quoted in Alaimo, 76)

In my research, ecomaterialism has provided critical tools for thinking through relationships rather than binary terms, thwarting previous critical conflations of all representations of rural life with mere nostalgia. The widespread critique of social construction that pervaded visual culture studies in the 1990s today seems coldly disengaged, as Alaimo writes, "with lived, biological bodies and the actions and significations of the nonhuman world." (Alaimo, 2016: 542)

Ecocriticism has come more recently to studies of art history and visual culture. Alan Braddock was an early advocate for ecocritical readings of 19th-century visual culture; he notes that "ecocriticism emphasizes ecological interconnectedness, sustainability, and environmental justice in cultural interpretation. It asserts the imbrication of all beings, artifacts, and matter-including humans and their creative works-within a dynamic mesh of relations, agents, and historical forces." (Braddock, 2015: 448) The importance of an ecocritical approach is at the heart of the volume *Ecocriticism and the Anthropocene in Nineteenth-Century Art and Visual Culture*, which I coedited with Emily Gephart. We brought together essays that explored, among many other things, the paradox that, just at the times when "resources were *extricated* irreversibly from their surroundings, scientists studied evidence of *inextricable* ecological relationships and postulated comprehensive narratives of the world's deep time, vast scale and dynamic flux." (Coughlin and Gephart, 2019: 5) Ecocriticism emphasizes that monetizing our relationship with this thing we call "nature" has resulted in a loss of understanding of our connections to the nonhuman world. As Raj Patel and Jason W. Moore write, the Cartesian revolution of the Enlightenment accomplished four major transformations: the valorization of binary thinking about nature and culture, the primary conception of substances as things (while ignoring the relationships between substances), the domination of nature through science, and the colonial project of global mapping and domination (Patel and Moore, 2017: 54). In the environmental humanities, the term "Capitalocene" has gained traction as an epochal term descriptive of this logic that has underscored human responsibility for the climate crisis. Moore (and many others) have critiqued the current use of the term "Anthropocene" to mark our era, because it focuses too strictly on the effects of fossil fuel usage that begins in the years around 1800: "this narrative is shaped by a peculiar kind of past/present binary: the whole of history, at least since the Neolithic Revolution, is cast into the dustbin of the 'preindustrial.' Most scholars are well aware that human civilizations transformed environments in significant ways well before the nineteenth century." (Moore, 2016: 90)

"Capitalocene" shifts the focus to the longer story of the global capitalist exploitation of "cheap nature" that harnessed naïve faith in modernity and progress to accelerate the extraction of monetary value from natural resources. Science played a role, from the Enlightenment, of making nature a thing, an Other in which capital accumulated, something that could be assessed, traded, and sold. Philosopher Timothy Morton deploys his own term "agrilogistics" to refer to this utilitarian attitude toward "resources": "agrilogistics promises to eliminate fear, anxiety and contradiction—social, physical and ontological—by establishing thin rigid boundaries between human and nonhuman worlds and by reducing existence to sheer quantity." (Morton, 2016: 43)

Examining the extraction of value from "cheap nature" in the Géniaux brothers' picturing of landscapes and labor reveals the centuries-old nature of this relationship in the entangled cultures of their worked Breton landscapes and laboring Breton bodies. Paradoxically, the widespread reproduction of their images rendered rural Brittany as both a ubiquitous image of the marginal survival of rural life and a material extraction site of seemingly endless natural resources drawn from the land and sea. What the material ecologies of their images articulate so clearly is the nature of materials and their transformations through human and animal labor. Matter that is dried, sliced, picked, reaped, quarried, boiled, and separated from its original form repeats throughout their work. For the remainder of this essay, I turn to particular images by the Géniaux that detail the extraction, production, or cultivation of three materials: hemp, slate, and salt.

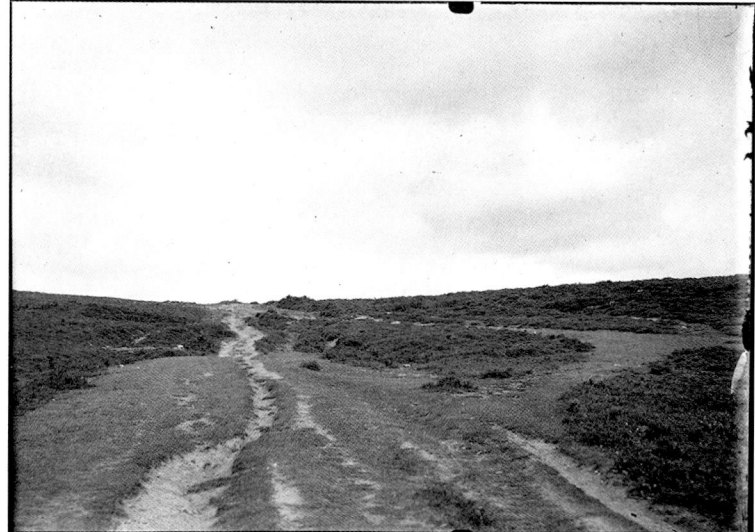

Figure 3.2

Paul or Charles Géniaux, *Paysage de Landes (Waste Landscape)*, ca. 1902–1905. Gelatin silver print, Musée de Bretagne, Rennes.

Hemp and Other Plant Matter

In their photograph *Paysage de Landes*, ca. 1902–1905, the Géniaux depict a typical Breton *lande* or moor. It depicts only a grazed, uneven, and eroded field with a worn path through the spare ground cover and a gray sky above. (fig. 3.2) Although the term *lande* roughly translates as moorland or heath, it also connotes other uncultivated or "wastelands" without evident agricultural productivity. Despite its appearance of wild and empty desolation, this was a thoroughly worked, human space: *landes* like this had been used by humans and animals for millennia. Peasants used every available plant that grew on the *landes*. Peat was dug from bogs for heating; even spiny gorse, broom, heather, and ferns were harvested for fuel or animal fodder and bedding. Farmers of the area cleared and burned these commons. Fields lay fallow for a time, then were planted and grazed in rotation in a relatively balanced practice that maintained and worked with their limited fertility. Through formal clearing or *défrichement*, rural spaces that were not already put to use in hedgerow-enclosed *bocages* either became extraction sites or were transformed to arable worked lands. Coastal wetlands and interior bogs were gradually drained to create grasslands or were worked for shellfish farming or salt harvesting. Although many of these sites were modest in acreage, the cumulative result was devastating. Over the course of the 19th and 20th centuries, 98 percent of Britany's *landes* were cleared, primarily for agriculture.

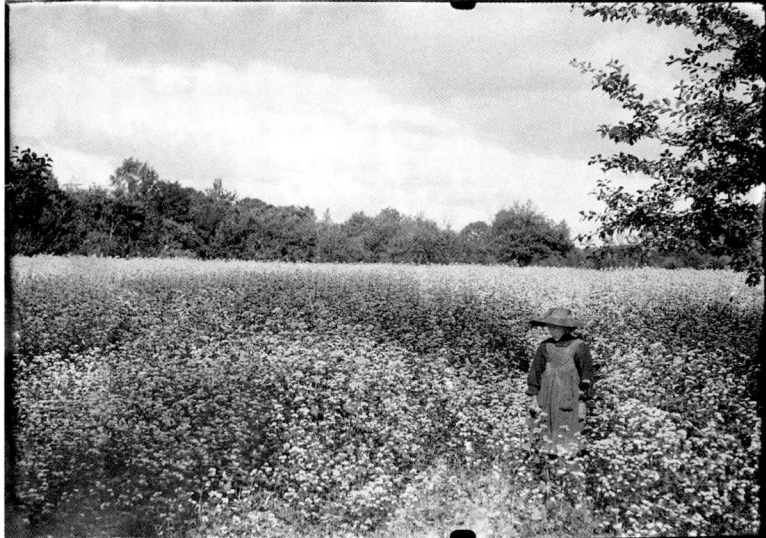

Figure 3.3

Géniaux brothers, *Champ de Sarrasin (Buckwheat Field)*, ca. 1902–1905. Glass negative, Musée de Bretagne, Rennes.

Prior to industrial agriculture and the production of chemical fertilizers, few crops flourished on the *landes* except for buckwheat (*sarrasin*) and hemp. Both of these crops appear in the Géniaux brothers' photographs. In one photograph, a child, perhaps already a harvester, stands in a field of flowering buckwheat, which stretches beyond the frame. (fig. 3.3) In two others (ca. 1902–1905), two young men use a horse-drawn mowing machine to harvest a buckwheat field. Originating in Asia, buckwheat was introduced in Europe sometime in the Middle

Ages—*blé noir* or "black wheat" was a foodstuff synonymous with the poverty of Brittany, as it gave peasants buckwheat crepes and black bread instead of refined baked goods made with white flour. Not a true grain, but a plant in the same family as sorrel, knotweed, and rhubarb, buckwheat grows well in sandy soil with a low nitrogen content, much like hemp. The Géniaux present the cultivation of buckwheat as an aspect of the everyday agricultural landscape.

Breton hemp and linen (which grew well on the coast) brought great wealth to Finistère in the booming textile trade of the 16th and 17th centuries. These crops were grown, processed, and finished in Brittany and were the materials from which nets, lines, ropes, and sails were made; these materials were central actors in France's maritime trade.[3] As Moore notes, the cloth trade is central to the emergence of capitalism, because both peasant labor and naturally derived resources were conceived as "Cheap Nature […] [which] toward the end of the seventeenth century […] reached deep into the countrysides of western Europe through protoindustrialization, centering on textiles." (Moore, 2016: 99) Until English cotton was industrially produced cheaply enough to become ubiquitous in the mid-19th century, Brittany exported textiles globally as an Atlantic trade commodity, especially to Latin America. Once Brittany's textile trade died out, the interior was deindustrialized (Ford, 1993: 34–36; Martin and Le Noac'h, 1998: 189). What the Géniaux show us in images of weavers, spinning linen, or binding hemp is the residual presence of a once profitable exploitation of the land. A product that was once global has now only local use, but it nevertheless persists in small-scale cultivation. As if re-enacting a page

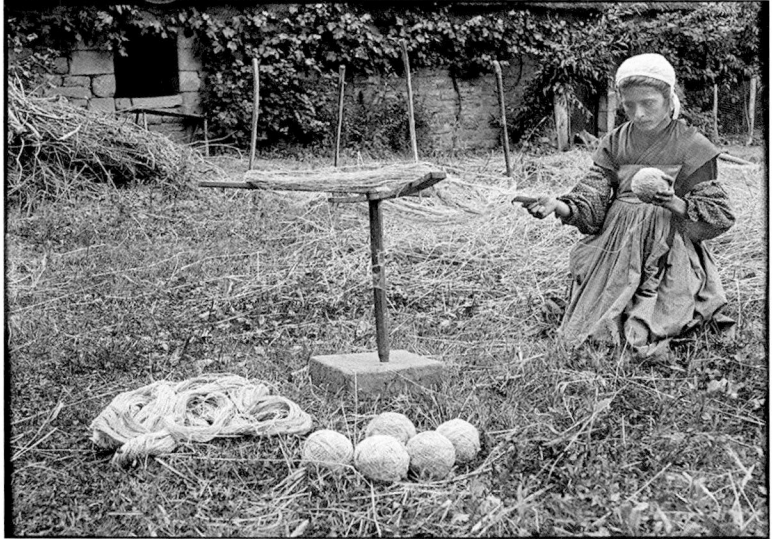

Figure 3.4

Charles Géniaux, *Jeune fille au dévidoir (Young girl with a linen skein winder)*, ca. 1902–1905. Glass negative, Musée de Bretagne, Rennes.

from Diderot's encyclopedia of preindustrial production, whose images repeat routines of rote labor in each stage of artisanal production, children wind linen skeins by hand (fig. 3.4); men and women bind bundles of raw hemp for drying that others later beat to loosen the seeds and to separate the usable fiber from the woody core of the stem (Sennett, 2008: 92). (figs. 3.5a and 3.5b)

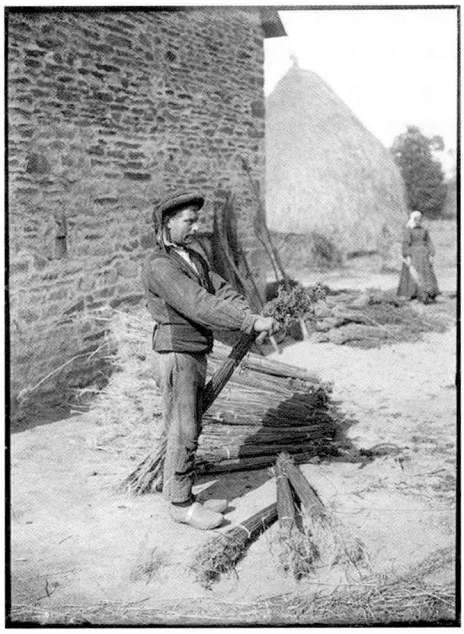

Figure 3.5a

Charles or Paul Géniaux, *Confection de bottes de chanvre (Making hemp boots)*, ca. 1902–1905. Glass negative, Musée de Bretagne, Rennes

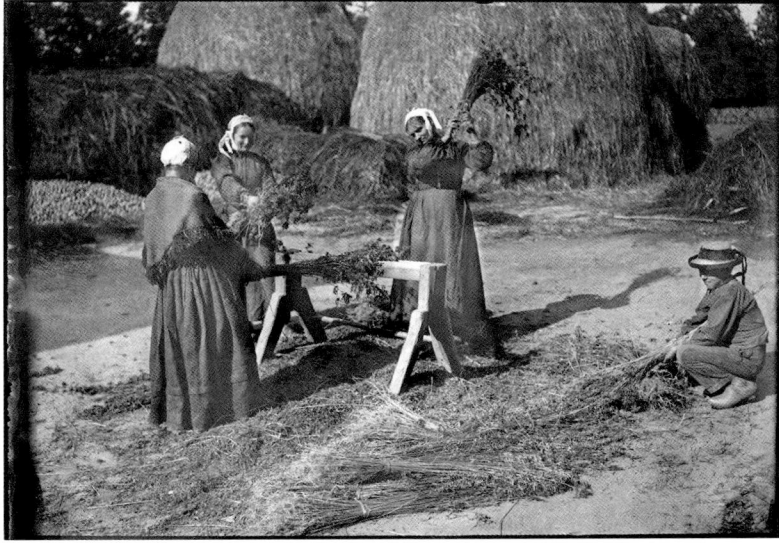

Figure 3.5b

Charles Géniaux, *Moisson battage (Harvest threshing)*, ca. 1902–1905. Glass negative, Musée de Bretagne, Rennes.

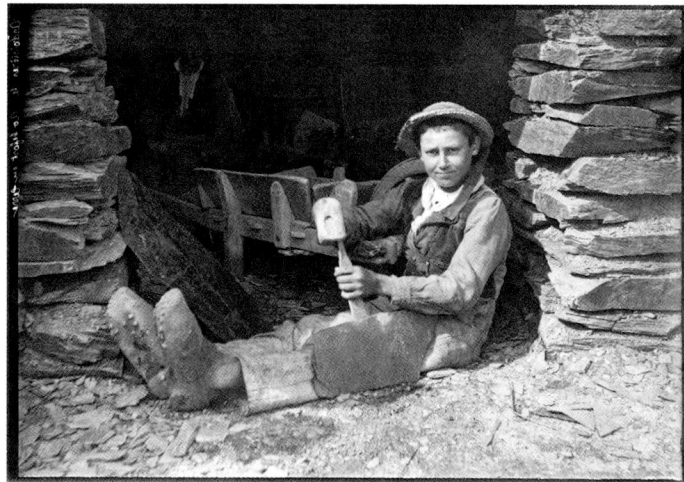

Figure 3.6

Paul Géniaux, *Ardoisières de Rochefort-en-Terre (Slate Quarries in Rochefort-sur-Terre)*, ca. 1895. Gelatin silver print, Musée de Bretagne, Rennes.

Slate

In contrast to the images of small-scale hemp processing or the weaver who works at home, Paul Géniaux produced very different images of the slate industry. Breton slate had been exploited since Middle Ages in sites all over the peninsula, but before the 19th century, sea transport was the only viable route. The early 19th-century canal system running from Nantes to Brest facilitated more mobility, and train lines that were extensive by the 1880s widened the market for Breton slate into Normandy and even to Paris. Most Breton slate was used for roofing; it rapidly replaced thatch as it became more accessible. Breton slate quarries reached their peak production in 1923 (Musset, 1940: 238). Paul photographed series of images of actively exploited slate quarries in 1895 and 1910 in Rochefort-en-Terre (in Morbihan, near one of their family homes) and in the village of Trélazé (near Angers). Rochefort was one of many Breton slate producing towns; in 1900, the quarry employed about five hundred people. In 1887, its four open quarries produced about sixteen million slates annually that were shipped out all over France (Lukas, 1978). Géniaux pictured a combination of manual and mechanized work. Men use equipment to slice slates; a boy in heavy wooden clogs gently taps out an individual slate; winches tow boxes of slate across an open quarry; or a machine is the only actor, standing in for human labor. (fig. 3.6) In an 1895 photograph of the slate works at Rochefort, a workplace with slate huts is temporarily vacated by its workers. (fig. 3.7) Dramatic diagonals emphasize both extraction and transport: a ladder perilously points downward into a quarry pit from which more slate will be extracted, and train tracks indicate the destination of the finished slates. In later photos from the quarries of Rochefort, ca. 1910, a quarry worker rides a large wooden crate (reinforced with metal) as it is being winched skyward to travel along a horizontal cable. (see fig. 3.8) In another shot, this same box is suspended above the horizon, and we understand the enormity of this endeavor through the relational scale of the human body. Quarries are unusual subjects for visual representation; they are removed landscapes, ruins, places whose

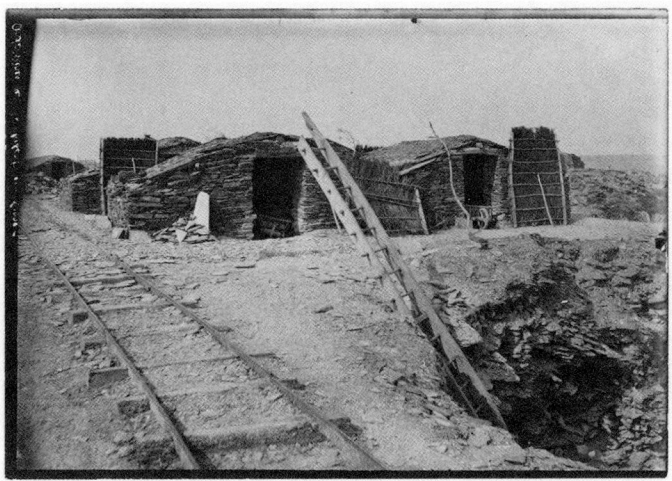

Figure 3.7

Paul Géniaux, *Ardoisières de Rochefort-en-Terre (Slate Quarries in Rochefort-sur-Terre)*, ca. 1910. Paper photograph, Musée de Bretagne, Rennes.

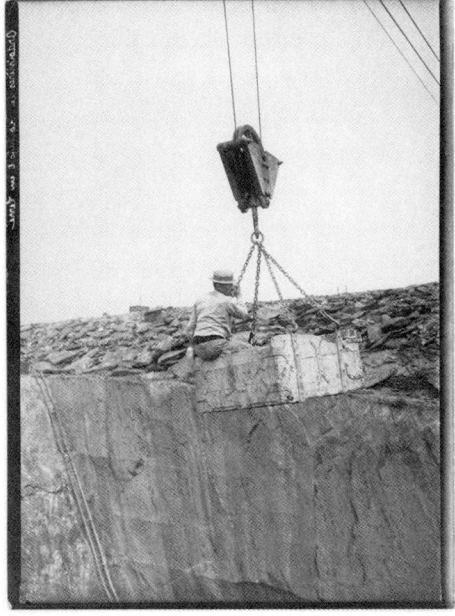

Figure 3.8

Paul Géniaux, *Ardoisières de Rochefort-en-Terre (Slate Quarries in Rochefort-sur-Terre)*, ca. 1910. Paper photograph, Musée de Bretagne, Rennes.

See also Plate 6.1.

material constituents have been "sourced" elsewhere (Coughlin, 2009). These later quarry photographs owe nothing to a picturesque notion of "primitive" Brittany, rather they picture the Capitalocene utility of its landscape as a site of material extraction that will be pursued as long as it is economically viable.

Salt

Salt making in the area of Guérande and Billiers is perhaps the most materially engaged labor and one of the industries most extensively photographed by the Géniaux brothers. Salt had been made in this region of France for millennia and, despite its large-scale production, harvesting techniques had changed little in 1900 (Kurlansky, 2002: 117). Gildas Buron, curator of the Musée des Marais Salants (Batz-sur-Mer) and the foremost historian of salt in the Guérande region, describes the first discovery of salt extraction in the area: crystals formed naturally in tidal pools and on rocks, and these were doubtlessly noticed by Neolithic people who gradually worked with this natural process in the Bay of Morbihan to produce more salt (Buron, 2001: 11).

Ecologically speaking, *marais salants* are encultered and controlled landscapes, marsh realms carved, directed, and maintained explicitly for the extraction of salt. Seawater is channeled through canals and basins to concentrate the salinity but also to lose its organic matter. In the process, the potential ecologies of the salt marsh (fish, eels, algae) are removed or blocked from the reservoirs that precede the final pans. Only in the heat and wind of summer was the evaporation of water possible in this area. Like an open-air factory, the salt marshes of Guérande were landscapes carved out of the wetlands, formed and maintained explicitly for the extraction of salt. Brittany's economy had long been entwined with salt production on its south coast. Historically, Breton saltworks had been enormously profitable as they answered both French and global demands for sea salt, especially in the North Atlantic cod fisheries (whose home ports were on Brittany's north coast) that grew in scale from the 16th century onward. It was not until after the French Revolution that the taxing of salt was reformed and the economics of salt making no longer favored Brittany (Buron, 2001: 108).

The Géniaux brothers followed male and female salt harvesters (*paludièrs* and *paludierès*, respectively) working alone as they rake the crystallized minerals from the surface of the pools (*fleur du sel*) or from the bottoms of the pans (*sel gris*). Most of their salt-making images are in the collection of the Musée de Bretagne, Rennes and the museum dedicated to saltworks, the Musée des Marais Salants, Batz-sur-Mer. In two photographs of women who balance on the edge of the gridded pans, there is an uncanny, commanding monumentality to the figures' confident stances. (figs. 3.9a, 3.9b) We see again a set of *corporatif* bodily movements that were learned through repetition, the result of collective knowledge and local practice. This careful bodily array is clearly demonstrated the use of the long-handled *lousse* that each harvester displays to the viewer in a pose that Géniaux might have encouraged or asked to her to hold. By showing the learned technique of her *métier* to the lens, she invites us to think about the material consequences and productivity of her actions.

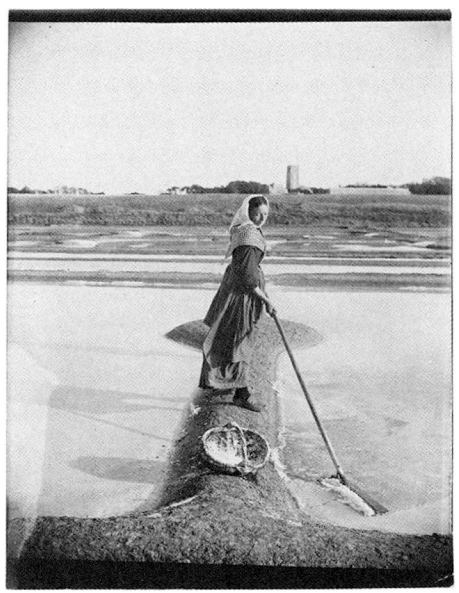

Figure 3.9a

Paul Géniaux, *Marais salants de Billiers prise de la fleur de sel (Salt marshes of Billiers, harvesting fleur de sel)*, ca. 1900. Gelatin silver print, Musée de Bretagne, Rennes.

See also Plate 6.2.

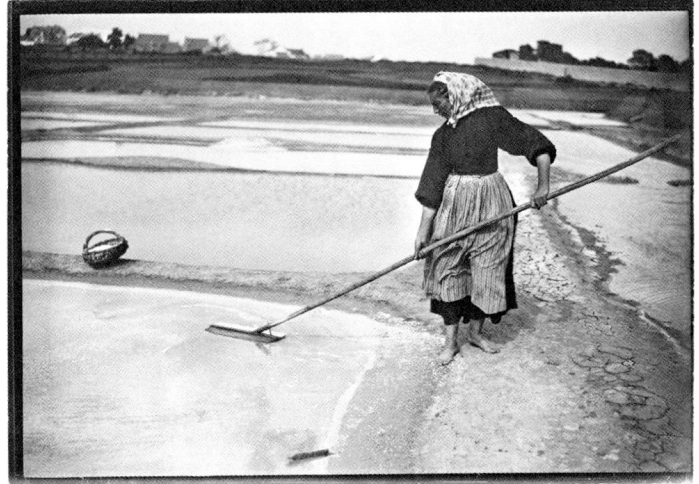

Figure 3.9b

Paul Géniaux, *Marais salants de Billiers prise de la fleur de sel (Salt marshes of Billiers, harvesting fleur de sel)*, ca. 1900. Gelatin silver print, Musée de Bretagne, Rennes.

See also Plate 6.3.

In the image of the *paludière* in profile, material contrasts are particularly striking. (see fig. 3.9b) Silver salts on this image's surface only needed a short exposure on this blazingly sunny day to register the dark skin of her face, long exposed to the same summer sun and wind that had crystallized the salt she skims from the surface. Her face and hair are framed by a light cotton kerchief (protecting her bright white *coiffe* beneath it). Over a somber dress is a striped apron, long since new or clean. Unlike painters or illustrators who preferred to depict Bretons in their most exotic festive costumes, these clothes are dirty, mended, and everyday.

Their salt-making technique had changed little over the centuries, yet the visual contrasts in the Géniaux brothers' image depend upon a modern suspension of light-sensitive silver on a dry plate in a gelatin emulsion. This technique, initiated in the 1870s, had, by 1900, replaced earlier salted paper prints. But it was no less material: one of George Eastman's findings of the 1880s, in the early manufacturing of dry plates, was that the bones of cattle raised on mustard plants produced superior, light-sensitive gelatin (Simmons, 2008: 33). Animal matter, crudely bioengineered, is crucial to the ubiquity and seeming inorganic (precise) nature of the gelatin silver print. The details of the Géniaux photographs ask viewers to consider and to associate the sensitivity of salts in the silver gelatin dry plate, the sensitivity of skin to sun, and sensation of tough and cracked feet desensitized to walking on salt. As Serenella Iovino writes:

> 'materiality' is the condition through which bodies act with and relate with each other, shaping other bodies [...] Reflecting on matter means reflecting on the modes of production and consumption of nature(s) as reservoirs of usable elements; it means reflecting on the way the matter of the world is embodied in human experience, as well as in human 'mind.' (Iovino, 2012: 76)

Apart from the image of the individual *paludière*—a favorite motif of both 19th-century artists and illustrators—another series of salt-making images depicts a much more massive scale of production. One image of salt piles or *mulons* presents huge, white, spiral mounds of salt that sit outside in rows on the edge of the marsh's grids, uncanny monuments to accumulation and extraction. (fig. 3.10) A windmill and horse-drawn cart in the background point to the animal labor in this landscape and the energy of the wind that aids the crystallization of the salt and powers the mill that pumps water or grinds grain. The foreground salt pile that initially resembles the output of modern manufacture is the result of thousands of human gestures of scooping, hauling, and dumping salt from pools of water. Although the massive mound mimics an eternal

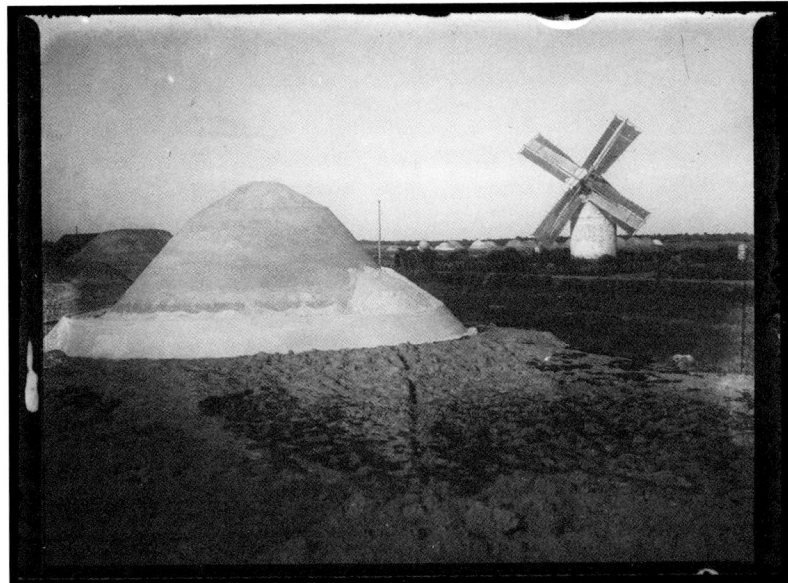

Figure 3.10

Charles Géniaux,
*Marais salants de Billiers
prise de la fleur de sel
(Salt marshes of Billiers,
harvesting fleur de sel)*,
ca. 1900–1915. Glass
negative, Musée de
Bretagne, Rennes.

monument, its matter, shaped through *corporatif* labor, only holds this form temporarily before being refined, packaged, and sold in small quantities. In 1900, Paul photographed inside the massive Benoît salt storehouses and refinery (Buron, 2001: 159). In these photos, workers rake, bag, and weigh salt. As Buron explains, at the time of the photographs, the Benoît brothers had recently opened their processing plant to standardize, bleach, and wash their product so that it might compete on a national market with mined salt from eastern France and sea salt from the Mediterranean. Like the slate quarry photos, there are a few examples from the salt factory where the gears and structures of the machinery seem to stand in for human labor, implying the modern mechanization of work. These images are not well known, and, as far as I have been able to discern, they were not widely distributed as were the images of traditional, individual labor in the salt pans.

Conclusion

With the rediscovery of so many of the Géniaux brothers' photographs in the past decade, we have just begun to evaluate the ways in which the brothers represented Brittany and its material ecologies. Material eco-criticism is one tool that may aid in describing the relationships between Bretons, their work, and their environment articulated in some of the Géniaux brothers' least studied images. Their images dematerialized through reproduction from analog indexicality to ubiquitous stock and postcard imagery in a way that was thoroughly modern, just as the materiality of the world they pictured in Brittany often seemed, on the surface, to be timeless. At times, the brothers collected images that broke away from the aesthetic of the picturesque and primitive, and revealed something of the changing relationships of the modern working-class people of Brittany to their immediate environment.

Notes

1. All translations from French mine unless otherwise noted. The majority of this essay was written in response to the 2019 exhibition of the Géniaux brothers' photography at the Musée de Bretagne, Rennes and the publication of the accompanying catalog. I could not have researched this essay without the generous collegiality of scholars in Brittany including Laurence Prod'homme, Gildas Buron, Hubert Chermereau, Gérard Berthelom, and Caroline Boyle-Turner. Bryant University librarian Sam Simas was an invaluable ally as was my dear colleague, Emily Gephart, and photo historian Joanne Lukitsch. Thanks also to research librarian Marie-Rose Prigent at the Centre de recherche bretonne en celtique (the Breton and Celtic Research Center) in Brest. Many thanks to the participants of the Ubiquity: Photography's Multitudes symposium in Rochester, New York, especially Jacob Lewis and Kyle Parry. Funding for this project was generously provided by a research stipend from Bryant University.

2. Prod'homme cites an unpublished biographic manuscript by Claire Géniaux, Charles's wife, who notes that he rejected what he thought of as the "low trade" of both photography and journalism, preferring to think of himself as a novelist or poet. She does not provide dates for his decision. See Claire Géniaux, *La vie d'un homme de letters Charles Géniaux*, (n.d.), 17.

3. The role of linen and hemp was extensively explored in a 2013 exhibition in Douranenez and in the accompanying volume, Anne Guirado, *Fibres Marines: Chanvre et Lin, hier et aujourd'hui* (Quimper: Editions Palantines, 2013).

Bibliography

Stacy Alaimo, "Nature," in *The Oxford Handbook of Feminist Theory*, eds Lisa Disch and Mary Hawkesworth (New York: Oxford University Press, 2016).

Stacy Alaimo, "States of Suspension: Trans-corporeality at Sea," *Interdisciplinary Studies in Literature and Environment*, 19, 3 (2012): 476–493.

Ariella Azoulay, *The Civil Contract of Photography* (New York: Zone Books, 2014).

Christian Bellec, Denise Delouche, and Anne le Roux-Le Pimpec, *100 métiers vus par les artistes en Bretagne*, exh. cat. (Le Faouët: Liv'éditions, 2017).

Jane Bennett, *Vibrant Matter: A Political Ecology of Things* (Durham, NC: Duke University Press, 2010).

John Berger, *About Looking* (London: Bloomsbury, 2009).

Nathalie Boulouch, "Photographier la Bretagne qui s'en va," in *Charles et Paul Géniaux*, ed. Laurence Prod'homme (Châteaulin: Locus Solus, 2019), 41–46.

Pierre Bourdieu, Marie-Claire Bourdieu, Loïc Wacquant, and Richard Nice, "The Peasant and Photography (1965)," *Ethnography*, 5, 4 (2004): 600–616.

Alan Braddock, "From Nature to Ecology: The Emergence of Ecocritical Art History," in *A Companion to American Art*, eds John Davis, Jennifer A. Greenhill, and Jason D. LaFountain (Hoboken: Wiley Blackwell, 2015), 1165–1215.

Gildas Buron, *Bretagne des marais salants* (Morlaix: Skol Vreizh, 2001).

Maura Coughlin, "Inevitable Grottoes: Modern Painting and Waste Space," *Iowa Journal of Cultural Studies*, 10 (2009): 25–41.

Maura Coughlin, "Millet's Milkmaids," *Nineteenth-Century Art Worldwide*, 2, 1 (Winter 2003), http://www.19thc-artworldwide.org/winter03/247-millets-milk-maids (accessed August 1, 2020).

Maura Coughlin, "Place Myths of the Breton Landscape," in *Impressionist France: Visions of Nation from Le Gray to Monet*, eds April Watson and Simon Kelly, exh. cat. (New Haven: Yale University Press, 2013), 67–78.

Maura Coughlin, "Votive Boats, Ex-votos, and Maritime Memory in Atlantic France," in *Cultures of Memory in the Nineteenth Century: Consuming Commemoration*, eds Amanda Mushal and Kathy Grenier (London: Palgrave, 2020), 97–122.

Alain Croix et al., *La Bretagne des Photographes. La construction d'une image de 1841 à nos jours* (Rennes: Presses Universitaires de Rennes, 2012).

Caroline Ford, *Creating the Nation in Provincial France: Religion and Political Identity in Brittany* (Princeton: Princeton University Press, 1993).

Alfred Gell, *Art and Agency: An Anthropological Theory* (Oxford: Clarendon, 1998).

Gustave Geffroy, *La Bretagne. Illustrations d'après les photographies de M.P. Gruyer* (Paris: Hachette, 1905).

Charles Géniaux, "The Human Hair Harvest in Brittany," *Wide World Magazine*, 4 (1900): 430–436.

Charles Géniaux, *La Vieille France Qui S'en Va* (Tours: Mame, 1903).

Charles Géniaux, "Naia, the Witch of Rochefort," *Wide World Magazine*, 3 (1899): 643–648.

Lucie Goujard, "Une jeunesse décadente et idéaliste. La maison d'édition Géniaux," in *Charles et Paul Géniaux*, ed. Laurence Prod'homme (Châteaulin: Locus Solus, 2019), 67–74.

Lucie Goujard, "Photographie pittoresque. L'influence des modèles esthétiques traditionnels sur les photographies de la pauvreté," *Apparence(s)*, 3 (2009), https://apparences.revues.org/1052 (accessed August 2, 2020).

Sophie Grossiord and Françoise Reynaud, *Petits Métiers et Types Parisiens vers 1900: Atget, Géniaux, Vert*, exh. cat. (Paris: Musée Carnavalet, 1984)

Anne Guirado, *Fibres Marines: Chanvre et Lin, hier et aujourd'hui* (Quimper: Editions Palantines, 2013).

Donna Haraway, *When Species Meet* (Minneapolis: University of Minnesota Press, 2008).

Michelle Henning, *Photography: The Unfettered Image* (Abingdon: Routledge, 2018).

Serenella Iovino, "Material Ecocriticism: Matter, Text, and Posthuman Ethics," in *Literature, Ecology, Ethics: Recent Trends in Ecocriticism*, eds Timo Müller and Michael Sauter (Heidelberg: Universitätsverlag Winter, 2012), 50–51.

Corinne Jeaneau and Gérard Berthelom, *Photographes Au Xixe Siècle: Les Nouveaux Imagiers De La Bretagne* (Spézet: Coop Breizh, 2006).

Mark Kurlansky, *Salt: A World History*. (New York: Penguin, 2002).

Bruno Latour, *Reassembling the Social: An Introduction to Actor-Network-Theory* (Oxford: Oxford University Press, 2005)

Yann Lukas, *Roches et minéraux de Bretagne* (Rennes: Ouest-France, 1978).

Jean Martin and Alain Le Noac'h, *Toiles de Bretagne: la manufacture de Quintin, Uzel et Loudéac: 1670-1830* (Rennes: Presses Universitaires de Rennes, 1998).

Charles R. Menzies, *Red Flags and Lace Coiffes: Identity and Survival in a Breton Village* (Toronto: University of Toronto, 2011).

Jason W. Moore, "The Rise of Cheap Nature," in *Anthropocene or Capitalocene?: Nature, History, and the Crisis of Capitalism*, ed. Jason W. Moore (Oakland, PM Press: 2016), 78–115.

Timothy Morton, *Dark Ecology: For a Logic of Future Coexistence* (New York: Columbia University Press, 2016).

Raj Patel and Jason W. Moore, *A History of the World in Seven Cheap Things: A Guide to Capitalism, Nature, and the Future of the Planet* (London and New York: Verso, 2017).

René Musset, "L'industrie de l'ardoise en Basse-Bretagne," *Annales de Géographie*, 49, 280 (1940), 236–238.

Griselda Pollock and Penny Florence, *Looking Back to the Future* (Amsterdam: G+B Arts International, 2001).

Laurence Prod'homme, ed. *Charles et Paul Géniaux: La Photographie, un Destin*, exh. cat. (Châteaulin: Locus Solus, 2019).

Laurence Prod'homme, *Charles et Paul Géniaux: Deux Frères en Photographie* (Lyon: Fage, 2014).

Laurence Prod'homme, *Reflets de Bretagne: Les Collections Photographiques du Musée de Bretagne* (Lyon: Fage, 2012).

Lucienne Roubin, "Savoir et Art de Vivre Campagnard," in *The Wolf and the Lamb: Popular Culture in France: From the Old Regime to the Twentieth Century*, eds Jacques Beauroy and Marc Bertrand (Saratoga, CA: Anma libri, 1977), 93–100.

Richard Sennett, *The Craftsman* (New Haven: Yale University Press, 2008).

Becky Simmons, "Amateur Photographers, Camera Clubs and Societies," in *Encyclopedia of Nineteenth Century Photography*, ed. John Hannavy, vol. 1 (London: Routledge, 2008), 31–35.

Helena E. Wright, "Photography in the Printing Press: The Photomechanical Revolution," in *Presenting Pictures*, ed. Bernard Finn (London: Science Museum, 2004).

Patrick Young, *Enacting Brittany: Tourism and Culture in Provincial France, 1871–1939* (Farnham: Ashgate, 2012).

4. "Our Best Machines Are Made of Sunlight": Photography and Technologies of Light

Niharika Dinkar

With the demise of analog photography, the workings of light, which seemed an obvious and transparent modality in an earlier era, have acquired a new salience. Instead of a transparent medium that seamlessly links seeing and knowing, light is shown as having agency and a textured materiality, both of which inflect bodies and spaces.[1] This resurgence is indicated in the recent spate of scholarship on the social and material cultures of light, the infrastructures enabled by light, colonial practices of light (which is my own point of entry into the subject), anthropologies of luminosity, and geographies of darkness.[2]

These interventions have questioned the apparent transparency and invisibility of light to examine the material culture it has spawned. They have also evaluated relationships between light's material forms and its symbolic valences. Such interdisciplinary dialogues have examined practices of light that move beyond its scientific role and its ideological and religious connotations, and instead pose questions about light's place in modernity, marked by the remarkable explosion in lighting technologies and the instrumentalization of light for the media and communication industries.

This chapter explores what lessons such material and cultural histories of light might hold for photography, which, as a medium borne of light, is necessarily implicated in those histories. There has been a resurgence of interest in considerations of light in photography from wider environmental histories, such as Joanna Zylinska's recent work on *Nonhuman Photography* (Zylinska, 2017). In this reappraisal of photography, Zylinska turns away from photography as "things humans do with cameras" to embrace imaging processes from which the human is absent, arguing for the existence of a "photographic condition," inasmuch as we are "all part of that photographic flow of things that are being incessantly photographed." (69) Zylinska poses the ubiquity of photography by viewing photographs as fossils and recognizing the formative role of light across various media—stone, clay, wax, or even skin (as in either sun or sunless tanning)—consonant with the emergence of the discipline of geology that saw the earth as a recording medium, or inscribed by light. This leads her to view photography as not a new process but a "'modern, mediated extension' of the ancient-long 'impressioning' activity enabled by light, soil, and various minerals." (111)

Around such an expanded definition of photography as an ubiquitous event enabled by the autonomous inscription of light upon various media, a host of claimants to the term "photography" have been posed in recent scholarship, in which the work of natural light supplements the common definition of photographs as imprints on paper. Scholarship on fossils as photographs has been the most prominent strand of these, examining the fossil as a product of the originary gesture of photography as a trace of light (Michaels, 2007). Geoffrey Batchen has mused upon photosynthesis as an organic world of light writing, and the Singaporean artist Ho Rui An has explored sweat as a bodily response to the sun to consider colonial labor as a particular form of sun writing enabled by empire (Batchen, 1997: 163; An, 2014). Such organic instances of light writing have been supplemented by studies such as that by Tania Woloshyn, which has examined the popularity of light therapy in Britain around the turn of the 19th century, when the health benefits of sunlight were sought to be replicated by devices such as the mercury vapor lamp and ultraviolet lamps (Woloshyn, 2017). While Woloshyn's book is an exception delving into relationships between natural light and artificial light, the emphasis on natural light in this strand of scholarship has posed an understanding of the autonomous agency of light and its production of material traces to reconsider photography as an organic process with little authorial intervention.

While this new direction of research, which is frequently propelled by ecological concerns, has encouraged an engagement with natural light in photography, there has been a simultaneous exploration of specific technologies of light. Among the earliest and most widely researched is the X-ray, which had been announced as a "new kind of light" by William Roentgen in 1895. The X-ray is nevertheless understudied given the phenomenal instrumentalization of light in contemporary media and society. Studies have built upon the specificity of X-rays as a form of light that lies outside the visible spectrum, and this has expanded to consider later technologies including CT scanning, magnetic resonance imaging, and positron emission tomography.[3] This work on medical technologies has been supplemented by scholarship on infrared light and its role in the surveillance and communication industries (Pierotti and Ronetti, 2018). Most significantly, Kate Flint's recent history of the flash and the particular modes of vision it has enabled, notably its role in crime and celebrity culture, has raised the question of visibilities enabled by artificial light as fundamentally different from that of the sun

(Flint, 2017). In tying together a material and cultural history of the flash as a specific technology of light, Flint's work also asks questions beyond essentialist material formulations of photographic light as comprised of and limited to photon activity (Frizot, 2007).

This second set of discussions on specific technologies of light has initiated a debate beyond solar light to consider questions around what Wolfgang Schivelbusch had deemed "the industrialization of light" in the 19th century and the place of photography within that (Schivelbusch, 1988). Indeed, as I suggest below, from its earliest days, photography had occasioned experimentation with artificial light employing a range of materials including saltpeter, quicklime, and magnesium, which were implicated in global networks of trade, scientific experimentation, commercial patents, and had wide-ranging uses in industries and activities that ranged from war to theatre. This history features prominently in photographic and trade journals in discussions about appropriate lighting, night photography, and the efficacy of different materials and devices for artificial lighting, yet it is rarely included in contemporary discussions of photographic light, where it is assumed to be an undifferentiated element that marks photographic paper.

Mikkel Bille and Tim Flohr Sørensen have argued for a need to "unravel how the actual *matter* and the *use* of light shapes experiences in culturally specific ways and why." (Bille and Sørensen, 2007: 266) Accordingly, instead of the historical predominance of solar metaphors that have dominated photographic discourse, this chapter asks how we might consider a more material history of photographic light, rooted in a terrestrial economy and distributed through commercial and trade networks, and what that might tell us about our modern experience of light and its industrial past. Photographic writing and imagery on light in the early decades of photography have traditionally foregrounded solar light, evinced in the names for photography as heliography or sun pictures, and this is accompanied by metaphorical associations of light with truth and divinity. Against such an allegorical approach to light, this chapter will draw upon a more prosaic material history of light for photography by examining three primary materials (quicklime, saltpeter, and magnesium) that were used for photography in its early history. The use of these materials brings photographic light into conversation with wider practices of artificial illumination in public life, because these materials were used for a wide range of activities that ranged from lighting homes and streets to theatrical lighting and practices of military mapping. Such an approach to photographic light attempts to follow Bille and Sørensen in tying the specific material economies of light to its cultural practices in public life. This aligns this study with the wider developments in lighting technologies in modernity to posit plural sources of light at the dawn of photography.

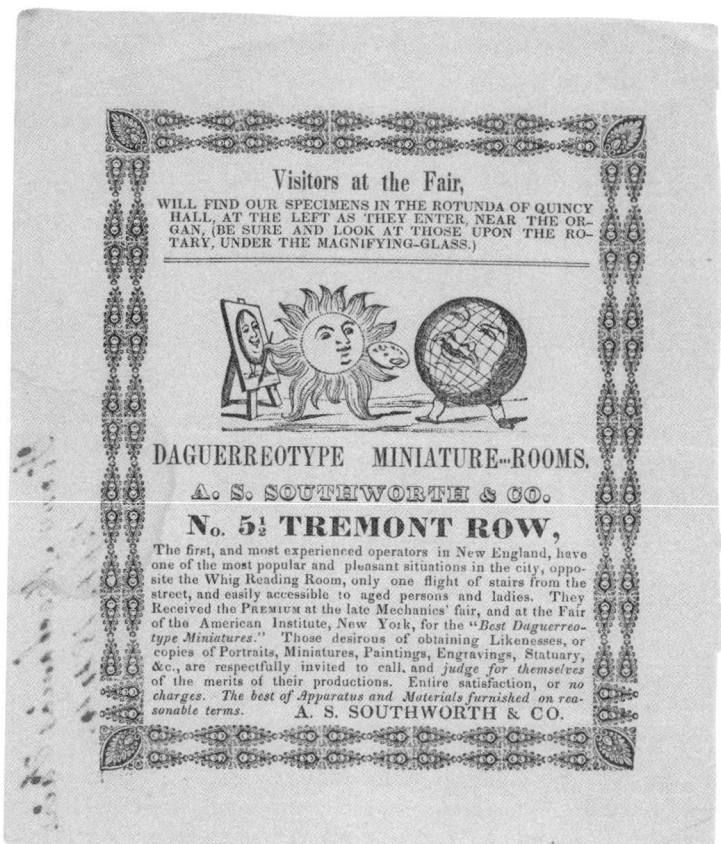

Figure 4.1

Handbill for A. S. South-
worth and Company,
"Daguerreotype, Miniature
Rooms, No. 5 1/2 Tremont
Row, Boston, Mass.," 1844.
Courtesy of Historic New
England.

Photographic Heliotropism

We have long known that early photographic discourse was explicitly
concerned with the sun. This is indicated in the early names of "sun
painting" or "heliograph," both of which foreground the role of sunlight in materializing the photographic image. First used by Nicéphore
Niépce, who presented his findings to the Royal Society in 1827 in a
"Notice sur l'heliographié," the word heliograph invokes the powers of
the sun. Of course, Niépce simultaneously confessed to being unsatisfied with the word. A notebook entry from 1832 toyed with alternatives.
Among the seven potential terms and the twenty potential prefixes and
suffixes he offered, neither *helio* nor *light* figured at all. Instead, he favored the Greek term *phusis*, or nature, which was conjoined with variations of copy as the suffix (Batchen, 1993).

Batchen presents the naming of photography as an epistemological choice, and it is intriguing to imagine how we may have viewed photography without the central role accorded to light. Among the numerous potential terms thrown up, alternatives like "sciagraph" (writing with shadows) or "calotype" (from the Greek *kalos*, or beauty) were briefly considered, but the adoption of John Herschel's term "photography" (first used in 1839 after Talbot's "photogenic drawing") drew upon the more capacious idea of light rather than the sun, even though, as I argue below, the overt equation of the sun with light did not entirely disappear.

The centrality of the sun in early photographic discourse was indicated in the many solar metaphors that abounded in writings and in caricature. In "Doings of the Sunbeam," Oliver Wendell Holmes paid homage to the "honest sunshine," endowing sunlight with the power to represent truthfully because the photograph "permanently recorded in the handwriting of the sun himself." (Holmes, 1863) Writers invoked the solar pencil, sun pictures, and "sunbeam art" in their paeans to photography, and visual imagery explicitly called attention to the sun.

The Boston-based daguerreotype studio Messrs. Southworth and Hawes employed a much-reproduced caricature of a flaming sun holding a palette painting the earth upon a standing canvas. (fig. 4.1) In use as early as 1844, it featured in advertising and handbills at trade fairs, and the same motif was also used by the New York–based Scovill Manufacturing Company for their advertising in 1850. Across the Atlantic, Cuthbert Bede, an English writer and illustrator who contributed to *Punch*, included variations of this jovial sun painting the earth in ink drawings included in *Photographic Pleasures Portrayed with Pen and Pencil* (1855), extending this popular understanding of the sun as the artist. In one version, *Phoebus Apollo portrait painter to General Earth*, he posed the flaming sun as the Greek god Apollo, or, explaining that if we were to "trace the science to its source, we might perchance discover that it arose amidst the sun-worshippers of the East, and its mysteries were presided over by the high priests of Apollo." (Bede, 1855: 16)

The sun was deemed the active agent in the photographic process that marginalized the role of the photographer. "The *sun* was the *artist*, the camera the vehicle, and the silver plate the canvas," claimed a member of the Liverpool Photographic Society in 1856 (cited in Green-Lewis, 1996: 60). Douglas Nickel notes that such invocations of the "sun as the artist" relied upon well-established literary, theological, and mystical tropes of the creative energies of the sun that shored up authority for the photograph as more than human (Nickel, 2002). Elizabeth Eastlake presents this view in describing the photographer as a "pilgrim of the sun," a magician who "attempted to enlist the powers of light in his service." (Eastlake, 1857: 246–247) Melissa Miles argues that this idea was consonant with Victorian ideas of gendered creative potential; Eastlake portrayed it as a distinctly masculine force impregnating the collodion film or the albumen-sheathed glass with its gaze:

> the great luminary concentrates his gaze for a few earnest minutes; with the albumen-sheathed glass he takes his time more leisurely still; but at the delicate film of collodion which hangs before him finer than any fairy's robe, and potent only with invisible spells—he literally does no more than wink his eye, tracing in that moment, with a detail and precision beyond all human power, the glory of the heavens, the wonders of the deep, the fall, not of the avalanche, but of the apple, the most fleeting smile of the babe, and the most vehement action of the man. (Miles, 2008b: 42)

If the sun as the artist arrogated a divine authority to the photograph, it also popularized the photograph as an objective representation against the subjective fancies of the painter. "Portrait painting is not what it used to be," lamented one account from 1843, "for since the sun has turned artist and taken to photography in partnership with Messrs. Claudet and Beard [a popular London studio], all the portrait painters under the sun have had a very powerful rival to contend against." (*The Comic Album*, 1843) It went on to mock the sun for not having the tact to "disguise any of those little defects of the countenance" that a painter would (*The Comic Album*, 1843).

The analogy of the "solar pencil" metonymically extended this imagery of the sun as the artist to the realm of language and writing. Commonly used in scientific contexts, it was adopted into popular writing by Lady Elizabeth Eastlake and Marcus Aurelius Root, among others, taking from Henry Fox Talbot's *Pencil of Nature*. Catherine Rogers has drawn attention to the long history of the idea of a "pencil of light," which natural philosophers since the 17th century had used to signify a ray of light striking an object (Rogers, 2002). Cuthbert Bede featured this imagery of the camera as writing with light quite literally on the cover of his *Photographic Pleasures*, which portrayed a man hunched over carrying his camera and a large pencil on his back as the sun smiles above them. The writing below adds, "Start into light and make the lighter start," lines drawn from contemporary poetry on the theatre and which signified the onset of sudden and instantaneous change (*Rejected Addresses*, 1813: 104).

Julia Margaret Cameron's photograph *Cupid's Pencil of Light* (1870) draws upon this legacy of the solar pencil but is notable in that it does not feature imagery of the sun itself; instead, it renders the power of solar light allegorically in the figure of Cupid bathed in a golden light, magically activating a photograph with a stylus. Both the Cupid figure and the mystical use of light grant the photograph a radiance that draws upon well-established mythological and divine attributes of light. In his examination of Talbot's epistemological presumptions, Douglas Nickel writes that the photograph was understood to be "responding to divine light and, by its very workings, manifesting divine intelligence," showcasing the technique as "human and divine, empirical and esoteric: "It united the two great divinities—the Sun and Nature—with Cartesian optics to engender a new form of natural magic." (Nickel, 139)

Melissa Miles has closely examined the romantic language associated with light in early photographic writing to similarly argue that there is a slippage between sunlight or natural light, the divine light of God and the objective truths accorded to the photographic image, in the coalescence of ideas attached to light in early photography. She points to the evidence of wide-ranging metaphors of light that populate photographic history, but contends that contemporary photographic discourse continues to reinscribe light "as a stable, fixed and extra discursive point of origin for the medium" in a heliotropic movement that consistently returns to the sun as a point of origin (Miles, 2008a: 98). Within this luminous foundation, relations of difference between light and dark, feminine and masculine, human and divine are resolved to reaffirm the sun as a masculine father figure and point of origin for photography, its creative energies usurping feminine generative powers (Miles, 2008a: 97–132).

Miles extends this heliotropic agenda of photography to a wider philosophical tradition, drawing upon Derrida's designation of metaphysics as essentially heliotropic in its conflation of light and truth. Derrida writes that "natural light, and all the axioms which it enables us to see, are never subjected to the most radical doubt," equating the sun with a divine light that serves as the founding metaphor of metaphysics: "The founding metaphor not only because it is a photological one—and in this respect the entire history of our philosophy is a photology, the name given to a history of, or treatise on, light—but because it is a metaphor." (Derrida, 1978: 27)

Miles's charge of an indifference to the mutability of light in photographic discourse is borne out in the heliocentrism of contemporary environmental histories of photography that continue to reinscribe light "as a stable, fixed and extra discursive point of origin for the medium." (Miles, 2008a: 98) The following section attempts to dispel the heliocentrism of discourses on photographic light by engaging with a material account of lighting sources for photography, employing materials that were aligned with wider developments in artificial lighting technologies and its transformations of urban spaces.

Technologies of Light

The well-established narrative of the central role of sun at the origins of photography has, however, ignored the simultaneous popularity of artificial lighting that was increasingly becoming an indispensable part of modern life, extending its tentacles into technologies and spaces that ranged from the military to theatre. In this section, I will take a look at three primary sources of light that photography relied upon in the early decades of photography (quicklime, saltpeter, and magnesium) to indicate how artificial lighting for photography was present at its earliest origins, and how these lighting technologies were in conversation with wider practices of illumination—for homes, theatres, public spaces, lighthouses, and magic lantern shows, for example.

As city spaces embraced public lighting projects that sought to conquer the night, the idea of "night photography" found increasing popularity, with the experimentation of materials and devices intended for its use after dark and in the long winter months, when sunlight could not be assured. Despite the paeans to solar light in canonical photographic histories, artificial lighting was used as early as 1839, and the desire to use commonly available lighting sources such as gas was voiced early on ("Drawing by the Agency of Light," 1843: 328). The first portrait photographs were taken by Antoine Claudet in 1840 with an oxyhydrogen lamp and soon featured commonly in exhibitions hosted by the Edinburgh Society of Arts.[4] Artificial light was acknowledged in contemporary accounts as well—while listing the exciting developments in "Photogenic [drawing] or the art of Photography," the *American Journal of Science and Arts* carefully pluralized the sources of light as "Pictorial delineations by light: solar, lunar, stellar and artificial." (*American Journal of Science and Arts*, 1839) In a paper read to the Society of Arts in February 1839, Andrew Fyfe listed his own experiments with a range of artificial sources including an oxyhydrogen blowpipe (limelight), "concentrating the light of a common fire with metallic mirrors," gas lamps, and a fish-tail gas burner, noting the photographs had longer exposure times but "all the richness of those taken by solar light." (Fyfe, 1839: 179)

The earliest photograph taken by artificial lighting is generally considered to be one by Captain Levett L. B. Ibbetson, a geologist and soldier. His daguerreotype of a coral taken through a microscope relied upon limelight as a source. However, this well-known factoid does not consider the use of artificial lighting for processing the photograph, either the preparation of photographic paper for calotypes, such as iodized paper that was crafted in candlelight, or the fixing process. Discussions of appropriate lighting in the darkroom were cautious about using artificial light such as candles or lamps, whose actinic rays (blue light) were hard to control; orange-colored glass was suggested as a more reliable method of blocking actinic rays ("A Catechism of Photography," 1858: 90).

Limelight or Drummond light was first exhibited between 1822 and 1823 at the Royal Society of the Arts by the scientist and chemist Goldsworthy Gurney, who displayed its brilliant effects produced by the special oxyhydrogen blowpipe he pioneered. It was obtained by passing a jet of oxygen through a flame of hydrogen, which was made to impinge upon a disk or cylinder of lime, to produce a bright light when brought to an incandescent state. The Scottish army officer and civil engineer Thomas Drummond saw a demonstration of this by Michael Faraday and engineered it to be used for the trigonometric survey of Northern Ireland he was working on. Early uses for mapping had relied upon Bengal light (a saltpeter-based compound) in Argand burners with parabolic reflectors; however, this was inadequate for measuring long distances. With the use of Drummond's apparatus, the survey, which depended upon a triangulation process to measure spaces, was able to cast light from a heightened space that could be observed up to sixty-eight miles away, with strong shadows visible at a distance of thirteen miles, greatly aiding the process of mapping in low or unstable light. This early use of limelight for the military mapping of the land was then extended to the exhibition of microscopic objects by projection onto a screen and thereafter gained greater popularity as part of magic lantern demonstrations.[5]

In 1839–1840, Captain Ibbetson used limelight for photographing microscopic objects, claiming that he made a daguerreotype in five minutes, when it would have taken him twenty-five in normal daylight. Reported in the *Westminster Review*, the article was accompanied by an engraving of the daguerreotype—an enlarged section of coral magnified twelve and a half times, which claimed to be the first daguerreotype to use artificial light ("Electrotype and Daguerreotype," 1840). The best-known use of limelight was, however, for theatrical performances; it was first used for an outdoor juggling performance in 1836 and then for stage illumination at the Covent Garden theatre in 1837. It continued to be popular through the mid-19th century, pioneering the use of spotlights for important characters that persists in its metaphorical use today. Among the most interesting experiments with limelight on stage included Charles Babbage and Michael Faraday's presentation of a ballet about natural science research and the rainbow in 1847. It employed dazzling limelight illumination using rotating glass filters in different colors, so the dancers' dresses reflected different colors without a change in costume (Gest, 1948).

While the bright light of oxyhydrogen lamps continued to be used for microscopic objects, magic lanterns, or cave photography, commercial uses of artificial lighting in the early decades employed the so-called

Bengal light patented in February 1857 by John Moule as Photogen. A compound that emitted a bluish light (that was sensitive to the wet collodion plates) and had a combustion time of about fifteen seconds, it allowed for shorter exposure lengths. It was particularly advertised to studios for portrait photography, and Moule claimed that, only four years after its patent, more than three hundred thousand portraits had been made in London alone, attesting to its popularity ("Newcastle Photographic Society," 1861: 224). Photogen was advertised broadly as "The special wonder of the age—the rival of the sun," even though critics deemed the results as "hideous portraits—ghastly and gravelike." (cited in Gernsheim, 1969: 427)

Like limelight's origins in military mapping, Bengal light also had a history in war. Bengal light's vital ingredient was saltpeter, a pyrotechnic that was also used in gunpowder, and which had long been used for signaling at sea. In the early 17th century, Bengal emerged as the world's leading supplier of saltpeter for gunpowder with English, Dutch, and French competing for its sources, and there is a rich colonial history of its extraction and trade that has been well chronicled (Frey, 2009; Brown, 2005: 25–50; Buchanan, 2005). Inasmuch as saltpeter fueled the military ambitions of colonial powers, its role in international trade cannot be emphasized enough, but it also had wide-ranging industrial applications from tanning and textile bleaching to metallurgy and food preservation. Bengal lights were used extensively for signaling in the American Civil War, and the term "blue light" acquired traction in military parlance, borne from its bluish flames of saltpeter, suggesting a host of meanings around patriotism and treason (Bartlette, 1859: 39).

Even as Photogen was patented for indoor studio use using a hexagonal glass lantern that channeled its smoke, Bengal lights continued to be used for celebratory outdoor lighting. At the inauguration of the Universal Exposition on May 6, 1889, the Eiffel Tower was lit up with Bengal lights, producing what one account called an "absolutely enchanting effect" with the wind blowing the flames, so it looked like the iron structure was on fire. A beacon on top of the tower and two projectors with carbon lamps added to the spectacular effect, indicated in the photograph taken at 9:30 at night, an engraving of which accompanied the report published in *The Scientific American*. The photograph showcased experiments with artificial lighting for photography outside the studio, and how that developed in conversation with public lighting projects ("Eiffel Tower," 1889).

Another significant source of artificial lighting in the early decades was magnesium, a metal whose volatility was noted in early laboratory experiments but was envisioned for photographic use only in 1859, with the first patent taken out in 1862. It was initially greeted with enthusiasm with reports deeming it "bottled sunshine!—portable daylight!"[6]—yet it was expensive to produce. In 1863, the Magnesium Metal Company was established in Manchester, and the first photograph using magnesium was taken in 1864, during a demonstration of its possibilities at the Manchester Literary and Philosophical Society.

Magnesium was easy to use inasmuch as it did not require a complicated apparatus and by 1865 was generally sold as both a ribbon and a wire that could be lit to produce a strong light. The development of the dry gelatin plate with faster emulsion speeds greatly reduced the amount of magnesium required, and the ease of a handheld wire made it a popular lighting source. In 1877, the cost of burning magnesium for over an hour was reduced to under one mark in Germany, the equivalent of around six dollars in 2020 (Vogel, 1887: 44–45). Experiments with burning powdered magnesium with potassium and sodium chlorate salts were pioneered by the firm Messrs. Gadicke and Miethe at the Berlin Society for the Advancement of Photography in 1877 pioneering "instantaneous photography." A brilliant burst of light that allowed for exposure times of one fortieth of a second allowed for photographing moving objects and the fumes were contained within a glass lantern ("Instantaneous Photography," 1887: 169–170). In 1883, a mixture of powdered magnesium and potassium chlorate was used as a flash, pioneering the flashlight technology we know today.

Among the most popular uses of magnesium in the early decades was the illumination and photography of underground caves and mines, which were a great source of fascination and could only be photographed using artificial light. In 1844, Henry Fox Talbot had hoped that photographs of the underground would "reveal the secrets of the darkened chamber" anticipating infrared photography and its technological promise of making visible hidden truths (Howes, 1989: xxi). While Photogen had also been used for this purpose—in 1861, Moule had sent two devices to Bengal to be used to photograph caves in India—magnesium was more widely adopted because of its dazzling brightness.[7] The Manchester-born photographer Alfred Brothers used magnesium to take photographs of the Blue John Cavern in Derbyshire in 1864, and this was followed by Charles Piazzi Smith's photographs of the Great Pyramid in Egypt in 1865. Across the Atlantic in 1866, Charles Waldack produced stereoscopic views of the Mammoth Caves in Kentucky, which were seven miles deep, using a mixture of magnesium filings and pulverized gunpowder to rave reviews: "Oh! Is not photography a great power? What else could creep into the bowels of the earth, and bring forth such pictures therefrom, as these?" (Cited in Flint, 2017: 22)

It was Nadar, however, who drew the greatest publicity for his photographs from the bowels of the Parisian catacombs using electric arc lights. Arc lights employed two carbon rods between which an electric current was passed, producing a spark, which caused the carbon to become incandescent and glow producing a brilliant white light. Talbot had experimented with this in 1851, and arc lights were adapted for studio photography using parabolic reflectors in 1854, with largely unfavorable results. Nadar toyed with arc lights from 1858 for studio photography, supplementing it with magnesium light and, in 1861, took a pile of fifty Bunsen batteries into the Parisian catacombs to power the arc lamps. Confronted with longer exposures of up to eighteen minutes in the dark passages, he was forced to give up on live models for mannequins, to emphasize the drama of living bodies against the ghastly bones hidden in the subterranean depths. He produced seventy-three photographs of the catacombs and twenty-three of the sewers, which were exhibited at the international exhibition in 1862 in London, where they captured the public imagination as some of the first photographs taken underground.

Chris Howes writes that, despite the popularity of Nadar's balloon photography, it was a secondary interest, the first being an investigation of the underground (Howes, 1989: 1). As Nadar himself affirmed: "The world underground offered an infinite field of activity no less interesting than that of the top surface. We were going into it, to reveal the mysteries of its deepest, most secret caverns." (Cited in Howes, 1989: 13) Like the "aerial vision" his balloon photographs produced, his interest in the underground equally represents a technology of sight aimed at unveiling hidden truths.[8] Rosalind Williams has attested to how journeys into the netherworlds represented "a modern version of the mythological quest to find truth in the hidden regions of the underworld," and photographic evidence of hidden interiorities likewise affirmed its powers to illuminate unknown worlds (Williams, 2008: 23).

Nadar's use of arc lamps pointed to the direction artificial lighting would take with the adaptation of arc lamps for street lighting with the Yablochkov candle in 1876, named after its founder Pavel Yablochkov. By 1878, major cities including Paris, London, and Los Angeles initiated public lighting projects using arc lights installed in exceptionally tall structures called moonlight towers. The harsh glare of the arc lamp was modified for studio purposes in London in 1877 by using reflectors to soften the light, and this use of electric light for studios gained ground at the Universal Exposition in Paris in 1878; by 1882, in addition to Paris, Vienna, Brussels, and Berlin had electric light studios.

To pull up some of these well-known sources of artificial lighting at the dawn of photography is to emphasize how they were part of the earliest experiments with light, of which we may consider photography itself as the best-known example. As such, what I have indicated is how closely these technologies of light for photography were in conversation with the wider practices of light, which extended from public lighting projects to theatre and military applications. What such a widespread use of lighting technologies suggests is that the familiar narrative of the role of light in photography was by no means limited to the sun and natural light—in fact, photography sits amid these wider conversations on technologies of light. My intention here is not to pit natural light against artificial light as two different sources, but to indicate the mutual imbrication of the two, to suggest that what was at stake here was an instrumentalization of light through a wide range of materials and devices. It is also to undermine narratives of the autonomous agency of light and the inevitability of the traces, to indicate that light was in fact manipulated in terms of the materials used. Crucially, light's manipulation was contingent upon economic and trade factors.

Investigating photography through its immersion in experiments with lighting technologies displaces the centrality of the sun in its origin narratives to pose a plurality of sources of light at play. While one may, in the final event, defer to the sun as what Michel Serres has called "the ultimate capital," it is imperative to acknowledge and situate the terrestrial attempts to replicate the sun, as it were (Serres, 1982: 173). Reza Negarestani takes a more radical approach in advocating against what he calls "heliocentric slavery" by proposing an ecology outside the empire of the sun: "The idea of ecological emancipation must be divorced from the simultaneously vitalistic and necrocratic relationship between the Earth and the Sun." (Negarestani, 2010: 3) Envisioning both the sun and the earth as dying, he calls for an end to the "monogamous relationship" that has been corrupted by capitalism's commerce in fossil fuels, by calling for opening up terrestrial life to wider cosmic contingency and play. Essentially a tragic acknowledgement of finitude, both human and earthly, Negarestani's views complicate the seemingly disparate economies of the sun and the markets it has sponsored. He deems oil the "black corpse of the sun" inasmuch as it is a product of sunlight and organic matter; in doing so, he ties the problematic fossil fuel industry to a solar history associated with divine light and truth (Negarestani, 2008: 26).

Negarestani's radical displacement of the sun encourages us to think critically about solar light as a source of energy as well as its formative role as a medium of photography and in photographic thinking. A recent initiative on "solarity" has similarly urged a critical look at solar energy, cautioning against its utopian promises and highlighting the unequal infrastructural distribution within which such promises are couched (Szeman and Barney, 2021). The authors bring up instead the question of how solar light is mediated by technologies and institutions, to pose solarity as a social condition that follows as a result of the political and economic choices made. Nicole Staroulienski proposes that, instead of thinking of sunlight as a natural, universally available resource, we need to account for it as both a socially mediated resource and a potential weapon, paying attention to the solar regimes it establishes (Starosielski, 2021).

While I have explored early photographic history's reliance upon solar light as a divine light, it is important to point out that even later re-evaluations, such as Zylinska's expansive understanding of an ubiquitous nonhuman photography that delineates a "photographic condition" beyond art practice, are also heliocentric in ignoring the developments spurred by the industrialization of light and its implications for photography. Zylinska is careful to note the altered character of light in the Anthropocene, inasmuch as it is reflected through the particulate matter and human-induced pollution that forms part of the atmosphere. However, inasmuch as the argument is driven by the primacy of a "light induced process of fossilization" as the ontology of the photograph, it does not acknowledge other technologies of light (Zylinska, 104).[9]

However, the origins of photography coincided with an industrialization of light, most visible in public and domestic lighting projects, but also heavily invested in the scientific and practical applications of light, which have only grown more entrenched in our contemporary world. The scientific instrumentalization of light has explored technologies of light beyond the visible spectrum for photographic imaging, and this has in fact been the source of some of the most dramatic new applications of photography. For instance, the shorter wavelengths of X-rays and ultraviolet light have spurred the photographs of bodily interiors associated with medical technologies, and the longer wavelengths of infrared light have been exploited for night vision cameras and thermal imaging associated with the surveillance and security industries, two of the most rapidly advancing industries that employ photographic imaging. Similarly, photolithographic technologies now used for the microprocessor and semiconductor industry (the manufacture of chips or integrated circuits that form the base of our current computing devices), have progressed from using the mercury vapor lamps of the 19th century to sophisticated excimer ultraviolet laser light. To consider the ubiquity of photography today is to engage with these developments in photography that employ technologies of light outside the visible spectrum or the electromagnetic spectrum.

Rahul Mukherjee's project on "radiant infrastructures" has taken this discussion of the electromagnetic spectrum further by addressing the vast architecture that has arisen around nuclear energy and the radioactive energy fields within which our lives are enmeshed (Mukherjee, 2020). While nuclear radiation itself is a product of the nonvisible spectrum of light, the detonation of atomic bomb releases a light that "exceeds all other man-made sources of light and is appropriately likened to a tiny star, indeed like a very small segment of the sun." (Butler, 1962: 489) Mukherjee's project does not address photography per se, but a number of artists and scholars have explored the impressioning acts of atomic light and the particular mark making it produces (Brian, 2015; *Flash of Light, Wall of Fire*, 2020). To disregard such sophisticated and consequential technologies of light in assessments of photography today is to ignore its widespread applications in military, industrial, and commercial culture. An examination of the ubiquitous "photographic condition" of our time therefore needs to contend with the multiple technologies of light beyond and within the solar in which our lives are enmeshed.

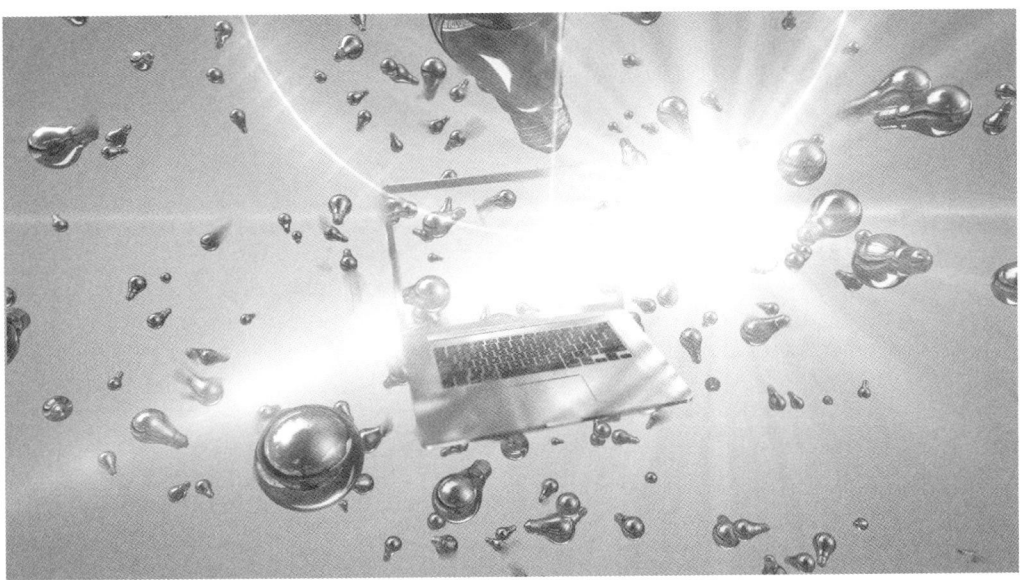

Our Best Machines Are Made of Sunshine

Hito Steyerl's video *Factory of the Sun* (2015) addresses many of these issues concerning the new applications of light for industrial and military use, warning us of a dystopian future in which light is wielded as a weapon. Like the initiative on solarity, the video expresses a disenchantment with the utopian promise of solar light and instead presents a narrative in which the control and capture of solar light defines contemporary and future modes of power. *Factory of the Sun* was first shown at the German Pavilion at the Venice Biennale in 2015 and poses a state in which Deutsche Bank officials have sped up the speed of light to gain advantages in financial trading and happen to kill three anti-accelerationist protestors in a drone strike. "Our machines are made of pure sunlight," begins the video, "electromagnetic frequencies / light pumping through fiberglass cables […] the sun is our factory."

Figure 4.2

Hito Steyerl, *Factory of the Sun,* 2015. Single-channel high-definition video, environment, luminescent LED grid, beach chairs, 23 minutes. Image CC 4.0, Hito Steyerl. Courtesy of the artist; Andrew Kreps Gallery, New York; and Esther Schipper, Berlin.

See also Plate 7.

Steyerl presents continuities between natural light and artificial light to reveal that, rather than the binaries of nature and culture, what is at stake is the instrumentalization of light—who is using light for what ends. (fig. 4.2) She takes Donna Haraway's dictum "Our best machines are made of sunshine" from "A Cyborg Manifesto" to frame a futuristic world where sunshine powers image economies of light that are controlled by a corporatized state. In Haraway's words:

> Our best machines are made of sunshine; they are all light and clean because they are nothing but signals, electromagnetic waves, a section of a spectrum, and these machines are eminently portable, mobile—a matter of immense human pain in Detroit and Singapore. People are nowhere near so fluid, being both material and opaque. Cyborgs are ether, quintessence. (Haraway, 1991)

Haraway asks us to consider sunlight beyond the visible spectrum including electromagnetic waves and their transmission of signals as the medium powering electronic communication devices. Steyerl's video adds in the perspective of human labor to ask how bodies are implicated in this image economy of light.

Steyerl's presentation of the sun as a factory powering the economy takes away the natural glow appended to the sun in early photographic discourse, but also in more contemporary paeans to clean solar energy. Instead, what it proposes is a world where the sun is not only the source for organic life, but also a factory that powers postindustrial communication and exchange. The protagonists in gleaming golden bodysuits serve as instruments of light dancing to house music against the remains of the Teufelsberg tower in Berlin. Used by the U.S. National Security Agency during the Cold War as a listening station to intercept communication across the Berlin Wall, the tower is rendered as antiquated ruin of surveillance mechanisms of the industrial past, amid the new economies of light. In this bleak technofuturist landscape that is Steyerl's distinctive topos, she presents dancing bodies as forced laborers as a motion capture studio grabs and converts their movements into energy—dance is not the joyous free movement of the body but a forced labor that extracts energy.

Steyerl presents a dystopic world powered by sunshine, where bodies are harnessed by the corporate state that has weaponized and instrumentalized light as an accessory of power. Yet, despite the futuristic topos that sets it within a world yet-to-come, such weaponization of light was foretold in the past. In his book *Atomic Light*, Akira Lippit had pointed to the nuclear bomb as a technology of light forged by the state, that burned "brighter than a thousand suns" in Robert Oppenheimer's memorable words (Lippit, 2005). There is now a considerable body of work that has explored the links between photography and nuclear light and the particular forms of indexical markings produced by radiation (Brian, 2015; Marcoń, 2011; Matheson, 2018).[10] I conclude, then, with the warning that this example represents—that a simplistic view of natural light in photographic studies and the paeans to "honest sunshine" have occluded more critical questions of technologies of light. If extinction and ecological concerns form a new horizon for photographic discourse, atomic light asks equally urgent questions about writing with light that an expanded definition of photography needs to address.

Notes

1. For a philosophical contestation of light as a transparent medium, see Cathryn Vasseleu, *Textures of Light: Vision and Touch in Irigaray, Levinas and Merleau-Ponty* (New York: Routledge, 1998).

2. See for instance, Wolfgang Schivelbusch, *Disenchanted Night: The Industrialization of Light in the Nineteenth Century*, trans. Angela Davies (Berkeley: University of California Press, 1988); Brian Bowers, *Lengthening the Day: A History of Lighting Technology* (Oxford: Oxford University Press, 1998); Craig Koslofsky, *Evening's Empire: A History of the Night in Early Modern Europe* (Cambridge: Cambridge University Press, 2011). See also the special issue edited by Tim Edensor "Geographies of Darkness," *Cultural Geography* vol. 22, no. 4 (2015): 559–565; Mikkel Bille and Tim Flohr Sørensen, "An Anthropology of Luminosity: The Agency of Light," *Journal of Material Culture* vol. 12, no. 3 (2007): 263–284; Tim Edensor, ed., "Sensing and Perceiving with Light and Dark, Special Issue," *The Senses and Society* vol. 10, no. 2 (2015); Chris Otter, *The Victorian Eye: A Political History of Light and Vision in Britain, 1800–1910* (Chicago: University of Chicago Press, 2008); Noam Elcott, *Artificial Darkness: An Obscure History of Modern Art and Media* (Chicago: University of Chicago Press, 2016); and Hollis Clayson, *Illuminated Paris: Essays on Art and Lighting in the Belle Epoque* (Chicago: University of Chicago Press, 2019).

3. A number of studies have explored the role of X-rays and later medical technologies, including Lisa Cartwright, *Screening the Body: Tracing Medicine's Visual Culture* (Minneapolis: University of Minnesota Press, 1995); Bettyann Holtzmann Kevles, *Naked to the Bone: Medical Imaging in the Twentieth Century* (New Brunswick: Rutgers University Press, 1997); and Akira Lippit, *Atomic Light: Shadow Optics* (Minneapolis: University of Minnesota Press, 2005).

4. Sir W. Newton's views of Undercliff, Isle of Wright, as enabled by artificial light are listed in "Photographic Exhibition at the Society of Arts," *The Art Journal* vol. 5 (1853): 56.

5. The association between the camera and the gun noted in many accounts is affirmed in the close relationships that emerge between the development of lighting technologies for military practices and their adaptation for photography. See, for instance, Paul Virilio, *War and Cinema: The Logistics of Perception*, trans. Patrick Camiller (New York: Verso, 1989).

6. An "old Edinburgh professor" is said to have exclaimed this on seeing its dazzling light. See "Magnesium: The True Method of Using It," *British Journal of Photography* vol. 23, no. 18 (January 7, 1876): 2–3.

7. See *Photographic News* (May 10, 1861): 224.

8. On the evolution of an aerial vision, see Caren Kaplan, *Aerial Aftermaths: War Time from Above* (Durham: Duke University Press, 2018).

9. The postscript to the book considers laser imaging technologies, deeming them postphotographic and offering the possibility to rethink our sources of energy and light; see pages 195–201.

10. See also the documentary film *Chernobyl: Chronicle of Difficult Weeks* (1986) dir. Vladimir Shevchenko, and Susan Schuppli, *Material Witness: Media, Forensics, Evidence* (Boston: MIT Press, 2020).

Bibliography

American Journal of Science and Arts, 37 (October 1839): 169–187.

Ho Rui An, *Sun, Sweat, Solar Queens: An Expedition*, 2014 (Performance at Kochi Biennale).

John Russell Bartlett, *Dictionary of Americanisms* (Boston: Little, Brown and Co., 1859).

Geoffrey Batchen, "The Naming of Photography," *History of Photography*, 17, 1 (1993): 22–32.

Geoffrey Batchen, *Burning with Desire: The Conception of Photography* (Cambridge, MA: MIT Press, 1997).

Cuthbert Bede, *Photographic Pleasures Popularly Portrayed with Pen and Pencil* (London: T. Mclean, Haymarket, 1855).

Mikkel Bille and Tim Flohr Sørensen, "An Anthropology of Luminosity: The Agency of Light," *Journal of Material Culture*, 12, 3 (2007): 263–284.

John O. Brian, ed., *Camera Atomica* (London: Black Dog Publications, 2015).

Stephen R. Brown, *A Most Damnable Invention: Dynamite, Nitrates, and the Making of the Modern World* (New York: T. Dunne Books, 2005).

Brenda J. Buchanan, "Saltpetre: A Commodity of Empire," in *Gunpowder, Explosives and the State: A Technological History*, ed. Brenda J. Buchanan (Aldershot: Ashgate, 2005), 67–90.

Clay P. Butler, "The Light of the Atom Bomb," *Science*, 138, 3539 (October 26, 1962): 483–489.

"A Catechism of Photography: The Dark Room," *Photographic News* (October 29, 1858): 90.

The Comic Album: A Book for Every Table (London: W.M.S Orr & C., Amen Corner, Paternaster Row, 1843).

Jacques Derrida, *Writing and Difference* (Chicago: University of Chicago Press, 1978).

Dolph Briscoe Center for American History, *Flash of Light, Wall of Fire: Japanese Photographs Documenting the Atomic Bombings of Hiroshima and Nagasaki* (Austin: University of Texas Press, 2020).

"Drawing by the Agency of Light or Photogenic Drawing," *Edinburgh Review*, CLIV (January, 1843): 309–344.

Lady Elizabeth Eastlake, "Photography," *London Quarterly Review* (April 1857): 241–255.

"The Eiffel Tower," *The Scientific American Supplement*, 705 (July 6, 1889): 11258–11260.

"Electrotype and Daguerreotype," *Westminster Review*, 34 (September 1840): 434–460.

Kate Flint, *Flash! Photography, Writing and Surprising Illumination* (Oxford: Oxford University Press, 2017).

James W. Frey, "The Indian Saltpeter Trade, the Military Revolution and the Rise of Britain as a Global Superpower," *The Historian*, 71, 3 (2009): 507–554.

Michel Frizot, "Who's Afraid of Photons?" in *Photography Theory*, ed. James Elkins (New York, London: Routledge, 2007), 269–283.

Andrew Fyfe, "Photographic Processes: Paper read before the Society of Arts, Edinburgh, March and April 1839," *New Edinburgh Philosophical Journal* (April to July 1839); reprinted in *American Journal of Science and Arts*, 37 (October 1839): 175–183.

Helmut and Alison Gernsheim, *The History of Photography: From the Camera Obscura to the Beginning of the Modern Era* (London: Thames and Hudson, 1969).

Ivor Gest, "Babbage's Ballet," *Ballet*, 5, 4 (1948): 51–56.

Jennifer Green-Lewis, *Framing the Victorians: Photography and the Culture of Realism* (Cornell: Cornell University Press, 1996).

Donna Haraway, "A Cyborg Manifesto: Science, Technology, and Socialist-Feminism in the Late Twentieth Century," in *Simians, Cyborgs, and Women: The Reinvention of Nature* (New York: Routledge, 1991), 149–181.

Oliver Wendell Holmes Jr., "Doings of the Sunbeam," *Atlantic Monthly* (July 1863): 1–15.

Chris Howes, *To Photograph Darkness: The History of Underground and Flash Photography* (Carbondale and Edwardsville: Southern Illinois University Press, 1989).

"Instantaneous Photography with Magnesium," *American Journal of Photography*, 8, 10 (October 1887): 169–170.

Akira Mizuta Lippit, *Atomic Light (Shadow Optics)* (Minneapolis: University of Minnesota Press, 2005).

Barbara Marcoń, "Hiroshima and Nagasaki in the Eye of the Camera: Images and Memory," *Third Text*, 25, 6 (2011): 787–797.

Neil Matheson, "Hiroshima-Nagasaki Remembered Through the Body: Haptic Visuality and the Skin of the Photograph," *photographies*, 11, no. 1 (2018): 73–93.

Walter Benn Michaels, "Photographs and Fossils," in *Photography Theory*, ed. James Elkins (New York, London: Routledge, 2007), 431–450.

Melissa Miles, *The Burning Mirror: Photography in an Ambivalent Light* (Melbourne: Australian Scholarly Publishing, 2008a).

Melissa Miles, "Sun-Pictures and Shadow-Play: Untangling the Web of Gendered Metaphors in Lady Elizabeth Eastlake's 'Photography,'" *Word & Image*, 24, 1 (2008b): 42–50.

Rahul Mukherjee, *Radiant Infrastructures: Media, Environment and Cultures of Uncertainty* (Durham and London: Duke University Press, 2020).

Reza Negarestani, "Solar Inferno and the Earthbound Abyss," in *Our Sun* (Milan: Instituto Svizzero di Roma, 2010): 3–8.

Reza Negarestani, *Cyclonopedia: Complicity with Anonymous Materials* (Melbourne: re.press, 2008).

"Newcastle Photographic Society," *The Photographic News* (May 10, 1861): 223–224.

Douglas Nickel, "Talbot's Natural Magic," *History of Photography*, 26, 2 (2002): 132–140.

Federico Pierotti and Alessandra Ronetti, "Beyond Human Vision: Towards an Archaeology of Infrared Images," *Necsus: European Journal of Media Studies* (Spring 2018), https://necsus-ejms.org/beyond-human-vision-to-wards-an-archaeology-of-infrared-images. Accessed December 15, 2019.

Rejected Addresses: Or the New Theatrum Poetarum (London: Printed for John Miller, 25 Bow-Street Covent-Garden and John Ballantyne and Co., Edinburgh, 1813).

Catherine Rogers, "W. H. F. Talbot, *The Pencil of Nature* and the Camera," *History of Photography*, 26, 2 (2002): 141–150.

Michel Serres, *The Parasite*, trans. Lawrence R. Schehr (Baltimore and London: Johns Hopkins University Press, 1982).

Wolfgang Schivelbusch, *Disenchanted Night: The Industrialization of Light in the Nineteenth Century*, trans. Angela Davies (Berkeley: University of California Press, 1988).

Nicole Starosielski, "Beyond the Sun: Embedded Solarities and Agricultural Practices," *South Atlantic Quarterly*, 20, 1 (January 2021): 13–24.

Imre Szeman and Darin Barney, eds, "Special Issue: Solarity," *South Atlantic Quarterly*, 20, 1 (January 2021): 1–188.

Herman Vogel, "About Artificial Light in Photography," *American Journal of Photography*, 8, 3 (March 1887): 44–45.

Rosalind Williams, *Notes on the Underground: An Essay on Technology, Society, and the Imagination* (Cambridge, MA and London: MIT Press, 2008).

Tania Woloshyn, *Soaking up the Rays: Light Therapy and Visual Culture in Britain, 1890–1940* (Manchester: Manchester University Press, 2017).

Joanna Zylinska, *Nonhuman Photography* (Cambridge, MA and London: MIT Press, 2017).

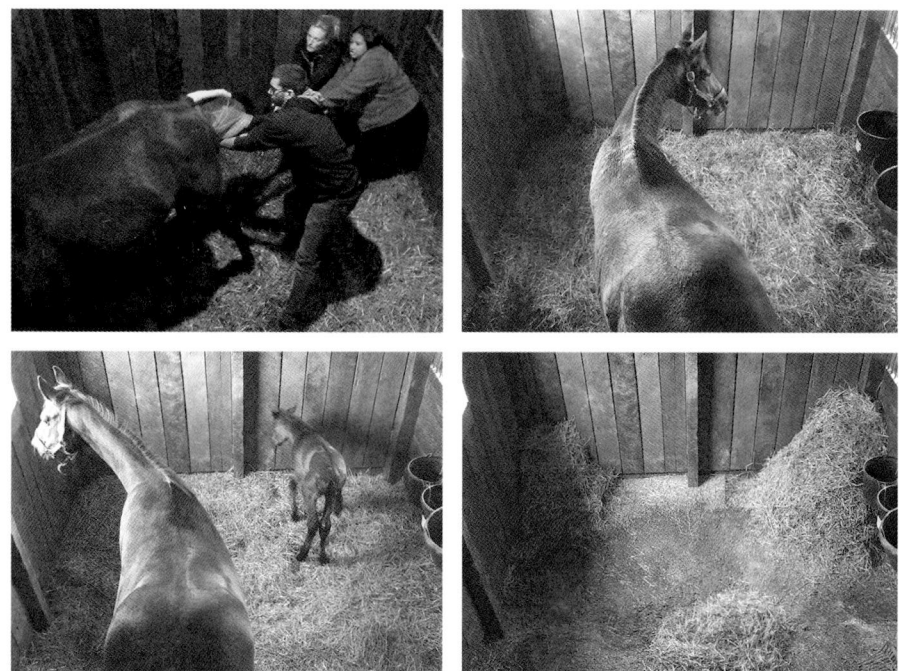

Figure 5.1

Joseph Moore, *Oversight/Rendered no. 18*, 2016.
Silver gelatin print, 8"×10". Courtesy of the artist.

5. Managing Time: Nonhuman Animal Labor in Photographic Images

Joseph Moore

In 1882, the French physiologist Étienne-Jules Marey captured the image of a gull in flight using his chronographic gun (Braun, 1993: 57). Contributing to the development of both cinema and camera-based biometrics, Marey utilized this apparatus to create a chronological record of birds in flight using a series of photographic images. In subsequent photographic inventions, Marey improved the level of detail captured as well as the precision of control of time intervals between images, making the graphing of the movement in later analysis more exact. Exposed in the meeting of Marey, the camera, the negative, and the bird is a web of social relations between human animals, nonhuman animals, and technology. These actors are not separate but overlapping and intersecting, from certain viewpoints conceptually, from others on a more material basis. The environment also belongs to this web of relations: an environment produced by these relations and, in turn, reproducing them. While the white, black, or metrological gridded background against which many of scientific photography's subjects during this time were photographed communicates an appearance of neutrality, it is neutral in appearance only. What appears as background or incidental is mobilized according to the desire to maximize positivist knowledge, on the one hand, and to use that knowledge in the accumulation of capital through the exploitation of labor, human and nonhuman, on the other.

In 2014, I began working on a photo series titled *Oversight/Rendered*. This work relies on an archive of images taken using unsecured Internet Protocol (IP) cameras connected to the internet. IP cameras are photo-computational devices, digital cameras that receive commands from and send images to other computers over a network. The image feed can be recorded and analyzed, often using a separate device, or simply used as a tool for nearly real-time observation. IP cameras are found in varying types of environments in locations around the world. I discover these feeds on an ongoing basis using a variety of tools, including software I developed. This mostly automated process of discovery ends with downloading a single image from each camera found. At the end of each session, I usually have between one hundred and two thousand images. I then shift to examining what I have found. I'm looking for cameras focused on nonhuman animals, and among each set, I usually find a few. Once I've found the kind of image I'm looking for, I record the camera that produced that image for twenty-four hours at one frame every ten seconds. This results in approximately 8,640 images that are added to my archive, which, as of January 2020, consists of around 3.5 million images. If the recording meets certain criteria, I then move on to the next part of the process. From 8,640 images, I select four to combine in digital image editing software, their layout always following a two by two grid. While certain formal aspects of my work seek to show historical continuity by referencing early motion photography and the aesthetics of conceptual photography, others attempt to disrupt any easy narrativization or easy placement within a historical continuum. This antinarrative aspect is carried out in the nonchronological placing of the four images. The images never follow the common narrative order found in various written languages of left to right, top to bottom or right to left, top to bottom. That composite digital image is then used to create a negative. Finally, I contact print the image onto silver gelatin paper in a traditional darkroom setting. This process and the resulting project come out of experimentation, an investigation into the materials of photography, the nonhuman animal's relationship to photography, (pre)cinema, and certain methods of camera-based analysis in development since the late 19th century.

In the work of Eadweard Muybridge, Étienne-Jules Marey, Félix Regnault, and others investigating the use of the camera as a tool for studying motion, photographic devices are produced to dissect continuous time into discrete moments. The freezing of bodies in motion would give scientists and artists ways of apprehending "nature," to be followed later by its conditioning. The best-known example is Muybridge's photographic sequences of horses in motion created in 1878 (Braun, 2010: 141). Although these sequences represent an important achievement in the development of camera-based biometrics, it is worth noting that the time intervals at which they were made were too irregular and the sampling rate too low to accurately graph and analyze movement without introducing the aliasing of motion. For example, the downstroke of a horse's hoof in an image might appear to be part of an upstroke (Braun, 1993: 53). Marey, inspired by Muybridge's work, would develop more sophisticated approaches that overcame the limitations of Muybridge's method. The first would be his *fusil photographique*, or camera gun, capable of recording a series of images at regular intervals of 1/720 of a second (Braun, 1993: 57). He would use this and other photographic tools of analysis to study birds in flight as well as other types of human and nonhuman animal movement. His findings and techniques would be used by his contemporaries and in future camera-based systems of analysis. For example, in 1895, contracted by the French military, Regnault applied Marey's findings in muscle elasticity to the study of military paces as a way to clarify the most efficient movement of troops (Braun, 1993: 104). Out of these techniques, the scientific management of industrial labor was also born, inspired by Marey but often carried out in a pseudoscientific manner by people such as Frederick Taylor and later by Frank and Lilian Gilbreth, who utilized and patented some of Marey's inventions but to very different ends. Whereas Marey wished his work to be used to establish universal scientific principles for the betterment of humankind, Taylor's and the Gilbreths' ultimate objective was the maximization of capital through the disciplining of labor. As Marta Braun writes in *Picturing Time*:

> Whereas Marey studied fatigue to increase the endurance of the individual, Gilbreth aimed at determining the standards for maximizing labor efficiency for the benefit of the company. Implicit, therefore, in Gilbreth's 'science' was the removal of such potential from the individual's own control. For Marey, science would unleash the energy of the animate machine. For scientific management, workers were part of a larger mechanism. Their potential was for the accumulation of capital; it could be made available only by fixed hours, systematic control, and the reorganization of labor. (Braun, 1993: 347–348)

In the above meeting of Marey, the bird, the camera, and the negative, the importance of distance should not be overlooked. Importantly, the chronographic gun allowed Marey to complete his analysis without making a physical intervention into the bird itself. Conforming to certain ideals of science that emerged during the second half of the 19th century—including an ideal in which science attempts to free itself from the subjective though the use of machines—Marey's work can be seen as emblematic of what Lorraine Daston and Peter Galison have termed "mechanical objectivity." (Daston and Galison, 1992: 82) In this and similar scenarios of scientific investigation and recording, standards of nonintervention, unbiased representation, and moral asceticism often come together in the representation of phenomena though photographic means. Mechanical objectivity attempts to negate the mediating presence of the observer, to remove human intervention. Standardization and averaging are an important part of these techniques as is the separation of the normal from the pathological. Much of the camera's valorization as an objective observer is still with us. Photographs are regularly used as evidence in the courtroom and other forums where deliberation and the building of consensus may be required. But when found in contemporary automated systems using artificial intelligence, the forum and the audience are replaced with computers whose goals range from deboning fish fillets (Mery et al., 2011) to discovering "threat objects" in luggage (Riffo et al., 2017). When seen as a passive receiver of reality—as a "pencil of nature"—the camera, when coupled with a computer, takes on additional value as a device for reporting a series of objective facts to be acted upon. The rationality of the camera and computer replaces causality with probability.

According to various estimates, the number of photographs taken every year is now over one trillion. Of course, this number is based on images taken by people for consumption by people: images coming from digital single-lens reflex cameras, tablets, camera phones, and other devices; images shared though services such as Instagram and Flickr. Other images go uncounted, such as those images not created for direct human consumption but used in various computer-controlled and computer-assisted processes, such as X-rays used in the nondestructive testing of materials and objects in semiautomated and automated systems of inspection. The one trillion figure also doesn't take account of photographs used in street cameras set up to automatically detect instances of petty crime (that is, if one can argue that these collections of data are ontologically photographs) (Tagg, 2009: 19). Jonathan Crary stated thirty years ago that

> [m]ost of the historically important functions of the human eye are being supplanted by practices in which visual images no longer have any reference to the position of an observer in a 'real,' optically perceived world. If these images can be said to refer to anything, it is to millions of bits of electronic data. Increasingly, visuality will be situated on a cybernetic and electromagnetic terrain where abstract visual and linguistic elements coincide and are consumed, circulated, and exchanged globally. (Crary, 1990: 2)

This is a situation in which traditional notions of photographer and audience unravel. Alongside the cultural artifacts of photography and cameraless photography, we have photographerless photography.

The kind of images I find in the video streams I record are both ubiquitous and unseen by most people. Like radio transmitted though the electromagnetic spectrum, we are surrounded by these images even if we lack direct access to them. Digital images are at once easy to distribute though the internet and so plentiful that they become hidden, concealed by design or eclipsed though their sheer mass. Through this work, I slow down some of these images—to hold them for a moment. I also wish to create a constellation of historical aesthetics and processes that are found in early motion studies, techniques dependent on this previous work, contemporary images, and the human and nonhuman

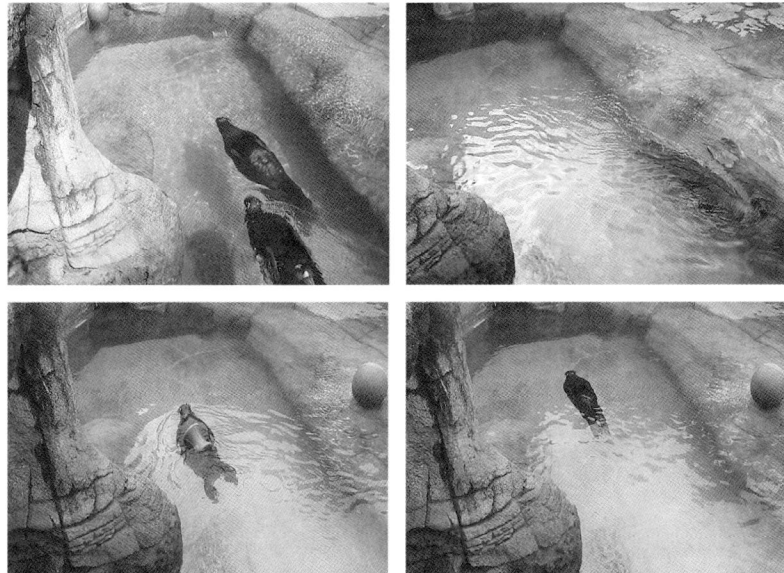

labor required in their formation. My desire to see the unseen, to bear witness to something missed or in the state of being lost, is accompanied by a knowledge of limits, that is, that which is lost and can never be found. Like a letter from the deceased, the past comes to us already too late. In the end, things remain shattered and fragmented. The whole is unavailable.

The word *oversight* in the title of my work draws on the double meaning of this autoantonym, a word with multiple meanings with at least one of those meanings being the reversal of another. Two of the definitions of oversight in the *Oxford Dictionary of English* are

2. a. The action of overseeing something; supervision, inspection, authority, management.
3. b. An accidental omission; a mistake made through inadvertence or negligence. Also: a person or thing which is passed over.

"Oversight" aptly describes the use of IP or webcams. These cameras are found in domestic settings, in places of work such as restaurants and shops, in settings of industrial production, and in places of places of leisure such as parks and sports arenas. Networked with other devices on the internet, they are among the billions of computational machines that make up the Internet of Things. These photocomputational objects work within disciplinary systems of inspection, authority, and

Figure 5.2

Joseph Moore, *Oversight/ Rendered no. 31*, 2017. Silver gelatin print, 8"×10". Courtesy of the artist.

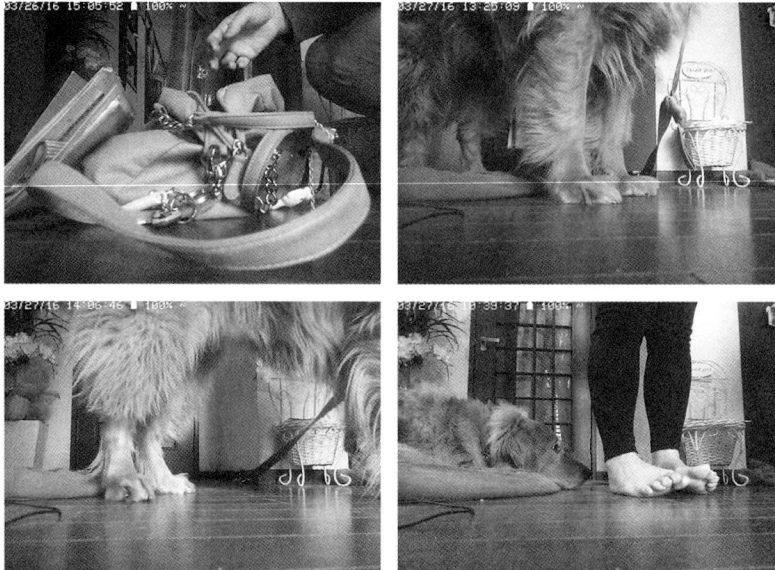

Figure 5.3

Joseph Moore, *Oversight/Rendered no. 27*, 2016. Silver gelatin print, 8"×10". Courtesy of the artist.

management for laborers. They are tools within the standardization of work and leisure time. Their proliferation into nearly all aspects of life appears, at times, total and unblinking. At the same time, these often poorly secured, unsecured, or incorrectly secured devices inadvertently allow anyone to view their transmissions with relative ease, an oversight that in some cases undoes the imagined security associated with these devices when they are marketed as "security cameras."

Using the camera as a means of discovering the unseen—of dissecting the part from the whole for further analysis—finds theorization in Walter Benjamin's notion of the optical unconscious. The optical unconscious might be described as the potential for increasing apperception though photographic means as an extension of the human sensorium. Benjamin lauds the ability of still photography and cinema to give viewers access to dimensions of scale and time previously unavailable, such as breaking down the continuous movement of a person into its constituent parts or magnifying the size of a flower. Each alteration gives the viewer access to something previously unknowable. In "Little History of Photography," he writes:

> Whereas it is a common-place that, for example, we have some idea what is involved in the act of walking (if only in general terms), we have no idea at all what happens during the fraction of a second when a person actually takes a step. Photography, with its devices of

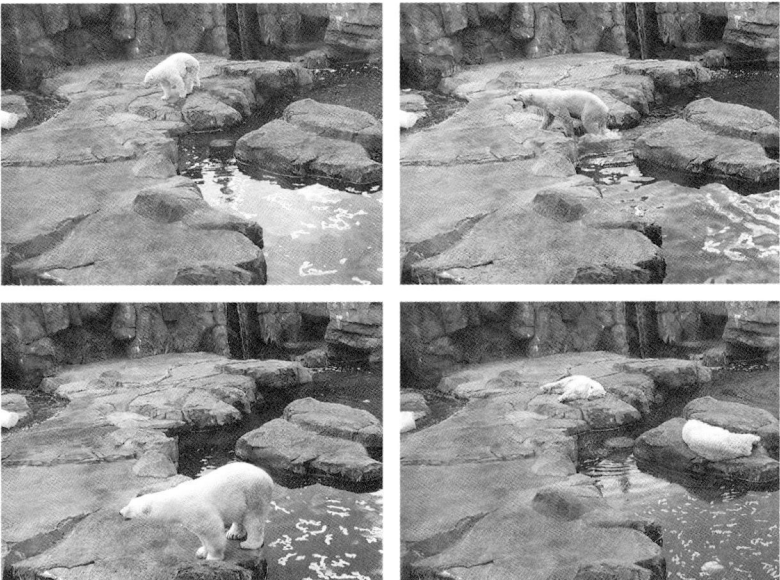

slow motion and enlargement, reveals the secret. It is through photography that we first discover the existence of this optical unconscious, just as we discover the instinctual unconscious through psychoanalysis. (Benjamin, 1999: 510–512)

Figure 5.4

Joseph Moore, *Oversight/Rendered no. 37*, 2018. Silver gelatin print, 8"×10". Courtesy of the artist.

Following Shawn Michelle Smith's work on the optical unconscious, I am interested in what can be revealed through photography and how this revelation is accompanied by a sense that there is always an additional unrecorded image. An excess in seeing is accompanied by an excess of the unseen. The chasm around each image remains. Like the edges that separate images in motion studies, their discontinuity is at once known and invisible. One might imagine that this knowledge of limit could satiate the appetites of certain positivist strains in still photography and moving images, especially those found in systems of criminal justice and the natural sciences. Instead, the seemingly infinite number of potentially knowable unknown images provides a reservoir to be tapped until the resources required for their production is exhausted. Where a world once existed, only its analogy remains. (fig. 5.4)

That last part of oversight's definition—"a person or thing which is passed over"—brings to mind other reasons for not seeing, such as a passing over due to forgetting, trauma, disavowal, or simply being a free or unpaid resource within capitalist accumulation. In *Capitalism and the Web of Life*, Jason Moore characterizes cheap and unpaid labor as a necessary aspect in the accumulation of capital and as immanent in the capitalist form of organizing relationships within nature. For Moore, this appropriated labor makes exploitation of wage workers possible. The online image world I draw from in *Oversight/Rendered* includes many such instances of appropriated human and nonhuman animal labor. These expand beyond the farm and include domestic spaces of affective labor in the family home, the human workers and nonhuman animal workers or performers at zoos and carnivals, and the animals engaged in scientific inquiry as workers or subjects in laboratories. As Moore states, "Every act of exploitation (of commodified labor-power) therefore depends on an even greater act of appropriation (of unpaid work/energy)." (2015: 54) Moore's account links with Smith's. Consider the exploitation of both unpaid and paid labor power in Moore and the optical unconscious as the perception of a "world only partially perceived" in Smith (2013: 4). In both cases, we have something that is seen, counted, noted as well as something that is unseen, unrecognized, and obscure. There are physiological limitations to sight and to imaging technologies. (For instance, film is a discrete medium and therefore does not capture the motion between frames.) But there is also a bracketing off of the world, consciously and unconsciously. The camera is pointed in a direction that corresponds with a need or desire to register that part of the world. What lies beyond the periphery is always more and required by this center, but its weight goes unregistered.

I borrow the other term in the title, *rendered*, from Nicole Shukin's book *Animal Capital*. Shukin traces the imbricated relationship between nonhuman animals and capitalist production on both the level of material production and in an economy of signs not separate from their material instantiation. Shukin writes that

> [r]endering signifies both the mimetic act of making a copy, that is, reproducing or interpreting an object in linguistic, painterly, musical, filmic, or other media […] and the boiling down and recycling of animal remains. The double sense of rendering—the seemingly incommensurable (yet arguably supplementary) practices that the word evokes—provides a peculiarly apt rubric for beginning to more concretely historicize animal capital's modes of production. (2009: 20)

The photographic prints in *Oversight/Rendered* engage with animal labor on both representational and material levels. The images of the animals, created though the reaction of silver halides to light, are embedded into the gelatin surface of the paper. This gelatin coating is made from the bodies of rendered animals: from bone, tendon, and offal. While the gelatin acts as a glue to coat the paper or celluloid with light sensitive

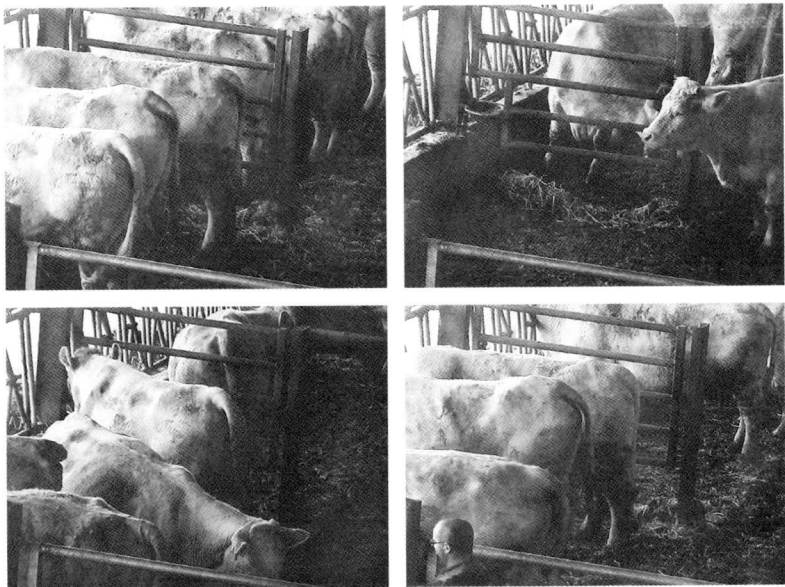

Figure 5.5

Joseph Moore, *Oversight/
Rendered no. 20*, 2016.
Silver gelatin print, 8"×10".
Courtesy of the artist.

material, the gelatin also increases the "animation" of the silver halide material. In 1925, a scientist working at Kodak, Dr. Samuel Sheppard, discovered that cattle who had eaten mustard seed produced gelatin that yielded better film speeds (Shukin, 2009: 109). This knowledge would in turn be used by producers of photographic materials in their highly controlled and systematized supply chain, which included Kodak's purchase of the American Glue Company in 1930, to be renamed the Eastman Gelatine Corporation (Shukin, 2009: 110). As a material that actively influences the sensitivity of silver halides, gelatin is "dead" at the same time that it actively "works" to create an image. This "work," both represented as an image and as a material substance, recalls a living being and its bodily labor congealed, creating a dialectical tension between life and death. In discussions of photography, the tension between the living and the dead is often remarked upon, but rarely with regard to nonhuman finitude or bearing in mind the at once dead and animate material of the photograph itself. Marx's notion of dead labor seems important here: the ossification of living labor in commodities such as machines and capital. There is an opportunity here to expand this to include the nonhuman as living labor in this process and to trouble easy ontological divides between life and death. (fig. 5.5)

In the creation and maintenance of this often unseen and sometimes invisible photographic landscape, we still find the appropriated labor of the animal. While silver gelatin paper might be seen as an anachronism

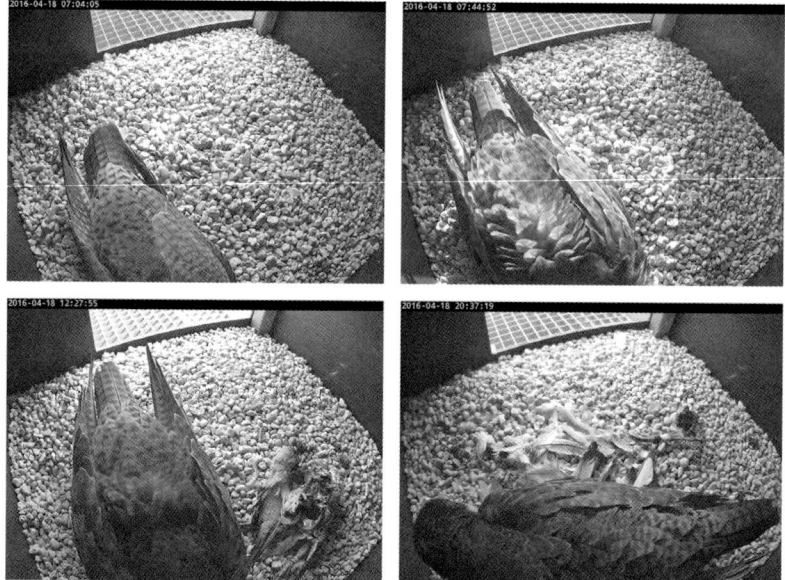

Figure 5.6

Joseph Moore, *Oversight/ Rendered no. 30*, 2017. Silver gelatin print, 8"×10". Courtesy of the artist.

in contemporary digital imaging practice, the use of gelatin and other animal-based products in the imaging industry has not disappeared (Kopacek, 2010: 436). The development of the color LCD television relied on previous discoveries in photography. For example, William Henry Fox Talbot's realization that dichromated gelatin and gum arabic became insoluble to water after exposure to sunlight formed the basis for a number of 19th-century photographic processes such as gum dichromate and carbon printing. Following Talbot over one hundred years later, the first color LCD television, sold by the Seiko Corporation in 1983, utilized a dichromated gelatin and dye to produce RGB color filters (Nishikawa, 2014: 75). That the Seiko Corporation was also a major manufacturer of lens shutters and watches serves as another point of intersection and overlap between the analog and digital, rather than a revolutionary break, as do the various recent patents filed that use gelatin in LCD production by the FujiFilm Corporation (Saneto et al., 2016). Likewise, one can see how Muybridge's camera-assisted analysis of a horse's gait in 1878 might be constellated with more recent uses of gait as an identifying attribute of individuals captured by CCTV cameras in criminal justice systems (Nirenberg et al., 2018: 293).

Through its use of web-based imagery and traditional printing, *Oversight/Rendered* points to the historical overlap between contemporary image-based technology—CCTV, image tracking, and biometrics, for example—and these techniques' historical precedents. Under this analytic, the labor of the cashier, the gestures of a pedestrian, and the lives of nonhuman animals exist to be recorded, graphed, and examined. The banal and the transcendent are distilled into a set of points in time. It is the lifeworld subjected to the efficiency of a slaughterhouse. Although *Oversight/Rendered* relies on the fragmenting of continuous time into the discrete in a way that echoes the historical examples previously mentioned, unlike them I wish to problematize the ordering and control that accompany a settled order and arrangement. (fig. 5.6)

Bibliography

Walter Benjamin, "Little History of Photography," *Walter Benjamin Selected Writings Volume 2, Part 2, 1931–1934,* eds Michael W. Jennings, Howard Eiland, Gary Smith (Cambridge, MA: The Belknap Press of Harvard University Press, 1999), 507–530.

Marta Braun, *Eadweard Muybridge* (London: Reaktion Books Ltd., 2010).

Marta Braun, *Picturing Time: The Work of Etienne-Jules Marey (1830–1904)* (Chicago: University of Chicago Press, 1994).

Jonathan Crary, *Techniques of the Observer* (Cambridge, MA: MIT Press, 1990).

Lorraine Daston and Peter Galison, "The Image of Objectivity," *Representations*, 40 (1992): 81–128.

Haruo Harada and Hiroshi Arisawa, Liquid crystal display element and manufacturing method thereof. U.S. Patent 7,903,203 filed November 9, 2007.

B. Kopacak, "ReLCD recycling and re-use of LCD panels," *Proceedings of the 2010 IEEE International Symposium on Sustainable Systems and Technology* (2010): 1–3

Domingo Mery, Iván Lillo, Hans Loebel, Vladimir Riffo, Alvaro Soto, Aldo Cipriano, and José Miguel Aguilera, "Automated Fish Bone Detection Using X-Ray Imaging," *Journal of Food Engineering*, 105 (2011): 485–492.

Jason W. Moore, *Capitalism in the Web of Life: Ecology and the Accumulation of Capital* (London: Verso, 2015).

Michael Nirenberg, Wesley Vernon, and Ivan Birch, "A Review of the Historical Use and Criticisms of Gait Analysis Evidence," *Science & Justice* (2018): 292–298, https://doi.org/10.1016/j.scijus.2018.03.002 (accessed June 9, 2021).

Michinori Nishikawa, "Alignment Films for TFT-LCDs: Development of Organic-Solvent-Soluble Polyimides," in *The Liquid Crystal Display Story: 50 Years of Liquid Crystal R&D that Led the Way to the Future*, ed. Naoyuki Koide (Tokyo: Springer, 2014), 75–80.

"Oversight," OED Online, March 2018, Oxford University Press, http://www.oed.com/view/Entry/135076?rskey=ekHpDG&result=1&isAdvanced=false (accessed April 20, 2018).

Vladimir Riffo, Sebastian Flores, and Domingo Mery, "Threat Objects Detection in X-ray Images Using an Active Vision Approach," *Journal of Nondestructive Evaluation*, 36, 44 (2017): 1–13. https://doi-org.ccny-proxy1.libr.ccny.cuny.edu/10.1007/s10921-017-0419-3 (accessed June 9, 2021).

Ryuji Saneto and Katsufumi Ohmuro, Liquid-crystal display device. U.S. Patent 10,156,754 filed January 20, 2016.

Nicole Shukin, *Animal Capital Rendering Life in Biopolitical Times* (Minneapolis: University of Minnesota Press, 2009).

Shawn Michelle Smith, *At the Edge of Sight* (Durham, NC and London: Duke University Press, 2013).

John Tagg, "Mindless Photography," in *Photography: Theoretical Snapshots*, eds J. J. Long, Andrea Noble, and Edward Welch (London: Routledge, 2009), 16–30.

6. In 1973: Family Photography as Material, Affective History

Mette Sandbye

We tend to equate the idea of ubiquitous photography with the digital, the internet, and the smartphone.[1] But the spread of photography into everyday life has happened in steps and phases ever since the invention of the carte-de-visite photograph in 1854, when portraiture became an integrated part of middle-class family life, identity formation, and the interchange and negotiation of social relations.[2] A major leap in terms of the production, consumption, and pervasiveness of ubiquitous everyday photography took place in the 1970s alongside the rapid development and expansion of capitalist welfare and consumer society in the Western world and concomitant technological improvements of camera technology. Nevertheless, relatively little has been written on this seminal period in the history of private photography.[3]

In the early 1970s, amateur photography exploded into what I will call a major period of "ubiquitous private photography," anticipating the much later digital revolution. The aim of this chapter is to point to the importance of this period in the history of everyday photography and, at the same time, to argue in favor of the family photograph as an important source for a material, affective understanding and writing of history. I will do this through a specific case study of one particular year, 1973, in one particular European country, Denmark. Inspired by Hans Ulrich Gumbrecht's *In 1926: Living at the Edge of Time*, I will simply ask how a study of private family photographs can add to a description of one particular year. With this specific year 1973 as my point of departure, I will study a sample of private everyday snapshot photographs with the aim to analyze what could be called complex affects of the everyday. Inspired by Gumbrecht's "take" on history, my aim is to dig out a slice of history of the Danish everyday in the 1970s, colored by a phenomenological interest in affect, feelings, bodies, and things, inspired by Daniel Miller, Richard Chalfen, and Raymond Williams, among others.

I thereby claim that the ubiquitousness of photography started much earlier than the advent of the digital and the internet. On the other hand, the new—digital—technologies and affordances have made us—and visual studies as such—regard photography not only or primarily as a representational technology. Rather, they have made us look into its "nonrepresentational," but nevertheless extremely important, aspects, to regard photography as a relational, dynamic, and transient practice creating material objects related to emotions and phenomenology. As such, the idea of ubiquitous photography is relevant for the whole history of photography. Insights from different periods, from the early Kodak heyday through the 1970s to "the digital now" can cross-fertilize each other across chronology. In many ways, it is the advent of digital photography that has made researchers look into photography—also of the past—as "a doing" related to *being* in social life and in the world (Larsen and Sandbye, 2013; Sandbye, 2013). Or, as the two editors of a recent anthology on *Digital Photography and Everyday Life* put it: "We suggest that photography is tied to both ways of seeing and representing, as well as to ways of acting and performing." (Cruz and Lehmuskallio, 2016: 4) The insights of digital and social media photography have made us look back into history and ask, as a pioneer in this field, Richard Chalfen, does: "What do ordinary people do with their cameras and personal pictures, as part of everyday life?" (Chalfen, 2016: xv)

The Digital Makes Us Look to History

Although the practice of everyday, personal photography is related to depicting the family, until recent decades, few have taken an interest in studying family photography. This "ubiquitous" genre of photography has been conceptualized in dualistic terms, considered either highly conventional, ritual, and selective in terms of motifs that are extremely redundant across class, gender, and geography *or* as invested with deeply emotional and highly individual, as well as private, psychological content. This duality is exemplified in the oppositional takes on photography by sociologist Pierre Bourdieu and phenomenologist Roland Barthes in their influential works, *Photography: A Middle-Brow Art* (1965) and *Camera Lucida* (1980), respectively. Whereas Barthes underlines the highly personal and emotional qualities in photographs, including the never-shown "winter garden photograph," Bourdieu and his fellow sociologists—studying family and amateur photography from the late 1950s and early 1960s—argue that family photography is an extremely coded, regulated, conventional, and ritualized genre. "The most trivial photograph," Bourdieu writes, "expresses, apart from the explicit intentions of the photographer, the system of schemes of perception, thought and appreciation common to a whole group." Bourdieu continues: "there is nothing more regulated and conventional than photographic practice and amateur photographs." (Bourdieu, 1990: 6–7)

In an article from 1980 in *The American Scholar*, James C. A. Kaufmann articulates this duality in an overall argument *against* taking an interest in "Learning from the Fotomat," as the article is called. Kaufmann's article is written in the aftermath of the explosion of the everyday photography that is the focus of my study. Kaufmann begins by recognizing the pervasiveness of family photography and family photo albums, but he warns that "comprehensive history is never the aim of the family photograph album." (Kaufman, 1980: 244) He argues that those kinds of photographs certainly represent feelings and emotions and that they serve as an aid to personal memory and can thus be of immensely personal value to those who take them and own them. However, to outsiders, they appear as "endless acts of conformity." (245) "Because family snapshots have deep meaning only for those who have somehow participated in their creation, they defy analysis by outsiders on all but the most superficial levels," Kaufmann argues, and we should therefore "feel hesitant about trying to interpret family snapshots in these albums. As traces of the past, they are virtually beyond our comprehension, unless, of course, they are our own albums." (246)

The background of Kaufmann's criticism is the image collection *American Snapshots*, published in 1977 (Graves and Payne, 1977). This book represents an early institutional interest in everyday snapshots that seemed to grow during the 1990s and early 2000s.[4] Common to most of these museum exhibition books and catalogues that were produced in this period was avoiding a deeper analysis of these images or including their sociological narratives. These ordinary snapshots were regarded and treated as a kind of poetic, semiartistic amateurism, as ambiguous haiku poems or open images with narrative indeterminacy. This is how, for instance, curator at the San Francisco Museum of Modern Art Douglas R. Nickel described them in the museum's 1988 catalogue *Snapshots: The Photography of Everyday Life* (Nickel, 1998). Alternatively, these images were seen as profoundly innocent, simple, and direct images, as collector Thomas Walther defines them in the catalogue for the Metropolitan Museum of Art's 2000 exhibition of private snapshots (Walther, 2000).

But the advent of Web 2.0 photography practices and albums in the 2000s forced academia to address the understanding and use of everyday photography and to therefore revise longstanding theoretical understandings of photography. These uses and distributions of digital images taught us to regard snapshot photographs as primarily social—and sometimes highly political—images, made to be shared with and looked at by other people, more than they are made as solitary, poetic, rarefied moments of domestic living. Cruz and Lehmuskallio argue in relation to digital practices:

Focusing contextually on material and visual practices helps us in reconsidering both photography (*What is it? How should it be understood, especially when taking digital forms into consideration?*), and everyday life (*What roles does digital photography take within everyday life?*). Digital photography, understood broadly, can thus be studied as a nexus that connects people in emotionally significant ways, as a family or as a group of friends, but, increasingly, also to current social and political movements. (Cruz and Lehmuskallio, 2016: 4)

The new digital practices can therefore also shed light on the use of albums and photographs before Web 2.0. In that sense, amateur or snapshot practices in the digital age can be said to theorize photography, making us realize aspects that we knew but that were not clear or explicit to us until after the advent of the digital. Here, photography is conceived and used as a primarily social, participatory, performative, and cultural phenomenon.

With industrialization and urbanization in the 19th century, the urban nuclear family was cemented as the main family unit. The family photo album dates back to the late 1850s, and it became common in both Europe and the United States in the 1860s among the new urban middle classes. In these early decades, the album typically included carte-de-visite portraits as well as commercially produced and sold portraits of celebrities. With the introduction of the Kodak camera in 1888, the family album became even more common and widespread, and it changed into a much more personal, often scrapbook-like, and more narrative format celebrating either the family as an entity or the story of the individual member. The practice of making family albums grew steadily throughout the 20th century, until the digital production, as well as storage, took over in the early 2000s (although the concept of "album" is often still used in digital storage formats). With the internet and social media, the "photo album" became a phenomenon often addressed to a wider public audience, whereas it—until then—had been a private object in the home primarily addressing the family members. From the late 19th century, members of the middle class were targeted as the prime consumers of the albums. Most often, men were the family photographers, but historically, women have been the primary producers of the material album (Siegel, 2010).

The family photo album is about social exchange and sharing, and it is an act of love and belonging. More philosophically put, studying family photographs historically through the insights provided by digital media might change our concepts of what authenticity and identity mean in relation to photography and make us develop a more thorough understanding of photography that is simultaneously an aesthetic medium, a historical document, and an emotional, existential, dynamic social practice. Today, photography taken with camera phones and shared via social media is used and represented as presence maker, family genealogy, identity construction, self-therapy, mourning work, social act of "reaching out," and a great deal more. Faced with these simultaneous and varied practices, we are forced to re-evaluate the museum practice represented by the examples mentioned above and to take another look at the kind of material that Kaufmann resisted in his criticism of the *American Snapshots* book.

The practice of "doing" digital photography has demanded new approaches to photography, keeping the many aspects of photography alive. At the same time, digital photography and social media have raised new problems related to the storage and archiving of photographs and therefore also for historical memory. I will thus argue that it is urgent to look into older forms of photography—as I do here—armed with these newer insights in order to keep both personal and collective memory alive, as Nancy Van House has argued: "A more traditional use for photos that is threatened, I argue, is personal and collective memory […] I fear that, as inaugural acts, digital technologies and social media have disrupted our memory regimes and the integrity of personal and collective archives and threaten images' traditional role as memory objects." (Van House, 2016: 276)

Keeping the Duality of the Material Floating

Martha Langford and Elizabeth Edwards both stress the way that family photographs are related to orality, to talking about the images. Edwards calls them "performative objects," and she invites us to think of them as material objects and to include processes of intention, making, distributing, consuming, discarding, and recycling photographs (Langford, 2001; Edwards, 2005: 39).

It is important to keep the dual sides of everyday photography not as separate and different approaches but as simultaneously existing aspects: the sociological, generic, cultural aspects as well as the highly individual side of family photography as a practice related to phenomenological aspects such as emotions, affects, and feelings. As an anthropologist interested in material culture, Daniel Miller has argued for keeping a constant eye on the diversity of materiality. In his 2010 book *Stuff*, Miller criticizes the philosophical division between particularity and universality, arguing that "one of the major dangers that besets the world today lies in the increasing dissociation of the two extremes." (Miller, 2008: 9)

Where Kaufmann isolates the aspects of emotions and feeling to something exclusively individual and private, more recent affect studies have taught us to look at feelings as deeply embedded in our experience as well as our construction of society.[5] It is important to regard family photography as a "structure of feeling," to use a much-cited term by Raymond Williams, which dates back to the production of my case study material. In a 1977 essay with that title, Williams argues against the Marxist cultural studies tradition of exclusively focusing on ideology, institutions, and systems to the exclusion of consciousness, lived experience, feeling, everyday social relations, and "what is actually being lived"—in short, structures of feeling. "We are talking about characteristic elements of impulse, restraint, and tone," Williams writes, "specifically affective elements of consciousness and relationships: not feeling against thought, but thought as felt and feeling as thought: practical consciousness of a present kind, in a living and interrelating continuity." (Williams, 1977: 131–132)

The "Third Leap" in Everyday Photography

Williams's advocacy for feelings and his bridging of feeling and thought as practical consciousness are highly relevant for my case study: the year 1973. Let me go back to this period that initially made Kaufmann react to the ubiquitousness of "Fotomat," as he calls the abundance of family photographic "material." In his 1983 book *La photo sur la cheminée: Naissance d'un culte moderne*, French photography historian Bertrand Mary analyzes popular photography's two major "leaps." The first takes place in the wake of Kodak's launch of the Kodak camera and the roll film in 1888 with the advertising slogan "You press the button, we do the rest," which made it easy and affordable for ordinary people to photograph. The second leap, according to Mary (who focuses mainly on Europe), was around World War I, when all the soldiers and their family members wanted to be photographed before the soldier went to war. The third leap, as I see it, and following the genealogy initiated by Mary, must be the late 1960s and the 1970s, when color film, the film cassette, the flash cube, and cheap camera types were introduced, first in the United States and shortly after also in Europe.

In her book *Irresistible Empire*, Victoria de Grazia describes how "America's hegemony was built on European territory," because the United States initiated a global traffic in values as well as commodities throughout the 20th century (de Grazia, 2005: 4). She has analyzed how what she calls the U.S. "Market Empire" established a new European democracy of consumption targeted at the middle class, and how American society represented an attractive model of society and modern life to European consumers, especially in the 1950s and 1960s. This can also be seen in the popularization of family photography in Europe.

In both Europe and the United States, the vast middle class was targeted as the prime consumers of photography and photo albums.

Mary states that, out of fifteen billion private photos produced worldwide in 1970, the United States alone produced six billion, so one could argue that this is the first period of really "ubiquitous photography." A fourth leap is, of course, today, when amateur snapshots flourish in the billions on a daily basis on the internet (Sandbye, 2014: 3–4). However, as already mentioned, not much has been written about the important third leap in the history of the family snapshot. The main reason is the abovementioned dual positioning of this kind of material in general. Another reason is that material from the 1960s and 1970s has not yet really been included in public archives. It is still mostly to be found in private homes. Further, it is likely that a lot has been thrown out due to the growth of the amount of photographs taken in the 1970s onward.

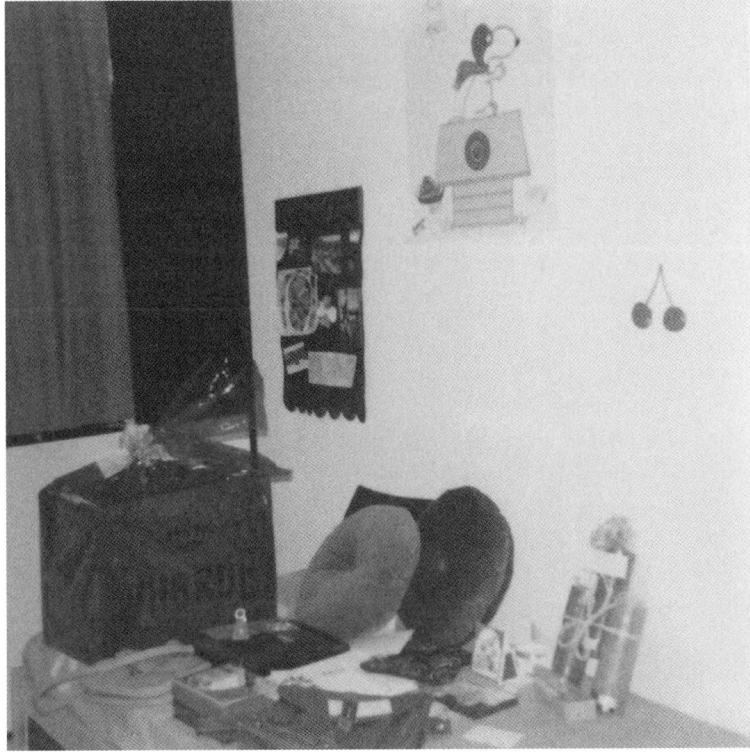

Figure 6.1

Anonymous, confirmation gift table with a Kodak Instamatic camera, Denmark, 1972.

In 1963, Kodak launched its series of inexpensive, easy-to-load Instamatic 126 and 110 cameras, which immediately became immensely popular, also in Denmark (Sandbye, 2004). (fig. 6.1) Between 1963 and 1970, more than fifty million Instamatic cameras were sold; this was the biggest success in Kodak's history (Tobin, 2013). Up until this point, people had trouble loading the camera with the film themselves; many things could go wrong, including false light and the film not rolling forward with each exposure. The Kodak Instamatic film came in an easy-to-load cartridge. At the same time that photography became accessible to people with low technological skills, even to smaller children, began the "black-boxing" and rendering invisible of the photographic technology, a process that seems to have culminated in today's everyday digital photo practice with the smartphone (Lister, 2016: 269). In 1970, Kodak introduced the flash bulb cube, and in 1972, came the much smaller compact Pocket Instamatic. More than twenty-five million Pocket Instamatics were produced in less than three years. Since the introduction of the "Kodak girl" right after the Box Brownie camera in year 1900, Kodak had underlined its cameras as easy-to-access-technology, and even in the early years, ads included images of children as camera operators. But with the Instamatic cameras, Kodak more directly targeted children in their advertisements, either showing them as photographers themselves or using their idols to pose with the camera, as with Michael Landon, the lead actor from the then globally popular television series *Little House on the Prairie* (1974–1982). To celebrate Kodak's 1980 centennial jubilee as "American Storyteller," as the campaign was called, multiple advertisements with the smiling actor posing with a pocket camera in hand stating experiences such as "Easy really does it…" were published in a variety of magazines such as *National Geographic*, *People*, *Time*, *Sports Illustrated*, *Reader's Digest*, and *TV Guide*.

Looking at Danish camera advertisements in the late 1960s and 1970s, this technological ease is most often underlined as well (Sandbye, 2004). In 1977, six programs were shown on Danish national television with the title "Better Images," all of them targeting these new amateur "shooters." Already in 1960, at least 20 percent of all Danish citizens owned a camera, a number that continued to grow through the following decades (239).

"What Did Your 1970s Look Like?": A Case Study

Since 1994, a private organization funded by public support has arranged a biannual (and now annual) history festival in Copenhagen, the capital of Denmark, under the title "Golden Days." Each festival focuses on a specific historical period. It started out with a focus on the last half of the 19th century, which was called "The Golden Days" in Denmark, but has since taken up periods in the 20th century as well. In 2016, the festival theme was the 1970s. The festival organization serves as an umbrella for events, concerts, and exhibitions arranged by museums and other cultural institutions, mostly with a focus on history and the fine arts, and these museums and institutions curate a few events themselves. Because I had been working on family snapshot photography from the 1960s and 1970s, but had had some problems finding material to study in public archives, I suggested a small project in collaboration with the festival in which we asked people to contribute their own private photographs under the headline: "What Did Your 1970s Look Like?" During the summer, people could upload their own private photos to the festival website, which was made public. When the festival opened in September (it lasted September 9–13), we had curated a selection of them to be published in the festival newspaper (twenty thousand copies), in an exhibition at the Copenhagen main public library, and as posters people could bring home from the exhibition. (fig. 6.2) When uploading, people could add small explanatory texts, which were used in the various public presentations as well.[6] Before writing the call for photographs, I identified four subthemes or recurrent motifs central to family photographs: holiday, family, home, celebration. People uploaded their photographs under these headlines. The exhibition was popular, the posters and the newspapers were widely distributed, and I presented a public interpretation of the material at the library.

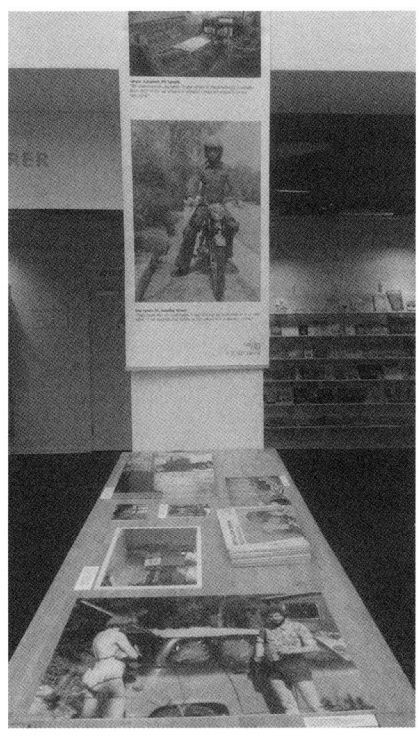

Figure 6.2

Layout from the exhibition at the Copenhagen main library during Golden Days, September 2016, including the free newspaper.

Gumbrecht's Study of 1926

I do not have direct access to the owners of my case study material (at least not anymore), but I do have their written comments. Many theoretical and methodological approaches can be used to address everyday photographs. To get my bearings on this heterogeneous material, I found inspiration in Hans Ulrich Gumbrecht's book *In 1926: Living at the Edge of Time*. This is a study of one (apparently randomly chosen) year, 1926. Gumbrecht calls for looking at the sensual side of historical experience in a study of the everyday worlds, lived experience, and public culture in this one year. He subtitles the book "An Essay on Historical Simultaneity," with the intention "to bring out dominant surface perceptions as they were offered by certain material phenomena" and to ask, "What can we do with our knowledge of the past once we have given up the hope of 'learning from history'?" (Gumbrecht, 1997, ix, xi)

Whereas Kaufmann regards the surface-ness of photography as an obstacle to even talking about photographs unless they are your own, Gumbrecht advocates for attention to surfaces,[7] although not surfaces that have to be penetrated to reach "Truth." (421) Gumbrecht's interest in surfaces is rather related to bringing forth "the sensual side of historical experience." (419) According to Gumbrecht, we have trespassed the idea of learning from history and understanding the past. Therefore, in principle, we can write about any year; we don't need to legitimize the specific moment of the past we choose to write about, which is why he simply made the choice to write about the year 1926. With a focus on "surface phenomenon" and "lived experience" (*Erleben*) as opposed to "experience" (*Erfahrung*) (431), Gumbrecht's book has an encyclopedic structure with the aim to construct "a rhizome rather than a totality" (435), because he realized the impossibility of representing the past. Inspired by Walter Benjamin's *The Arcades Project* and Gustave Flaubert's *Dictionary of Received Ideas*, he lists in alphabetical order a lot of surface appearances and objects related to "everyday-worlds." (418)[8] They are organized and presented alphabetically in three major sections. The first is what he names "arrays," meaning all sorts of rather concrete phenomenon and objects such as airplanes, bullfighting, and telephones. Common to them is that they are all related to artifacts and activities involving the body. Secondly, Gumbrecht orders them into what he calls "codes," which are binary pairs of feelings or abilities related to the arrays, such as action/impotence, male/female, silence/noise, and authenticity/artificiality. He also uses the terms "discourses" and everyday cultures in connection with these "binary codes," which he sees as "principles of order within the unstructured simultaneity of everyday-worlds." (435) Finally, as his third ordering principle in this encyclopedia of early modernity, he looks for phenomena that imply what he calls "codes collapsed" (349) These are areas where the "codes" he so apparently easily identifies seem to disappear into "areas of malfunction and entropy." (435) An example could be male-female oppositions, resulting in gender trouble, often implying "a potential for change." Exactly the collapse of male-female codes—as Gumbrecht calls it—were typical for the 1920s (for instance, seen in the concept of the new woman and the boyish *la garçonne*) as they were in the 1970s (in the wake of the women's liberation movement), which my case material also showed, but pairing of the authenticity/artificiality or the individuality/collectivity can be recognized as well.

This method of framing a whole year, and indirectly a larger period around it, as I intend to do on a much smaller scale as well (although Gumbrecht strictly warns about making diachronic interpretations), is described in the introductory chapter called "User's Manual" as well as in the chapter called "After Learning from History" toward the end of the book. In these two explanatory chapters, Gumbrecht states that he aims for a strictly descriptive discourse to bring out the surface perceptions offered by the material as concretely as possible, to avoid the traditional didactic idea of "learning from history."[9]

Strangely enough, Gumbrecht is not interested in including photographs in his compilation of 1926 "surface" phenomenon and objects "because they produce an effect of immediacy which easily overwhelms," as he puts it (425). He is also eager to underline that he is not developing a method to analyze history. Nevertheless, in search of a take on my material from the Golden Days event, I am inspired by Gumbrecht's "ordering" method, combined with a wish to challenge him on his aversion toward photography. What I take from Gumbrecht is a dual attentiveness both to the discourses, or codes, in which ordinary photographs are enmeshed, and to the complexity of the very same discourses or codes, which most ordinary photos contribute to, too, and which therefore also make them transgress more traditional sociological strata. Photographs are much more than discourse.

Everyday Photography in the 1970s

The images in my case study date from the whole decade. But 1973 was a rather focal year in the period. After a 1972 referendum, Denmark entered the European Union in January 1973; the government agreed to a law about free abortion; car-free Sundays were decreed for almost three months at the end of the year due to the global oil crisis; two lesbians were married on national TV—just to mention a few events pointing to the fact that "The times they are a-changin'," as Bob Dylan had predicted in 1964. All these facts can be studied in history books, but I would argue that a "surface" study of "ubiquitous" everyday photography from the 1970s can complement history books and bring forth subtle details and insights—"structures of feeling"—related to bodies and their interaction with ordinary objects in their lives.

Let me describe two pairs of photos that were chosen for both the newspaper and the exhibition. The first pair appears under the theme "Family." Both images are from 1972. (figs. 6.3 and 6.4) One is called "Father matching the baby carriage"; the other, "My family." The father photo was sent in by the mother of the baby in the carriage. In the rather long accompanying text, she explains that the father had time to take care of the baby, because he had refused going to military service, that the baby carriage was given to them as social aid, and that they had painted the black carriage yellow and red. The couple used the carriage to agitate against the E.U. referendum later the same year; the mother describes people's surprise when they looked into the carriage and

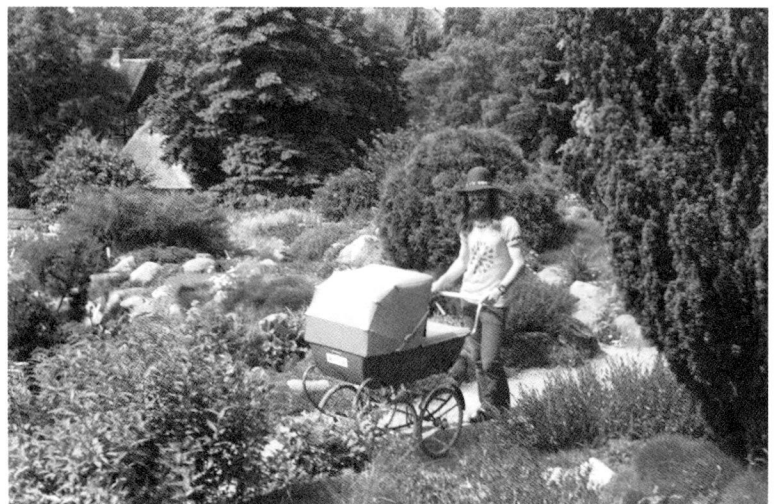

Figure 6.3

Anonymous, Theme Family: "Father matching the baby carriage," Denmark, 1972.

See also Plate 8.1.

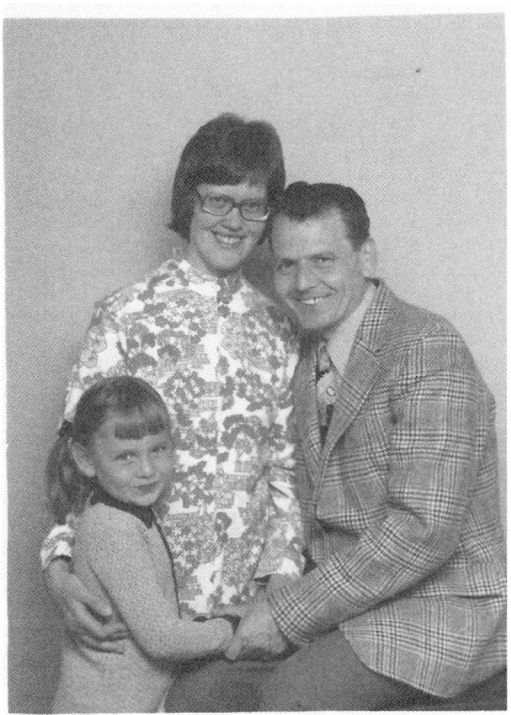

Figure 6.4

Anonymous, Theme Family: "My family," Denmark, 1972.

found a baby instead of propagandist material. We see the longhaired young father wearing a hat and a yellow T-shirt and red pants matching the colors of the carriage. They are walking in a botanical garden. In another photo from 1971, we meet the newlywed couple in front of the city town hall dressed informally in ponchos and "unisex" clothes. The other family-themed photo comes with a short text written by the now adult daughter in the photo: "This photo is taken at the photographer's studio, it shows my family (before they divorced in 1975)." In many ways, this seems like a more "ordinary," middle-class family compared to the "hippie" father. They are standing close together, holding each other as a triangular unit with the mother as the center, smiling. However, whereas the "hippie" couple is newly wedded and thus sticking to the idea of the nuclear family, this second couple is approaching divorce. Where the hippie father has long hair, here the mother seems to slowly be breaking up conventions with her short hair and her patterned loose blouse. The mother of this family had a job as manager at a childcare institution and earned more money than the father of the family, which enabled her to move to a larger house when they divorced. Here, we might bring Gumbrecht's binary codes of what is considered typically male versus typically female into mind and his pointing to the subtle collapse of binary codes seen in everyday culture.

The second pair is from the "Holiday" section. (figs. 6.5 and 6.6) The first is entitled "Swedish twist bread, 1977." The text, written by a now seventy-two-year-old man, describes how "my partner and I often spent vacations at a farm in Sweden with good socialist friends." It asks us to notice the pile of cigarettes and cigars in the middle of the photo and the little boy's Chinese cap, which his father had brought home from a long train trip from Copenhagen to Hong Kong. In the photo, we see two women and a boy making twist bread at a bonfire. In the middle, we see a man taking a photograph in the direction of the photographer of the "Swedish twist bread" photo. Both the little boy and the photographing man have rather long hair, and both are wearing caps. The latter could be taken for a 19th-century prop, but it was a socialist fashion at the time. All are wearing jeans and sweaters, no matter gender and age. The other photo is called "Car trip to Austria, 1972." The text is written by of one the now adult girls in the photo, "Camping equipment. Photo of my father and two elder sisters, I am wearing a Tyrolean dress." The photo represents the major wave of ordinary people traveling to southern Europe in the late 1960s and 1970s, either in their own car or by charter flights, as many of the other color photos in my case study represent. (Another annotation to another photograph reads "First trip to 'the South.'") Photography has always been related to traveling, but in this period, there was a growth in tourism and travel, and photography became a particularly important and widespread part of conquering

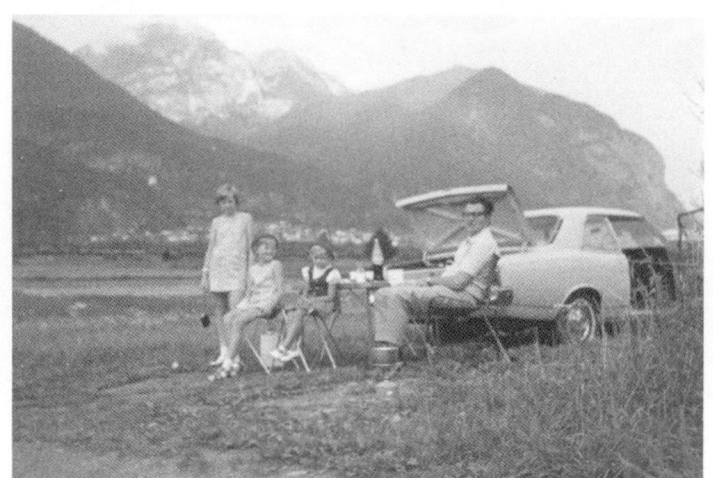

Figure 6.5

Anonymous, Theme Holiday: "Car trip to Austria," Denmark, 1972.

See also Plate 8.2.

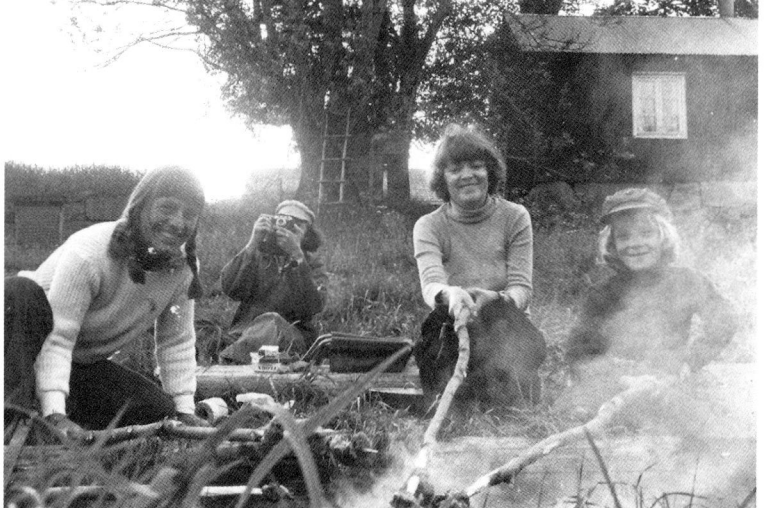

Figure 6.6

Anonymous, Theme Holiday: "Swedish twist bread," Denmark, 1977.

and understanding the new and the foreign. As opposed to today, when people would probably not have lunch with their own camping equipment that close to the car, there seems to be a certain pride in including the car in several of the photos. Together with other newly acquired status symbols such as the refrigerator, television, and record player, this is often seen in family photos in the period. In addition, we see a change in dress codes with the older girls' short, "streamlined" dresses.

Of course, the case study sample includes formal and ritual family posing. Nevertheless, most of the photographs, in fact, show much more ordinary situations, objects, and interiors: cooking (with new electronic equipment) among parents and children; father and son digging out soil in front of the newly constructed standard house; the new record player; a whole family playing in the first snow; the teenager's own photograph of her room including a cat poster, smart new furniture, and her beloved older male cousin dressed in purple, pink, and yellow; a toddler eating in a very "dirty," independent way in a living room in front of both a poster of Karl Marx and an old-style bourgeois-looking piece of furniture; a smoking father playing chess with his daughter; going to a music festival; close-ups of new (often homemade, often colorful) clothes; a father in his forties and teenage daughter sowing and knitting together. These motifs also point to the ubiquity of photography at the time: that it has become much cheaper to produce and thus also a much more common part of everyday life, where people photograph their everyday doings.

Arrays, Codes, and Breakdown of Codes

It would lead too far in this context to go into a deeper, close analysis of the many photographs and the small texts. Rather, my contribution here is exemplary and more meant for inspiration than it is comprehensive. More recently, there have been many movies about the 1970s, most often centered on the rebellion of the young hippies against their bourgeois backgrounds or parents. This duality was also clear in the photographs, and some of them were probably chosen by their owner in retrospect exactly because they seemed to underline this particular and most often talked about aspect of the 1970s as a time of unrest and upheaval. However, as my two apparently "opposing" samples articulate, the oppositions were not all that clear.

In line with Gumbrecht's notions, several "arrays" appear in the material. These include new forms of clothes, patterns, and colors; new bodies such as topless women at the beach, men with long hair, a man with a baby carriage, a man sewing informal wedding dresses; an interest in the "exotic" related to traveling, such as belly dancing, camel riding, airplanes, and mountains; modern implements, which had suddenly become affordable, such as cars, record players, new one-floor standard houses in the suburbs, new electronics. A variety of codes can be outlined related to these motifs and themes: eternal values versus modernity, nonmateriality versus (welfare society and consumer) materiality, past versus present, sticking to the local versus interest in difference and the exotic, authenticity versus artificiality, active women versus posing women, the beautiful versus the insignificant, formality versus informality, children as children versus children as small grown-ups, feminine men versus active, masculine men.

These oppositions are not necessarily played out in different images but can be seen in the same image, which therefore also points to a "breakdown of codes" in the period related to notions of gender (male-female), generations (children-teenagers-young adults-older adults), the value of consumer society goods such as cameras, cars, and Kitchen Aids. For instance, in Figure 6.1 (1972), the confirmation gift table, clearly photographed in a new, one-floor, suburban, mass-produced, middle-class, standard house, we see the new Kodak Instamatic, a cassette tape recorder, a poster with the American cartoon figure Snoopy, a color scale of green, brown, red, and orange, and then the big box wrapped in red cellophane. It is a wooden, old-fashioned beer box, provided (the text explains) by the uncle, who owned a grocery store. In the 1970s, this kind of recirculation of "ordinary" things and materials was in fashion and, at the same time, seen as a political statement (as it is today).

In one image from 1970, we meet two topless women (mother and daughter) at the beach with their boyfriends. (The mother's partner was not the father of the daughter.) The daughter writes that her mother filed for divorce after more than twenty years of marriage, "because mom had had enough of being a housewife." She and her new partner in the photo were "Rudolph Steiner enthusiasts and vegetarians." In another photo, a woman poses with her two sons in the living room of their new house. The furniture is a mixture of heavy 1930s armchairs (probably inherited), new streamline design furniture in leather and steel, a "Morocco" leather pillow (maybe bought on vacation), and a wall "rya" rug showing the "Sun Chariot," a well-known Danish national heritage museum object dating back to the bronze age. The living room has a huge window, probably facing the garden. It is covered by a thin white curtain in a modern kind of polyester material, which lets some of the exterior light in, but also closes out the outside. Here, Gumbrecht's code pair authenticity/artificiality is highly relevant, as well as modernity/tradition. In this image alone, a lot of the abovementioned codes and breakdown of codes take place, as I see it. The old heavy furniture, the curtains, and the Sun Chariot motif point to maintenance of traditions such as history and the family as a private unit sealed from the outside, modernity, and change. The Morocco pillow, the streamline modern furniture, and the many modern materials in the house all point to modernity and openness to the new and unfamiliar—just as the two vacation images described above do.

Much more could be said from a close reading of how the bodies in the photos pose, behave, wear themselves, are clothed, and touch each other (or not); what people find worth taking pictures of; how homes are decorated, and so on. As already mentioned, historically, women were album producers and thereby the prime narrators of the family history. In *Gender of Modernity*, Rita Felski has argued that we should take an interest in domestic experiences as well as alternative outcomes expressing women's experiences such as diaries or magazine novellas in order to complement and give nuance to the now canonized story of modernism and modernity written from the perspective of male as well as avant-garde culture (Felski, 2009). As Daniel Miller has pointed out in his study of material culture in British households, it is important to focus on the diversity of what is studied, so that one "does not reduce to sociological categories or labels, or for that matter colloquial categories or labels." It does not matter "what one learns from knowing the class, gender, and origin of people" as much as "what one doesn't learn from these things." (Miller, 2008: 292)

Conclusion

Family and everyday photographs represent both cultural differences and sociological strata. They also represent unarticulated differences to those, as well as more universal and philosophical endeavors to articulate questions of emotions, identity, memory, and family. Whether taken by a child or an adult, they have clearly also been used to understand, come to terms with, and negotiate the "codes" of the period, and many of my examples from the 1970s represent much more subtle nuances and breakdown of codes within a single image. This kind of material has not really been collected in public archives. As I argue, this period likely represents the first period of ubiquitous everyday photography. For this reason, it might never be included in "the archive," simply because of the already huge amount of images from the period in peoples' homes and personal archives. Or because they have already been thrown out.

Therefore, the ubiquity of everyday photography is double. It—"the digital period" in particular—has opened our eyes to new approaches to photography as a social, communicative event. A major achievement of the tradition of visual culture studies in general has been a shift of interest from structural to more cultural concerns at the level of everyday life and a focus on images not as static entities but as social and dynamic objects and cultural doings, such as my short analysis above has shown. As Lisa Cartwright and Marita Sturken underline in their visual culture reader,

> as we humans give meaning to objects, so too do the objects we create, gaze on, and use for communication or simply for pleasure have the power to give meaning to us as well as in the dynamic interaction of social networks. The exchange of meaning and value between people, on the one hand, and the objects and technologies in their worlds, on the other, is interactive and dynamic. This means that artifacts such as images and imaging technologies have politics and agency. (Cartwright and Sturken, 2009: 3)

However, this development has also had consequences, and the stakes are therefore not only methodological but also a matter of storage, of keeping photographs alive as memory keepers and identity supporters, both on a personal and on a societal level. It seems that a companion to the increasing ubiquity of photography is a decline in the actual archiving of photography. This is partly due to the enormous amount of images threatening to bury us in unorganized piles, partly due to technological challenges—from 1970s color photographs losing their quality (or being kept in plastic folders that threaten to destroy the images after some decades) to the increased speed of new digital storage systems replacing each other. Nancy Van House, Martin Hand, and others have pointed to this dilemma regarding digital photography. However, one of my points here is to draw the attention even further back into history, to the "ubiquitous phase" of the 1960s and 1970s, still important for the memory construction of modern lives in the decades that followed. Pointing to photography as a "doing" and as a social activity does not exclude talking about memory and the archive in relation to everyday photography, and we must keep both intentions in mind when we deal with everyday, ubiquitous photography.

Family photos from the 1970s have not yet entered public archives. Today, where private family photos are stored in digital forms and shared on social media, it is also imperative to collect and to take an interest in the materials that came before, and which might otherwise disappear in attics or trash bins and thus lose their role as "mirrors with a memory," as the early pioneers named photography.

Notes

1. See, for instance, Martin Hand, *Ubiquitous Photography*. Here, in fact, Hand also suggests that "this is not the first moment in history when photography has been considered 'ubiquitous.'" (Hand, 2012: 4)

2. See, for instance, Elizabeth Anne McCauley, *A. A. E. Disdéri and the Carte de Visite Portrait Photograph*.

3. Terms such as private photography, amateur, personal, vernacular, snapshots, family photography, and everyday photography are all used about more or less the same kind of images—as they will be used in this contribution. I have chosen not to use one term but the term that fits best in the context of the sentence context. Therefore, I will primarily use the terms "family" and "everyday."

4. Some examples are *Snapshots: The Photography of Everyday Life* (San Francisco Museum of Modern Art, 1998); *Other Pictures* (Metropolitan Museum of Art, 2000); *Close to Home: An American Album* (J. Paul Getty Museum, 2004); *Snapshots: From the Box Brownie to the Camera Phone* (Museum of Photographic Arts, 2005); *The Art of the American Snapshot* (National Gallery of Art, 2007); Michel Frizot and Cédric de and Veigy, *Photos trouvées* (Phaidon, London: 2006); Christian Skrein, *Snapshots: The Eye of the Century* (Ostfildern-Ruit: Hatje Cantz, 2004).

5. By such names as Sianne Ngai, Sarah Ahmed, Judith Butler, and Lauren Berlant.

6. When uploading, people agreed to have their text and photos published during the festival. Each person could upload a maximum of ten photos. We discussed how we could most easily collect the material, and, for economical and practical reasons, we opted for the digital upload. People's private photos from the 1970s are analog, so we were dependent on people making the effort to either scan or take a digital re-photograph, which of course was an obstacle. Due to this, and due to the fact that the call for photos was announced during the summer vacation period, only around sixty people participated in sending in their private photos. I realize that this is not at all a complete and general survey of "typical" (if this would even exist) Danish family photos from the 1970s. Nevertheless, it was enough material and of such a variety that we could make the exhibition and that I allow myself to draw some conclusions, as I do here.

7. In the introductory "User's Manual."

8. The notion of everyday world is inspired by Husserl's notion of "Lebenswelt."

9. At the same time, Gumbrecht polemicizes against Foucault's discourse theory, New Historicism's "poetic" subjectivity (416), and Constructivism. Summing up this criticism would require more space than I have in this context.

Bibliography

Pierre Bourdieu et al., *Photography: A Middle-Brow Art* (Cambridge: Polity Press, 1990).

Lisa Cartwright and Marita Sturken, *Practices of Looking: An Introduction to Visual Culture*, 2nd ed. (Oxford: Oxford University Press, 2009).

Richard Chalfen, "Foreword," in *Digital Photography and Everyday Life: Empirical Studies on Material Visual Practices*, eds Edgar Gómez Cruz and Asko Lehmuskallio (London: Routledge, 2016), xv–xxi.

Edgar Gómez Cruz and Asko Lehmuskallio, "Why Material Visual Practices?" in *Digital Photography and Everyday Life: Empirical Studies on Material Visual Practices*, eds Edgar Gómez Cruz and Asko Lehmuskallio (London: Routledge, 2016), 1–16.

Victoria de Grazia, *Irresistible Empire: America's Advance Through Twentieth-Century Europe* (Cambridge, MA: Belknap Press, 2005).

Elizabeth Edwards, "Photographs and the Sound of History," *Visual Anthropology*, 21, 1+2 (Spring/Fall, 2005): 27–46.

Kenn Graves and Mitchell Payne, foreword by Jean Shepherd, *American Snapshots* (Oakland: Scrimshaw Press, 1977).

Hans Ulrich Gumbrecht, *In 1926: Living at the Edge of Time* (Cambridge, MA: Harvard University Press, 1997).

Martin Hand, *Ubiquitous Photography* (Cambridge: Polity Press, 2012).

James C.A. Kaufmann, "Learning from the Fotomat," *The American Scholar*, 49, 2 (Spring 1980): 244–246.

Martha Langford, *Suspended Conversations: The Afterlife of Memory in Photographic Albums* (Montreal: McGill-Queen's University Press, 2001).

Jonas Larsen and Mette Sandbye, "Introduction," in *Digital Snaps: The New Face of Photography*, eds Jonas Larsen and Mette Sandbye (London: IB Taurus, 2013), xv–xxxii.

Martin Lister, "Is the Camera an Extension of the Photographer?," in *Digital Photography and Everyday Life: Empirical Studies on Material Visual Practices*, eds Edgar Gómez Cruz and Asko Lehmuskallio (London: Routledge, 2016): 267–274.

Bertrand Mary, *La Photo sur la Cheminée: Naissance d'un Culte Moderne* (Paris: Métailié, 1983).

Elizabeth Anne McCauley, *A. A. E. Disdéri and the Carte de Visite Portrait Photograph* (New Haven: Yale University Press, 1985).

Daniel Miller, *Stuff* (Cambridge: Polity Press, 2010).

Daniel Miller, *The Comfort of Things* (Cambridge: Polity Press, 2008).

Douglas R. Nickel, *Snapshots: The Photography of Everyday Life* (San Francisco: San Francisco Museum of Modern Art, 1998).

Mette Sandbye, "Looking at the Family Photo Album: A Resumed Theoretical Discussion of Why and How," *Journal of Aesthetics & Culture*, 6 (2014): 1–17.

Mette Sandbye, "The Family Photo Album as Transformed Social Space in the Age of 'Web 2.0,'" in *Throughout: Art and Culture Emerging with Ubiquitous Computing*, ed. Ulrik Ekman (Cambridge, MA: MIT Press, 2013), 103–118.

Mette Sandbye, ed., *Dansk Fotografihistorie* (Copenhagen: Gyldendal, 2004).

Elizabeth Siegel, *Galleries of Friendship and Fame: A History of Nineteenth-Century American Photograph Albums* (New Haven and London: Yale University Press, 2010).

Tom Tobin, "Kodak Instamatic camera turns 50," *USA Today*, March 29, 2013, https://eu.usatoday.com/story/tech/2013/03/29/instamatic-camera-50-years/2034585 (accessed January 29, 2020).

Nancy Van House, "Outlook: Photographic Wayfaring, Now and to Come," in *Digital Photography and Everyday Life: Empirical Studies on Material Visual Practices*, eds Edgar Gómez Cruz and Asko Lehmuskallio (London: Routledge, 2016), 274–283.

Thomas Walther, *Other Pictures: Anonymous Photographs from the Thomas Walther Collection* (New York: Twin Palm Publishers, 2000).

Raymond Williams, *Marxism and Literature* (Oxford: Oxford University Press, 1977).

7. Where Is My Photo? A Study of the Representation of Tehran in the Work of Contemporary Iranian Photographers

Mohammadreza Mirzaei

Photographing Tehran

The second half of the 2000s is the period of Iran's photographic revolution, fostered by an environment in which digital cameras and social media led to the photographic process becoming less expensive and more democratic.[1] Greater internet access allowed young people to discover more about topics in international photography, one of which included documenting the city and its historical and human dimensions. In this first decade, a new generation of artists chipped away at the unified front of contemporary Iranian art, creating pieces outside of the common assumptions of work by Iranian artists represented in Western art institutions (that is, Iran's domestic contradictions, human rights issues, cultural characteristics and symbols, primitivism, politics, and exoticism).[2] Following this development, the domestic audience for contemporary art grew. In response, a new group of buyers and gallery owners emerged with different motivations apart from the global art market. In turn, this made the art scene of Iran seem even more active than usual.

New social, technological, and economic conditions led to a surplus of interest in photographing Tehran. The city that had been neglected and ignored for years by Iranian photographers became a foundation for art, supported by the city's gallery scene. By studying notable examples of gallery photographs of Tehran, I will question the reasons behind the emergence of the urban landscape as a popular genre in Iranian photography. This emergent genre stands in stark contrast to mainstream Iranian photography from the previous decade, which had given priority to staged photography and pictorial approaches that expressed particular political messages. While political conflicts in Iran are still effective in the formation of urban documentary, I intend to position these photos in their social context. These new photographs of empty streets in Tehran can be seen as a response not only to the political situation but also to the changes in the policies of photographing Tehran.

Following Mahmoud Ahmadinejad's second victory in the 2009 presidential election, the massive crowd of protesters that took to the streets of Tehran testified to the political power of those who believed the election result was fraudulent. As with any political protest of the modern era, the representations of the protests that the media transmitted were as important as the protests themselves. In a country with restrictions imposed on foreign and domestic reporters, images captured on the streets by ordinary citizens and published on the internet became a window into the bustling streets of Tehran. Clearly, under such circumstances, those in power enforced restrictions on the distribution and circulation of photography. Therefore, photographing life on the street, even with a cell phone, was not be as easy as it had been before.

Protest photographs taken by these citizen photographers are unarchived and are still in dire need of scholarly attention. However, we still have access to some examples to understand the phenomenon better. The available pictures found under the hashtag #iranelection on Twitter can clarify the restrictiveness of photographic ubiquity in 2009 Tehran.[3] For instance, there is a photo, with crooked framing, perhaps because the photographer was hiding the camera to not be caught by authorities. Taken in downtown Tehran, the photograph shows the street full of people, with some holding banners of green, a symbolic color for the 2009 protesters. Reading this picture, it is essential to recognize the streets full of people as evidence of political power. As the Iranian writer Amir Ahmadi Arian writes, "any political conflict between people and the government in any era is and will be about the place of politics." (Arian, 2014: 33) As he discusses, the government attempts to limit such activity to specific buildings, such as the ministries and the related buildings. To occupy the streets, therefore, is to show disembodiment, "to show an emergence of a desire to change." (34) That is why even the photographic representation of such a desire is considered dangerous by the government.

It is in the context of the 2009 protests that photographing Tehran became a trend for Iranian art photographers such as Mehran Mohajer, Mohammad Ghazali, and Sasan Abri. While the political references in the titles and statements are bold, do these images have the same function of the mentioned images transmitted in social media? Images produced and shared by citizen photographers were both a form of information and a means of resistance, while photographs displayed on the walls of the city's galleries resist the label of documentary in a variety of ways. Inspired by Mehran Mohajer, an established Iranian photographer who has taught in several institutions in Tehran, several emergent photographers used urban landscapes to reflect on the medium of photography. These artists chose viewpoints and manipulated the representational qualities of their images to create a void with an absence of details in their images. As T. J. Clark writes, the medium can appear "most characteristically as the site of negation and estrangement." (Clark, 1982: 152) As Clark identifies, the medium dialectically represents the materiality of the work of art and also a place to explore negation. This negation comes from the absence of certain qualities such as depth, figuration, and details. Such absences become meaningful in the works of Iranian photographers showing in galleries after 2009, making the audience acutely aware of what these photographers are not supposed to show in their pictures. What we have instead is a glimpse into a rarely seen face of Tehran as a defamiliarized city.

The statements accompanying the projects or the titles could fill these spatial and visual absences with sentiments of grief and fear such that the manifestation of the desire to change turns to an image of failure and its emotional implications. In those cases, the distinction is beyond the one between the representation of the presence of people with pictures of empty streets; it is indeed in making the representation of empty streets an elegy for the packed ones. Of course, it is fair that, with limited political discussion, the relevant discourse could be reduced to the expression of feelings. However, as I will discuss, such romantic approaches by Iranian photographers are challenging, as demonstrations of fear and representations of empty streets can be in line with the wishes of the "power."

Where Is My Photo?[4]

Mehran Mohajer's *Tehran, Undated* is an important series in Iran's photography scene, because it shifts the urban landscapes of Tehran from the margins to the center of the art scene. In the 1990s and in the early 2000s, straight photography—and to be more precise, works that examined medium specificity—rarely played a central role in an Iranian photo series. Audiences and critics approached photographic works instead through painterly criteria (as in Bahman Jalali's later series *Image of Imagination*, 2000–2008), performance (like Sadegh Tirafkan's *Persepolis*, 1995–1998), or studio mise-en-scène (such as Shadi Ghadirian's *Qajar*, 1998). In contrast, Mohajer's practice involves testing the different capacities of the medium, selecting the apparatus as one of the consistent subjects of his photography. In this way, we can define his photography as emerging from a practice about "photography itself" that aligns with the historical ideals of straight photography.

In 2008, Mohajer began the series *Tehran, Undated*, examining the process and act of taking pictures. (fig. 7.1) In this project, he used a pinhole camera, a primitive version of a photographic apparatus without a true lens. The main limitation of this practice is that it requires a long exposure time, which means that a lot of detail and motion will be lost in the resulting images. This is quite in line with Mohajer's interest in absence, which is a theme found in different formal and conceptual arrangements throughout his work. For instance, absence takes priority in his use of vast, centrifugal negative spaces in some of the photographs of Tehran and Isfahan in *Urban Landscapes* (1990); in these images, with emphasis on the photograph's frame, he chose the space between buildings as the subject of his photographs, leaving what we know as the image of these cities out of the frames. Emphasizing photography's power of transparency, he photographs newspapers in envelopes in *Photograph/Newspapers* (2000), or a damaged TV covered with a newspaper in *The Light is Out, The Room is Dark* (2003). Alternatively, he deploys an exaggerated shallow depth of field to force an absence of detail in *Nothingness* (2012). Pressing further, Mohajer chooses to omit the bustle of city life quite effectively in *Tehran, Undated*. The formation of weird reflections due to the long exposure time, or the creation of vast negative space caused by the photographer sticking either to the walls or the ground, helps the photographer to make it a "concept": hiding a noisy city like Tehran while capturing the spirit of the city.

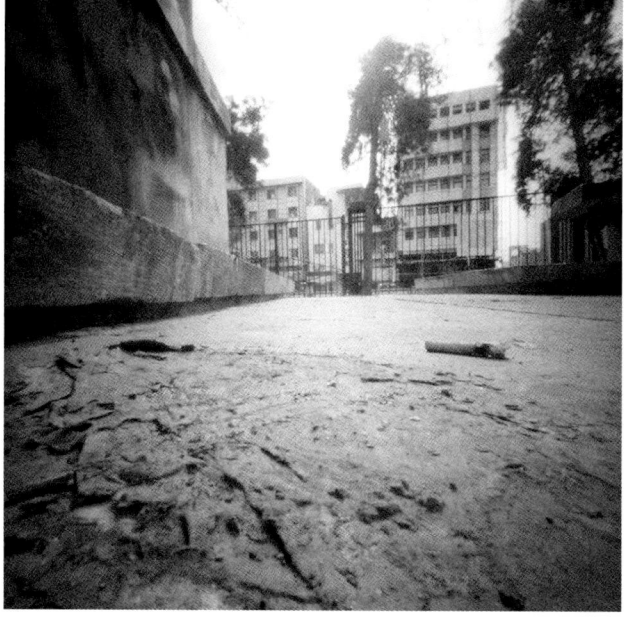

Figure 7.1

Mehran Mohajer, *Tehran, Undated*, 2008. Pigmented inkjet print on fine art paper, 76 cm×76 cm. Courtesy of the artist.

See also Plate 9.

Mohajer's photographs of the city were exhibited in 2009, during a period when Tehran experienced protests and unrest for months. Mohajer frankly said that he took the photographs a year before those events, and in a note accompanying the exhibition, he identified his work as an homage to the early 20th-century photographer of Paris, Eugène Atget (Mohajer, 2019). The context in which any photograph is exhibited, however, changes its meaning. Mohajer's photographs were like images of an abandoned, burned-out city with no sign of the noisy tumult of Tehran's unrest in them. Due to the long exposure times, Mohajer leaned on walls or situated the camera on the ground, which gives these photographs their extraordinarily unusual angles. Could these perspectives be the various viewpoints of the protesters? Furthermore, the limited detail of the photographs is eerily similar to those taken by mobile phones in Tehran, which at that time were the only means available for broadcasting what unfolded in the streets.

Journalist and critic Fabio Severo wrote an essay in *Dide Magazine* about *Tehran, Undated*. Severo writes, "Our visitor always seems to be seeking protection from a wall, a shop window, sometimes by lying on the ground. The spaces are wide, but the view is oddly narrow, almost hindered. And yet those places feel like they're inhabited by countless stories, events, lives." Referring to the 2009 unrest, Severo reiterated that what one first makes out from the low-quality mobile photos taken by protesters in Tehran at that time was something wholly absent in Mohajer's photographs: the streets were packed with people. He continues:

> *Tehran, Undated* puts us in front of that image, empty roads filled with movement, memories, thoughts. It also asks the viewer to fill them again, to picture how to walk on them, which turn to pick, which shelter to seek. There is a stillness full of noise in those alleys. But the truth is that, from where we stand, we can only imagine it. (Severo, 2010)

Interpretations and glosses laid onto Mohajer's photographs by their display context changed the series from an homage to Atget to an urgent political commentary. Consequently, it caused younger photographers such as Mohammad Ghazali and Sasan Abrit to notice this sociopolitical potential, founded upon the photographer's subjectivity in interacting with his society, specifically through the genre of the urban landscape. Mohajer was already active in teaching in the leading art universities in Tehran, and many of these photographers were his former pupils.[5] These young photographers were interested in Mohajer's questions on the photographic medium, and they tried to express the theme of absence through various pictorial tactics. Nevertheless, instead of seeing what was happening in Tehran's streets, they chose "not seeing" as their strategy. While these photographers were numerous, the result of their work was quite unlike the ubiquity of images by citizen photographers, which escaped censorship to be transmitted in the first weeks of the protests. Those pictures of a turbulent, animated city, with people occupying the streets, were antiaesthetic yet nonetheless striking given their historical importance. In direct contrast, art photographers remade the city to be empty and in many ways aestheticized this emptiness. Nevertheless, these photographs are implicitly claimed by the photographers themselves to be political and resistant to a disciplinary force, just like those images by citizen photographers. Mohajer's work, however unwittingly, benefited by providing an open-ended visual equivalent of the muted voice. In the projects that followed, the political tone became apparent, and the photographers then directed the audience's reading.

Figure 7.2

Sasan Abri, *Conjunctivitis*, 2012. Pigmented inkjet print, 86 cm×84 cm. Courtesy of the artist.

See also Plate 10.1.

Sassan Abri's *Conjunctivitis* is one of those projects and was exhibited at Silk Road Gallery in 2012. (fig. 7.2) Like Mohajer's earlier series, Abri's photographs lack detail and photographic sharpness. To achieve the abovementioned absence, Abri used a Polaroid camera and manipulated the image during the photographic processing stage. Afterward, he scanned his images before blowing them up on a computer to print in an oversize format (86×84 cm). In spite of their size, there is little concrete detail to see in these large, reproduced Polaroids. Representation in the photographs is problematized, yet their extreme red and blue tones manage to create formal harmony.

A distinction between Abri's and Mohajer's projects is that Abri has recognizable symbols of and references to the Iranian regime—the Islamic Republic of Iran's flag, for instance, or a watchtower. These signs provide the context for political readings of the photographs. Abri names the series *Conjunctivitis* with reference to an infection of the eye, and with a vague, cautiously worded statement, Abri connects the photographs and their title to the experience of fear. He writes, "This is no simple chemical reaction; it is fear's insidious effect. A fear born from the constant view of distant states extended so very near. So distant that they are invisible, indecipherable, yet so close, that their shapes create fear."[6] Here, the series' title and its statement restrict and orient the viewer's reading, filling the void in the pictures by creating a cause-and-effect relationship between image and word. While the statement issues a claim to confront and critique authority, the image ends up showing what "power" hopes to see: empty streets—that is, the negation of what previous citizen photographers captured of the crowded protests in 2009. It is no accident that these highly aestheticized photographs found their display in a gallery in Farmanieh, one of the most expensive neighborhoods of Tehran; its market proximity offers a sense for how such works, even with their political connotations, could be sellable to a particular social class in Tehran.

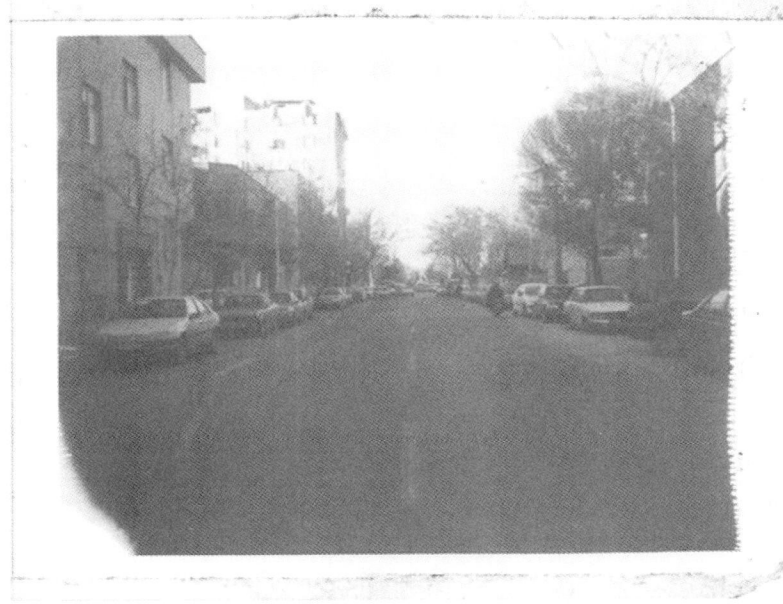

Figure 7.3

Mohammad Ghazali, *Tehran a Little to the Right*, 2010–2013. Expired Polaroid film, 8.5 cm×10.5 cm. Courtesy of the artist.

See also Plate 10.2.

Mohammad Ghazali's series, *Tehran a Little to the Right*, exhibited at Assar Gallery a year after *Conjunctivitis*, shares similarities with Abri's own project. (fig. 7.3) For this series, Ghazali stands in the middle of the street while capturing his photographs. In most of them, we are faced with a similar perspective. He, too, makes use of formal and spatial absences, here created within an emphasis on chemical manipulation. He uses expired Polaroid film and bleaches the left-hand side of his images erratically. The damage is less severe in some of the works of the series, but the process nevertheless continues. In the last few images of the series, with the sequence suggested by Ghazali in the show and the PDF provided on his website, almost nothing is definite, and most of the frames are empty.[7] Like Abri, Ghazali invokes Tehran's unrest in the series text, written by the writer Akram Afshar as a letter to the Czech novelist Milan Kundera. Facing opposition from the gallery, the text wasn't displayed in the gallery but was published a year later in the journal *Landscape Stories*. Afshar writes:

> To be honest, this isn't a typical letter. It is a friendly heart-to-heart, perhaps written to draw your attention to the events, which took place in … Tehran is the capital city of my country, Iran. And the reason for …, which shared results similar to those of the Prague Spring. (Ghazali, 2014)

The letter's censored parts—replaced in the text with ellipses—find an analog in the bleached spaces of Ghazali's photographs, and, as with the text, the viewer is compelled to fill them with specific political references. The photographs represent city streets whose connotations and connections to recent events remain unclear, just as unclear as the reasons behind his use of expired film. Nevertheless, under one image, the artist writes the location and date, "Tehran, 2010," linking the photographed locations and the content of the text. What is the link between the bleached left side of the photos and political parties in Iran? Although Ghazali risks several indirect references to Tehran's turmoil, this reading depends greatly on Afshar's text. A different exhibition statement, or the absence of Afshar's letter (which did occur for the exhibition), turns these photographs into another project entirely. For instance, let's imagine that this is a series in which the photographer has been photographing locations where he made memories with an ex-lover. The burned-out parts of photos could be both a symbol of burning love and a loss of memory. In this reading, the left side, of course, is the place from where the heart of our sensitive photographer would have been torn out. Thus, this speculative context doesn't let the audience fill the absence with their own experience of post-2009 Tehran. Yet one does not have to imagine an alternative scenario or speculate further, given the Polaroid's colorful saturation and warmth, and the obsolescence of the film that Ghazali chooses. Ghazali's photographs, like Abri's, first and foremost look beautiful and desirable. Their romantic aesthetics stand in stark contrast with images taken by citizen photographers and the social realities of the time.

Figure 7.4

Mehran Mohajer, *Closed*, 2013. Pigmented inkjet print on fine art paper, 60 cm×90 cm. Courtesy of the artist.

See also Plate 10.3.

So far, I have discussed the influence on contemporary photography by Mehran Mohajer's *Tehran, Undated*, which came to incorporate new meaning in the context of Tehran in 2009. Mohajer himself was also influenced by a certain mood in Iranian photography, creating a series called *Closed*. (fig. 7.4) In this series, some obstacles are placed in the camera's way, in front of the views of the city; for instance, a piece of tape placed in front of the camera's view that works like an obstructive dam. We can consider the series as a response to the closed social and political atmosphere of Iran in those days. This time, unlike in *Tehran, Undated*, Mohajer offers his clear intentions in his statement: "These photos are the result of these years." (Mohajer, 2013) The refusal of simple readings, which we can see in Mohajer's best works, is instead replaced here with a cause-and-effect relationship between the title and text, on the one hand, and the photographs themselves, on the other. Also, the visibility of certain objects, such as a satellite dish—a media broadcast technology that is illegal in Iran—leaves no choice but for the audience to read a certain political meaning. While the series is visually appealing, almost like a modernist monochrome, its sociopolitical function tends to demonstrate the claustrophobia of the contemporary social atmosphere.

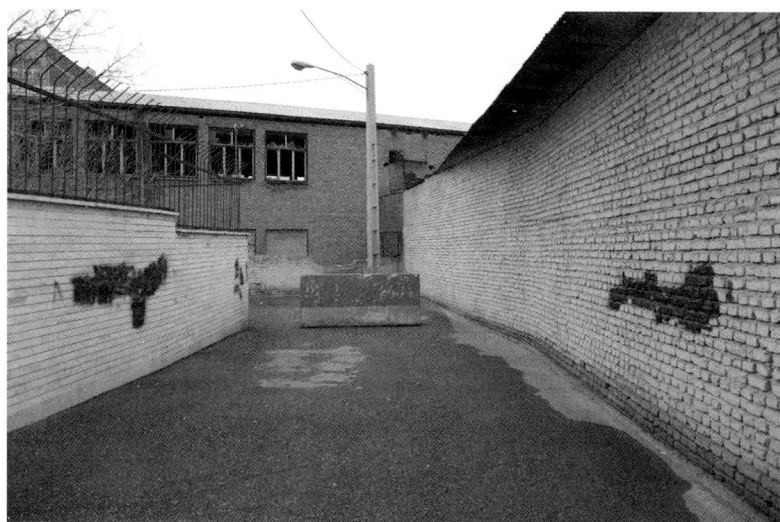

The artist Ehsan Barati takes a different approach in *The Other City*, which was exhibited at Azad Art Gallery in 2013. (fig. 7.5) Just like Abri and Ghazali, Barati is Mohajer's pupil. Unlike his mentor and his peers, however, his work does not critique the representative qualities of photography through formalism. Like the Situationist International of 1960s Paris, he plots four paths in four different directions in Tehran. Following these new cardinal directions, Barati tries to distance his camera from Tehran's official face, forcing him to portray the city's reality that is perhaps less visible. His photographs are empty of people, too, but in this case, because he encounters urban spaces that are left empty. Despite the fact that Barati photographs the city of Tehran, he omits geographical indicators and recognizable landmarks as much as possible. There is no statement or title to invoke a political reading, yet interestingly, viewers are compelled to see the works as commenting on Tehran's general political atmosphere in the wake of 2009. The last photo in the series shows a dead-end alley, where we find an abandoned green block (again, green was the symbol of Iran's freedom movement and the protesters of 2009). There are some slogans written by the police on the walls, which, ironically, have become unintelligible. Toward the background stands a building whose windows are all broken. This image, and the spirit in the architecture, gives news of an ending. Presenting this series in 2013, when the protests of that time had faded, it seems to portray a city with no life in it. The only things left are boredom, violence, and the disappointment of empty streets.

Photographers Mehrdad Naraghi and Hannaneh Parvin (the latter another pupil of Mohajer) infuse Tehran with atmospheric mystery and emotional intensity in their recent series. In *The City*, which was exhibited at Ag Galerie in 2015, Naraghi gives an apocalyptic quality to Tehran, too, but with two significant differences from Barati's *The Other City*. The first is that Naraghi works with Tehran's official face, including photographs of Tehran's recognizable urban views that are rendered in deep grays or blacks. Whether through digital manipulation or camera exposure, Naraghi obtains deliberately underexposed photographs. The result is similar to Mohajer's expression of absence in *Tehran, Undated*. Secondly, the urban void is then filled with the photographer's own words, accompanying the photographs as his statement. At first glance, the project seems to address issues such as air pollution and other environmental concerns, but upon further examination, it becomes clear that the photographer's desire is to relate these urban environments to postelection turmoil. Here is Naraghi's short statement:

My city is one ravaged by the storms, an unrecognizable city, with undefined inhabitants concealed within its grayness. Dazed and confused, with gaping mouths and struggling to breathe. Unconcerned but smiling at another's misery. Neither breaths sighed return to be breathed nor are desires fulfilled; greyness overwhelms. My city is the endless rule of grey.[8]

The tone is primarily emotional, expressing the grays of the photographs. One considers a symbolic quality to them as well; gray is supposed to be symbolic, not simply a symptom of the camera's exposure or evidence of air pollution. The reduction of Tehran to an emotional condition is a risky approach, and instead of confronting the viewer, it might appease them. This affect, when perceived in the series as a whole, draws away from the striking form of the first few photographs.

A work by Hananeh Parvin, exhibited at Ehsan Gallery in 2015 as *The Glass City*, is similar to Naraghi's *The City*. If Naraghi attempts to cover up detail with either exposure or processing, Parvin takes to the urban landscape as already full of visible and invisible barriers. Here, glass always stands between the lens and the city, from the windshield of a car to the plateglass of a bus station. This reminds us of Mohajer's *Closed*, while for Parvin the layer between lens and cityscape has become transparent here. It also has similarities with Abri's *Conjunctivitis*, because signs with everyday meanings are emphasized in Parvin's pictures. This includes a red cross emblazoned on glass that offers atmosphere to the city, or a "No Parking" sign amended with "sending students abroad" written underneath, speaking to the brain drain of the city's citizens. Other photographs of lines and scratches on glass take the image into abstraction, distorting the relationship between figure and ground. Yet Parvin's Tehran also gets caught up in sentimentality, and it seeks to represent absence in the city. Some pictures lapse into pictorialism, and others fail to avoid a different trap: one of sociopolitical sloganeering, pointing to the citizens' brain drain. Like other series discussed in this chapter, *The Glass City* tends to distance itself from the burst of ubiquitous representations of Tehran following the political turmoil in 2009.

One long-term project among these cityscapes is Arash Hanaei's *The Capital*, which began in 2009 and lasted until 2015. In practice, Hanaei chooses a similar strategy in escaping the documentary photography of Tehran that recorded the political moment, using pictorial exaggerations like those employed by Parvin and Naraghi. The results, however, cast Hanaei as completely distinct from those photographers. He uses a process of graphic elimination, and his pictures avoid faithfully representing Tehran. However, he boldly emphasizes specific details that open up the possibility for more complex questions to emerge. Employing detailed digital techniques, he removes parts of the photos, and he turns the leftovers into surfaces or architectural outlines. Hanaei's images ultimately become similar to panels from a two-tone, black-and-white comic strip, a format that achieves textual comprehension through captions and speech bubbles. In Hanaei's work, however, there is no sign of such texts to guide us. We are faced with a location in a cartoon world where the only legible signs are advertisements and religious slogans, which seem to have been reborn in this world from scratch. In Hanaei's Tehran, commercial billboards and murals of war martyrs are not dissimilar, and the juxtaposition of ideological messages and brand slogans veer toward the absurd. Putting comic strip graphics—often cast as immoral, sexually promiscuous, and violent by critics—to work on a city rife with conflicted messages points to what is eliminated from the official face of the city. Putting real-life heroes in a medium that is home to fantastic and imaginary stories creates a striking contradiction. Hanaei tacitly suggests that those heroes, who have always been displayed prominently on the media outlets of authority, are characters in a larger story, suggestive of a comic narrative that goes beyond the history of art photography and its subjective connotations.

Conclusion

In the past decade, more than at any other time, Tehran has been one of the more vibrant subjects of photography in Iran. The presence of Mehran Mohajer, as an active photographer and as an educator in the leading Iranian institutions, compelled a new group of Iranian photographers to represent Tehran within particular medium-specific approaches meant to capture the city and its many absences. Absence in post-2009 Tehran became more meaningful and representative of many events, emotions, and stories that do not project the official face of the city. However, as discussed in this chapter, many Iranian photographers fill this absence with specific narratives and poetics, which seems to be a challenging strategy. Aestheticized images, with overloaded emotional statements about sadness and fear, thus became a commodity in the Iranian art market.

A criticism often leveled at contemporary Iranian art since the 1990s—namely, its oversimplification of sociopolitical issues to be quickly packaged and transmitted to an international audience—can also be applied to the way in which these photographers interact with Tehran.[9] Both of these manifestations of new Iranian art can be strangely considered as visually attractive products for their respective audiences with different tastes, especially in the context of the growth of galleries and the art market in Iran since the mid-2000s.

While this chapter analyzes photographic series exhibited in Iran's artistic mainstream, displayed on the walls of various Tehran galleries, there were also series that, for different reasons (including censorship), never had the chance to confront audiences in such spaces. (Mehraneh Atashi's *Tehran's Self-Portraits* is one significant example of a series missing gallery exposure.) Yet we should not forget how photography today is produced and consumed on monitors or mobile screens and finds its audience in this way. The images of Tehran recorded by citizen photographers did so without thinking about the main currents of Iranian art, and their work necessitates its own historical and critical analysis. While there have been restrictions on the transmission of such images, photos of the 2009 protests can still provide necessary context for understanding the capabilities of the medium today. Those intrepid photographers of the street have just as much to add to our definition of documentary photography as they do to that of contemporary art photography.

Notes

1. The cheaper process helped many photographers who did not attend BFA programs to work without needing to learn the darkroom process or have access to it. Many Iranian photographers hold workshops in private institutions (such as the Mahe Mehr Institution in Tehran), and young photographers still benefit from this critical and theoretical environment.

2. These categories are borrowed from an analysis by Iranian critic Iman Afsarian (Afsarian, 2016: 507).

3. Unfortunately, not everyone used a hashtag with their pictures.

4. "Where is my vote?" was a motto used during the protests in Tehran after the 2009 Iranian presidential election, in which protesters demanded the removal of Mahmoud Ahmadinejad from office.

5. For instance, University of Tehran, Art University, Azad University, and the Mahe Mehr Institution.

6. This statement was installed on one of the walls in the gallery.

7. See http://mohammadghazali.com.

8. This statement was presented in the gallery accompanying Naraghi's photographs.

9. For instance, see the articles by Majid Akhgar, Iman Afsarian, and Vahid Hakim in *Herfeh Honarmand Quarterly Magazine* no. 33 (2010).

Bibliography

Iman Afsarian, "Tars-i Aqab Māndigī, va Mikānīsm-i Difā'ī," in *Dar Justujū-yi Zamān-i Naw: Darāmadī bar Tārīkh-i Intiqādī-i Hunar-i Mu'āṣir-i Īrān*, vol. 2, ed Iman Afsarian (Tehran: Herfeh Honarmand Publications, 2016), 503–515.

Amir Ahmadi Arian, *Sho'ār Nivīsī bar Dīvār-i Kāghazī* (Tehran: Cheshmeh Publications, 2014).

T. J. Clark, "Clement Greenberg's Theory of Art," *Critical Inquiry*, 9, 1 (1982): 139–156.

Mohammad Ghazali, "Iran," *Landscape Stories*, 16 (2014), http://magazine.landscapestories.net/en/archive/2014/iran/projects/mohammad-ghazali (accessed September 1, 2021).

Mehran Mohajer, *Basteh*, exh. Cat. (Tehran: Azad Art Gallery, 2013).

Mehran Mohajer, *Dide Magazine*, 7 (October 2010), http://www.didemag.com/07/00.htm (accessed December 20, 2019).

Fabio Severo, "On Foreign Roads," *Dide Magazine*, 7 (October 2010), http://www.didemag.com/07/00.htm (accessed December 20, 2019).

8. Evidence of Feeling: Race, Police Violence, and the Limits of Documentation

Catherine Zuromskis

Over the weekend of June 8, 2019, another cell phone video briefly went viral. As it begins, William Ewell, a twenty-four-year-old Black man, is seen kneeling on a street corner in Hawthorne, California, with his hands behind his head. Behind him are a cluster of police cars and armed police officers. At least five of the officers are sheltered behind the open doors of the police cars, pointing their guns at Ewell. The videographer, Sky Holsey, introduces the scene to her viewers, panning across the intersection and pointing out the officers and their guns. She then tries to de-escalate the situation, alternating between announcing that she is filming, coaching Ewell to not to move or resist because "they will shoot you," and asking the officers "is all that really necessary?" As the situation continues, she becomes increasingly distraught. She states that her boyfriend was killed by police in 2015 and pleads, "Can somebody put your guns down and please come get him?" After about two minutes, the police approach Ewell, handcuff him, and lead him over to a police car. One officer approaches Holsey in an apparent attempt to both calm her down and block the view of her camera. He explains mildly, "We are just detaining him, OK? We're not saying he's a suspect, but we are just trying to figure out what's going on, alright?" She continues to film for another few minutes as Ewell is questioned, and once it is apparent that the mortal danger has passed, the video switches off.

Holsey's video follows a long and troubling history of images of the exploitation, suffering, and death of Black citizens that goes back to the dawn of photography, and even before. But the current prevalence of cell phone cameras and social media networks has made the production and circulation of such videos ubiquitous and relentless. Increasingly, citizens have sought to mobilize technology to document and publicize the ongoing harassment, assault, and killing of Black civilians by mostly white law enforcement, and once recorded, individuals feel increasingly compelled to watch and share. Over the past decade or so, the murders of George Floyd, Eric Garner, Oscar Grant, Antwon Rose, Keith Lamont Scott, Alton Sterling, and Walter Scott have all been captured on cell phone video by relatives, friends, or bystanders. Diamond Reynolds livestreamed the death of her boyfriend Philando Castile on Facebook to an audience of millions after he was shot in his car by a cop during a traffic stop. Police dashcam, body camera, and surveillance camera footage surrounding of the deaths of Daniel Prude, Tamir Rice, Michael Brown, Christian Taylor, Terrence Crutcher, Laquan McDonald, Stephon Clark, and Atatiana Jefferson circulate in the news media and proliferate on video-sharing sites such as YouTube. And there are other, less lethal but equally unjust examples—Sandra Bland's cell phone video of Texas state trooper Brian T. Encinia threatening her with a stun gun at a traffic stop before her arrest (she later died in jail of an apparent suicide); a teenage bystander's video of McKinney, Texas police officer Eric Casebolt physically assaulting fifteen-year-old Dajerria Becton at a pool party; a Rochester, New York police officer's body camera documented his handcuffing and pepper spraying of a nine-year-old-girl when she resisted being put into a police car. Indeed, by comparison, Holsey's video of the arrest of William Ewell barely registers. It received some coverage in the twenty-four-hour news cycle immediately after the video surfaced, but given the comparative lack of sensational content (no one was killed or seriously injured, Ewell was released with a citation shortly after his arrest), the media and the public quickly moved on.

The impulse to make, share, and view these documents seems fairly straightforward. Cameras have long been figured as ideal witnesses. They are distinct from other media technologies, because they offer a mechanical, indexical, and indiscriminate trace of what appears before the lens. As Roland Barthes famously insists of photography, one "can never deny that the thing has been there." (Barthes, 1981: 76) Andre Bazin takes it even further, describing the photograph as "the object itself" and cinema as "objectivity in time." (Bazin, 1960: 6) And while the digital video of a cell phone camera lacks the true indexicality of an analog photograph or film frame, Janna Houwen has convincingly posited, evoking Barthes, a "rhetorical reality effect […] by way of formal features that signify veracity, documentary, and authenticity." (Houwen, 2017: 27) Thus, even as recent scholarship has begun to raise questions about the primacy of indexicality in theorizations of lens-based media (Elkins, 2007) and the accuracy of journalism has been called into question in the "post-truth" era, our practical understanding that the camera image is an objective representation of reality appears largely unaffected. The documentary trace is still figured as a factual account of the incident it depicts. This faith in the evidentiary function of the camera, combined with the increasingly ubiquitous presence of cameras in everyday life has spurred a flourishing culture of citizen journalism and advocacy for police body cameras in hopes that increased visibility will lead to a more transparent and just exercise of police (and other) authority.

Yet while our faith in camera technologies to provide incontrovertible evidence persists, the legal authority of the camera witness is less assured. On early New Year's Day of 2009, several passengers on a stopped Bay Area Rapid Transit train in Oakland, California documented with their cell phones as, on the platform, transit police officer Johannes Mehserle shot a handcuffed and prone Oscar Grant in the back. Harrowing as the footage was, at trial, Mehserle verbally testified that he had meant to reach for his taser and not his gun, which largely outweighed the damning visual evidence. Mehserle served less than fifteen months in prison for involuntary manslaughter. Despite the livestream of Philando Castile's suffering and death after being shot five times at point blank range—the video received nearly 2.5 million views on Facebook within the first twenty-four hours—as well as dashcam footage of the shooting, officer Jeronimo Yanez was acquitted of all charges related to Castile's death. After viewing Ramsey Orta's graphic cell phone footage of officer Daniel Pantaleo pushing Eric Garner to the ground and choking him to death, a Staten Island Grand Jury failed to produce even an indictment for Pantaleo.[1] Video documentation has also failed to produce a conviction, and in some cases even an indictment, in the deaths of Keith Scott, Alton Sterling, Terrence Crutcher, Tamir Rice, Freddie Gray, Michael Brown, Sandra Bland, Christian Taylor, Antwon Rose, Stephon Clark, and Daniel Prude, and officers who were convicted in similar cases have, overall, received remarkably light sentences for their crimes. Indeed, as Louis-George Schwartz has compellingly shown, motion picture documentation has long required strategic positioning to serve effectively as evidence, and it is equally susceptible to counterpositioning by attorneys who seek to call this kind of evidence into question. (Schwartz, 2009) As in the case of the failed prosecution of the four Los Angeles Police Department officers who were captured on video beating Black motorist Rodney King in 1991, the camera image of the crime may be emotionally moving, it may bring the viewer viscerally close to the horrific act, sparking anguish and public outrage, but as hard legal evidence, such traces prove to be stunningly unstable and open to interpretation.

The ubiquity of such videos paired with their repeated legal inefficacy has significant implications for the presumed evidentiary function of lens-based media. The issue here is not simply that the promise of objectivity and juridical authority in the camera image is and has long been a false one. Almost from the moment of its invention, photography's potential as a form of visual evidence was met with equal parts enthusiasm and skepticism. (Mnookin, 1988) From photography's inception, critics have understood that the camera could lie and embellish. Visual documentation of crime scenes has evolved accordingly, developing an extensive list of rules, procedures, and best practices designed, among other things, to minimize the distortions and biases injected into the image by the human camera operator. Citizen journalists often fail in this regard. In one radio interview, for example, Carlos Miller, author of *The Citizen Journalist's Photography Handbook* and founder of the organization Photography Is Not a Crime, was asked to offer a quick primer on amateur cell phone documentation. Miller cautioned would-be citizen journalists, above all, to keep quiet. All too frequently, he states, cell phone videos of police brutality are corrupted by vocalized expressions of outrage, empathy, and despair on the part of the videographer (Gladstone, 2015). Yet, as Miller's guidelines suggest, it is difficult to keep quiet. American politics, particularly surrounding issues of race, have so long operated in the realm of affective relations it is difficult to consider an alternative response.

I argue that, even as it has the potential to undermine the legal authority of the evidentiary trace, this affective response is also central to the appeal of this form of documentation. At once an impassioned plea for justice on the part of the videographer and, for the viewer, a means of confronting and "experiencing" the brutality of that injustice by proxy, these viral videos of police violence constitute a complex new form of visual evidence, one that is defined not by the ontological properties of lens-based media producing factual accounts, but by various and intersecting histories, social conventions, and political ideologies grounded in emotional response. In what follows, I will situate this evidentiary form within historical debates surrounding documentary images of atrocity, conventions of vernacular film and photography, and the visual culture of race in America. In so doing, I suggest that, contra the culturally constructed fantasy of a disciplined democratic society maintained through the ubiquity of citizen journalists with cell phones and police body cameras, this evidentiary mode privileges affective connection to, over legal justice for, the victim. And while these images have the potential to galvanize resistance to the institutional forms of white power they represent—as so vividly occurred around the documentation of the murder of George Floyd in summer of 2020—they also demand a more complex, situational, and ambiguous understanding of evidentiary technologies.

Images of Violence

The camera image of Black suffering and death as both a touchstone for emotional experience and a site of interpretive negotiation has a long history in America. From the daguerreotypes and cartes-de-visite of Black slaves circulated by the abolitionist movement, to the graphic lynching photographs of the late 19th and early 20th centuries used to propagate narratives of white supremacy and Black criminality in the Jim Crow–era south, to the photographs of Emmett Till's mutilated remains published in *Jet* magazine—widely cited for catalyzing the civil rights movement—the indexical image of Black suffering and death has been effectively mobilized both for and against Black communities in the United States.[2] But while such images of Black death may be, as Leigh Raiford suggests, an iconic part of American visual culture, the proliferation of smartphones and surveillance cameras, and the fluid accessibility of digital networks and social media, have increased the visibility of such images and brought new and distinct contexts of articulation to their consumption. Almost everyone has a cell phone camera in their pocket, and the impulse to pull it out and start shooting is now ingrained in everyday culture.[3] Once captured, social media platforms such as Facebook and Snapchat, as well as dedicated software and networks like the American Civil Liberties Union Mobile Justice app and the Photography Is Not a Crime website facilitate the wide and immediate circulation of these images to an eager public.

This, in turn, has given birth to a thriving secondary culture of appropriations, re-enactments, and memes from both the right and the left. Video stills and snapshots of victims grace murals, shrines, and clothing as forms of mourning and remembrance. They inspire artistic interpretations such as Henry Taylor's painting, *THE TIMES THEY AINT A CHANGING FAST ENOUGH!* (2017) included in the Whitney Biennial, and Ryan Coogler's heart-wrenching 2013 film *Fruitvale Station* (winner of the Sundance Grand Jury Prize and Best New Film at Cannes). They guide the language of protest against the structural inequalities that sanction these crimes. Hoodies like the one worn by young Trayvon Martin on the night he was shot by neighborhood watchman George Zimmerman were donned in protest by the Miami Heat basketball team and members of Congress. Eric Garner's last words, "I can't breathe," became a rallying cry for Black Lives Matter, inspired a song by the feminist punk band Pussy Riot, and emblazoned an iconic T-shirt worn publicly by athletes and celebrities from National Basketball Association all-star LeBron James to acclaimed filmmaker Ava DuVernay.

At the same time, reactionaries and countermovements such as Blue Lives Matter create their own rhetoric and iconography around these images. After Garner's death, counterprotesters wore and sold shirts emblazoned with the slogans "I CAN breathe, thanks to the NYPD" and "Breathe easy, don't break the law." Videos of police violence ground what Donte Newman calls the "ambivalent discourse" of conservative posters on social media, who present themselves as sympathetic and unbiased by stating sympathy for the individual Black victim, while maintaining that "the shooting had absolutely nothing to do with race." (Sangillo, 2018)

Conservative media pundits frame evidentiary traces as subject to inter-pretation, describe victims of police shootings as "no angels," and cite instances of petty theft, resisting arrest, or perceived moral failings as justification for murder. While presented under the thin veil of rational interpretation, these counternarratives from the right stoke, and are, in turn, fueled by race panic and righteous anger over the potential loss of white power held in the promise of racial justice. Thus, like the activism and outrage from the left, these reactionary responses draw on the visual spectacle of Black death as a symbolic anchor for impassioned and affective political discourse.

Questions about the political implications of looking at images of violence and atrocity have long concerned scholars of photography. On the one hand, as Susan Sontag emphatically argued, photographs of suf-fering and violence are no mere passive representations, and are often constructed and wielded to humiliate and subordinate the photograph-ic subject, as was the case with lynching photography or the more re-cent example of photographs of prisoner torture at Abu Ghraib prison. (Sontag, 2004)[4] If we take this idea to heart, then the act of looking itself implies a form of participation in the spectacle of Black suffering and, with it, the subtle effacement of the white violence that causes that suf-fering.[5] As John Berger cautions in his still bracing essay on the graphic photojournalism of the Vietnam War, even if one is troubled by such images, the moment of arrest or shock inspired by photographs of agony may also be the very thing that distracts the viewer from engaging in real political change. (Berger, 1991) Worse still, images of suffering may inure us to violence such that we cease to feel much at all.

On the other hand, failing to confront the severity of the problem and tuning out bad feelings that may also undermine new political realizations is equally problematic. In her book *The Civil Contract of Photography*, Ariella Azoulay posits an obligation on the part of the spectator to acknowledge the insistent presence of the subject and heed the call to "recognize and restore their citizenship." (Azoulay, 2008: 17) Moreover, as Sharon Sliwinski demonstrates, photography is itself foundational to human rights, a concept that "did not emerge from the abstract articulation of an inalienable human dignity but rather from a particular visual encounter with atrocity." (Sliwinski, 2011: 58) As Meg McLagen and Yates McKee suggest, central to this activist potential of photography is precisely its ability to provoke emotional response; the photograph combines "evidentiary truth value" with "affectual address […] to mobilize sentiments of anger, shame, and outrage." (McLagen and McKee, 2012: 19)

Ultimately, as these scholarly debates make clear, the question of whether it is just to look at images of atrocity has no clear answer, and the social and political value of such traces has everything to do with the particularities of the image and where and how it is encountered. In her book *Humane Insight*, for example, Courtney R. Baker finds in images of atrocity instances of both exploitation and political resistance. (Baker, 2017) The lynching photographs of the early 20th century were originally produced by professional photographers and amateur snapshooters alike as a means of asserting white dominance over Black populations in the American South. Yet they were also significantly repurposed first by Ida B. Wells and the National Association for the Advancement of Colored People and later in the exhibition and book *Without Sanctuary* in efforts to raise awareness and bring the violent practice to an end. (Allen, 2000) While none of the many antilynching bills proposed in U.S. Congress ever passed, it is clear that the visceral response to these violent images helped coalesce a national community of opposition through the iconic visual representation of the lynched Black male body.[6] By offering a less restrictive and, importantly, more situational consideration of how specific images have been presented and represented over time, Baker demonstrates various ways that images of Black suffering and death have been used effectively, if imperfectly, to inscribe Black bodies within the ideological construct of humanity.

However, for all the echoes of iconic images of past Black suffering and death in contemporary images of police violence, the latter is also distinct, both for the technological frameworks in which it circulates and the sociopolitical phenomena those frameworks help to facilitate. Indeed, in a later essay in the *Los Angeles Review of Books*, Baker offers a decidedly less measured response to recent depictions of police brutality against African Americans. Titled "The E-snuff of Alton Sterling and Philando Castile," this essay suggests that the current twenty-four-hour news cycle and the proliferation of social media platforms wrest images of Black suffering and death from the control of those who might present them in a sympathetic or effective manner. She writes:

> Contexts of care and of justice are absent and at times anathema to the mass media entities that carelessly circulate these images for titillation or profit [...] As long as these images and videos are published alongside cries that blue lives matter and queries about black-on-black crime and recitations of the victims' irrelevant criminal histories, they have no place in the public sphere. (Baker, 2016)

The indexical image of Black suffering and death, then, is neither inherently exploitative nor fundamentally humanizing—or rather, it is perhaps always a bit of both—but vital to its meaning and political efficacy (contra the totalizing rhetoric of theorists like Sontag) is a careful consideration of the media frameworks through which one encounters the image.

In this regard, the issue is not just that digital media platforms are unruly or careless (though they often are), but that lens-based media both analog and digital, as well as the digital networks through which images circulate, are themselves ingrained with racial bias. (On the racial bias of the internet, see Daniels, 2018; Nakamura, 2008; and Noble, 2018a.) From the oft-cited Google Gorilla Glitch (where Google's image algorithm repeatedly identified images of Black people as apes), to the Shirley cards created by Kodak to calibrate their color film to best represent white skin tones, visual media technologies have so long been encoded with racial bias, that it is all but impossible to separate the two. As Lisa Nakamura argues, "racism is less a virus in the internet's body than it *is* that body." (Nakamura, 2014: 269–270) These media biases are all the more insidious for being naturalized via the rhetoric of technological objectivity—the mechanical camera-eye that looks indiscriminately, or the algorithm that supposedly circumvents implicit bias. And while the internet and social media have, in certain instances, proved a vital network for progressive political activism and reform—many cite the Arab Spring uprisings between 2010 and 2012—as Nakamura and Safiya Noble have shown, the biases embedded in these technologies serve equally as a cover for racist representations circulated under the guise of good digital citizenship and free markets. (Nakamura, 2014; Noble, 2018b: 147) Whatever original intentions lie behind the production and dissemination of images of police violence against Black civilians, they cannot be considered outside of the technological and algorithmic frameworks of the internet and social media that circulate, promote, and even monetize their consumption.

First Person

Equally important to the contextual meaning of these cell phone videos, as well as their ubiquity and viral appeal, is their vernacular status. I use the term "vernacular" here to describe the agency of the amateur cameraperson as opposed to the professional journalist or automated surveillance camera. While vernacular photography, film, and video are most often associated with the private or domestic realm (family snapshots and home movies), it is useful to consider the effect of vernacularity on citizen journalism, in which the amateur camera captures an event of historical and political import. Imagery such as Alice Seeley Harris's photographs of colonial atrocities in the Congo Free State, the Zapruder film of the assassination of John F. Kennedy, the Rodney King tape, and cell phone documentation of the ravages of the 2004 tsunami in Aceh province, Indonesia are justly iconic as instances in which an amateur bystander with a camera was able to capture what the press could not or chose not to.[7] As this range of examples suggests, citizen journalism also has a long history, and while the ubiquity of the camera is often cast as a digital phenomenon, the development of amateur snapshot, home movie, and video cameras, beginning with the introduction of the Kodak camera over a century ago in 1888, has had an equally profound influence on the proliferation of lens-based media and in daily life. Yet the popularization of cell phone cameras has dramatically facilitated this kind of documentation in recent years. The term "citizen journalism" suggests a kind of crowdsourcing of gathering news. More everyday people on the ground with cameras means more coverage and more diversity of perspectives; thus, citizen journalism is often celebrated for its democratic potential in creating a more open and transparent society. However, it is also necessary to emphasize the way the vernacular status of these images frames what they depict.

On the one hand, the cell phone video, like various lens-based media before it, gives the assurance of truth, based in its ability to depict reality with technical precision, indiscriminateness, and objectivity. While in actuality, the truth value of lens-based media is less an ontological certainty than a system of beliefs surrounding technology, empiricism, and social control, this does not diminish their utility as cultural indicators of truth across social institutions from the sciences to systems of disciplinary control to the press. (On the shifting epistemologies of photographic indexicality, see Gunning, 2008 and Kember, 1998.) In the words of the popular hashtag, "pictures, or it didn't happen." Moreover, vernacular traces often seem even more incontrovertibly true, because, as spontaneous, sometimes even accidental documents produced outside the conventions and ideologies of the professional press, they function as "raw data," free of media spin. Like much of the rhetoric surrounding the naïve "snapshot aesthetic" in late 20th-century art photography, citizen journalism is often framed as a kind of journalism at degree zero, completely absent of motive, style, or ideology and thus factually pure.[8] As such, the amateur status of the image or footage seems to enhance the evidentiary authority of the camera.

At the same time as its vernacular status seems to purge the cell phone video of media bias, it also, somewhat paradoxically, emphasizes the subjective point of view of the person behind the camera and thus invites the viewer to experience what it shows in a more intimate way. This is particularly pronounced in instances like Reynold's livestream of Castile's death or Holsey's video of Ewell's arrest, in which the person filming also narrates the unfolding events from an individual perspective. In both cases, the video is a manifestation of the videographer's own trauma, one that the viewer is invited to engage and experience through the video (however impoverished it may be in comparison to the actual event). But even in cases in which the videographer stays silent, the knowledge alone that a video was shot by an amateur amplifies what Barbie Zelizer has described as the "subjunctive voice" of the news image, one that invites speculation, interpretation, and emotional engagement with the event it represents. (Zelizer, 2010: 23) While documentary and photojournalism have long employed narrative and sentiment to engage and inform the public—John Grierson, who coined the term, candidly defined documentary as "the creative treatment of actuality"—no genre is more suffused with affect and intimacy than vernacular snapshot photographs and home movies and videos. (Grierson, 1933: 8) These kinds of images are both products and representations of interpersonal intimacies. (Zuromskis, 2013) Citizen journalism fuses the sentimental narrative of public events conventionally associated with documentary visual media with the more personal and individualized intimacies of the snapshot or home movie. These traces seem to put the viewer at the scene of the crime in a specifically embodied and affecting way. To view the video is to bear witness and to feel alongside the bystander on the sidelines of history. As a result, these amateur traces seem both more authentic and more poignant, compelling the sympathetic citizen to connect viscerally and emotionally to the victim's humanity, innocence, and suffering.

This is not to say that this is the conscious intent of the person behind the camera. Many of the cell phone videos currently circulating online were filmed by anonymous bystanders, so when it comes to the motive to film, one can only speculate. And in cases where the videographer is known, media coverage tends to focus on the violent act itself rather than the choice to document it, indicating that, at least from the point of view of a major news outlet, the need for visual documentation is a given. However, what little has been reported suggests that, for documenting witnesses who are also people of color—such as Diamond Reynolds, who livestreamed the aftermath of the shooting of her boyfriend, Philando Castile; Ramsay Orta, who filmed the death of Eric Garner; and Rakeyia Scott, who documented the shooting of her husband Keith Lamont Scott—turning on the camera was first and foremost a defensive act. *The New York Times* reported that Reynolds began to livestream the aftermath of Castile's shooting, because she feared for the well-being of herself and her young daughter in the back seat of the car. (Smith, 2017) A feature on Orta in *The Verge* states that, while Orta now regrets making the video (in large part because of alleged retaliation from the New York Police Department), he "knew from experience that anything could happen during these interactions. And so, for him, it had become a form of self-defense to film the police." (Jones, 2019) And as CBS news anchor Gayle King recounted from her interview with Scott, the choice to pull out her phone came out of fear and anticipation of a violent outcome: "she said 'that's what you have to do these days.'" (CBS

This Morning, 2016) In such instances (we might also include Holsey's video), the mobilization of the camera is as much about the act of filming itself as a form of nonviolent resistance against an aggressor empowered by legal authority as it is about creating factual legal evidence for a future date. As David LaRocca argues, considering both Scott and Reynolds among other amateur documentarians:

> The motivation—the 'ethical impulse'—to grab a camera and start rolling [...] does not issue from some noble desire to 'bear witness' for history, or some political motivation to advocate for a position [...] Rather, the ethical impulse in these cases appears to emerge at a private, existential level [...] The camera [...] becomes a kind of proxy force for private inscription, and thereby a space in which to encode one's ownmost potentiality (always a matter of life and death). (Larocca, 2017)

This suggests that, in keeping with other instances of vernacular film and photography—family snapshots and home videos—the cell phone video, even in a life-and-death situation, functions as a form of affective retaliation and self-preservation. (Zuromskis, 2013) The act of filming is as much about making a signifying gesture in the present as it is about producing a stable objective document for the future. Even in the face of death, Reynolds's impulse to film asserts some modicum of control over the narrative and connects her traumatic experience to those of others.

Once produced, however, the vernacular status of these videos is central to their virality. For many, the circulation of this particularly compelling and affecting kind of footage represents a sympathetic political act. For outraged liberal citizens, the videos may be troubling and difficult, but the lure of bearing witness, of seeing through the eyes of the bystander and testifying to that experience is strong and goes largely unquestioned. Yet this same impulse to click, to view, and to share can never be entirely separated from the violence that the images represent, and indeed, the racist ideologues that circulate and consume images of Black suffering to fuel and profit from racist sentiment. As one conflicted reader of Baker's *Los Angeles Review of Books* piece wrote in the comments section, "In a moment of outrage, I posted the video [of Castile's death] and my horror. Then little by little I felt worse and worse until it was clear to me that I was perpetuating violence. I took it down and apologized, too late, I am afraid." (Baker, 2016) Often, and even with the best of intentions, the emotional impulse, grounded in the conventions of vernacular documentation, is first, to look, to show, to share, and to bear witness, so one might acknowledge the feelings that looking engenders. Only later does one consider what the implications of that need to see might be.

Evidence and Feelings

While I do not mean this essay as a challenge to the felt encounter with a documentary image, it is nevertheless important to emphasize the ways in which the same qualities that we may find particularly moving in cell phone videos of police violence, prompting us to click and share, may also undermine their function as evidence. Feelings have an insidious way of undermining factual evidence. In her book *The Emotional Politics of Racism*, Paula Ioanide explores contemporary epistemologies of white ignorance and how obscure evidence of structural racism in society. She notes that "being presented with evidence about systemic injustices of [...] racism rarely has the effect of changing the minds and actions of people who are emotionally invested in holding onto their beliefs, identities, and worldviews." (Ioanide, 2015: 11) In her analysis of yet another case of police brutality against a Black man, the torture of Haitian immigrant Abner Louima by New York Police Department officer Justin Volpe in 1997, Ioanide shows how the retelling of an event may engender sympathies only for specific victims, or worse, tap into "guilty enjoyments of voyeuristic sadism or other emotional economies that justify Black people's violation." (Ioanide, 2015: 64) This is equally an issue in the legal arena. On the face of it, a video documenting a crime in progress would seem to be a powerful and damning piece of evidence. Yet, as Baker and others make clear, the impact of the image is always contingent upon its framing. The grand jury investigating the case of Eric Garner were clearly able to look at Orta's video and see something other than an innocent Black man strangled to death by a police officer on a public street.

And while the transcripts for the Garner grand jury remain sealed, we may gain insight into how this came to be by looking at the 1992 trial concerning the Rodney King beating. As numerous studies of the case have discussed, the acquittal of the four officers who brutalized King was not in spite of, but facilitated by, the vernacular video of the crime. (Nichols, 1994; Gooding-Williams, 1993; Alexander 1994; Schwartz, 2009) The defense presented the jury with numerous stills from the video, dissecting it in detail to make the case that an obvious act of police brutality was instead a procedurally legitimate act of law enforcement to restrain a potentially dangerous civilian. As even a passing familiarity with the present media environment makes clear, no evidence is impervious to interpretation and ideological reframing, and stereotypes of menacing Black men are routinely trotted out in legal and media discourse as justification for racist violence. As Khalil Mohammed argues, the entrenchment of white racial imaginings about Black criminality is so strong that even in the face of hard data—a ProPublica report that Black men are twenty-one times more likely than white men to be killed by law enforcement—attitudes remain unchanged (Muhammed, 2014). Returning to the evidentiary failures of these documentary traces, we might say that, despite its obvious indexicality, the photographic or filmic image may, paradoxically, fail to show us what it shows us and only affirm what we already feel we know.

Why, then, do these images continue to have such cultural currency even among those who are appalled by what they represent? Certainly the feelings of outrage and injustice that one may stir through the visual consumption of images of Black suffering can lead to political action, as they did, quite effectively, for the abolitionist movement, the civil rights movement, and most recently Black Lives Matter protests in the aftermath of the deaths of Eric Garner, George Floyd, and others. At best, as Azoulay argues, images of suffering and atrocity place an obligation on the spectator to redress the wrongs depicted in the image. But this "civil contract of photography" requires one to push beyond affective modes of "empathy or mercy," toward a more regulated and political "covenant for the rehabilitation of [the subject's] citizenship." (Azoulay, 2008: 17) We must be wary, then, about too easily associating emotional response with ideal outcomes and action. Moreover, as Baker suggests, the murders of Castile and Sterling disseminated to the world via cable news and social media are entirely different from Mamie Till-Mobley's decision to allow postmortem photographs of her son Emmett to be published in a weekly news magazine geared explicitly to African American readers. That the Sterling or Castile footage was made as an act of documentary resistance and may be viewed with sadness or outrage, does not, in itself, control the framing of these images in a way that imagines useful alternatives. Moreover, the ubiquity of these sensational images of Black suffering in the current media landscape may ultimately reiterate, or worse, intensify, comfortably familiar narratives of static and systemic racial inequality in America.

Western culture has long employed representations of victimized Black men and women to drum up white sympathies. In *Seeing Through Race*, his groundbreaking study of photography and the civil rights movement, Martin Berger points to the long history in the United States and abroad of making the complexities of racism more accessible and digestible to a sympathetic white audience through images of passive Black men (or women), victim to white aggressors and beholden to white defenders. (Berger, 2011) As vital as photography was to the civil rights struggle in the United States, Berger makes clear that image of stoic Black children marching to newly desegregated schools or of Black men standing passively in front of lunging police dogs and fire hoses, equally "impeded efforts to enact—or even imagine—reforms that threatened white racial power." (Berger, 2011: 7)[9] Media narratives surrounding the deaths of figures such as Grant, Garner, Castile, and

Floyd often conform to similar tropes, tacitly reiterating conventions of white power and conditioning the behavior of Black citizens. Press surrounding the death of Castile, for example, often highlights his job as a nutrition services supervisor at a Montessori school as evidence of his gentle and caring character. A widely circulated smiling photograph of him and a colleague from the school yearbook shores up accounts of his disposition. Garner's apparent genial nature makes him a similarly appealing, tragic figure. In the tributes following his death, Garner was frequently described not only as a dedicated husband and father but also as gentle, kind, a "big teddy bear" and "a neighborhood peacemaker." (McDonald, 2014; Peltz, 2014) In Orta's video, though Garner is clearly agitated, he is at pains to stay reserved, even polite in his encounter with Pantaleo in both word and gesture. *Fruitvale Station* presents yet another portrait of a genial but passive Black character in Oscar Grant (played by Michael B. Jordan). Availing himself of many familiar tropes—child victims; the kid from the wrong side of the tracks who just wants to make good; stoic, mournful Black mothers (two of them); and, in the Grant character, a "magical negro" figure shown on multiple occasions selflessly helping and protecting white people—director Coogler constructs a deeply affecting but uncritically normative depiction of racial injustice. And countless media reports on the death of George Floyd emphasize the poignant detail that he called out to his late mother with his dying breaths. In comparison to other, more "complicated" victims—Michael Brown, for example, whose death seemed easier for the media to justify because of his altercation with a convenience store clerk and Darren Wilson's grand jury testimony that he had a face "like a demon" (*State of Missouri v. Darren Wilson*, 2014)—the stories of Floyd, Castile, Garner, and Grant fit the familiar mold of Black martyrdom.

I mean this in no way as a challenge to the characters of these men or a critique of nonviolence as a mode of political resistance. Nor am I immune to the emotional lure of these narratives. But I do want to draw attention to the way that such cultural texts operate via existing racist conventions that highlight white agency—as both aggressor and potential liberator—and necessitate the polite subservience of Black citizens. While Berger shows that the emotional politics of Black suffering is nothing new, it seems particularly urgent in the present moment, when liberal feelings of righteous outrage are provoked and expressed through the same images and technological networks that have also facilitated a powerful resurgence of white nationalism. By simply ignoring this contiguity, by desiring encounters with bad feeling and asserting them in public forums like social media and popular culture, white liberals (myself included) also cultivate good feeling about ourselves as white liberal political agents and ultimately reinforce the structures of white power.

Conclusion

We arrive, then, at something of an impasse. Cell phone videos chron-icling the epidemic institutional violence against Black civilians in the contemporary United States both reiterate the spectacle of Black suffering and hold the potential to coalesce opposition to institutional racism. They allow for a profound and affecting mode of bearing witness to crimes that they also fail to redress. As such these images both am-plify a sense of social and political urgency surrounding race and high-light the failures of technology and visual culture to effect political alternatives. Yet returning to Azoulay's civil contract of photography, I am compelled to explore the possibility that these contemporary im-ages of police violence might be framed and presented in other, more effective ways, ways that might check the carelessness and individuali-zations of the current media landscape and oblige its viewers to engage the humanity and complexity of its Black subjects on a structural level. Such a project requires a more considered and situational engagement with the nature of documentary technology, the frameworks in which they are presented, and how we receive and interpret them.

This means, first, that we must question our remarkably persistent faith in indexical media. It may seem counterintuitive given how much more publicized these kinds of incidents are thanks to the ubiquity of the cell phone camera and the fluid networking of social media. The revolutionary potential of such technological forms is enticing, but, as is evident in the case of the Rodney King video, no techno-logy is self-determining. Our relationships to cameras and the traces they produce have always been historically contingent, economical-ly motivated, and politicized, be it the citizen journalist's cell phone video or the police body camera. To understand these media as sim-ply objective, indexical, and therefore productive of knowledge (rather than reflective of ideology) is to grossly oversimplify their social func-tion. While there is potential in turning cameras on those in power to monitor their behavior, advocating for more police body cameras or sharing video evidence on social media has not and will not, *in itself*, prevent police violence merely by exposing it. In a moment when feel-ings override facts, we must resist the notion of an uncomplicated, authentic visibility.

Second, we must attend more carefully to our agencies as specta-tors. This could mean heeding Azoulay's directive to "watch," rather than simply look at the photograph, activating our engagement with and responsibility to the subject in videos of police violence, resisting the spectacle of Black suffering and seeking out and indicting systemic white violence. It could also mean following Baker's lead and delib-erately turning away, not as a refusal to engage but as an intentional engagement via refusal. Or we might follow the brilliant work of Tina Campt, who urges us to "listen" for the frequencies of tension within images that do not fit so neatly into binaries of honorific and repressive (Campt, 2017). Citing Allan Sekula classic essay, "The Body and the Archive," Campt's argument builds on the idea that both honorific and repressive images occupy the same "shadow archive" in which everyone is marked and identified (Sekula, 1986). Rather than get caught up in the binary opposition of honorific and repressive, good and bad images, Campt's work suggests that we seek out more complex and ambiguous visualizations of Black futurity, images that highlight the tensions and "effortful equilibrium" of Black life.

I will close, then, with one example of what this kind of complex and ambiguous visualization might look like in the work of Black American cinematographer and video artist Arthur Jafa.[10] Jafa's lauded video works are assembled largely from still images and video footage found on internet platforms such as YouTube (alongside instances of Jafa's own lyrical footage) and set to musical accompaniment. Jafa's work presents images, vernacular and otherwise, in what John Akomfrah has dubbed "affective proximity" to one another to create a more complex and crafted visual experience, one that complicates the stability of any single depiction within it and immerses the viewer in the "effortful equilibrium" of Black life. Jafa's best-known work, the joyous, traumatic, beautiful, gutting 2016 single-channel video *Love is the Message, The Message is Death* immerses the viewer in a range of intimate and iconic images of Black life and culture. In addition to familiar videos of police brutality and Black suffering, *Love is the Message, The Message is Death* includes powerful images of uplift, as well as many that encompass both joy and trauma: President Obama singing "Amazing Grace" during his eulogy for Reverend Clementa Pinckney after the Emanuel African Methodist Episcopal shooting in 2015; dreamily static footage of iconic powerful Black women like Hortense Spillers, Angela Davis, and Aretha Franklin; shaky home videos of Black people death dropping and twerking in clubs and living rooms; a Black couple wading through the floodwaters of Hurricane Katrina. Huey Copeland has described *Love is the Message, The Message is Death* as a form of antiportraiture. While the piece is replete with images of both beauty and suffering, the images come so rapid-fire that, Copeland suggests, they "hedge against the visual capture of Black folks, while throwing light—and shade—on viewers' implication in the digital ecologies through which those images circulate and dis/appear." (Copeland, 2018)

Jafa's video work is steeped in all kinds of affects. While *Love is the Message, The Message is Death* is ecstatic and traumatic, his 2013 video *APEX*, is more anxiety-provoking and unsettling. An eight-minute sequence of still images (mostly photographs) set to a relentless, mechanical techno track ("Minus" by DJ Robert Hood, which feels like a heartbeat racing out of sync with itself), *APEX* offers split-second glimpses of monsters from science fiction and horror movies, the microscopic and the telescopic, David Bowie and Mickey Mouse, and brutal historical images of Black bodies tortured and mutilated. The effect is queasy-making, pulse-quickening, and exhausting. It challenges the impulse to keep looking and to turn away, simultaneously.[11] When images of true horror appear, they emerge and disappear too quickly to be fully comprehended. They function neither as transparent evidence of specific historical events nor as affective spectacles of Black death—instead, they haunt me, obliging me to recognize the civil contract of photography without the catharsis of full understanding.

The affective response to *Love is the Message, The Message is Death* in particular has been so strong that Jafa himself has expressed ambivalence about its success. In an interview with *The Guardian*, he mused, "I started to feel like I was giving people this sort of microwave epiphany about blackness […] After so many 'I cried. I crieds', well, is that the measure of having processed it in a constructive way? I'm not sure it is." (Gebreyesus, 2018) Yet considered alongside his other works, *Love is the Message, The Message is Death* seems less epiphanic and more elusive. Images of Black suffering and death (particularly explicit in *APEX*) are contextualized through Jafa's affective proximities, but in such a way that they can remain necessarily fluid and unfixed, visible, but also, to evoke Krista A. Thompson's groundbreaking work on "video light" in Black diasporic culture, interrupting, disrupting, and blinding. (Thompson, 2015) Rather than seeking out uncomplicated innocent victims as icons for mourning and outrage, it is in contexts like these where indexical traces of Black experience are replicated and reframed within a more complex, contradictory, and fluid space of consumption.[12] In these aesthetic frameworks, the vernacular video of Black suffering and death may begin to find the necessary contexts of care and control that might reconfigure technological networks of consumption and display and challenge the dominant narratives of white power. And perhaps it is here that we might begin to feel and imagine a future that is different from the present.

Notes

1. Perhaps the only decisive action the video produced was the New York Police Derpartment's possible retaliation against Orta, who has repeatedly alleged police harassment and trumped-up arrests for minor offenses. Orta completed a four-year prison term in 2020, making him, as reporter Juan Gonzalez noted in 2016, "the only person at the scene of Garner's killing who will serve jail time." (Goodman and González, 2016)

2. As Leigh Raiford suggests (citing Coco Fusco), not only do such photographs "produce race," but "the negation/annihilation of black people in act and image is constitutive of American identity." (Fusco, 2003: 60; Raiford, 2011: 17)

3. This is not exclusive to instances of police violence. As one feature on Diamond Reynolds reported, "She had always found it cathartic to broadcast her life" and continued to do so, via friends' social media accounts even after her lawyers advised her to close her own. (Saslow, 2016)

4. Sontag also explored this idea in *On Photography*, where she highlighted what she saw as the essential violence and incrimination of photography as a medium. Citing the distance it imposes between photographer and subject and the visual dominance of photographer over subject, she likens the camera to a gun, describes the photographic act as "sublimated murder," and declares unequivocally that "there is an aggression implicit in every use of the camera." (Sontag, 1973: 15)

5. As Richard Dyer has argued, Whiteness has long been constructed as an invisible racial position (Dyer, 1997). Parallel to the invisibility of Whiteness is what Hortense Spillers describes as the "theft of the body" of Indigenous and African peoples during the colonization of the New World and the slave trade. (Spillers, 1987: 67) The objectification and othering of the Black body, absent Black subjectivity and agency, in American visual culture is central to the ongoing invisibility and dominance of Whiteness as a racial category.

6. Leigh Raiford describes lynching imagery as iconic for the way they have been reproduced by Black agents in both art and culture and have come to be "a constitu-

tive element of black visuality." (Raiford, 2011; 18–19) While the practice of lynching in America had largely ended by the 1960s, racially motivated torture and murders like those of Michael Donald in Mobile, Alabama (1981), James Byrd, Jr. in Jasper, Texas (1998), and Alize Ramon Smith and Jarron Keonte Moreland in Moore, Oklahoma (2018) bear many of the features that distinguished lynching as a practice earlier in the century. What is notably missing is the integral function of visual spectacle. As Dora Apel notes in case of Byrd, the crime was so horrific and shameful that no photographs of the body were ever published. (Apel and Smith, 2007: 74–75)

7. The history and political actions spurred by citizen journalism was chronicled in the Bronx Documentary Center's 2016 exhibition *New Documents*.

8. Here, I evoke Geoffrey Batchen's use of the term "photography degree zero," after Roland Barthes's 1953 book *Writing Degree Zero*, to describe an approach to writing "that attempts to achieve a neutral or 'zero degree' of form—a form of writing that, like most photographs, denies it even has a form." (Batchen, 2011; 5) For an extended discussion of the purity and naïveté of the snapshot aesthetic, see Jonathan Green's special issues of *Aperture* on the topic (Green, 1974: 6).

9. Similar arguments about the narrative conventions surrounding representations of the civil rights movement have been made by Raiford (2011) and various authors (particularly Edward Morgan) in Raiford and Romano (2006).

10. I am grateful to Tina Campt for introducing Jafa's work to me in her thoughtful and compelling keynote at the Reframing Family Photography conference at the University of Toronto, September 21–23, 2017.

11. It bears noting that others have very different responses. In Jafa's massive recent monograph, John Akomfrah describes dancing with joy at a screening of *APEX* (Akomfrah, 2018: 71).

12. On the liquidity of Blackness in the cultural sphere, see Raengo et al. (2019).

Bibliography

John Akomfrah, "It Is in the Brewing Luminous," in *A Series of Utterly Improbable, Yet Extraordinary Renditions*, ed. Arthur Jafa (London: Serpentine Galleries, 2018), 67–94.

Elizabeth Alexander, "'Can You Be BLACK and Look at This?': Reading the Rodney King Video(s)," *Public Culture*, 7 (1994): 77–94.

James Allen, ed., *Without Sanctuary: Lynching Photography in America* (Santa Fe: Twin Palms, 2000).

Dora Apel and Shawn Michelle Smith, *Lynching Photographs* (Berkeley: University of California Press, 2007).

Ariella Azoulay, *The Civil Contract of Photography* (Cambridge: Zone Books, 2008).

Courtney Baker, "The E-Snuff of Alton Sterling and Philando Castile," *Avidly*, July 8, 2016, http://avidly.lareviewofbooks.org/2016/07/08/the-e-snuff-of-alton-sterling-and-philando-castile/ (accessed February 18, 2021).

Courtney Baker, *Humane Insight: Looking at Images of African American Suffering and Death* (Urbana, Chicago, and Springfield: University of Illinois Press, 2017).

Roland Barthes, *Camera Lucida: Reflections on Photography* (New York: Hill and Wang, 1981).

Geoffrey Batchen, *Photography Degree Zero: Reflections on Roland Barthes's Camera Lucida* (Cambridge, MA and London: MIT Press, 2011).

André Bazin, "The Ontology of the Photographic Image," *Film Quarterly*, 13, 4 (1960): 4–9.

John Berger, "Photographs of Agony," in *About Looking* (New York: Vintage International, 1991), 37–40.

Martin A. Berger, *Seeing through Race: A Reinterpretation of Civil Rights Photography* (Berkeley: University of California Press, 2011).

Tina Campt, *Listening to Images* (Durham, NC: Duke University Press, 2017).

Huey Copeland, "B.O.s 1 / Love Is the Message, The Message Is Death," *Black One Shot*, June 4, 2018, http://asapjournal.com/love-is-the-message-the-message-is-death-huey-copeland/ (accessed February 18, 2021).

Jessie Daniels, "The Algorithmic Rise of the 'Alt-Right,'" *Contexts*, 17, 1 (February 2018): 60–65

Richard Dyer, *white* (London and New York: Routledge, 1997).

James Elkins, ed., *Photography Theory* (New York: Routledge, 2007).

Coco Fusco, "Racial Times, Racial Marks, Racial Metaphors," in *Only Skin Deep: Changing Visions of the American Self*, eds Coco Fusco and Brian Wallis (New York: International Center of Photography in association with Harry N. Abrams, Inc., Publishers, 2003), 13–48.

Brooke Gladstone, "Breaking News Consumer's Handbook: Bearing Witness Edition," *On the Media*, WNYC Studios (June 12, 2015).

Robert Gooding-Williams, ed., *Reading Rodney King/Reading Urban Uprising* (New York: Routledge, 1993).

Amy Goodman and Juan González, "Two Years After Eric Garner's Death, Ramsey Orta, Who Filmed Police, Is Only One Heading to Jail," *Democracy Now!*, Pacifica Radio (July 13, 2016).

Jonathan Green, ed., "Special Issue on The Snapshot," *Aperture*, 19, 1 (1974): 1–128.

Ruth Gebreyesus, "Why the Film-Maker Behind Love Is the Message Is Turning His Lens to whiteness," *The Guardian*, December 11, 2018, https://www.theguardian.com/artanddesign/2018/dec/11/arthur-jafa-video-artist-love-is-the-message (accessed February 18, 2021).

John Grierson, "The Documentary Producer," *Cinema Quarterly*, 1, 2 (Autumn 1933): 7–9.

Tom Gunning, "What's the Point of an Index? Or, Faking Photographs," in *Still Moving*, eds Karen Beckman and Jean Ma (Durham, NC: Duke University Press, 2008), 23–40.

Janna Houwen, *Film and Video Intermediality: The Question of Medium Specificity in Contemporary Moving Images* (New York: Bloomsbury, 2017).

Paula Ioanide, *The Emotional Politics of Racism: How Feelings Trump Facts in an Era of Colorblindness* (Stanford: Stanford University Press, 2015).

Chloé Cooper Jones, "Fearing for His Life," *The Verge*, March 13, 2019, https://www.theverge.com/2019/3/13/18253848/eric-garner-footage-ramsey-orta-police-brutality-killing-safety (accessed February 18, 2021).

Sarah Kember, *Virtual Anxiety: Photography, New Technologies, and Subjectivity* (Manchester: Manchester University Press, 1998).

"Gayle King Interview with Rakeyia Scott," CBS *This Morning*, CBS (October 13, 2016).

David LaRocca, "Shooting for the Truth: Amateur Documentary Filmmaking, Affective Optics, and the Ethical Impulse," *Post Script: Essays in Film and the Humanities*, 36, 2 & 3 (2017): n.p.

Soraya Nadia McDonald, "Friends: Eric Garner Was a 'Gentle Giant,'" *The Washington Post*, December 4, 2014, https://www.washingtonpost.com/news/morning-mix/wp/2014/12/04/friends-eric-garner-was-a-gentle-giant/ (accessed February 18, 2021).

Meg McLagan and Yates McKee, eds, *Sensible Politics: The Visual Culture of Nongovernmental Activism* (Cambridge: Zone Books, 2012).

State of Missouri v. Darren Wilson, Gore Perry (Grand Jury Vol V, 2014).

Jennifer Mnookin, "The Image of Truth: Photographic Evidence and the Power of Analogy," *Yale Journal of Law & the Humanities*, 10, 1 (Winter 1988): 1–74.

Khalil Gibran Muhammad, "Darren Wilson: America's 'Model Policeman,'" *The Nation* (November 29, 2014), https://www.thenation.com/article/archive/darren-wilson-americas-model-policeman/ (accessed February 18, 2021).

Lisa Nakamura, "'I WILL DO EVERYTHING That Am Asked': Scambaiting, Digital Show-Space, and the Racial Violence of Social Media," *Journal of Visual Culture*, 13, 3 (December 2014): 257–274.

Lisa Nakamura, *Digitizing Race: Visual Cultures of the Internet* (Minneapolis: University of Minnesota Press, 2008).

Bill Nichols, *Blurred Boundaries: Questions of Meaning in Contemporary Culture* (Bloomington: Indiana University Press, 1994).

Safiya Umoja Noble, *Algorithms of Oppression: How Search Engines Reinforce Racism* (New York: New York University Press, 2018a).

Safiya Umoja Noble, "Critical Surveillance Literacy in Social Media: Interrogating Black Death and Dying Online," *Black Camera*, 9, 2 (2018b): 147–160.

Jennifer Peltz, "In Neighborhood, Anger at Chokehold Death Decision," *Marin Independent Journal*, December 3, 2014, https://www.marinij.com/2014/12/03/in-neighborhood-anger-at-chokehold-death-decision/ (accessed February 18, 2021)

Alessandra Raengo et al., "Liquid Blackness: A Research Project on Blackness and Aesthetics," *Liquid Blackness*, February 12, 2019, http://liquidblackness.com/lb-original-about-page/ (accessed February 18, 2021).

Leigh Raiford, *Imprisoned in a Luminous Glare: Photography and the African American Freedom Struggle* (Chapel Hill: UNC Press Books, 2011).

Leigh Raiford and Renee C. Romano, eds, *The Civil Rights Movement in American Memory* (Athens, GA: University of Georgia Press, 2006).

Eli Saslow, "For Diamond Reynolds, Trying to Move Past 10 Tragic Minutes of Video," *The Washington Post*, September 10, 2016, https://www.washingtonpost.com/national/stay-calm-be-patient/2016/09/10/ec4ec3f2-7452-11e6-8149-b8d05321db62_story.html?utm_term=.59d573dde936 (accessed February 18, 2021).

Louis-Georges Schwartz, *Mechanical Witness: A History of Motion Picture Evidence in U.S. Courts* (Oxford and New York: Oxford University Press, 2009).

Gregg Sangillo, "whitesplaining on Facebook: PhD Student Donte Newman Looks at Race and Social Media," *American University: Communications and Marketing*, April 10, 2018, https://www.american.edu/ucm/news/20180409-newman-research.cfm (accessed Feburary 18, 2021).

Allan Sekula, "The Body and the Archive," *October* 39 (1986): 3–64.

Sharon Sliwinski, *Human Rights in Camera* (Chicago: University of Chicago Press, 2011).

Mitch Smith, "In Court, Diamond Reynolds Recounts Moments Before a Police Shooting," *The New York Times*, June 6, 2017, https://www.nytimes.com/2017/06/06/us/castile-police-shooting-facebook-trial.html (accessed February 18, 2021).

Susan Sontag, *On Photography* (New York: Farrar, Straus and Giroux, 1973).

Susan Sontag, "Regarding the Torture of Others: Notes on What Has Been Done—and Why—to Prisoners, by Americans," *New York Times Magazine* (May 23, 2004): 25–29, 42.

Hortense J. Spillers, "Mama's Baby, Papa's Maybe: An American Grammar Book," *Diacritics*, 17, 2 (1987): 64–81.

Krista A. Thompson, *Shine: The Visual Economy of Light in African Diasporic Aesthetic Practice* (Durham, NC: Duke University Press, 2015).

Barbie Zelizer, *About to Die: How News Images Move the Public* (New York: Oxford University Press, 2010).

Catherine Zuromskis, *Snapshot Photography: The Lives of Images* (Cambridge, MA: MIT Press, 2013).

9. On Photographic Ubiquity in the Age of Online Self-Imaging

Derek Conrad Murray

In fact, everyone will agree that desire is not only longing, a clear and translucent longing which directs itself through our body toward a certain object. Desire is defined as trouble... troubled water remains water; it preserves the fluidity and the essential characteristics of water; but its translucency is 'troubled' by an inapprehensible presence which makes one with it, which is everywhere and nowhere, and which is given as a clogging of the water itself.

—Jean-Paul Sartre, *Being and Nothingness* (Sartre, 1993: 378)

In a 2019 *New York Times* op-ed entitled "What Does It Mean to 'Look Like Me'?," philosophy professor Kwame Anthony Appiah pondered the importance of recognition in visual culture—and more pointedly, the potential impact of seeing one's physical corollary represented on screens and in popular forms of media. As Appiah recounts, the refrain, "I just want to see someone like me" represented in mainstream visual culture is a commonly uttered—if not entirely cliché—retort, so often recited by entertainers of color when asked why they do what they do:

The playwright Tarell Alvin McCraney, explaining what drove him to create the new television drama series 'David Makes Man,' which follows the life of a black boy in a public-housing project, observed: 'John Hughes made several movies that depicted the rich interior lives of young white American men and women. I just want the same for people who look like me.' The comedian Ali Wong inspired the writer Nicole Clark to confess that she 'didn't think she liked stand-up until a few years ago, when I realized the problem was the lack of comedians who look like me and tell jokes that I "get."' (Appiah, 2019)

Appiah is right to point out that this popular notion alludes to what the philosopher calls a "kinship of social identity": it functions as a means to express in-group cultural commonalities. Though it may speak to a desire for recognition that is easily articulated, we must also acknowledge that group identity and the solidarities it calls for have always been more aspirational than a tangible reality. Appiah's consideration of this representational problem argues that we may need to complicate what it means to see people who "look like me," while acknowledging the fallaciousness and impossibility for images to capture the complexities and ideological slippages of identity.

The aspirational dimensions of recognition in the visual realm, of which Appiah speaks, resonates in many ways with self-imaging online, most commonly articulated in the visual form known as the selfie, or digital self-portrait. The now ubiquitous term has become synonymous with our 21st-century, techno-crazed society, even while the act itself has been maligned as a puerile and largely vacuous visual expression. Common on social media sites such as Facebook and Instagram, the selfie has become a powerful means of self-expression, encouraging its makers to share the most intimate and private moments of their lives. The popularity of self-imaging online is unprecedented, yet within popular journalism, the selfie is reviled and regarded as a shallow expression of online narcissism. I have written previously about the more political and socially engaged dimensions of online self-imaging, while considering the gendered implications of both the act, and its common (mis)characterization as a largely female-driven form of communication (Murray, 2015). While many of the more radical mobilizations of the selfie are produced by women, it is not, contrary to dominant discussions, a uniquely female act. Despite that fact, popular discourses have largely characterized the selfie as a symptom of a narcissistic society, or they have asserted that those who make selfies are themselves suffering from mental health disorders (Murray, 2020).

In response to the aforementioned tendency, this chapter argues for a reassessment of digital culture's impacts on contemporary life, while simultaneously considering how certain constituencies have responded to the increasing presence of new technologies. I acknowledge that the utopian promise of digital culture has, in many respects, contributed to the dismantling of democracy and is complicit in the rise of inequality and the erosion of privacy. By exploring the impact of digital utopianism in the visual realm, this research explores how young women have responded to the ubiquity of new technologies as a means to assert a sense of personal value, recognition, and empowerment. The representational expressions of marginalized groups online have often functioned as a counterpoint to the dominant culture's tendency toward devaluing, misrepresentation, and erasure—though these expressions have nonetheless absorbed digital mediums, making productive use of their participatory networks and interactive platforms. One of the more generative aspects of self-imaging online is its engagement with new forms of image-making in the 21st century that utilize (and often weaponize) individuated, participatory, and interactive practices as a powerful means for social engagement. Ultimately, the aim is to explore the impact of digital technology on contemporary life from an anti-utopian perspective that is lucid about the implicit identity politics expressed within the often fraught and misinterpreted act of online self-imaging.

The critical framework for this essay explores the notion of desire under the ubiquity of digitalism. In contemplating this thematic, I tend to think of desire (and the self-image) in terms of *desiring the self*. Moreover, I critically position the selfie as one of intense intimacy: as a form of self-fashioning that is often about attempting to assuage feelings of lack, of isolation, and of alienation—as a means to love oneself. For that reason, this essay takes a more speculative approach that investigates the self-imaging of women of color, not as an effort to generate external sexual desire (something that beckons), but rather to create a framework in which they begin to desire themselves: to create a representational system of value for subjectivities who experience persistent devaluing and/or erasure—a phenomenon that we might regard as a *romance with the self*. These expressions flourish under a constant pejorative threat of ridicule and pathologizing rhetoric. For that reason, there is a great need to understand the logics that drive the ubiquity of self-imaging in online cultures as a tool for self-definition.

The Ubiquity of Culture

As a 21st-century social phenomenon, the selfie has an interesting relationship with both technology and culture. The degree to which one bears down upon the other historically, and in the present, is a complex and enduring discussion. In this case, however, I question whether the selfie tends to prioritize culture over the concerns of technology—ultimately, propelling the self-image to the forefront of social discourse. My engagement with ubiquity is informed by recent debates concerned with the conjunction between identity and culture—as well as by a more generalized set of popular characterizations of the selfie as an ever-present, inescapable, and insidious social scourge. My formulation breaks from film scholar Christian Metz's well-known writings on ubiquity, which are more specifically engaged with the psychodynamics of cinematic spectatorship (Metz, 1982; Hodge, 2015: 55). That said, the derisive, often articulated characterization of the selfie has greatly impacted my writing on the topic, in addition to my thoughts on the photographic self-portrait in general. Metz has discussed what he calls cinemas "gifts of ubiquity," which alludes to the all-consuming omnipresence of the camera; its uncanny ability to "be anywhere and see anything." (Hodge, 2015: 54) In photographic discourse, the ubiquity of digital imaging in online cultures has ushered in what could be characterized as a postphotographic media landscape—in which the photographic medium thrives, but without the veracity of its more traditional use value. Utilizing Metz's theorization, the spectator's identification is with the camera, and therefore, a greater attention should perhaps be given to unpacking the viewers relationship to the act of looking, as opposed to the perceived narcissism of the representational subject.

Metz's formulation of the scopic regime explores the relation between cinema and voyeurism, as a means to rethink psychoanalytic framings of fetishism and the complexities of subjectivity. Many of his observations can illuminate the psychodynamics of self-imaging online. For Metz, "the practice of cinema is only possible through the perceptual passions: the desire to see," which suggests it is implicitly interconnected with the scopic drive, scopophilia, and voyeurism (Metz, 1982: 58). What I find most salient in Metz's concept is the notion that cinematic spectatorship (which is essentially an act of looking) is voyeuristic, yet interpolated by exhibitionism by the subject of representation. In other words, there are two drives that compel the act of cinematic spectatorship: a desire to be seen and a voyeuristic gaze. These interconnected drives are equally complicit and not dissociated from one another. As Metz suggests, the subject of representation (the one who is looked at) is not a passive presence, which implies a certain consent. He argues that this form of looking is an inherently participatory act. Voyeurism, in a strictly Freudian sense, obviously suggests an active viewer and a passive, unaware subject. Metz, on the other hand, looks at cinematic spectatorship as reciprocal in the sense that subjects perform with an awareness that they will be looked at. In his formulation, however, there is a distinction to be made between the cinema and live theatrical performance, as it pertains to consent: "In the theater, actors and spectators are present at the same time and in the same location, hence present one to another, as the two protagonists of an authentic perverse couple." (63) The scholar makes a delineation between the theatre and the cinema, as it pertains to consent, suggesting that cinema is perhaps more voyeuristic than theatre, largely due to the absence of the subject/performer: "In the darkened hall, the voyeur is really left alone (or with other voyeurs, which is worse), deprived of his other half." Ultimately, Metz intimates that (as it pertains to theatrical and cinematic spectatorship) there are both active and passive roles in the exercise of the scopic drive. In the context of viewing cinema, the spectator is still a voyeur, since there is something to see, called the film, but something in whose definition there is a great deal of 'flight': not precisely something that hides, rather something that *lets* itself be seen without *presenting* itself to be seen, which has gone out of the room before leaving only its trace visible there.

Cinema therefore exercises what he calls an *unauthorized* scopophilia. The selfie is implicitly consensual, or perhaps it encourages what could be called, following Metz, an *authorized* scopophilia. Despite the perceived narcissism, there is a kind of agreement between the subject and viewer; there is an implied consensus that one is to look, and the other to be looked at. The tension around, or societal loathing for, selfies taps into a relation that Metz illuminates, which is the perversity of looking. Metz's scopic drive acknowledges something very base in the act of looking, which is its connection to desire and ultimately to sexual drives. Freud characterized these sexual impulses as "ego drives," which he linked to narcissism. There are, of course, many reasons why looking at others would imply the sexual, but as Freud insisted, the sexual drives are perverse, and paradoxically, always remain more or less unsatisfied (59). Perhaps it is the perverse dimension of looking at others (the never-satiated sexual drives), and not the narcissism of the subject of representation, that vexes. In keeping with Metz's formulation, there are two drives that compel the act of producing and consuming selfies: a desire to be seen and a voyeuristic gaze. Therefore, the selfie is also intertwined with the perceptual passions. What is so socially treacherous about the desire to be seen? Is it the narcissism of the image-maker/subject, or is it something more connected to the viewer's desire?

Within popular discussions of online self-imaging, it is precisely the way the act tends to recuperate the politics of identification that generates tension. And as mentioned, the apparent narcissism of the selfie is commonly referred to as something that cheapens and demeans. In my critical approach to the highly personal and intimate expressive dimension of the selfie, I see the possibility for self-transformation: a form of identification that is not a series of fixities and reductions (a kind of dumbing down of the self), but rather a subjectivity that is changing and in constant flux—what we might characterize as a transcendental subject. But, reduced to its most base and pejorative interpretations, the selfie is perhaps a sign of culture run amok, a symptom of a societal descent into the politics of identity.

The idea of culture has consistently been a much-debated topic throughout the 20th and 21st centuries, if not also an issue of increasing contestation. In the last two decades in the United States, visual culture studies has emerged as a vibrant cross-disciplinary field spanning the arts, humanities, and social sciences. Informed, in many respects, by cultural studies in the United Kingdom, visual studies (in its current form) has not always been embraced, despite its increasing prevalence. In certain respects, visual culture studies, at least within art history, was treated as an unwanted guest that arrived late and stayed too long. But as scholar Margaret Dikovitskaya reminds us, visual culture studies has been around since the 1960s, despite its seeming newness:

> An interdisciplinary field, visual studies came together in the late 1980s after the disciplines of art history, anthropology, film studies, linguistics, and comparative literature encountered poststructuralist theory and cultural studies. Deconstructionist criticism showed that the academic humanities were as much artifacts of language as they were outcomes of the pursuit of truth. The inclusive concept of culture as 'a whole way of life' became the object of inquiry of cultural studies, which encompassed the 'high' arts and literature without giving them a privileged status. As a result of the cultural turn, the status of culture has been revised in the humanities: It is currently seen as a cause of—rather than merely a reflection of or response to— social, political, and economic processes. (Dikovitskaya, 2006: 6)

To Dikovitskaya's point, what we now call visual culture studies has also been informed by the interrelated fields of visual communication, visual anthropology, and visual sociology: all arenas concerned with both culture and the visual. Without belaboring the debates, contestations, and disciplinary and methodological boundaries, it arguably goes without saying that the tensions around visual culture studies are perhaps more related to *culture* than to its visual dimension. That culture is the source of antagonism is not a huge surprise. Cultural studies in Britain, most notably associated with Stuart Hall's post-Gramscian theoretical approach to hegemony, has gone on to define current conceptualizations of visual culture studies across the arts and humanities. However, Hall's writings on cultural identity tended to view identity not as static, but determined by a process of perpetual transformation. The notion that identity is not a fixed essence—but rather a chosen identification or a means of positioning—had a profound impact on the development of visual culture studies in the United States. But, among its many interventions, cultural studies enabled the study of visuality to be expanded in terms of its objects of study, its geographic scope, and the deepening of its engagements with identity and representation (Hall, 1990; Hall, 2007).

However, British cultural studies, despite its early formulations in the 1950 and 1960s, really took shape as a multicultural-era response to the horrors of political conservatism under Margaret Thatcher's reign as prime minister (1979–1990). Among its lasting interventions, British cultural studies solidified a set of theoretical and methodological approaches for the consideration of race, gender, and sexuality. The rise of identity discourses in U.S. universities, and the increasing presence of departments in the arenas of gender and sexuality studies, African/African American and Black studies, as well as Chicano/Latinx and Asian studies (among other disciplinary formations), have brought with them needed change within the academy—while also facing persistent institutional instability. A dimension of that instability is, at least in part, due to an increasing sentiment both in academia and within cultural politics that the academy has become irrecoverably entrenched in a toxic brand of liberalism. The spectrum of these concerns reflects a range of often contrasting agendas—from the self-reflexivity of notable left-leaning scholars, to the ideological demagoguery of the political right. Nonetheless, such critical reflections have become increasingly prevalent and now threaten the institutional longevity of these departments. This threat has been exacerbated by the rise of neoliberalism within the U.S. university system and the continued diminishing of the arts and humanities, in favor of the science, technology, engineering, and mathematics fields. But arguably what is more important here is the perception that academic liberalism has become hackneyed and trite: that it has devolved into a kind of liberal dystopia, which engages in institutional hand-wringing around a set of lefty positions on diversity, inclusion, and tolerance—while lamenting the presence (or absence) of the *underrepresented* and the *vulnerable*. These terminologies have become the lingua franca of liberal tolerance as institutional optics (Vedder, 2018). Within certain segments of the intelligentsia (perhaps most notoriously reflected in the work of scholars such as Jordan Peterson, professor of psychology at the University of Toronto), there is an increasingly vocal pushback against academic liberalism. These counterarguments often lament the presence of institutional browbeating around politically correctness, such as race discourse and feminism, or the use of proper pronouns for transgender and genderqueer constituencies. Of course, these positions are well known, as they populate the national media and extend far beyond academia.

The problem is that *culture* itself has gone on to signify the evils of identity and diversity: terminologies that are arguably more reflective of intellectual and institutional positioning—and the galvanizing of a progressive image—rather than any substantive commitment to equity. While the liberal university has become a bastion of tolerance-based sentimentality, on a structural and demographic level, it has a long way to go in its commitments against forms of discrimination. British Australian scholar Sara Ahmed suggests that the function of so-called "diversity work" within liberal institutions is the need to both generate and project the *right image*, as a corrective to the *wrong* one: arguing that perception is more important than the problem itself, which is the continued presence of structural inequity (Ahmed, 2006: 104). Slavoj Žižek has leveled an even more pointed critique of this apparent problem in his questioning of the tendency toward tolerance-based posturing within liberal multiculturalism. Žižek's more cynical position argues that the liberal multiculturalist's basic ideological operation is the "culturalization of politics," a condition upon which the celebration of (and identification with) cultural differences masquerades as political action (Žižek, 2008: 660). This tendency toward tolerance, as opposed to equity, is certainly the problem, because it represents a contradictory or hypocritical tendency toward an institution's stated commitments (its progressive ethos) and the continued presence of structural inequality and bias.

To the above point, *culture* masquerading as *politics* has become a dominant feature of far-left scholarship, particularly in the humanities, and to a certain degree in the arts. In fact, the term *culture* is a trigger that (for many intellectual and cultural commentators) signifies what is increasingly regarded as a kind of hysterical or psychotic liberalism that is ultimately ineffective. In his writing on the ubiquity of culture, Jefferey Williams argues that culture has extended beyond the perception of its nonessential function—its ornamental role, so to speak. "In classical aesthetics," he writes, "culture is defined precisely by its uselessness and detachment from ordinary life." (Williams, 2014: 45) The scholar's argument is interesting, largely because he initially characterizes culture as a frivolity:

> The traditional idea of culture as high art conceives of culture as something like the flowerbed. While we might appreciate and value artifacts we deem beautiful, they are not essential to our primary physical needs. In a no-nonsense, colloquial view, culture is ornamental, secondary to if not a frivolous distraction from the real business of life.

Williams draws upon this analogy as a means to explore the *rise* of culture as central to intellectual and social life: that it has become politics. Informed by a Marxist framing, he laments that culture has, in his estimation, reached beyond its intellectual and historical positioning as tertiary to politics, economics, and business.

Williams's initial framing of culture as a kind of aesthetic diversion, and not as a central historical antagonism, is fascinating. In a sense, it captures a certain frustration around the contradictions of academic liberalism and its particular mobilization of culture (*as politics*). On the other hand, it tends to step around the toxic weaponization of culture—as a potent form of social engineering—throughout the 19th and twentieth 20th. It is clear, however, that Williams is more concerned with the phenomenon of culture's increasing predominance and politicization in contemporary life:

> We speak of proclivities within a society, such as 'sports culture,' 'car culture,' 'hip-hop culture,' or 'mall culture.' In political discourse, culture describes the tenor of society, such as 'the culture of complaint,' 'the culture of civility,' or 'the culture of fear,' and societies are defined by their cultures, such as the 'culture of Islam,' 'the culture of democracy,' or 'the culture of imperialism,' which generate their politics. In criticism and theory, culture, whether indicating race, class, nationality, ethnicity, gender, sexuality, abledness, locality, or taste, determines human identity, which in turn designates political interest. In short, 'culture' has shifted from ornament to essence, from secondary effect to primary cause, and from a matter of disinterested taste to a matter of political interest. Consequently, pursuits that study culture, like literary or cultural criticism, have claimed greater political importance to society. (46)

Fifty years ago, Raymond Williams charged criticism to look at the conjunction of "culture and society." Now it seems that culture *is* society, interchangeable as a synonym for social interests, groups, and bases. Culture has shifted from a subsidiary (if special) role to primary ground, inverting the standard model of base and superstructure. Even a social theorist such as Pierre Bourdieu, who persistently foregrounded the significance of class, conceived of class less as a matter of material means than of taste, disposition, and other cultural cues.

The ubiquity of culture that Williams speaks of holds a special resonance when considering self-imaging in the 21st century, because, as mentioned, it is an expression that (in the case of certain constituencies) encourages the mobilization of culture, as a political or socially engaged act. If we give credence to the feminist mantra, *the personal is political*, then we can begin to understand why the "selfie," for many young women, generates such malice in public discourse. I argue that what the selfie does (its operation, so to speak) is to make culture visible—to render it indispensable and of foremost importance. Culture is *always* the problem; but it's not what the selfie *is*, but what the selfie *does* that is the vexation. So, when we ponder the ubiquity of the online self-image, perhaps what we're seeing is Žižek's "culturalization of politics" rendered visible via an extremely personalized engagement with digital technology. The very act of making oneself a public spectacle has undeniably political ramifications and associations, particularly when mobilized by minoritized and socially maligned communities. The almost hysterical fixation with self-articulation, identity formation, and self-fashioning—not to mention the rapacious need for fame and cool—is indeed troubling. I have no argument there. Yet we might think of these expressions of technological self-affection not merely as the visual culture empire or as empty expressions of narcissism, but rather as a means to simply exist in a profoundly alienating and extremely intolerant world.

The Selfie and Its Discontents

In 2013, the *Oxford Dictionary of English* announced *selfie* as the word of the year—a distinction that has inaugurated its introduction into the public consciousness. A selfie has been defined as a photograph that one has taken of oneself, typically one taken with a smartphone or webcam and uploaded to a social media website. Despite the increasing ubiquity of the term—and the popularity of the act itself—the tendency has been to position online forms of self-imaging as culturally corrosive, pathological, and even mortally dangerous. As a result, the selfie debate has evolved from a lighthearted discussion about the perils of technology and consumption to the pathologizing of the image-maker. The aim here is to give insight into a contemporary discussion about the impact of technology and social media as a means to disseminate and share images. The term selfie, in its popular usage, is meant to delineate a particular engagement with technologies of image-making, a phenomenon that has led to public debate about the potentially corrosive effects of technology on our individual and collective selves.

There is, on the other hand, a continued need to explore the political, ideological, and aesthetic complexity at the heart of the selfie phenomenon, and contemplate whether the urge to compulsively self-image in the 21st century is mere narcissism or if it holds the potential for more redemptive meanings. Moreover, there is a significant amount of serious scholarship being done on the subject of digital self-portraiture (primarily in the social sciences and communications), but most of it is *not* engaged with the visual. While there is a need for scholarship that is innovative, knowledgeable, and insightful about online self-imaging as a social, economic, and technological phenomenon, there is a paucity of research that is engaged with digital self-portraiture *as* representation. Scholars Edgar Gómez and Ellen Thornham make a contrasting argument, suggesting that placing undue attention on self-representation is to ultimately miss the point:

> We argue that contemporary understandings of selfies either in relation to a 'documenting of the self' or as a neoliberal (narcissistic) identity affirmation are inherently problematic. Instead, we argue that selfies should be understood as a wider social, cultural, and

media phenomenon that understands the selfie as far more than a representational image. This, in turn, necessarily redirects us away from the object 'itself,' and in so doing seeks to understand selfies as a socio-technical phenomenon that momentarily and tentatively holds together a number of different elements of mediated digital communication. (Gómez and Thornham, 2015: 1)

Gómez and Thornham's position is a widely held one across the spectrum of social sciences research—even while the selfie, as a highly personalized representational act, speaks directly to discourses around recognition, as well as to the *kinship of social identity* that Appiah describes: that pesky need to *see oneself* imaged. Needless to say, the interpretive quandary posed by these contrasting approaches alludes quite troublingly to the relation between the individual consumer and the rapacious forces of technocapitalism that bear down upon them. Scholar Henry Giroux compellingly argues that "freedom has become an exercise in self-development rather than social responsibility," further intimating that the tendency toward neocapitalist privatization and voracious consumerization have served to erode the public good (Giroux, 2015: 155).

Giroux tends to view the selfie phenomenon as a troubling sign that "a vision of the good society has now been replaced with visions of individual happiness characterized by an endless search for instant gratification and self-recognition." (156) He further states that "the personal appears to be the only politics that matters in providing both emotional gratification and a tangible referent for negotiating social problems." Giroux's central concern here is the decimation of individual privacies, engendered by the state and the corporate sphere. He argues compellingly that there is an "increasing view of privacy on the part of the American public as something to escape from rather than preserve as a precious political right." To that point, the willingness of consumers to give over their most personal information is a hallmark of the social media phenomenon: a feature of 21st-century life that, as Giroux laments, acculturates the masses into the intrusion of consumer-based surveillance practices. There is really no productive counterpoint to this argument, as we come to grips with the manner in which technology has created new and more invasive means to exert its control. The scholar acknowledges that, while the selfie does not offer up the types of information that is most concerning, it does, in fact, transform the self into a matter of public concern. "Privacy has mostly become synonymous with a form of self-generated, non-stop performance—a type of public relations in which privacy is valued only for the way it makes possible the unearthing of secrets, a cult of commodified confessionals and an infusion of narcissistic, self-referencing narratives." (157) Many commentators have lamented what is perceived as a societal descent into self-obsession and the shallowness of individual posturing. And the selfie is the perfect foil for these concerns. We can, of course, utilize online self-portraiture and image-sharing as a barometer for the hegemonies of state and corporate surveillance. But perhaps, we need to look more closely, particularly as we acknowledge that, throughout history, the tools meant to dominate have often been weaponized against those very dominating forces. While not attempting to uncritically redeem the selfie phenomenon of its troubling dimensions, I argue that the personal is *still* political, even while the capitalist subject wrestles with the threats posed by techno-capitalist aggression.

The more cynical interpretations of the selfie/influencer debate share a central conceit that concerns me, which is not simply what I would characterize as a careless, or callous, disregard for the deeply personal motivations for self-imaging—but rather the disdain articulated around the private desires expressed in individual images. There is much more interest in viewing the selfie judgmentally as a social scourge of sorts, as a representational phenomenon defined by a society in which private citizens don't feel they exist without photographic evidence. In fact, the negation of individual desire extends beyond this contemporaneous discussion. Yet we must come to terms with this insistent need to characterize desire as a disruption or as a regressive tendency that fosters, as Judith Butler argues, "philosophical myopia, encouraging one to only see what one *wants*, and not what *is*." (Butler, 1999: 3) Within this particular discussion, such attitudes take the shape of expressed misgivings about the rapaciousness of neoliberal capitalism, while ignoring the human longings and desires for recognition that emanate from these forms of representation. Butler expresses a critical concern regarding the philosophical tendency to "obliterate" desire through the formulation of "strategies to silence or control it." (2)

The domestication of desire in the name of reason or, more aptly, the constructed philosophical split between reason and desire, is the subject of Butler's ire—as it expresses a contradictory moralism. Desire is in fact the operation implicit to the act of self-imaging; desire is its modus operandi. The envisioning of desire is not the antithesis of tacit knowledge, any more than there is an irrational desire. And as Butler asserts, "there is no necessarily irrational desire, no affective moment that must be renounced for its intrinsic arbitrariness." That implicit arbitrariness of desire externalized is what intrigues me about online self-imaging: that tension between consciousness and self-consciousness that offers up the intimacies and longings of an individual. The photographic self-portrait is an intensely psychological image that mobilizes (or, more aptly, weaponizes) the returned gaze in the process of self-conception.

In response to less charitable characterizations of online self-imaging, I argue that it is not just desire (the desire of the Other) that unsettles, but rather the self-eroticizing and objectification: what is perceived as a narcissistic self-display that positions the female body as a fetish object. This articulated expression of female agency *is* scopophilic, but its voyeuristic pleasures are self-fixated—even while visually acknowledging (through a performed femininity) that the female body (in representation) is not her own, but a matter of public concern. Female bodies are always subjected to the gaze and always rendered *the object* of popular representation. Even though the visual codes of female display are manipulated to grand effect, there is an implied pleasure in directing the gaze back upon itself, while playing with the "to-be-looked-at-ness" that Laura Mulvey theorized in her famous essay on visual pleasure (Mulvey, 1989). Rather than reject the passive female/active male binary, implicit to the selfie is a claimed pleasure—an active *jouissance* of sorts—that gestures toward a femininity that is beyond repression, despite its many glaring contradictions.

Lacan's *jouissance* (or the pleasure principle) functions as a limit of enjoyment. It is a repressive law meant to prohibit the subject from experiencing too much pleasure, but the consequence is that the subject is locked in an eternal struggle to transgress the imposed boundaries. The subject's attempt to transgress the pleasure principle does not lead to more pleasure, but pain itself: a type of suffering or *painful pleasure*. This suffering is what Lacan calls *jouissance*. In essence, *jouissance* represents a paradox, in that subjects becomes conflicted with their own pleasure and derive satisfaction in the suffering brought about by the pleasure experienced (Lacan, 1981: 183).

Jacques Lacan first developed his concept of an opposition between *jouissance* and the pleasure principle (what Sigmund Freud calls the pursuit of enjoyment) in his seminar The Ethics of Psychoanalysis (1959–1960). Lacan argued there is a *jouissance* beyond the pleasure principle, a *jouissance* that compels subjects to constantly attempt to transgress the prohibitions imposed on their enjoyment—to go beyond the pleasure principle. Yet, according to Lacan, the result of transgressing the pleasure principle is not more pleasure, but pain, because there is only a certain amount of pleasure that the subject can endure. Beyond this limit, pleasure becomes pain, and this painful principle is what Lacan calls *jouissance*. *Jouissance* is therefore suffering.

Female Jouissance, Self-Love, Desire, and Recognition

Lacan's model has become a powerful metaphor for the contradictory tensions between pleasure and guilt: a paradox that informs individual action, but also larger social relations. It is precisely the opposition between enjoyment and pain, vis-à-vis the imaging and visual consumption of Otherness that is of interest to this investigation. What happens when difference (in this case, the female body) enters into the realm of representation, in a cultural climate in which gender inequity is a persistent problem? As a key psychoanalytic concept in Lacan's building upon Freud, the concept of *jouissance* is phallocentric and rooted in the repression of masculine pleasure. However, as woman is configured as lack (as nonuniversal), there is what can be called a female *jouissance*, or more appropriately the *jouissance of the Other*. Lacanian feminism has been extremely generative in terms of our application of this concept—not least because the French philosopher's writing was instrumental to the linguistic turn in poststructuralism of the 1980s. As Nina Lykke points out, "French theorists became important sources of theoretical inspiration for the continued feminist struggle against biological determinism." (Lykke, 2010: 97) She continues: "Some feminists found Lacan's orientation toward language a particularly useful aspect of his reinterpretation of Freud's psychoanalysis."

French feminist writer Hélène Cixous's formulation of Lacan's *jouissance* is more concerned with a woman's pleasure: asserting that *jouissance* is the root of a woman's creative power, and its suppression restrains the female subject's expressive potential. Therefore, we might think of feminist *jouissance* as a kind of transcendent state that signifies freedom from societal repression. Scholar Jane Gallop offers a similar interpretation:

When jouissance becomes an emblem of French feminine theory, however, it is specifically identified as non-phallic, beyond the phallus. But even though jouissance is specified as feminine, the tendency to stiffen into a strong, muscular image remains. The difference between jouissance and pleasure is generally understood to be one of degree: jouissance is stronger and so the person who experiences it is stronger, braver, less repressed, less scared. Fear also appears in conjunction with jouissance in an English translation of French feminism, but in a different form. The editors of New French Feminisms state, in a footnote, that "[jouissance] is a word used by Hélène Cixous to refer to that intense, rapturous pleasure which women know and men fear." Here, the two are conjoined but divorced: we have jouissance, and they fear it. If jouissance is defined, as it is by Barthes and the women, as a loss of self, disruption of comfort, loss of control, it cannot simply be claimed as an ego-gratifying identity, but must also frighten those who "know" it. As jouissance becomes a banner and a badge for French feminine writing, the accompanying fear or unworthiness is projected outward and we—militant and bold—lose the ambiguous link to fear and emotion, which are catapulted beyond the jouissance principle where it might even be their momentary fate to take up residence in that mediocre and unworthy word, "pleasure." (Gallop, 1984: 114)

In response to Gallop and the critical framings of other notable Lacanian feminists, we can see how *jouissance* can be mobilized in the service of dismantling gender-based repressions. *Jouissance* holds a particular fascination when unpacking the role that difference plays in the representational schemas of a society in which gender hierarchy is fundamental to the social, economic, and political order. I find these theorizations incredibly useful when contemplating the psychological implications of the photographic self-portrait. As Amelia Jones asserts, there is "something fundamental about the body in relation to the image, something that, indeed, provided the major impetus to the development of photographic technologies: the desire for the image to render up the body *and thereby the self* in its fullness and truth." (Jones, 2006: xiv) Jones makes a salient point about the technology of the camera as means to render the body via the manipulation of light:

Being an indexical trace of the body before the camera, then, the photograph promised to return the represented body to some kind of authentic state. Because the photographic portrait documents the embodied trace of the self (with the mind made visible only through its body-sign), it highlights both the inextricability of body and mind and the fact that we often access the self via its visible— corporeal—form, a form we want to serve as guarantor of the body. The photographic portrait seems to reaffirm the body's never-ending 'thereness,' its refusal to disappear, its infinite capacity to render up the self in some incontrovertibly 'real' way. (xiv–xv)

What Jones argues for here is a more nuanced engagement with our relation to the representation of bodies—further suggesting that we have an attachment to their presumed legibility, that there is a desire for the body and image to function as a clear reflection and indicator for ideo- logical meanings. In other words, we often interpret and engage others through their appearances, which is the basis for stereotyping, racism, and forms of social discrimination (xvii). Kwame Anthony Appiah, in his thoughts on recognition and popular representation, suggests something similar, that the need for a representative image of ourselves similarly requires certain reductions that are ultimately less about see- ing *someone who looks like me*, as they are a dubious confirmation of one's existence. The types of self-images circulating online (selfies and influencer portraits) "deploy technologies of visual representation to render and/or confirm the self (paradoxically: objectifying the self so as to prove its existence as a subject), and the way in which these technologies expose the inexorable failure of representation to offer up the self as a coherent knowable entity." (Mulvey, 1989: 19) The self-fashioning of desire implicit to the online self-image fulfills that "primordial wish for pleasurable looking" that Mulvey articulates, fully indulging the scopophilic and narcissistic pleasures of recognition.

The vast and ubiquitous landscape of selfies and influencers is by no means strictly female, though I assert that the most urgent and progressive interventions online are driven by women. In fact, I have written before that, within the female-driven landscape of "selfie-laden" blogging and influencer culture, the spectacle of female bodies is the dominant driving force. But these images may constitute a new love affair (to borrow Mulvey's terminology) between the image and self-image. And it is true that the visual power of online self-portraiture is rooted in a type of pleasure that is voraciously claimed: an oppositional desire and enjoyment in oneself as a response to a culture of devaluing and misrepresentation (Murray, 2015: 22). This enjoyment is bound up in a conglomeration of intersecting affects around self-love, desire, and the need for a mutual recognition: one in which both the subject of representation and the viewer/consumer enjoy the visual pleasures of the self as spectacle. This reciprocity is likely the driving force behind the selfie/influencer matrix: that it enables both the subject and viewer/consumer to gaze lovingly upon that which has historically been denied—the imago of the devalued and the underrepresented, presented within the glitzy motifs and the vacuity of consumer technocapitalism.

Bibliography

Sara Ahmed, "The Nonperformativity of Antiracism," *Meridians*, 7, 1 (2006): 104–126.

Kwame Anthony Appiah, "What Does It Mean to 'Look Like Me'?," *New York Times*, September 21, 2019, https://www.nytimes.com/2019/09/21/opinion/sunday/minorities-representation-culture.html (accessed April 15, 2020).

Judith Butler, *Subjects of Desire: Hegelian Reflections in Twentieth-Century France* (New York: Columbia University Press, 1999).

Margaret Dikovitskaya, *Visual Culture: The Study of the Visual after the Cultural Turn* (Cambridge, MA: MIT Press, 2006).

Jane Gallop, "Beyond the *Jouissance* Principal," *Representations*, 7 (Summer 1984): 110–115.

Henry Giroux, "Selfie in the Age of Corporate and State Surveillance," *Third Text*, 2, 29, 3 (2015): 155–164.

Edgard Gómez and Ellen Thornham, "Selfies Beyond Self-Representation: The (Theoretical) F(r)ictions of a Practice," *Journal of Aesthetics & Culture*, 7, 1 (2015): 1–10.

Stuart Hall, "Cultural Identity and Diaspora," in *Identity: Community, Culture, Difference*, ed. Jonathan Rutherford (London: Lawrence & Wishart: 1990), 220–237.

Stuart Hall, "Cultural Studies and Its Theoretical Legacies," in *The Cultural Studies Reader*, ed. Simon During (London: Routledge Press, 2007): 33–44.

James Hodge, "Gifts of Ubiquity," *Film Criticism*, 39, 2 (Winter 2015): 53–78.

Amelia Jones, *Self/Image: Technology, Representation, and the Contemporary Subject* (London: Routledge, 2009).

Jacques Lacan, *The Four Fundamental Concepts of Psychoanalysis*, trans. Alan Sheridan (New York: W.W. Norton & Company, 1998).

Nina Lykke, *Feminist Studies: A Guide to Intersectional Theory, Methodology and Writing* (London: Routledge, 2010).

Christian Metz, *The Imaginary Signifier: Psychoanalysis and the Cinema*, trans. Celia Britton, Annwyl Williams, Ben Brewster, and Alfred Guzzetti (Bloomington: Indiana University Press, 1982).

Laura Mulvey, "Visual Pleasure and Narrative Cinema," *Visual and Other Pleasures* (Bloomington: Indiana University Press, 1989).

Derek Conrad Murray, "Notes to Self: The Visual Culture of Selfies in the Age of Social Media," *Consumption Markets & Culture*, 18, 6 (2015): 490–516.

Derek Conrad Murray, "Selfie Consumerism in a Narcissistic Age," *Consumption Markets & Culture*, 23, 1 (2020): 21–43.

Jean-Paul Sartre, *Being and Nothingness*, trans. Hazel E. Barnes (New York: Washington Square Press, 1993).

Richard Vedder, "Are Most Universities Truly 'Liberal' Or 'Progressive'? Rhetoric vs. Reality," *Forbes*, December 10, 2018, https://www.forbes.com/sites/richardvedder/2018/12/10/are-universities-truly-liberal-or-progressive-rhetoric-and-reality/#51bed93b1452 (accessed May 13, 2020).

Jeffrey Williams, *How to Be an Intellectual: Essays on Criticism, Culture, and the University* (New York: Fordham University Press, 2014).

Slavoj Žižek, "Tolerance as an Ideological Category," *Critical Inquiry*, 34 (Summer 2008): 660–682.

10. Parafiction and the New Latent Image

Kate Palmer Albers

What do you think of when you imagine a photograph? What does it look like? Do you conjure one from your past, perhaps a favorite childhood photograph, or one of a parent or a grandparent before you knew them? Or perhaps it is one you anticipate making, imagined in the moment that you pull out your phone to snap a picture. Either way, whether for remembered, imagined, or anticipated photographs, our cognitive faculties enact a complex set of associations to conjure such a mental image: we not only draw on our own networks of personal images (our own archives), we also draw on the vast sea of photographic images we have encountered. Nearly all of these images exist in correspondence with other forms of information, whether memories of events, particular sensory experiences—of smell, of emotional warmth or distance, of physical movement or other visceral encounters, of music or sound—or knowledge gleaned through words, text, captions, narratives, histories. On occasion, we might imagine photographs that don't exist, may never exist, or once existed but don't any longer; these may be moments of inspiration, speculative fantasies, or ruminations filled with longing or loss.

In two recent projects, WDCH *Dreams* (2018) and *Archive Dreaming* (2017), the media artist Refik Anadol (b. Turkey, 1984) extends the parameters of this imaginative exercise, asking what would happen if a computer imagined a photograph based on all the photographs and information it had encountered. Would that image be a memory? A dream? A hallucination? Would it be a photograph at all? Throughout his projects, Anadol has brought his fascination with the expressive potentials of data into the realms of human memory and architecture, asking how viewers might engage with the relatively abstract complexities of algorithmic possibility via a physical immersion in the perhaps more recognizable realms of human-scaled architecture. Anadol's work consistently seeks to operate in a newly defined space, one that pivots precisely at an intersection of massive quantities of data and human perception.

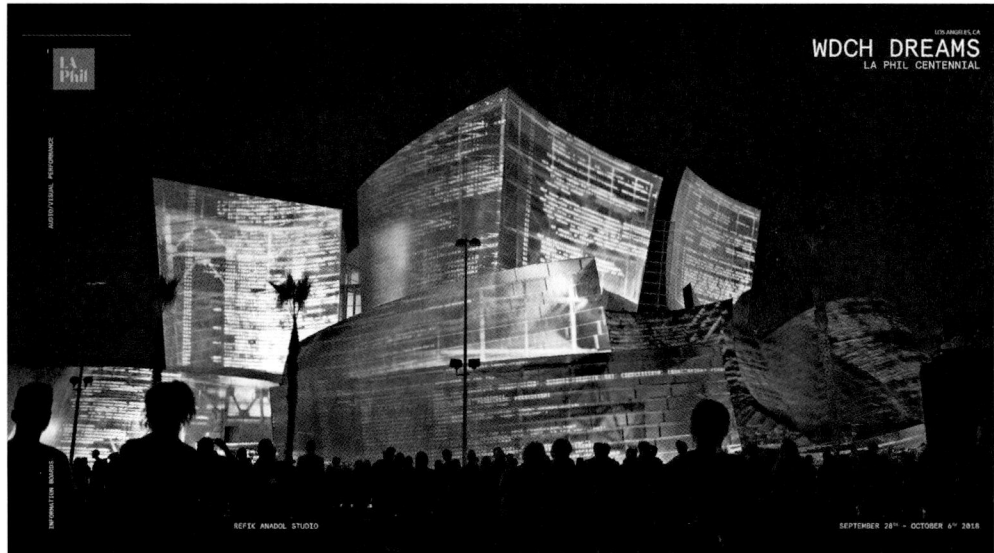

Figure 10.1

Refik Anadol, *WDCH Dreams* (performance documentation), 2018. Multi-projection site-specific video installation, 12-minute loop. Courtesy of the artist.

These particularly photographic questions emerge from a distinct set of material operations and experiments in visualizing archives (and, thus, history and memory). Andadol's provocative refiguring of what "counts" as photographic reflects a current inability of language to describe, and thus perhaps to fix, the meaning of a new form of generated image production. Language in this uncertain state reflects, too, the assumptions, the expectations, and the desires of makers and viewers.

WDCH Dreams premiered in downtown Los Angeles as public art installation, urban spectacle, and community event. Each night, for ten nights, architect Frank Gehry's iconic Walt Disney Concert Hall was activated by Anadol's forty-two projections, each meticulously calibrated to the dynamic shapes of the building's extraordinary exterior. Unfolding in a sequence of three visual chapters given structure by periodic textual interludes (Chapter 1: Memory; Chapter 2: Consciousness; Chapter 3: Dream), the projected images collectively told, in a twelve-minute narrative cycle, the story of their own creation. (figs. 10.1 and 10.2) At the start, scrolls of color photographs travel up the sides of the building's facades; they are familiar and repetitive, evoking the scores of personal snapshots on any iPhone or computer desktop, echoes of our own visual archives, writ large. Images of photo albums and outdated recording technology scroll by as well, and always more photographs, in escalating quantities. In this early sequence of the performance, the building's exterior reflects (via projection) the data that Anadol's neural network has received. Like many other institutions, Walt Disney Concert Hall has digitized its extensive analog archives, a

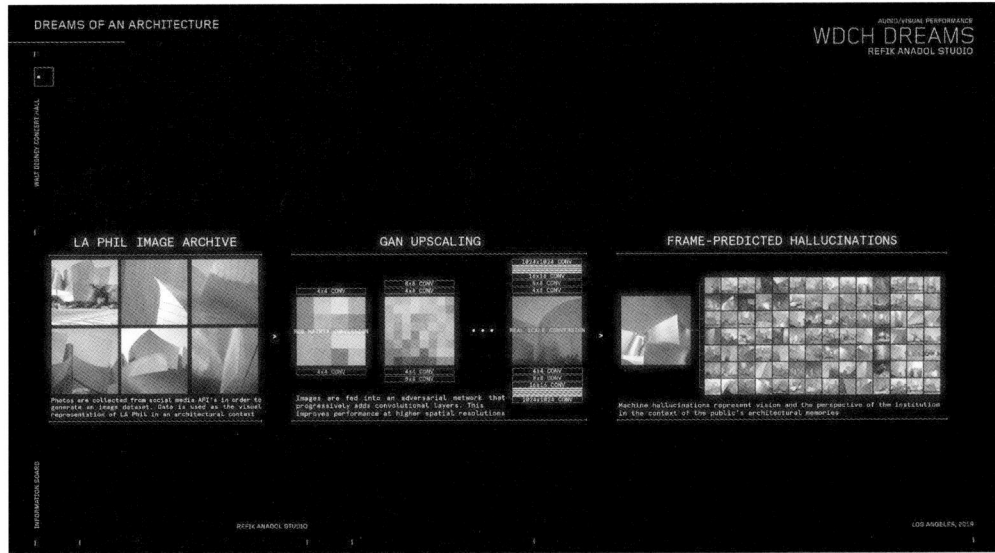

material shift that can have a profound effect not only on the accessibility of those records but also on the manner in which they are interpreted and, thus, understood. The source material of this newly configured archive, all told, comprises nearly forty-five terabytes of image, video, audio, and metadata, all in digital form.

The initial projection of this original material comprises Chapter 1: Memory. The chapter concludes with the visualization of its own jarring upload sequence: a cacophony of chaotic sound, data, video, and image. From here, the network is activated and Chapter 2: Consciousness begins. Individual images become a mass of data, layered into impossible quantities, images that merge into a sinuous geometric structure, abstraction in motion, a series of viscerally dynamic yet technologically cool biomorphic forms and structures that play upon the exterior skin of Gehry's architecture. The visuals become swirling, porous, and organic, evoking a mix of the embodied and the networked. They are irresistibly photogenic, as they morph through an inventory of forms. Nearly all of the spectators are compelled at one point or another to record, with their own phones, these strangely beautiful and sensuously abstract images. Finally, Chapter 3 launches the dream, the neural network's generative mode. A thick neural net evokes movements and pathways; it reveals an interior architecture that leaks and seeps forms. It is a moment of strange vulnerability (and, even stranger, of empathy) for the neural network, as it offers its own imaginings for public view, extending a notion of "this is what I can do, this is how I imagine a photograph." The projected images become strangely hallucinogenic and a little bit

Figure 10.2

Refik Anadol, *WDCH Dreams* (presentation detail), 2018. Multi-projection site-specific video installation, 12-minute loop. Courtesy of the artist.

See also Plate 12.

unnerving as not-quite-human forms seem to struggle to cohere into something recognizable. The intriguingly experimental moment soon yields to a return to both narrative and visual familiarity, a grand and celebratory finale featuring the (recognizably human) conductors of the Los Angeles Philharmonic.

Anadol's collaborators matter: in this site-specific commission, he operates within the relatively safe harbor of an august cultural institution (the Los Angeles Philharmonic) in a celebratory moment (its hundredth anniversary) for an audience (Angelenos) who, outside of the opening night gala, have likely had only a cursory engagement with the Los Angeles Philharmonic's long history. And while both the core and crescendo of Anadol's narrative adheres to the celebratory and triumphant nature of the work's commission, the project nevertheless, and perhaps despite itself, fundamentally evokes counternarratives of authority, the ethics of representation, and the emerging possibilities—both poetic and fraught—of human–machine collaboration.

The point is illustrated in some alternatives. To start, imagine that Anadol's custom technology, developed in collaboration with Google's Artists and Machine Intelligence program, was directed toward a different institution and with a different commission in mind. What if the projection, rather than dwelling on the archives of an august cultural institution, had dwelled instead on the archives of the Federal Bureau of Investigation, or, more locally, the Los Angeles Police Department—a department with a deep legacy of racial profiling and violence? If the data set were comprised of mug shots, crime scene documents, and psychological profiles, what different interpretive languages might be necessary? How might audiences react to "dreamed" or "imagined" or "fictive" archival photographs in those contexts? Given the deep history of critical texts on the restrictive nature of representation within archives of power (Tagg, 1988; Sekula, 1986), and the strong reservations even a casual observer might have about the ethics of "producing" "memories" from archives that have already been shown to be systemically racist and oppressive both in origin and practice, dramatically different stakes would be at play. The Los Angeles Philharmonic provides a kind of cover for the more rigorously ethical and philosophical questions that the technology suggests, but that the project evades and, to some degree, actively resists. Indeed, in Anadol's vision, "the archive" is performed, and made spectacularly visible. The public work is, by its very terms of existence, separate from the archive's material origins. Viewers are not meant to actively engage or explore, but to be spectators.

In the public performance, the "look, but not too closely" spirit of the piece is a matter of practicality that the demands of large-scale public installation art may seem to require. Yet the ethos extends into the smaller, interactive installation. Inside the Walt Disney Concert Hall lobby, viewers may spend up to ten minutes at a time with smaller-scale iterations of the archive visualizations, which are, in an intimate gallery space, parceled into visual and auditory components, accessible as a curated subset. As with the exterior projections, Anadol is at his best conveying the awesomeness of massive scale. Not unlike the philosophical and art historical emergence of the concept of the sublime, Anadol's visualizations are both beautiful and somewhat terrifyingly vast in their complexity. A viewer of either is not unlike the figure in Caspar David Friedrich's classic *Wanderer Above the Sea of Fog* (ca. 1818), standing apart from, yet awed by, the massive scope of nature's beauty and terror. In the radically more intimate scale of this smaller viewing gallery, a viewer—feeling figured as a discrete individual rather than a participant in a public community spectacle—experiences the visualizations close at hand. In one, a vast network slowly reveals itself, as the viewer seems to move dimensionally "through" clusters of data, which are comprised of vast quantities of individual photographs visualized in a kind of space-time dimension. When encountering the unexpected sight of this star cluster visualization of the photographic archive at hand, I was as awestruck as I've ever been at the (latent) potentials of volume and depth of an archival accumulation. Yet in Anadol's projections and visualizations, the viewer is continually held at arm's length, simultaneously beckoned and kept at a distance. The question arises whether this distance indicates safety or a dangerous unknowability. Archives have the capacity to serve as powerful sites of historical engagement, with material that can be mobilized to facilitate critical inquiry into complex historical dynamics, such as the relationship of preservation and cultural value. But collections don't do this on their own: they must be activated, and the method of that engagement can produce vastly different results.

At their most effective, Anadol's projections provide a space from which to reimagine the ethics and aesthetics of memory production and historical engagement, our relationship to images and even what it means to see. Moreover, given the newly configured material dimensions of Anadol's data, these questions require frameworks and language to both evoke and address the complexities at hand, whether visualized or suggested.

To that end, Anadol's machinic collaboration may be situated within the long trajectory of artists drawn to the generative possibilities of the fictive photograph. We can go back to nearly the origins of the medium to establish this persistently fertile territory: to the French photographer Hippolyte Bayard's irresistible, and entirely fictional, *Portrait of a Drowned Man*, a direct positive print made at the tender date of 1840. On the front of this print is a portrait of Bayard himself, feigning death—slumped, shirtless, open to interpretation. On the back, Bayard addresses the viewer directly via a lengthy text. Showing his dark sense of humor, he starts with a complaint that he has not received enough credit for his efforts in the project of photography's invention. He then explains that the dead body in the photograph is *his own*, as he playfully recognizes the limitations of photography—it can't evoke the sense of smell, for instance—and he uses a mix of text and image to engage the viewer in his dark photographic fantasy.

Bayard's gesture, his combination of text and image, played on the delightfully proximate, yet ultimately tenuous, relationship between reality and its photographic representation. This photograph also suggests a foundational contradiction in the medium: because of photographs' enduring and persistent adhesion to some kernel of "truth" or reality, photographic images are all the more compelling and provocative a medium through which to conjure—whether slyly or blatantly—speculative scenarios.

This type of fictive archival engagement persists widely in the contemporary realm.[1] To cite one example, the artist Zoe Leonard created *The Fae Richards Photo Archive* in the early 1990s. The series is exhibited as an installation of an apparent photographic archive and was published as a little book, too, a form that establishes a connection to the personal album. (fig. 10.3) Leonard visually refers to past photographic processes, and much of the delight of the project comes from the skill and thoroughness with which she mines and mimics particular photographic genres, whether scrapbook imagery, publicity stills, or newspaper photojournalism. In *The Fae Richards Photo Archive*, Leonard masterfully spoofs the look of a range of types of photographic prints one might find in an archive: 1930s commercially printed snapshots, for instance, faithfully reproducing the format and tone of the time; or a midcentury film still; or a candid from the 1950s, which differs from those from the 1930s.

Fae Richards, it turns out, despite this persuasive photographic evidence, is fictional. She was initially created for *The Watermelon Woman*, a 1996 film by Cheryl Dunye. In the film, the protagonist goes on an archival hunt to discover a Black lesbian actress from the 1930s and 1940s. The actress's life is inspirational to the protagonist, who speaks movingly about the thrill of finding a role model, a predecessor in the film industry whose identity and experience as a Black lesbian woman she really relates to, and the power of that precedent. Though a viewer of the archive in exhibition or a reader of the book may never learn this, in the film it is ultimately revealed that it's all made up: there is no archive, no actual historical figure for her to relate to, no history or document to discover. As a narrative, the story of Fae Richards is equal parts heartbreaking and optimistic; it is the fantasy that a queer woman of color would have achieved fame and success in 1930s and 1940s Hollywood. As Dunye has noted, "Sometimes you have to create your own history."

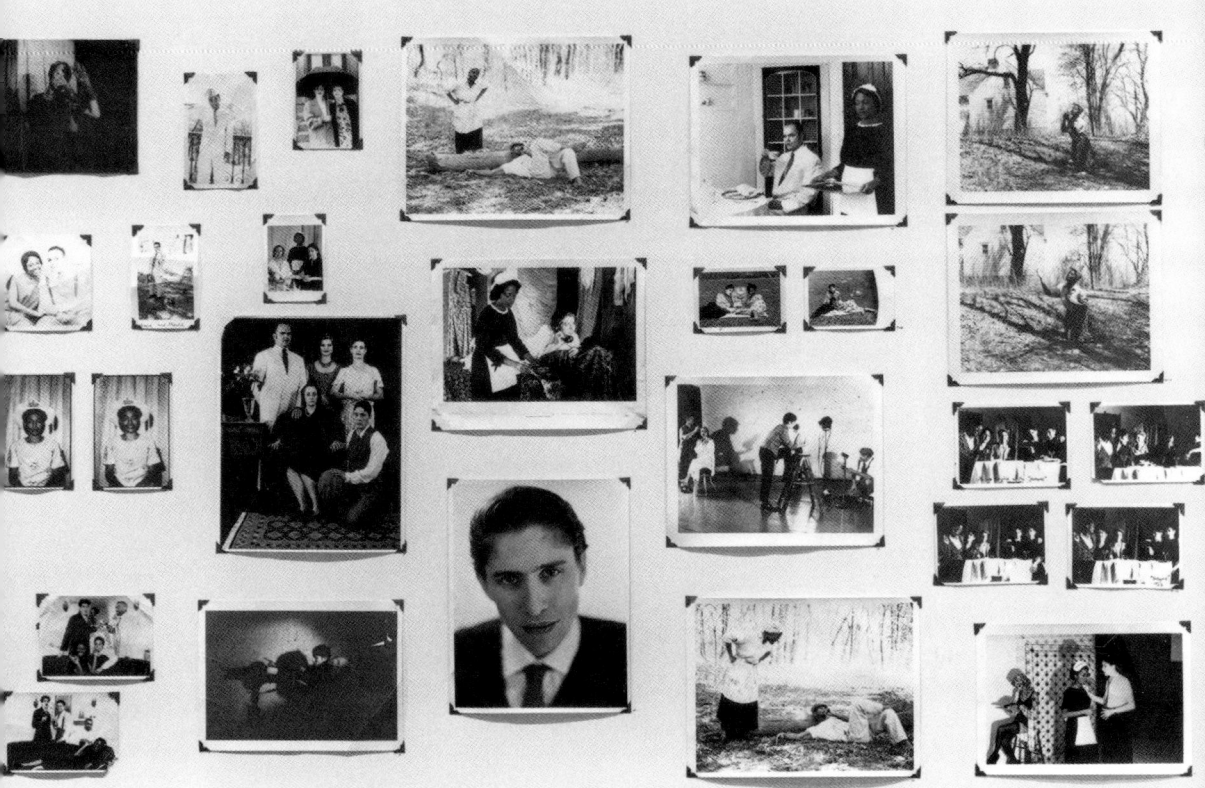

The art historian Carrie Lambert-Beatty has usefully described these realms of practice as the "parafictional," describing a rich history of artists' engagement at the slippery, yet fertile, intersections of plausibility and fiction. The parafictional, for Lambert-Beatty, is "a bit outside" the category of fiction. It "has one foot in the field of the real"; it is a mode in which "real and/or imaginary personages and stories intersect with the world as it is being lived"; and it produces fictions that "are experienced as fact." (Lambert-Beatty, 2009: 54) As these examples suggest, parafictional practices activate the work of artists, cultural critics, historians, archivists, and curators; they disrupt and redirect discourse through cultural interventions, art performances, creative hacking, invented histories and documents. These legions of conjured identities and invented personas are given voice to achieve political and aesthetic ends, often connected to the redressing of historical omissions, marginalized histories, or otherwise suppressed stories and narratives not easily found in either archival record or public discourse. At its most potent, the parafictional achieves the daunting challenge of maintaining a productive and uncomfortable uncertainty while shattering the possibility of a pre-existing status quo.

Figure 10.3

Zoe Leonard, *The Fae Richards Photo Archive* (detail), 1993–1996. 78 black-and-white photographs, 4 color photographs, 6 pages of typed text on typewriter paper, dimensions variable. Installation view, 1997 Whitney Biennial, Whitney Museum of American Art, New York. © Zoe Leonard. Courtesy of the artist; Galerie Gisela Capitain, Cologne; and Hauser & Wirth, New York.

See also Plate 13.

But core to Lambert-Beatty's analysis is an unspoken assumption that the creators of the parafictional are human. In Anadol's work, his collaborator in the creation of parafiction is distinctly machinic: the artificial intelligence capacity of a neural network that, while initially "trained" by a human programmer, operates one step away from human control. While Anadol controls the information from which the neural network learns as well as the coding for that information to be regenerated into new images and sounds, what happens between input and output is the opening up of a new terrain. I would like to suggest that this terrain functions effectively—both conceptually and practically—as a new mode of the latent image. In analog chemical photography, the latent image is the image that has been recorded on film but has not yet been developed, is not yet visible. The latent image exists as a physical and chemical reality yet is not visible to human eyes; as such, it exists slightly outside of time, in a distinct yet unfixed temporal relationship with both the original subject and the viewing audience.

One of Anadol's collaborators describes the neural network's hallucinated (or dreamed, or imagined) images as "inter-images." (McDowell, personal conversation, 2019) These "inter-images" function as a new form of latent image. That is, "inter-images" emerge from spaces between the data, existing as possibilities adjacent to the images of human memory (i.e., photographs), likely to appear but not already existing. This spatial description of the emergence of dream images is not a bad description of how humans, too, conjure and create new images, from latent spaces adjacent to the images we already know and understand. Incrementally, we add to a collective set, and hopefully, from time to time, new forms emerge, and we recognize an original quality. In a parallel way, Anadol's projections may be most provocative when they open a space for considering that temporal relationship between images not existing and existing. That creation is just as fundamentally mysterious in the machinic as in the human.

Although "photographic" images that are generated from the data memories of other, earlier images might seem futuristic, in fact, they are already being generated. Speaking to the algorithmic technology already in the basic visual processes of the phones we carry and use every day, artist Hito Steyerl has described a distinction between representational and newly speculative modes of photography:

A representational mode of thinking photography is: there is something out there and it will be represented by means of optical technology ideally via indexical link. But the technology for the phone camera is quite different. As the lenses are tiny and basically crap, about half of the data captured by the sensor are noise. The trick is to create the algorithm to clean the picture from the noise, or rather to define the picture from within noise. But how does the camera know this? Very simple. It scans all other pictures stored on the phone or on your social media networks and sifts through your contacts. It looks through the pictures you already made, or those that are networked to you and tries to match faces and shapes. In short: it creates the picture based on earlier pictures, on your/its memory. It does not only know what you saw but also what you might like to see based on your previous choices. In other words, it speculates on your preferences and offers an interpretation of data based on affinities to other data. (Steyerl, 2014)

Like the neural network that works as Anadol's collaborator to "dream" or "hallucinate" new images, these speculative images can also be conceived as "inter-images." In these cases, Steyerl continues:

The link to the thing in front of the lens is still there, but there are also links to past pictures that help create the picture. You don't really photograph the present, as the past is woven into it. The result might be a picture that never existed in reality, but that the phone thinks you might like to see. It is a bet, a gamble […] a mixture of conservatism and fabulation. (Steyerl, 2014)

In this new form of latency, this "mixture of conservatism and fabulation," the temporal interlude between not existing and existing is characterized not by a pause of anticipation, but by a productive mode of association impossible to disassociate from prior sight and knowledge. In this framework, the activity of interpreting the archive is deeply embedded in the act of image creation. The emerging project of how we understand and interpret these images is an open question. If we, as a culture, are going to have any meaningful critical engagement with the data systems that are growing all around us, and, by extension, the massive quantities of images they are producing, reconfiguring, and inventing, we can start with the sense of awe that Anadol elicits. But we must go one step further: we must also have experiences that give us a sense of ownership, a sense of investment, and a sense of critical engagement with the copious data that surround us, with the possibilities and potentials of activating these documents and these histories in creative and generative modes that inspire agency rather than passivity. We can't just be captivated by a sense of awe. We must be propelled by it.

Notes

1. Other notable projects in this realm are as varied and diverse as William DeLappa's *The Portraits of Violet and Al* (1973), Joan Fontcuberta's *Fauna* (1987) and *Sputnik* (1997), Yinka Shonibare's *Diary of a Victorian Dandy* (1998), and Christian Boltanski's early books, to name a few.

Bibliography

Carrie Lambert-Beatty, "Make-Believe: Parafiction and Plausibility," *October*, 129 (Summer 2009): 51–84.

Allan Sekula, "The Body and the Archive," *October*, 39 (Winter 1986): 3–64.

Hito Steyerl, "'Politics of Post-Representation': In Conversation with Marvin Jordan," *DIS Magazine*, June 2014, http://dismagazine.com/disillusioned-2/62143/ hito-steyerl-politics-of-post-representation/ (accessed June 9, 2021).

John Tagg, *The Burden of Representation: Photographies and Histories* (Minneapolis: University of Minnesota Press, 1988).

11. Dispersal and Denial: Photographic Ubiquity and the Microbial Analogy

Kyle Parry

"Pictures succumb to uniformity as they flow ceaselessly across our screens, going viral and generating an omnipresent sense that we are being submerged or surveilled. Photography is everywhere."
— from the introductory wall text for *Snap + Share: Transmitting Photographs from Mail Art to Social Networks* (2019)

"Everything is everywhere: but the environment selects."
— Lourens Baas-Becking, *Geobiologie of Inleiding Tot de Milieukunde* (1934)

Is photography really everywhere now? What drives so many observers to insist that it is? Why do so few resist the notion? What advantages might there be in nuancing received wisdom around the supposed pervasiveness of cameras and photographs? For whom could a better grasp on forms of digital photographic *dispersal*—and their inevitable corollary, forms of digital photographic *denial*—matter most?

That critics, curators, and scholars increasingly portray photography as ubiquitous is far from surprising: there isn't just more photography with each passing year—millions more cameras, trillions more images, ever faster and more frequent photo sharing—there are also ever more occasions through which to see, talk about, visualize, and sell photography. With the rise of digital cameras, smartphones, and social media, seemingly everyone is a shareholder in what Susan Sontag called the "photographic enterprise," and seemingly no situation is immune to the possibility of a photograph being taken. (Sontag, 1977: 3) Images can travel with incredible speed from one corner of the globe to the other. To use your computer or smartphone is to have a lens staring at you. On certain apps, you don't just post photos as a form of expression; you rapidly exchange photos as a means of conversation, or you regularly share photos as a matter of social survival. The institution of photography is now as much about representing the world as it is about being in all places and for everyone who would want to speak and show and remember. Even when actual cameras are not physically present, there are still effects from the awareness of the possibility of being photographed (Azoulay, 2015: 19). In short, ubiquity claims persist because photography *is* hypercommon, hyperabundant, and hyperinfluential.

Still, it remains curious that there is so little critical questioning around the manifestly dramatic proposition that photography is now *everywhere*. Indeed, at least as far as I am aware, only a handful of writers have voiced alternatives, and only briefly at that, effectively referring to differences of degree.[1] None of this would be much cause for concern were it not for the ubiquity claim's considerable vulnerability to critique. For one thing, there are plenty of meaningful gaps in the map. There are, for instance, many locations across the globe that photography either barely reaches or does not reach at all, such as places beset by poverty or war, or contexts in which cameras cannot physically operate, such as the Earth's interior. There are also numerous social, political, and cultural restrictions around photography across the planet: who can use cameras and social media (by age or gender or economic access); what types of photographs can be taken and distributed (whether because of censorship, copyright, or other barriers); what kinds of subjects or genres will receive attention and endorsement (based on prevailing norms or what type of person presents what). If anything, the sheer abundance and availability of photography makes it all the more plain that many types of events and circumstances continue to *not* receive photographic treatment, whether because of active restrictions (archival materials, museum holdings, secret prisons, secret wars) or because of forbidding conditions (such as events of slow and structural violence, the dispersed natures of which make them difficult to photograph).[2] In other words, it doesn't take much to see that the proposition that photography is everywhere is an exaggeration in the extreme. Although photography is in many, many places, it is by no means in all places.

The ubiquity claim is also vulnerable along critical and conceptual lines. This is the potential that ubiquity claims are fantasies of imagined, final circumstances rather than politically and philosophically nuanced interpretations of actual, unfolding ones. Such flights of analysis do not necessarily warrant approval, as though they were basically forgivable instances of hyperbolizing through the frame of everywhereness (of the kind one might know from when something spills in the kitchen, and a family member heartily exclaims that the offending substance has gotten *everywhere*). Indeed, to say, without qualification, that photography is ubiquitous risks reinforcing an implicit premise that the only worlds that truly matter are those in which this appears to be the case, those worlds in which selfies, espresso snaps, sunsets, or other seemingly hallmark digital photographic forms are frequent and pervasive. Everything else (and everyone else) falls outside the everywhere that matters to apprehend and interpret.

The point here is that, even if one were to accept the hyperbolic nature of ubiquity claims as necessary or forgivable, one would still have to answer for what Ulrik Ekman, speaking of ubiquitous computing, has characterized as the ubiquity concept's silent freight (Ekman, 2011: 7).[3] Whether applied to computing, photography, or still other institutions, ubiquity is not, in this rendering, an empty and neutral conceptual vessel. Instead, it is an insidious vehicle for premises and orientations that serve to warp and limit perceptions and interpretations of culture, people, and place. Unqualified ubiquity endorses a false sense of universality (such and such is everywhere, as in everywhere that matters to me to think about). It produces a sense of finality (reaching the status of everywhere means reaching an effectively uncontestable, total presence). And it undermines the essential question of *differential* distribution—the actual variation and inequality in the reach of photography or, in the opposite sense, the legitimate desire among certain publics to avoid or contest some or all aspects of that reach. So often couched in terms of democratization, unqualified ubiquity claims work against that very ambition.

The problem at hand, then, is how to respond to a persistent paradox within the world of contemporary photography: the simultaneous abundance of digital ubiquity claims and the dearth of critical questions thereby. The first and most obvious way to respond would be to refuse the above lines of critique and simply fall in line. One would accept as given the real-world applicability and necessity of the notion of ubiquity, and one would proceed to invoke that notion as necessary, either ignoring or dismissing the supposed problems of silent freight. A second option would be to do the opposite and refuse all ubiquity claims tout court. One could argue, for example, that it is absurd to claim that anything— apart from, say, gravity—is everywhere. Alternatively, one could elaborate the critique I have only just sketched, linking the problem of ubiquity with long histories of racialized, ethnocentric, neoliberal, and imperialist discourses. As books like *Provincializing Europe* attest (Chakrabarty, 2000), such discourses take contingent particulars as essential givens. In so doing, they undermine and forestall more vibrant, democratic, and liberatory conceptions and conversations.

As sympathetic as I am to both takes on ubiquity, I nevertheless favor a more uncertain, middle path. Rather than accepting or rejecting ubiquity claims outright, we find ways to critically reconceptualize them. We do so on the idea that there must be some reason that the concept of ubiquity has had its way, yet this needn't mean that the concept ought to continue to have its way in exactly the same way. Other approaches to this essential matter of radically wide distribution must be possible. The question is how we ought to construct those alternative approaches, and what we ought to do with them in turn. Somehow, these approaches must do justice to the manifest abundance and influence of digital (and nondigital) photographic forms while also negotiating the inaccuracies and harms—universalization, naturalization, erasure—in exactly such an enterprise. Such newly vivified theories of ubiquity will not, it seems to me, emerge through strict adherence to available modes of analysis and debate. Rather, they demand rethinking the terms through which we conceive questions of hypersaturation and hypercommonality in the first place. What is needed, in short, is direct, unorthodox, critical, transversal, and pragmatic thinking capable of reframing ubiquity without failing to recognize the undeniable attraction, actual real-world responsiveness, and critical and intellectual advantages of the concept.

Strange as it feels to write, I find crucial means for such thinking by shifting away from the most obvious dramatis personae—cameras and photographs—and instead moving toward the creatures that tend to dwell within and upon these and countless other objects: microbes. (fig. 11.1) Also called microorganisms, microbes are organisms (and organism-like entities) that defy human vision. Among the earliest life forms to have evolved, they include familiar entities like bacteria, fungi, and viruses as well as less familiar ones like archaea and protists. Microbes can be single-celled, multicellular, or acellular, and there are interesting cases of microbes that form colonies of many different organisms unified into a living whole that is, nevertheless, not considered an individual organism. Microbes serve all manner of critical ecological functions, from the recycling of nutrients to the removal of

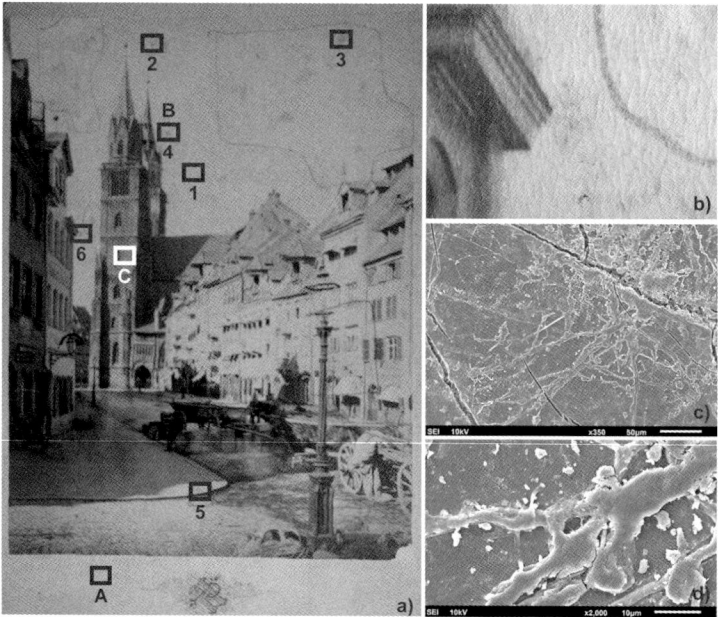

Figure 11.1

Puškárová et al., Documentation of the presence of fungal hyphae on albumen print from "Microbial communities affecting albumen photography heritage: a methodological survey," February 11, 2016. Creative Commons Attribution 4.0 International License.

contaminants. As the COVID-19 pandemic made tragically plain, however, certain microbial forms can radically undermine or even destroy bodies, communities, and economies.[4] (Of course, the pandemic also made plain that there are factors other than the pathogen, many of them preventable and many of them unevenly distributed across race, gender, and class, among other categories.) Estimates of the number of species of microbes vary widely, from hundreds of millions to perhaps even one trillion species in total, with hundreds of thousands of these being viruses in the oceans and something on the order of five million species of fungi (Bakalar, 2016; de Jesus, 2019; Hawksworth and Lücking, 2017). The distribution of these hyperabundant life forms is nothing short of astonishing. Where there is water—and this includes mineral veins deep beneath the ocean floor—there is microbial life.[5]

As things stand, the intellectual association between photography and microbes is both rich and restricted. On the one hand, there is the problem of material decay; certain microbes eat pictures (Puškárová et al., 2016). On the other hand, there is the microbial analogy of *virality*: certain images (or events or ideas) manage to become extremely widespread in a manner reminiscent of both computer viruses and actual viruses.[6] First used in 1999 in relation to marketing, the viral analogy provides a crucial frame through which to understand aspects of contemporary photography and indeed digital photographic ubiquity. Among other things, virality speaks to the events of spread that further entrench the presence of not just certain images but of images in general. Not only that, the metaphor of virality serves as a waypoint for a host of important lines of inquiry around *contagion* in which, as Tony D. Sampson summarizes, "financial crisis, social influence, innovations, fashions and fads, and even human emotion are understood to spread universally like viruses across networks." (Sampson, 2012: 2)[7] Nevertheless, metaphors of virality and contagion are not themselves sufficient for a direct inquiry into the conceptual foundations of digital photographic ubiquity. This is because those metaphors tend to emphasize networks, events, and transmission (key for understanding digital visual culture) rather than geographies, conditions, and densities (key for understanding questions of pervasiveness). Indeed, rather than explicitly address the broad "sea of content" (or what I prefer to call the dispersal and denial of photographic forms), virality tends to emphasize (Sampson's book notwithstanding) the remarkable "exception" that manages to achieve visibility and spread (Nahon and Hemsley, 2013).[8] By contrast, my own current notion of a valuable microbial intervention into debates around photography turns on precisely this question of what is—and isn't—"everywhere."

By way of a chance encounter amid research for this book, the alternative I have in mind is a nearly century-old concept in microbiology.

Commonly called the "ubiquity hypothesis," the concept first took root in 1934, when the Dutch scientist Lourens Baas-Becking sought to expand upon ideas first promulgated by his predecessor, Martinus Beijerinck.[9] "Everything is everywhere," Baas-Becking writes, "but the environment selects." (Baas-Becking, 1934) The gnomic statement became something of a mantra for microbial biogeography, the field of scientific study that explores the distribution of microbial life across the planet. This statement indicates a key difference between the distribution of macroorganisms, which includes creatures such as crows and redwood trees, and what Baas-Becking is here calling "everything," which means any microbial "taxon"—any group of one or more populations seen by biologists to form a unit—from bacteria and fungi to viruses and protists. For *macro*organisms, history and geography play crucial roles in which taxa are found where. For instance, although crows can travel many places (at times seemingly "anywhere"), they cannot necessarily get to or sustain themselves in all places; both how they evolved and where they evolved continually condition where members of the species can and cannot arrive and reside. With *micro*organisms, the situation is far different. Microbes can travel by wind, water, and other means throughout all manner of planetary habitats, from clouds and forest canopies to mammals' guts and the bottom of the ocean. (One of the more striking examples of the dispersal capacity of microbes I have come across is a form of bacteria that thrives near deep sea vents lodged in a person's belly button.[10]) In other words, microbes confront little to no dispersal constraints. And thus, according to the Baas-Becking hypothesis, microbial taxa should be understood as fundamentally and characteristically *ubiquitous*. (This term is indeed specifically employed by microbiologists.)

What is crucial here is the generative double move: the simultaneous assertion and qualification of the proposition of ubiquity. Everything, as in every microbial taxa, can disperse anywhere, but this does not mean that there are no observable differences in local and global distributions of particular types of microbes. It's just that the key determining factor in which taxa endure where is neither history nor geography (as is the case with macroorganisms). Rather, it is what is here called "environment." Particular taxa persist where they persist due to the features of particular habitats, which is to say because of distinct, local, life-sustaining conditions, such as temperature, availability of water and nutrients, or levels of sunlight.[11] Certain conditions support certain microbial taxa and not others. In a phrase, *microbial taxa can arrive anywhere, but they don't necessarily endure everywhere.*[12]

Over the nearly one hundred years since its introduction, the ubiquity hypothesis has occasioned both perennial citation and increasing skepticism within its field of origin. Some microbiologists see the hypothesis as accurate at best or necessary at worst, as though microbial biogeography would not now enjoy the legitimacy or productivity it now does without this core principle. Others, calling attention to strong evidence of at least a few instances in which geographical factors affect the distribution patterns of particular microbes and microbial communities, portray the proposition as imprecise and misleading, with one scientist going so far as to argue that "everything is everywhere" is a "siren song" that "gets us nowhere" (Fierer, 2015) and several others using their studies, such as one on the distinct makeup of microbial life in Antarctica (Vyerman et al., 2010), as occasions to assert the unreliability and false allure of the aphoristic claim.

From the position of concern I have laid out—that is, this concern to respond through critical reconceptualization to the paradoxical abundance of and lack of criticality around digital ubiquity claims—a turn to the Baas-Becking hypothesis could seem both odd and precarious, not only because I risk converting a scientific concept into mere metaphor but also because, as I have just indicated, the concept itself is (according to some at least) outdated and unreliable. However, there is good precedent for exactly this kind of exercise. Among the most thoroughgoing is found across the work of the philosopher Gilles Deleuze. For Deleuze, the apparent trouble with a given scientific proposition might be a sign of its conceptual potential.[13] That is to say, there are what Deleuze describes as "inexact yet completely rigorous" scientific notions that "scientists can't do without" but "which belong equally to scientists, philosophers, and artists." (Deleuze, 1995: 29) These notions are marked by an "excess of sense" that "can be mobilised in contexts that are distinct from the one in which they are usually (and justifiably) used." (Voss, 2013: 201) Although this practice of conceptual transplantation does come with "dangers"—for instance, the scientific concept might be uncritically applied, or it might simply function as a fruitless metaphor—careful use can yield considerable philosophical and pragmatic reward.[14] The key thing to do is to take from these inexact concepts "a particular conceptualizable character which itself refers to non-scientific areas." (Deleuze, 1986: 129)[15] That "conceptualizable character"—that quantum of insight or provocation, that useful reframing, whatever it might be—can then take on new life. As a result of such transference, inexact scientific concepts come to generate, as Daniela Voss puts it, "a movement of thought that transcends their usual sphere of application and arouses a synthesis with new conceptual components in another sphere." (Voss, 2013: 201)

Following on Deleuze and others' precedents, my contention isn't that this enduring aphorism from the world of microbial biogeography holds some magical solution to the silent freight of photographic and other ubiquity claims. Nor am I saying that the time has come to finally recognize that photography equals microbes (however willing to pursue this analogy I remain). Rather, I look to the Baas-Becking hypothesis for what it can imperfectly afford. This is an "inexact" concept that can lead to better thinking and conceptualizing than has heretofore been possible. It is an unsteady means toward useful "movements of thought" that have otherwise proved elusive.

Dispersal is one key, microbe-inspired starting point for a new movement of thought around ubiquity. By and large, when writers or curators say that photography is ubiquitous or "everywhere" (such as in the statement I've used as the first epigraph to this chapter), they leave the central term unspecified. "Photography" is a kind of conceptual mass or critical abstraction without much if anything in the way of qualities, components, or tensions. It is as though photography were some univocal thing à la God or seawater, the same in every place, not differing in what it is, just a perpetually reproduced and continuous entity that stretches across the entire globe with only the most minor variation. The notion of "everything is everywhere" does not provide some readymade rejoinder to that blunt casting of a complex, internally contradictory, and still evolving medium, institution, practice, and enterprise. But it does point to a viable, interesting, and indeed necessary alternative. It does this because "everything" refers to all manner of different species, subspecies, and species assemblages, in other words, to *taxa*. These taxa are everywhere not because they are actually everywhere, but because there is a constant, remarkable, and powerful "dispersal capacity" at work among them. Microbes disperse with spectacular speed and ease across all manner of habitats, spaces, climates, and times.

Such an emphasis pays off when "inexactly" translated into the context of photography. To speak of photographic ubiquity in a more precise and productive fashion is not to speak of photography in its pervasive and continuous presence; it is to speak of *the stunning and proven dispersal capacity of photographic forms*, a capacity that is not strictly limited to the digital era, but, which, as this collection shows, has manifested throughout histories of photography and undergone a recent, massive intensification. Early on, it is the remarkable, border-crossing dispersal of the fervor to fix a lens-based image. Soon, it is the slow but steady (and frequently destructive and exploitative) distribution of cameras to ever more places across industrial and imperial worlds. Then it is the flying fast of snapshot photographs, not absolutely widely saturated but present in an increasing number of homes and hands. And yet further on, reaching into the digital era, when smartphone cameras are readily snatched out of pockets and into situations, there emerges the apparent lack of immunity of any time or place or event from photography, with seemingly all places touched with at least one or the other photographic form that is, in turn, ready to assert and even reproduce itself.

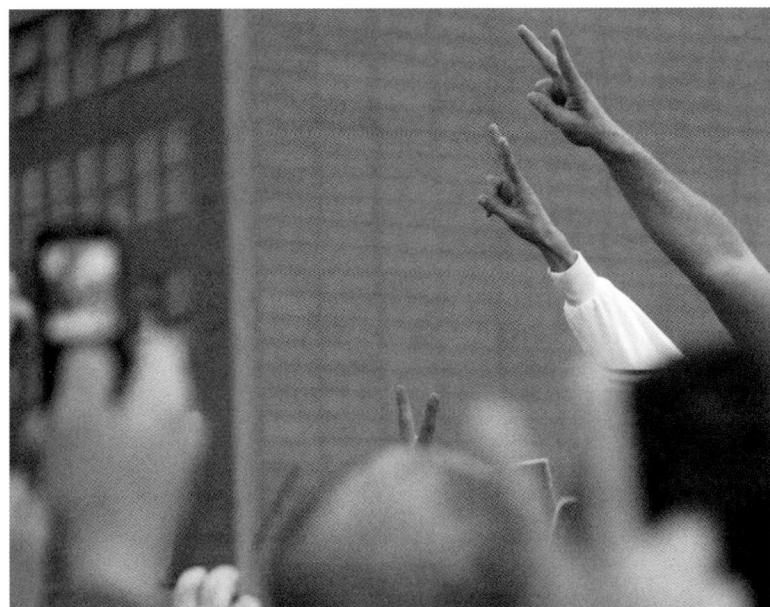

Although the concept and metaphor of virality to some degree alludes to photography in this fashion, at the end of the day it is a metaphor dedicated to single, sudden, fast, and exceptional dispersal. What really needs emphasis is the constant spreading and distribution of many different types of photographic forms. *That* constancy, that way in which not some but effectively all hours of the day, one can bear witness to the dispersal and perpetuation of one after the other photographic "taxa"—that is what deserves to occasion the otherwise risky and freighted frame of everywhere. Without such a dispersal-centered vision of photographic ubiquity, we fall short in our vision of abundance and saturation, stuck with the beginnings of a hyperbole, not actually attending to the sprawling and multifaceted force that we imperfectly gather under the banner of "ubiquitous photography." *With* a dispersal-centered vision, on the other hand, both the history and the theory of photographic hyperabundance open to more possibilities for description and questioning. Like (but not exactly like) a strain of bacteria in people's guts, the habit of making a "peace" or "V" sign for the camera, once largely concentrated in certain regions in East Asia has become a physical commonplace. (fig. 11.2)[16] Like (but not exactly like) a virus that mutates into more transmissible variants, the smartphone camera comes to variously mimic, supplement, and kill off forms of personal memory across increasingly many cultural settings. Like (but not exactly like) an invasive fungus, technologies for the surveillance of communications, locations, and faces (including one that creates a "temporary surveillance scene") ride the winds of profit and power from one country to another.[17] Time and again, that is, photographic forms (as well as their cognates in other media) find ways to spread and to perpetuate, sometimes causing surprise and consternation for the extent to which they now reach, other times functioning all too quietly and successfully to yield much in the way of attention or fear, much less countermeasure. Extraordinary dispersal, effectively ignorant of social and cultural borders, persists with such speed, reach, and variegation as to *seem* to add up to an uninterrupted "everything is everywhere."

And yet dispersal isn't everything. Once again, the Baas-Becking hypothesis provides an imperfect but necessary resource for conceiving of why this is so. In the first half of the aphorism, one gets a powerful notion of the incredible and effectively ubiquitous dispersal capacities of microbial species and of particular species assemblages, a notion which can then translate into a transformed vision of photographic forms circulating and reproducing with remarkable global reach. In the second half of the hypothesis, however, is a more agonistic picture: a fact of any habitat across the planet is the simultaneous receiving and *repulsion* of microbial taxa. That is to say, the members of certain taxa will *not* be welcomed into the fold; they will not persist and reproduce in this habitat, because that habitat does not provide sufficiently conducive conditions. These microbes stop short, they die, they go dormant. As much is happening all the time and "everywhere." And this leads to an important, alternative movement of thought. Zooming out to the widest possible perspective, working to consolidate something of a potentially "conceptualizable character," one comes to the proposition that *the inevitable other side of widespread dispersal is widespread denial.* Microbial taxa are constantly and pervasively spreading; microbial taxa are also constantly and pervasively failing to take hold.

In this observation about the microbial world is a valuable excess of sense. That excess can be directed toward an alternative and extended vision of photographic abundance in which *the facts of sheer quantity, speedy dispersal, and widespread presence are also the reality of all manner of negative processes: spurning, refusing, blocking, losing.* Something as simple as a selfie stick provides an immediate entrance into this way of thinking. For a long time, the selfie stick was a quite limited form, restricted to a few inventive people extending the reach of their cameras through improvised means, or, in the case of Hiroshi Ueda, through a "telescopic extender" for a "compact camera," invented in the early 1980s, that never took off.[18] (fig. 11.3) Soon after the smartphone became "ubiquitous," however, the now mass-produced selfie stick (unfortunately for Ueda, not his patented version) found its most appropriate vector; the practice of extending an appendage outward to produce a photograph of one's self, one's background, and potentially some fellow travelers became a

FIG.17a

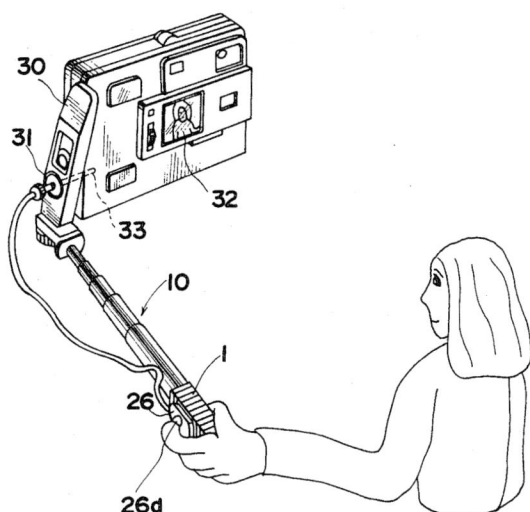

Figure 11.3

From Hiroshi Ueda et al., "Telescopic Extender for Supporting Compact Camera." Patent US4530580A, filed January 17, 1984.

widely dispersed (if also often derided) presence on the photographic scene. While critics spoke of seeing selfie sticks "selling out everywhere," the apparatus only further incited the general mockery launched at self-imaging. Of course, it didn't take long for this fervor to subside. A telescopic apparatus for self-imaging became less common, necessary, or desirable. A period of considerable spread—the participation of an evanescent photographic form (a tool and a practice) in digital photographic ubiquity qua dispersal—gave way to a period of denial and decay. Not only did fewer people find themselves wanting to carry selfie sticks around, but numerous museum and tourist sites saw fit to ban their use.[19] The selfie stick continued to "arrive" in various contexts of social life, from the solemn memorial to the rowdy sporting event, and it also continued to be useful for certain bodies at certain times. But the selfie stick did not endure in the numbers it once did. Instead, an alternative suite of photographic forms remained dominant in these and other places (including long-tested forms like simply extending one's arm to take a self-image or even the habit of partaking in a social experience without self-imaging at all). Meanwhile, adjacent and competing forms, such as Snap's "selfie drone," lay in wait, preparing themselves for both dispersal and (presumably) eventual denial.

If one way to observe the interplay of dispersal and denial is to focus on a formerly widespread photographic form, another is to dwell on a particular site at which ubiquitous (as in ever and widely dispersing) forms intersect and interact. Serving to frame *Snap + Share*, a rich

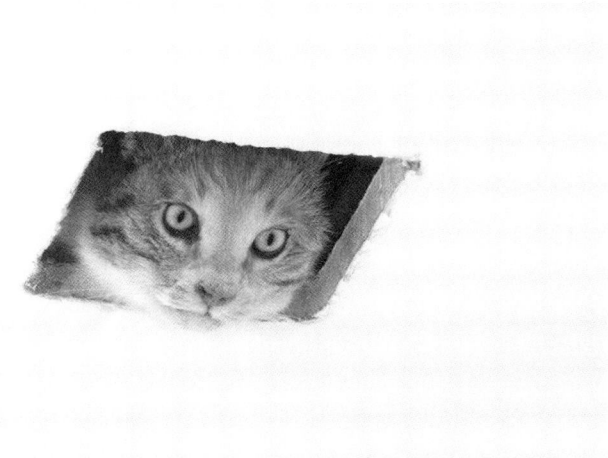

Figure 11.4

Eva Mattes and Franco
Mattes, *Ceiling Cat*,
2016. Taxidermy cat,
polyurethane resin, hole,
San Francisco Museum
of Modern Art, photo-
graph by Katherine Du
Tiel, CC0 1.0 Universal
(CC0 1.0) Public Domain
Dedication.

See also Plate 15.

(though markedly apolitical) exhibition led by Clément Chéroux on
the history of photography through the lens of sharing, the chapter's
first epigraph emerged at one such site, the San Francisco Museum of
Modern Art (commonly called SFMOMA).[20] (Selfie sticks were banned
there, too.) Sure enough, until the uncontrollable spread of a virus called
SARS-CoV-2 made it impossible, to look around this museum on any
given day was to see the workings of hyperabundant photography, with
photos as likely to be taken and shared across the galleries as out in the
courtyards or even within the colorful bathrooms.[21] Watched by both
official surveillance cameras and the photography-ready eyes of smartphone users (and, during *Snap + Share*, those of Eva and Franco Mattes's
taxidermy version of the internet's viral ceiling cat), the museum space
was effectively pervaded by the consciousness of the possibility of being
seen and photographed, or what the exhibition refers to as "an omnipresent sense that we are being submerged or surveilled." (fig. 11.4)
(One could also ask whether certain artists represented in this museum and others have tended to negotiate ubiquity by creating works
that lend themselves to visual travel by way of official and unofficial
documentation.)

Nevertheless, like any other "environment," SFMOMA was also shot
through with various kinds of actual and consequential photographic
denial. Visitors' desires aside, photos could be taken but only at particular times and at particular distances. Certain kinds of photos did not fit
the general habit. Certain kinds of photographers, whether due to socio-
economic or other factors, rarely arrived to take photographs. For all the
availability of photography, certain artworks received little to no photographic attention, or, if they did, those photographs did not see much in

the way of public circulation. At the same time, certain artworks within sfmoma also spoke to forms of rejection and selectivity that take place beyond the walls of the museum, including differential access to place and image, which is to say the photographic selection (or deselection) enforced by violent restrictions on citizenship, movement, and agency. In *Where We Come From*, for instance, Emily Jacir undertakes actions that her work's immediate protagonists, Palestinians exiled from their homeland, cannot, from watering a tree in one person's village to playing soccer with the first Palestinian boy the artist encounters.[22] (fig. 11.5) As Jacir documents these actions through individual photographs yoked to the protagonists' requests, she propels these images across borders to share and reshare them, initially through museum display alone but eventually also through the digital reproduction of excerpts from the artwork and, in the vein of ubiquity, through the ongoing documentation and social media sharing undertaken by museum visitors. Although it is not Jacir's intention per se, as her work assembles the profoundly uneven distribution of citizenship and agency, it also testifies to a persistence of photographic negation that sfmoma, like many other agents of photographic discourse, has heretofore tended to overwrite through its more normative framing of photography as a "fundamentally democratic" and universally available medium.[23]

Figure 11.5

Emily Jacir, *Where We Come From (Iyad)* (detail), 2001–2003. American passport, 30 texts, 32 c-prints, and 1 video, dimensions variable. © Emily Jacir. Courtesy of San Francisco Museum of Modern Art.

See also Plate 16.

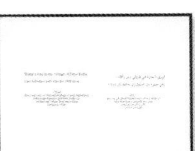

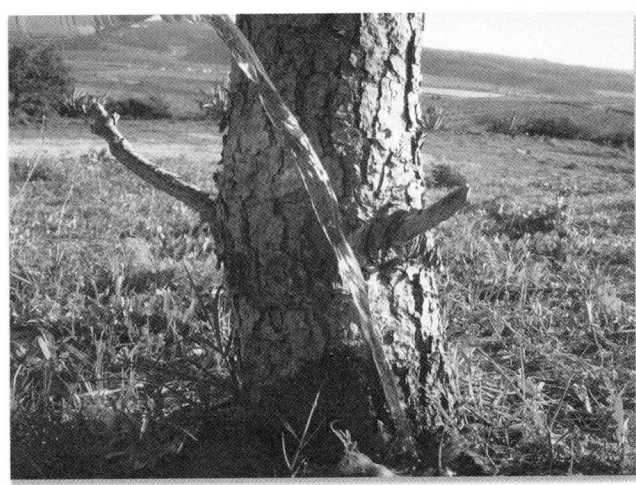

Beyond following a form and contemplating sites lie several other means of mapping and analyzing the dynamics of dispersal and denial that constitute digital ubiquity, including comparing distributions across cultural and geographic contexts. Alternatively, one could shift from an empirical to a prescriptive mode, considering both what photographic forms *ought* to ubiquitously disperse *and* what photographic forms ought to be resisted, refused, drawn down, denied. Of course, certain projects within photographic theory already do something to this effect. In Ariella Aïsha Azoulay's *Potential History*, for instance, there is a general proposition of photography as having been ubiquitously destructive throughout its history, with this destruction justified by the assumption of "imperial rights," including a "right to take" photographs and to do so in "worlds that were 'opened up'" by "imperial agents." (Azoulay, 2019: 282–283) Part of the prescriptive counter to this is an argument for both alternative dispersals (photography in the mode of "worldly sovereignty") and actively chosen denials (a call for a "general photographic strike") (Azoulay, 2019: 388, 285).

As a different example, for Kaja Silverman, the widely dispersed habit of framing photography as a kind of "taking" is challenged by a call to foster alternative language and thinking around photography as *receiving* (Silverman, 2015: 14–15, 24–26). Active and important and named as such in the early days of the medium, the mode of photography as receiving has, in the eyes of Silverman, long been spurned in favor of an approach to photography that seeks to command and control the world's light—and the beings who dwell within that light—by extracting and fixing views. At the same time, the effectively dormant vision of photography qua welcoming and waiting—evident in projects such as Abelardo Morell's camera obscura compositions—has the potential to spread and proliferate. While photographic postures marked by humility, openness, and what Silverman calls "the miracle of analogy" might not, as it were, outcompete those centered in taking and extracting, they might nevertheless find harbor and influence in more contexts than before.

My point is not that Azoulay, Silverman, or others addressing photography in its planetary reach are somehow secretly dependent on a microbial analogy. Rather, in reconceiving the terms of their writing through the notions of dispersal and denial, and in seeing the possibility that prescriptive (and political) work is possible through such repatterning, I elaborate what this chapter has sought to offer by way of an inexact analogy: revivified visions of photographic surfeit that retain the best aspects of ubiquity claims—including the attention they bring to the reality and import of astonishingly widespread photographic distribution—but that also work to avoid the forms of critical and conceptual harm that have so far been their silent freight.

Notes

1. Martin Hand, for instance, says photography is everywhere, but it is not everywhere "in the same way" (Hand, 2012: 12). Ariella Aïsha Azoulay says there are places, like disaster zones, where "the subjects of disaster are sentenced to be photographed rather than to photograph themselves." (Azoulay, 2015: 19)

2. See, for instance, Rob Nixon's *Slow Violence and the Environmentalism of the Poor* (Nixon, 2011).

3. Ekman writes, "Whether in cultural theoretical or technical discourses, the terms of 'ubiquity,' 'pervasiveness,' and 'ambience' come silently freighted with a notion of totalizing universality or even certain ontological and metaphysical remainders (altogether abstract idealizations and/or excessively essential or substantial extensions). Both the editors and the authors contributing to this special issue approach this as a call for ongoing deconstruction and reconstruction, not least in the sense that remainders and implications of onto-theological and sovereign ideological notions must be questioned reasonably so as to be put under critical erasure in one or more ways." (Ekman, 2011: 7)

4. On the often-overlooked ecological functions of viruses, see Rachel Nuwer, "Why the World Needs Viruses to Function," *BBC Future*, June 17, 2020, https://www.bbc.com/future/article/20200617-what-if-all-viruses-disappeared.

5. The oceanographer Brian Glazer puts it this way: "When we find water here on Earth—whether it be ice-covered lakes, whether it be deep-sea hydrothermal vents, whether it be arid deserts—if there's any water, we've found microbes that have found a way to make a living there." (Ghose, 2015)

6. There are multiple other instances in which media and viruses have been linked. One example is Jean Baudrillard's concern that television had become a "viral, endemic, chronic, alarming presence." (Baudrillard, 1981: 30) Another is Douglas Rushkoff's notion of a "media virus" that circulates hidden agendas under the veneer of enrapturing content (Rushkoff, 1994). For further reading along these lines, see the recent interdisciplinary volume *Endemic: Essays in Contagion Theory* (Nixon and Servitje, 2016).

7. While Sampson engages these microbial and epidemiological terms, he joins Deleuze in refusing to frame this engagement as metaphorical or analogical (see footnote on Deleuze below). On the one hand, Sampson parallels existing discourses on contagion, as when he writes, "This is a world awash with hormones and consumer goods, making people happy or sad, sympathetic or apathetic, and a space in which affects are significantly passed on, via suggestions made by others, more and more through networks." (5) On the other hand, in dialogue with the sociologist Gabriel Tarde, Sampson seeks to develop a nonrepresentational approach that can "disentangle contagion theory from the mechanistic limitations" that he perceives in memetics and theories of the crowd (87). Drawing on concepts from Deleuze and others, Sampson argues that the "universality of contagion needs to be understood […] as independent of unifying mechanisms and analyzed accordingly through the relationalities and associations established between singularities." (89) His account departs from others on virality and contagion by emphasizing "forces of relational encounter in the social field." (4)

8. For the authors of these words, Karine Nahon and Jeff Hemsley, "viral events" are ubiquitous, but they are also the "exception." "[E]ven in their ubiquity," they write, "viral events are the exception while the vast majority of content remains obscure. Viral content is what stands out as *remarkable* in a sea of content." (Nahon and Hemsley, 2013: 2)

9. Maureen A. O'Malley provides an excellent summary of the history of the microbial ubiquity hypothesis in a 2008 article (O'Malley, 2008).

10. According to the documentary *Life on Us: A Microscopic Safari* (2014), a swab of a subject's navel for the Belly Button Biodiversity project at North Carolina State University revealed the presence of a bacteria typically seen at deep ocean vents called *Dermacoccus abyssi*.

11. Tom Fenchel and Bland J. Finlay put it this way: "habitat properties alone are needed to explain the presence of a given microbe, and historical factors are irrelevant." (Fenchel and Finlay, 2004: 777)

12. Although this is not a statement found in microbiology contexts, I find it a fruitful way to sum up the point for present purposes. I am grateful to microbiologist Karen Ottemann for her feedback on my outsider attempts at summarization.

13. Another key precedent (unrelated to and of a different order and kind than that of Deleuze) is found in Christina Sharpe's 2016 book *In the Wake: On Blackness and Being*. Sharpe finds in the scientific concept of "residence time" the means to articulate otherwise elusive perspectives on historical repetition and saturation. Sharpe also speaks of residence time in literal

(and haunting) terms when she discusses the continued presence in the ocean of elements (like sodium in the blood) from the bodies of enslaved people who were thrown—or who jumped—overboard during the Middle Passage (Sharpe, 2016: 41).

14. It is important to note that Deleuze and his frequent collaborator Félix Guattari do not see such a practice as the use of science as metaphor. Rather, for these two thinkers, "there are no metaphors only concepts and occasions of their use which can involve either the unexpected extension, transformation or variation of an existing concept or, in extreme cases, the coinage of new words to express novel concepts." (Patton, 2006: 32) According to Daniel Smith and John Protevi, "Deleuze and Guattari's refusal to recognize that their work contains metaphors is due to their struggle against the 'imperialism' of the signifying regime, a major theme in both *Anti-Oedipus* and *A Thousand Plateaus*: not every relation between different intellectual fields can be grasped by the most common notions of 'metaphor,' reliant as they are on the notion of a transfer of sense from primary to secondary signification." (Smith and Protevi, 2020) For present purposes, I refer to my use of the Baas-Becking hypothesis as analogical.

15. One observer described this practice in microbial terms, referring to "the need to think through other fields, to reconfigure a body of discourse—or an antibody like Deleuze's for that matter—by infecting it with viruses from other locales, because thinking through different disciplinary terrain produces decisive differences." (Harris, 2000: 27) For an example of work in this vein, see *Narrating the Catastrophe* (Saorsa, 2011).

16. For a helpful account of the history and appeal of this gesture, see Dhvani Solani, "Why Does Basically Everyone Do This V-Finger Peace Thing in Photos?," *Vice*, March 31, 2021, https://www.vice.com/en/article/k7a4za/v-sign-fingers-peace-vagina-pose-photo.

17. According to Ryan Gallagher, technology for building mass dragnets has been "increasingly finding its way into the hands of security forces in undemocratic countries where dissidents are jailed, tortured, and in some cases executed." A related technology called HawkEye serves as a "temporary surveillance scene." It "scans people as they walk past the camera and compares images of their faces to photographs contained in 'multi-million-level databases' in real time, triggering an alert if a particular suspect is identified." See Ryan Gallagher, "Middle East Dictators Buy Spy Tech from Company Linked to IBM and Google," *The Intercept*, July 12, 2019.

18. See Vibeka Venema, "How the Selfie Stick Was Invented Twice," *BBC World Service*, April 19, 2015, https://www.bbc.com/news/magazine-32336808 and United States patent number US4530580A, "Telescopic extender for supporting compact camera."

19. See Sasha Lekach and Suzanne Ciechalski, "Don't Even Think About Bringing Your Selfie Stick to These Tourist Destinations," *Mashable*, July 29, 2017, https://mashable.com/2017/07/29/selfie-sticks-banned-travel-tourist-destinations.

20. Situated on the unceded ancestral homeland of the Ramaytush Ohlone peoples, visited by over a million people per year, as of 2020, the San Francisco Museum of Modern Art held over seventeen thousand photographic works from 1839 to the present. On the role of European-caused infection—including "gastrointestinal disease, measles, influenza, syphilis, tuberculosis, typhus, and diphtheria"—in the devastation of Indigenous peoples via Mission San Francisco and other mission sites, see *Our Better Nature: Environment and the Making of San Francisco* (Dreyfus, 2008: 27–28).

21. As I write these words, SFMOMA is closed due to the COVID-19 pandemic. The museum is also confronting demands for structural reconfiguration. On the movements against inequality and structural racism at SFMOMA, including those in support of Taylor Brandon, a former employee whose critical comment was removed from an Instagram post by the museum, see Hakim Bishara, "SFMOMA Accused of Censoring Black Voices After Removing Comment by Former Employee," *Hyperallergic*, June 2, 2020, https://hyperallergic.com/568331/sfmoma-george-floyd-instagram-comments-disabled and Hakim Bishara, "SFMOMA Workers Call for Major Reform During Public Board Meeting," *Hyperallergic*, September, 4, 2020, https://hyperallergic.com/586207/sfmoma-workers-call-for-major-reform-during-during-public-board-meeting.

22. Emily Jacir, *Where We Come From, 2001–2003*, Collection SFMOMA, Accessions Committee Fund purchase.

23. As of 2020, the SFMOMA web page on photography states: "Photography is everywhere. It is in the museum, but it's also on city walls, in magazine pages, and on our phones. Practiced by all—amateurs, professionals, and artists, no matter their geographic, social, or ethnic backgrounds—photography is fundamentally democratic." See https://www.sfmoma.org/artists-artworks/photography.

Bibliography

Ariella Azoulay, *Civil Imagination: A Political Ontology of Photography* (New York: Zone Books, 2015).

Ariella Aïsha Azoulay, *Potential History: Unlearning Imperialism* (New York: Verso, 2019).

L.G.M. Baas-Becking, *Geobiologie of Inleiding Tot de Milieukunde* (The Hague: Van Stockum & Zoon, 1934).

Nicholas Bakalar, "Earth May Be Home to a Trillion Species of Microbes," *New York Times*, May 23, 2016.

Jean Baudrillard, *Simulacra and Simulation*, trans. Sheila Faria Glaser (Ann Arbor: University of Michigan Press, 1981).

Dipesh Chakrabarty, *Provincializing Europe: Postcolonial Thought and Historical Difference* (Princeton: Princeton University Press, 2000).

Clément Chéroux, *Snap + Share: Transmitting Photographs from Mail Art to Social Networks* (New York: Cernunnos, 2019).

Gilles Deleuze, *Cinema 2: The Time-Image*, trans. Hugh Tomlinson and Robert Galeta (Minneapolis: University of Minnesota Press, 1986).

Gilles Deleuze, *Negotiations, 1972–1990*, trans. Martin Joughin (New York: Columbia University Press, 1995).

Philip J. Dreyfus, *Our Better Nature: Environment and the Making of San Francisco* (Norman, OK: University of Oklahoma Press, 2008).

Erin I. Garcia de Jesus, "Hundreds of Thousands of Marine Viruses Discovered in World's Oceans," *Nature*, April 25, 2019, https://www.nature.com/articles/d41586-019-01329-w (accessed May 2, 2020).

Ulrik Ekman, "Interaction Designs for Ubicomp Cultures," *The Fibreculture Journal*, 19 (2011): 1–30.

Tom Fenchel and Bland J. Finlay, "The Ubiquity of Small Species: Patterns of Local and Global Diversity," *BioScience*, 54, 8 (August 2004): 777–784.

Noah Fierer, "'Everything is everywhere…' gets us nowhere," *Fierer Lab* (blog), June 28, 2015, http://fiererlab.org/2015/06/28/everything-is-everywhere-gets-us-nowhere (accessed June 1, 2020).

Tia Ghose, "Why Is Water So Essential to Life?" *Live Science*, September 29, 2015, https://www.livescience.com/52332-why-is-water-needed-for-life.html (accessed June 1, 2020).

Martin Hand, *Ubiquitous Photography* (Cambridge: Polity, 2012).

Paul A. Harris, "Using Knowledge: Denuding the Deluded, Including the Excluded," *Amerikastudien / American Studies*, 45, 1 (2000): 23–32.

David L. Hawksworth and Robert Lücking, "Fungal Diversity Revisited: 2.2 to 3.8 Million Species," *Microbiology Spectrum*, 5, 4 (2017): 1–17.

Karine Nahon and Jeff Hemsley, *Going Viral* (Malden, MA: Polity Press, 2013).

Diana R. Nemergut, Steven K. Schmidt, Tadashi Fukami, Sean P. O'Neill, Teresa M. Bilinski, Lee F. Stanish, Joseph E. Knelman et al., "Patterns and Processes of Microbial Community Assembly," *Microbiology and Molecular Biology Reviews*, 77, 3 (2013): 342–356.

Kari Nixon and Lorenzo Servitje, eds, *Endemic: Essays in Contagion Theory* (London: Palgrave Macmillan, 2016).

Rob Nixon, *Slow Violence and the Environmentalism of the Poor* (Cambridge, MA: Harvard University Press, 2011).

Maureen A. O'Malley, "'Everything Is Everywhere: But the Environment Selects': Ubiquitous Distribution and Ecological Determinism in Microbial Biogeography," *Studies in History and Philosophy of Science Part C: Studies in History and Philosophy of Biological and Biomedical Sciences*, 39, 3 (September 2008): 314–325.

Paul Patton, "Mobile Concepts, Metaphor, and the Problem of Referentiality in Deleuze and Guattari," *Thamyris/Intersecting*, 12 (2006): 27–46.

Andrea Puškárová et al., "Microbial Communities Affecting Albumen Photography Heritage: A Methodological Survey," *Nature Scientific Reports*, 6, 1 (2016): 1–14.

Douglas Rushkoff, *Media Virus!: Hidden Agendas in Popular Culture* (New York: Ballantine Books, 1994).

Jac Saorsa, *Narrating the Catastrophe: An Artist's Dialogue with Deleuze and Ricoeur* (Bristol: Intellect Books, 2011).

Daniel Smith and John Protevi, "Gilles Deleuze," *The Stanford Encyclopedia of Philosophy* (Spring 2020 Edition), ed. Edward N. Zalta, https://plato.stanford.edu/archives/spr2020/entries/deleuze (accessed May 1, 2020).

Christina Sharpe, *In the Wake: On Blackness and Being* (Durham, NC: Duke University Press, 2016).

Kaja Silverman, *The Miracle of Analogy or The History of Photography, Part 1* (Stanford: Stanford University Press, 2015).

Susan Sontag, *On Photography* (New York: Farrar, Straus and Giroux, 1977).

Daniela Voss, *Conditions of Thought: Deleuze and Transcendental Ideas* (Edinburgh: Edinburgh University Press, 2013).

Wim Vyverman, Elie Verleyen, Annick Wilmotte, Dominic A. Hodgson, Anne Willems, Karolien Peeters, Bart Van de Vijver, Aaike De Wever, Frederik Leliaert, and Koen Sabbe, "Evidence for Widespread Endemism Among Antarctic Micro-organisms," *Polar Science*, 4, 2 (2010): 103–113.

12. That Liking Feeling: Mood, Emotion, and Social Media Photography

Michelle Henning

Flipping

It is 11:45 at night. I am moving between writing this chapter, writing emails, and checking Instagram. Earlier this evening, I posted a video of a strange Italian stage performance I saw a week ago. Checking it now, I see that I have two "likes," which is nice. I see a red and black graphic image announcing that a musician is doing a show in New Zealand. I don't know what to think about the image, but I "like" it, because I like her music and want to support her.

I swipe to a promoted photo of happy students at my university (Instagram always seems to promote my own university to me) and a friend's photo of a cat. I tap to "like" the cat. My friend repeatedly posts pictures of the cat, so liking it is a way of saying, "I like that you are still doing this—keep it up." Next is a drawn image by someone I find a bit odd. I don't know him except via Instagram. I don't tap, because I don't want to encourage him.

It's actually laborious listing each image I see, as it slows down the speed at which I look at them, and I have to adjust my fingers between the gestures needed for typing on my laptop, and those needed for swiping the mobile phone screen, which also starts to darken and lock if I don't keep touching it.

Touch screens are part of the disappearing of the interface. They encourage the user to feel "at one with the machine." (Davies, 2017: 41) By writing the above, I have lost this sense of oneness, and I struggle to describe and analyze my experience of using Instagram. Just as if I were trying to summarize each shot of a film while watching it, I have ceased to be absorbed. I have broken the flow. The app itself was perhaps doing a better job, however crudely, of capturing my experience in the flow, because it is, in part, an affect-capturing technology. As William

Davies explains in his work on "mood capture," social media platforms are designed to register our experience without interrupting it (39). He says that such platforms allow emotion, not to be represented, but to be performed, or played out (46). Another writer, Ricky Crano, suggests that, instead of focusing on what is represented, or even how users describe their experience, we should consider our physical engagement with these images, through gestures of scrolling, swiping, and tapping (Crano, 2018: 1134). This behavioral performance has become the basis of another kind of description of what I am doing, one I would perhaps not recognize, but which feeds back into my own interactions, changing the order of the images placed before me, prompting me to act in specific ways, promoting certain products to me.

When I say I "liked" something, I mean I tapped on a tiny heart icon for a host of different reasons: to be polite, to register approval, to support, as well as to actually express the fact that I like the image. My daughters would say I should do it to be polite, to not hurt someone's feelings and never, never, "like" an old post, because it implies you are a stalker. Actually, I do it to encourage, and by not tapping, to discourage, a certain kind of photographic or image-posting habit. I sometimes tap the heart on images I don't particularly like to support or encourage the person who has posted them. Then again, if I dislike a picture, I might not tap, because I don't want them to think I enjoy that sort of thing.[1] "Liking" turns out to be very complicated. But Davies's argument would suggest that, from the point of view of mood capture, this does not matter: Instagram's algorithm does not have to be able to distinguish between the different motivations I have for "liking." Intentions, drives, desires are not at issue here.

In a short time, I flip through a lot of images. I am aware "flip" is a term that does not exactly describe my finger sliding on the screen, as it is a gesture related to magazines. Nevertheless, I am conscious of a similar feeling. Paul Frosh writes that inattention is both embodied and learned—he points out that we know how to watch television or flip through magazines without having to think about it (Frosh, 2012: 129–130). I move through Instagram or a magazine, puzzled at this, dismissive of that, making a mental note of this, smiling at that. I generally pick up a magazine in the waiting room of the dentist's or doctor's or at the hairdresser's. If I am not actually bored, at least I have nothing pressing to do.

Instagram, like other social media, has a tendency to eat up even the smallest in-between times. I check it because it seems to be calling to me. It is needy; it wants my attention. Using techniques pioneered in the casino, in gambling machines, it is designed to pull me back into the flow, to keep me looking, tapping, swiping (Davies, 2017: 42). There is the attraction of liveness: something new is always appearing; these images are not still. Even those that are not GIFs or videos are still animated, in the sense that new images are always arriving. The introduction of Instagram "stories" has added an extra layer of liveness, since these are more ephemeral, disappearing altogether rather than slipping further down the feed.

These images work in sequences. People create running jokes: one musician I know photographs hotel dressing gowns that are always placed by the hotel staff with one sleeve stuffed inside the lapel, like Napoleon. People make the most of repetition: the same view from a window, the same wall with light falling on it. The image is not singular but cumulative, ongoing. As Daniel Palmer says, "aggregations of images are increasingly more important than individual images." (Palmer, 2013: 59)

What I have just described I would call a set of practices. Someone writing in a different field, perhaps in the sciences, might think of these as behaviors. But "behaviors" can only be described as if from the outside, and the term makes no assumptions about intention, control, or motivation. By contrast, "practices" suggests something developed over time, a relationship with materials and instruments that is collaborative and requires that we yield to one another, but allows for myself and the phone and its software to have tendencies, preferences, motivations, and agency. My description of these practices hints at something broadly shared: what I do, many others do, since there are certain constraints and possibilities built into the mobile phone and the app I am using. My description also hints at something more narrowly collective: informed by culturally specific ideas of sociable interaction, politeness, and so on. Finally, it suggests characteristics that are idiosyncratic and cannot easily be extrapolated beyond myself, my tastes, my particular anxieties and motivations. That is, my "thick description" of my own Instagram use is not a description of a typical experience. The ubiquity of social media photographs conceals a diversity of practices.

As the analogy with the magazine suggests, any interaction with photographs could be thought of in this way, as a set of practices with certain moods, different kinds of affective intensities, different name-able emotions linked to them. We could write, and indeed people have written, thick or thin descriptions of the encounter with the magazine at the doctor's waiting room or the photograph on the art gallery wall or the billboard in the street. However, the stakes of this kind of description have radically changed. For one thing, the scale has changed: mobile phones are now the primary objects on which we encounter images we call photos, and, while I will go on to critique the ways in which photography and media theorists describe the ubiquity of digital images, it is nevertheless true that the numbers of images in public circulation has grown massively. The ways we use and exchange them have changed, too. The practices I just described are also being tracked and described, even if only as "behaviors," through the built-in systems of the phone's hardware (the accelerometer, gyroscope, and proximity sensor) and the software of Instagram, which records and responds to my posts, "likes," comments, swipes, and tags. How do we make sense of our everyday encounters with photographs in this context, and in relation to this other, automated analysis?

Flooding

I am walking through the city at night. I am alone. A building glows brilliant green above me, like an alien spacecraft. I am here, now. I stop walking. I take my phone out of my pocket. Students push past me in the dark. I hold up the phone and compose an image, so nothing except the building and the sky can be seen. I am reminded of another photograph I once took in Italy. It is raining and the phone is wet. The touch screen, which is a replacement, is not very responsive. I want to share what I see; I wanted to be with someone, perhaps. But, this way, I can control the interpretation: I can say it was this green, this glowing, like a spaceship, and you will have to take my word for it. On Instagram, I write #nofilter. The next day, I walk past it, and it is glowing pink. I don't photograph it again, not because pink is inferior to green, but because I have no plans for a series.

My practice with Instagram is material and embodied, involving more than fingers, eyes, and brain. It takes place in a place, with a pause mid-walk, arms held in a particular way, body blocking the passage of other bodies. At the same time, it communicates to an absent other or several absent others, either in the same moment (elsewhere) or in the future. It might even be part of a dialogue with a past self. I am also one of those Instagram users who treat it as a kind of minor art practice, involving ideas, compositions, visual experimentation, and a developing body of interconnected work.

In this chapter, I want to attend to the gestural, conversational, social uses of photographic images and move away from an emphasis on the overwhelming volume of images. As Annebella Pollen suggests, instead of being considered en masse, as something we are drowning in, social media photographs might be addressed as ways of saying "hi," of acknowledging and giving presence to others (Pollen, 2016). I propose to shift perspective from a putative overwhelmed "we" to the "we" who are engaged in phatic communication, that is, in using utterances, or in this case photographic images, to establish and maintain sociable connections (Frosh, 2012: 133). As Nathan Jurgenson writes, photography has become central to the gestures and expressions that "make up the substance of our lives." (Jurgenson, 2019) Thinking about this as a practice means also considering what is happening beyond and prior to the making of the image—as Daniel Miller observes about photographs taken at a teenage party, and posted online: "Taking a photograph has become rather like holding a drink—a key mode by which everyone acknowledges how much fun they are having." (Miller, 2016: 87)

Numerous commentators, from academic theorists to photographers, would agree with Martin Lister when he argues that "we are drowning in images." (Lister, 2013: 11–12; Lister 2016) Though Lister cautions against abandoning the attention to the image itself, he does raise the question of how, in the face of this excess, locking down on a single image can be useful. This is all the more pertinent because these proliferating images seem to be largely throwaway: if they are as Daniel Rubinstein and Katrina Sluis describe them, a kind of speech, or as Crano calls them, "gregarious," they also seem to be trivial, without content, mere chitchat (Rubenstein and Sluis, 2013; Rubenstein, 2005; Crano, 2018). No wonder, then, that so many writers in photography theory have, over the past two decades, moved away from semiotic analysis and close reading and emphasized that new methods, new ways of speaking about the photographic must be developed.

However, the assumption of the overwhelming nature of the sheer number of images is, in my view, limiting the ways in which we understand new photographic practices. In several recent writings, I have discussed the watery language of a "torrent," "deluge," "flood," or "tsunami," and this has also been addressed by writers such as Pollen, Rubenstein and Sluis, Joanna Zylinska, Mark Andrejevic, and Ghislain Thibault (Henning, 2018: 130–134; Henning, 2018: 137–139; Pollen, 2016; Rubenstein and Sluis, 2013; Zylinska, 2017; Andrejevic, 2013; Thibault, 2015). Such metaphors imply that we are overwhelmed by images. They are so seductive that even critics of this discourse resort to them: Andrejevic writes of "a populace enjoined to rely on their emotions, their gut instinct, and their thoughtless thoughts, to anchor themselves in a flood of information." (Andrejevic, 2013: 98) In other words, theoretical discussions of the proliferation of images are often couched in a terminology that suggests a broader negative view of the visual, of photography, and of what used to be termed mass culture. They reveal a suspicion or denigration of mass images, and of chat or phatic speech.

"Flood" has long been a term used to describe population, migration, mobs, and crowds; the hysterical crowd is also linked to notions of femininity and the female body as fluid, unbounded, and in need of constraint (Theweleit, 1987; Huyssen, 1986). Anxieties about the crowd permeated 20th-century thinking about "mass culture" and especially discussions about the circulation of images and the rise of the information society.[2]

These anxieties reveal other fears: about the fragility of existing hier-archies, about the threat of mass participation in culture, and about a potential counterinvasion of Western culture by the populations and cultures of colonized societies (Henning, 2018a: 146–148; Henning, 2021: 89–91). Concerns about too many images quickly recall a sense of a dominant culture under siege. Moreover, if people do feel anxious and overwhelmed in the face of huge quantities of images and data (and I do not think this is the only or even the most prevalent affective re-sponse to our rich surfeit of visual culture), this is not necessarily an effect of pure quantity. As Geert Lovink has suggested (drawing on Bifo Berardi's work), "information overload" is not so much a symptom of the overabundance of information as an issue of workload in a competi-tive capitalist society (Lovink, 2011: 30). Visual abundance is not in itself overwhelming; we can observe blades of grass, flowers, or stars without panic. It would be a different matter if we were required to count them.

To think in terms of drowning, then, is to conceive of oneself or oth-ers as losing control, being in too deep, with far too much to do; and to imagine images as invading or attacking. The term "drowning" is used by the overworked and stressed, by professional photographers who find themselves struggling to gain attention for their images in the midst of so many others, and, it seems, by academics trained in the fine, close analysis of visual culture, trying to distinguish which (if any) objects now deserve this kind of attention. Instead, I suggest that photographs in social media that seem so ubiquitous need to be understood in terms of their singularity for individuals actively engaged in making, looking at, and sharing images and text on social media and in terms of their embeddedness in social practice.

Extracting

I open Instagram, to pass the time. I see a birthday post for a girl I know from drama class, "like" it because it's a sweet post—I think she looks good with her current haircut. It makes me think of her birthday party I went to last year. Scroll down and get an advert for a new Scooby Doo film—it looks awful. I think it's marketed for a much younger audience than the original Scooby Doo as they've given all the characters children's voices. Scroll down. Jeremy Corbyn has posted a pic of one of his tweets about the gender pay gap. I "like" it to show my support. I go on the comments section and read the arguments between people saying the pay gap does / doesn't exist. This irritates me, so I decide to stop reading them and look at my DMs. I go on the group chat. Zach has sent a post from

@depopdrama; where the buyer says they live in Wales, and the seller says they charge extra for postage outside the UK. I "like" the post, and his comment to show him that I think it's funny.

I'm bored.

My daughter's descriptive account of what she does with Instagram reveals intentions ("to pass the time," "to show my support"), motivations ("it's a sweet post"), memories (a birthday party), feelings (irritation, boredom), and decisions (to stop reading). It also suggests a drifting, fragmented set of thoughts and opinions, moving from haircuts to film criticism, from politics to jokes. Imagine this from the perspective of the software gathering data and you have a series of behaviors: open Instagram, "like," scroll down, and so on. In addition, the phone is gathering information about her location and movements.

(Auto)ethnographic accounts reveal the diverse meanings and experiences of cultural practices. There are a growing number of anthropological and ethnographic studies of social media use, which increasingly pay attention to the visual aspects of social media interactions (Miller, 2016: 45–121). However, the real significance of this event is arguably not in the human experience at the level of the interaction, but in the algorithms recording and responding to this interaction. In the context of the so-called "big data" markets, of what Shoshana Zuboff calls "surveillance capitalism" and Nick Srnicek describes as "platform capitalism," it might seem that the visual characteristics of this pervasive visual culture are largely irrelevant, little more than a superficial means to attract us and keep us interacting, and that what we are doing with it is less significant than what it is doing with us. Theorists argue that we become involuntary unpaid laborers, a human resource, producing the raw data of our own affective experiences to be translated into behavioral predictions and exchanged on what Zuboff calls "behavioral futures markets." "We are the sources of surveillance capitalism's crucial surplus: the objects of a technologically advanced and increasingly inescapable raw-material-extraction operation." (Zuboff, 2019)

Zuboff argues that behavioral data analytics are the technical realization of B.F. Skinner's radical behaviorist vision, alchemically transforming data that was supposedly waste into the gold of engineered behaviors. Data markets thrive on certainties, offering clients (such as political parties or commercial entities) "guaranteed outcomes." In contrast to this powerful underlying purpose, social media photographs are often viewed as light and insignificant (Cubitt, 2021: 25). Social media photographs often use standardized and repetitive formulas: the off-the-shelf "filters" are designed to add atmosphere, for example, by mimicking older photographic techniques. They may be made and posted, and then skimmed through, thoughtlessly and quickly. But writers point to their simple and trivial emotional character as a defining quality: Lister writes that, if digital photo-sharing is a kind of speech, it is "one composed of little exclamations, 'oohs' and 'ahs,' nods, chuckles, pointings in several directions, silent mutterings to the self." (Lister, 2014: 11–12) Crano suggests that the social media image belongs to what Barthes called the *studium*, that realm of "unconcerned desire, various interest, [and] inconsequential taste." (Crano, 2018: 1128) Though Barthes's own example was a press photograph taken in Nicaragua in 1979, the implication is that deep feeling (being *moved*) is substituted by a less substantial emotional engagement.

Certainly, data markets have far-reaching political effects, and their products are used to engineer our experiences. But this does not mean that their operations merit attention to the exclusion of our own experience of interacting with social media. The assumption that our affective and haptic engagement is more trivial than the underlying hard economic reality echoes not only the flawed Marxist model of a cultural superstructure and economic base, but also an old model of a supposedly "feminine" social realm concerned with visual distractions and "eye candy." As with the use of flooding metaphors, the idea that the image is a superficial distraction from a deeper process is limiting and gendered: we are left with an impression of an unbearable lightness and innocence of the feminized surface, and a dark and sinister world beneath. Social media becomes the bridge over which the little goats naïvely trip-trap while beneath lurks a troll. If these supposedly trivial interactions are the "waste" or byproduct that data markets value so highly, it is worth paying serious attention to our everyday affective experiences of social media.

Feeling

My mood fluctuates almost imperceptibly: vague pleasure at a photograph of a painted pink sky, irritation at a video ad for coconut scourers. What kind of profiling could have identified me as interested in housework? The incompetence, at least, is reassuring. I sense calm with a still image, agitation at video, more so with sound. No wonder I find TikTok a sensory onslaught. Reading a debate in the comments about whether a musician was "fat-shaming" another, I feel a slight anxiety, then a little guilt at noticing a message I have not replied to, annoyance at another ad (with the imperative "shop now!" beneath it), mild shame at scooting past another ("Don't let them kill our precious bees"). These nuances of mood are subtle and transient. Sometimes, I can be moved by an image or post I see online, but right now there are too many switches in tone and emotion to feel anything much for long. I don't feel the emotional pull of a novel or a film, nothing builds to much. But this flatness is strangely calming, because, today, I have been feeling something bubbling in me, a kind of suppressed anger that I had to prevent from spilling into my work emails, or conversations with my family. It is a miserable, rainy February, and we are in the midst of a lockdown. More than 100,000 people have died of COVID-19 *in the* UK. *The collective mood seems to swing between sadness, frustration, anger, and resignation. I can't face the news. I am looking to Instagram to be distracted from myself and my own feelings by dipping into the lives of other people.*

Social media platforms prioritize photographs and other images (graphics, video clips), recognizing that visual "content" drives use and popularity, but also on the assumption that they are an effective means to provoke and to circulate certain kinds of feelings.[3] Increasingly, our behaviors and our images are taken as symptoms or expressions of feeling, as part of a growing attention to affect and emotion in computing. The field of "affective computing," for instance, attempts to build emotionality into computers, and to write algorithms that can discriminate between emotions. Meanwhile, sentiment analysis, mood capture, "emotion recognition," and "opinion mining" use computational techniques to analyze online social exchanges (Picard, 1997; Poria et al., 2018; Scherer et al., 2010). As Richard Coyne argues, "the word 'emotion' and emotional concepts (such as happiness, sadness, anger, and fear) have increasing currency in the context of ubiquitous digital media." (Coyne, 2016: 29) The new interest in emotion comes from the recognition that emotion drives decision-making and therefore behavior, as well as from the view that emotion is a key component of intelligence (Andrejevic, 2013: 38).

These new analytic techniques largely depend on psychological and biological accounts of emotion in which intentions play a minimal part, and in which the point of view of the feeling person is mostly irrelevant. Observing an organism interacting with its environment, the behaviorist sees only stimulus and response, bracketing off any idea of an inner life as irrelevant or nonexistent (Williams, 1983: 44). The behaviorist approach to emotions treats them as discrete and universally shared, and connected to biologically determined responses to stimuli. The attractions of this are not hard to see, because responses to stimuli can be detected and measured (Leys, 2010: 81, 89).[4]

Sentiment analysis techniques also commonly classify people using psychological profiling techniques that were intended for therapeutic purposes. As Luke Stark explains, psychometrics—the measurement and scoring of behaviors to produce psychological profiles—becomes a means to renders the human subject legible, interpretable, and malleable on both an individual and a collective scale (Stark, 2018: 207). Applied to social media photography, these analytical techniques model what is happening when we take, view, respond to, and exchange photographs on social media platforms, without reference to our own understandings of what we are doing. They rely on the behaviorist view of emotions as observable characteristics of "a physical organism and its circumstances," treating emotions as legible and measurable, either via written expressions such as "I am feeling…" and taps on a happy or sad face icon, or indirectly, via behaviors (Charles et al., 2011: 3).

Stark challenges the popular assumption that it is the accuracy of profiling that is worrying—the fact that platforms could use reactions to gauge an individual's mental state or their sexual preferences. What matters more is the "performative power" of these profiles, their ability not to classify but to provoke (Stark, 2018: 213). They are part of an ongoing effort to engineer behaviors in order to transform mood. Moods and feelings are diagnosed and produced or orchestrated via correlations made across vast amounts of data. Predictive analytics (such as Amazon's recommendation system) that depend on representation exist alongside nonrepresentational, real-time analytics in which users' reactions immediately inform changes in the affective atmosphere of the social media "feed." (Davies, 2013: 39) Davies discusses how the use of emoji-style buttons and "liking" looks like crude qualitative data capture (yes/no, happy/sad), but is actually more about the production and performance of emotion (46). The (ideally) light, flowing quality of interactions with social media images lends itself to time-sensitive tools that aim to "capture" mood with minimal intervention and to manipulate mood on the fly.

This manipulation of mood is a kind of "mood work," a term Ben Highmore uses to describe the production of shared affective atmospheres in all sorts of contexts, including air travel and cinema (Highmore, 2017). We are currently in the midst of widespread mood work, a concerted intervention in individual and collective mood, something more widely understood since the 2016 election in the United States, the 2016 referendum on Britain's membership of the European Union, and the 2018 news coverage of the activities of Cambridge Analytica (Stark, 2018: 205–206). However, as Highmore's examples suggest, mood work has long been pervasive, albeit on smaller scales or in less automated ways. Mood work is not necessarily always controlled or predictable, and our devices do not simply track our moods and then shape them, but inform them in uncontrolled ways: for example, the frustrations of a touch screen in the rain or in bright sunlight, the embarrassment of a phone call or alarm in a silent meeting, or the sense of boredom or reassurance induced by repetitive hand movements.

As I suggest above, mood is not simply an individual matter, but links the personal and particular with what is collective, cultural, and social

(Highmore, 2017).[5] As mediated political events influence public mood, it is tempting to think of the mood work of social media in terms of mass manipulation, but where mood is collective, it is not necessarily a matter of manipulation and contagion. Coyne points out that we bring our own moods to media, rather than being "just passive receivers of moods that are foisted upon us," and he writes that "to tune in to the mood of the crowd is not necessarily to acquiesce to its dictates." (Coyne, 2016: 3, 54) Sara Ahmed questions the concept of affective contagion, arguing that it "tends to underestimate the extent to which affects are contingent"; she also argues that an affective atmosphere is not merely "out there," not already in a crowded room when we enter it, but also the consequence of "the angle of our arrival." (Ahmed, 2010: 36, 37)[6] We each experience atmosphere differently, read it differently because of our own subjective moods and our own existing orientations. To understand mood, emotion, and affect in relation to social media means to think in terms of atmospheres and to include not only the observably present but also "the suffusion of the ordinary with fantasy," linking material experience with things that are more ephemeral, from the temperature in a room to hopes and fears, values and imaginings (Ahmed, 2010: 30; Berlant, 2011: 14, 15). Against a behaviorist and instrumental approach to emotions, we might address mood and emotional expression in social media photography as extending beyond individual images and platforms, rather than properties belonging to them.

Close

The photograph depicts a girl from the waist up. She holds a black cat in her arms and gazes down at it. The cat stares straight into the camera. The girl casts a faint shadow on the wall to her right; on the left, the wall is brighter, as if a light is aimed directly at it. The cat's body is awkwardly arranged, she cradles him like a baby, but one leg sticks up and his tail points down at a sharp angle. The photograph appears to be a family snapshot, except that the photographer has engaged the eyes of the cat rather than the girl and has placed her against a plain green background. Still, the overly pink skin tone, the dull lighting, and a blown-out highlight on the wall to the right suggest this is not a professional portrait. There is something sentimental about the picture, as the girl smiles fondly at the cat. This sentimentality seems contradicted by the cat's gaze, which is ironic and challenging, as if he is aware of the indignity of his position. It also seems to be contradicted by the girl's jacket, which is covered in metal studs.

Writing against the view (held by some in the digital humanities) that only big data sets can yield reliable results, Barbara Herrnstein-Smith has emphasized the value of the practice of close reading, "the ability and disposition to read texts attentively, one by one," in an era of corporate, computational communication, in which "texts of all kinds are turned to manipulative ends with digitally multiplied effectiveness." (Smith, 2016: 69) Yet there is also a case to be made that, taken one by one, contemporary visual images are less "manipulative," or less sophisticated in their manipulations than they once were, and that contemporary visual culture does not lend itself to close reading.

Take, for example, advertising imagery. As Zuboff recounts, the markets in behavioral data grew from attempts to secure advertising revenue to fund digital media after the dot-com bubble of the 1990s. Around 2006, Google started to use behavioral data, previously regarded as useful information for improving services, as a means to match ads to users. This transformed not only the internet but also advertising, which became more heavily invested in behaviorism. Previously, the advertising industry had been interested in the workings of the human mind, understanding advertising as the "art of persuasion" and setting out "to stir the stream of consciousness." (Gill, 1954: 11) Advertising photography used an array of techniques to appeal to conscious and unconscious desires, directly addressing the inner lives of individuals in order to encourage them to consume. This approach to advertising seems to have peaked in the 1990s, and it virtually disappeared around the time that online marketing techniques pioneered by Google took off (Schwartzkopf, 2009). Meanwhile, in academic contexts, studies of advertising are largely superseded by studies of brands and marketing and public relations.

In its heyday, advertising emphasized creativity as a means to attract buyer attention and appeal to desire—the latter often understood in psychoanalytic terms. This provided rich pickings for the cultural theorist, who could have fun bringing to light the Freudian content of elaborate photographic campaigns. My own early lectures used examples of cigarette campaigns (Benson and Hedges, Marlboro, and Silk Cut), showing how they channeled the physical desire for a cigarette and the anxiety about health into sexual desire and the desire to take risks, to live on the edge. While the ostensible purpose was to critique and defuse manipulative imagery, the irony was not lost on us: we were training people not just to analyze ads but to potentially produce them. Even so, it would hardly be surprising if photography theorists were nostalgic for a time when close reading of highly constructed and elaborate images yielded such fruits. These are rare and exotic peacocks in a public domain now dominated by apparently throwaway and careless amateur imagery and bland stock photography. In this context, the uses of images, and the data they generate, seem to have become richer and more complex than their symbolic content.

However, the risk is that, without close reading, a culture cannot be understood. Without close reading, pictures such as the one described above can be reduced to mere expressions of emotion. In emotional computing, it seems that the belief that the arts are "emotional" gives rise to the false assumption that images directly express the feeling of the person who made or displayed the image (and therefore that feelings might be diagnosed from images).[7] Writers in the fields of emotional and affective computing seem to oppose emotion to reason or cognition, and they associate images with emotional "contagion," despite the fact that this is a contested and specifically expressionist aesthetics. Twentieth-century writers on art and aesthetics challenged this theory: both Ernst Gombrich and Nelson Goodman pointed out that it is based on the notion of a natural correspondence between colors and forms and emotional response that disregards the role of cognition and culture. Gombrich drew on early cybernetic theory to describe structural differences (gamuts, modalities, and scales) in the meanings we attribute to affects (Gombrich, 1963: 69). Goodman suggested that "in aesthetic experience the emotions function cognitively," that what we call "expression" is an indirect and metaphorical process, so when we say a picture "expresses" sadness, what we mean is not that the picture *is* sad, but that it "metaphorically exemplifies" sadness (Goodman, 1976).[8] Metaphors, however, do not lend themselves to sentiment analysis and mood tracking, because they are not observable as behaviors and, because, by definition, they are indirect and not literal.[9]

Can a sentimental picture be simultaneously ironic? Following Goodman, to depict a fond girl is not necessarily to express fondness, nor does a picture express irony because I find it ironic, any more than it expresses irritation because it irritates me. Pictures are cultural artifacts, and even photographs require cultural knowledge (here, of genres of sentimental imagery, family snaps, and online cat photography) to understand what work they may do in the world. As with the atmosphere in a room, we can read the mood of a picture differently, approaching it from our own angles and subjective moods. But a close reading helps to reveal how the picture participates in a larger culture without necessarily being the result of a coherent set of intentions.

Thick

You are going to a party wearing a jacket that you have had since you were little. Now, it fits very tightly, but it still looks great. I want a photograph of you in it. You pick up the cat, who is a regular photographic accessory.

But it's not such a good photograph—you are too self-conscious, and the lighting is bad. The cat, who always rises to the occasion, turns his yellow eyes toward me in a glare. I want to put it on Instagram. I ask your permission. Where does this desire come from? I barely know, except I have a sense that if I don't put it on Instagram, I may as well not take it. I don't need connection. I need approval. Even while I don't approve. Your skin is too pink, the wall is not green enough, the pose is wrong, the cat—well, the cat is great, but there is a lot of cat competition out there. I post it on Instagram, and I write underneath "That cat! That jacket!" A friend replies "That girl!" I had given her the cue. Did I post it to feel clever?

The anthropologist Clifford Geertz famously placed the practice of "thick description" at the heart of the interpretation of culture (Geertz, 1973).[10] Thick description addresses what people are up to, and even where it is not penned by participants, it draws on their own understanding of what is happening. By contrast, "thin description" describes only what a person is observably doing, without reference to what they or their coparticipants understand themselves to be doing (the data trails "mined" by the phone and by Instagram might be understood as thin description, for this reason). The job of the ethnographer is to tease out "a stratified hierarchy of meaningful structures," to situate the thin bones of what is happening ("a woman photographs her daughter and a cat and posts the photograph on Instagram, checking the responses it receives") within the interpretative frames and practices of the wider culture (Geertz, 1973: 7). The ethnographer makes skilled but "second and third order" interpretations (15). The subject's intentions matter (they are a knowing participant in the culture), but they are insufficient. What makes my activity meaningful, according to Geertz, is neither my conscious intentions nor unconscious motives, but the fact that it is a material and "ideational" activity drawing on skills, gestures, materials, and habits that are "socially established" and "publicly shared." (10, 11) More recent commentators, drawing on feminist materialist traditions, might add that what these mutually entangled technologies and bodies are up to is materially as well as symbolically transformative (Coleman, 2014).

If close reading flourishes where images are semiotically rich, "thick description" appears to be most effective where cultural practices are sufficiently "deep," the term Geertz uses to describe the kind of play involved in the Balinese cockfight. Geertz points out that not all cockfights involve "deep play." Rather, deep play is connected with the high stakes of the fight, meaning both the gambling stakes and the cultural significance that accompanies it—"the migration of the Balinese status hierarchy into the body of the cockfight." (Geertz, 1973) If we ignore the data dredging it fuels, my Instagram use would seem to be low stakes and shallow. It is a form of sociable play, but neither the affective engagement nor the symbolism run deep: though I am participating in cultural practices linked to social status (such as taking and displaying photographs of my children), I would be pushing it to claim (as Geertz does of the Balinese cockfight) that it draws on every level of my cultural experience. Even to narrate the event of my taking a photograph seems to overstate its significance. While the cockfight, according to Geertz, is a "blood sacrifice" in which Balinese masculinity is deeply invested, which renders intelligible and felt "their involvement with rage and the fear of rage," my participation in Instagram is driven by more low-level, albeit persistent passions (confusion, self-doubt, a vague desire for approval).

Writing about feelings of being disconcerted or unfocused, Sianne Ngai asks, "isn't this feeling of confusion about what one is feeling an affective state in its own right?" (Ngai, 2005: 14) My self-questioning in the passage above, my own uncertainty about my motivations for posting the image, should not be taken at face value. The fact that I do not know exactly what I am feeling, nor what I am expressing via the photograph, is also a kind of affect. Ngai links this to a sense of "loss of control"—I have an unsettling sense that I am being programmed by the camera phone or the platform. As Vilém Flusser puts it, I feel myself to have become a "functionary" of the photographic apparatus (which here includes Instagram, the camera, and photographic rituals) (Flusser, 2000: 24–25). At the same time, as Ngai observes, such a feeling also "often heralds the basic affect of 'interest' underwriting all acts of intellectual inquiry." (Ngai, 2005: 14) At the point that I sense that I do not know what I am feeling, emotion and cognition intertwine; I note the attempt to orchestrate my mood, and I begin the questioning that underpins this chapter. I wonder about the diverse practices of social media photography, their relation to automated "data dredging" and "mood capture," and my relationship with the algorithms that "feed" me social media images.

It is clear that I am participating in a set of cultural practices, and this set has its own distinct varieties of affect. The fact that my engagement is being provoked, prodded, and encouraged by an adaptable and responsive technology suggests that we need to understand this technology and its infrastructures as participating in this culture, rather than just mediating it. This cultural participant is in some ways remarkably able and in some ways remarkably poor at "reading" my moves. It recognizes and produces bodily practices (mediated as data) (Clough et al., 2015: 154). It sorts huge and "seemingly unrelated" sets of data to produce "novel relations." (157) It is a powerful agent in the flow of everyday living—inculcating new habits and gestures, appealing to inchoate desires, marking and molding the experience of time, performing mood work almost continuously. It "sees" the images in play but only as triggers or stimuli.

It can quantify the "grip" an image has on me and give me more of that, yet it knows nothing of how the image matters to me, where "matters" refers both to signification (what the image means to me) and to affect.[11]

José Van Dijck describes social media algorithms as "inscriptions of sociality": each algorithm is different, because "a Like is not a Retweet" yet they share the same "social norms and cultural logic." (Van Dijck, 2013: 157–158) They are ideal service economy workers, hooking sociability directly to sales. They are devoted to the goals that Van Dijck identifies as common to most platforms: "popularity, hierarchical ranking, neutrality, quick growth, large-traffic volumes and fast-turnover." (158) These algorithms are facilitators, whose values I mostly choose to overlook or to manipulate for my own ends (for example, by trying to promote an event, a friend, or myself) until such moments that they, too, openly reveal themselves in all their crassness. Once, for example, a personal Apple iMessage that I wrote about David Bowie's death turned his name into a hyperlink to albums for sale, as if the recipient might take that sad opportunity to do a spot of online shopping. One of the strange things about Instagram, since its takeover by Facebook, is the way it punctures its own illusion. Before—when the feed was in chronological order rather than organized according to what the algorithm calculates I want to see—I had a sense of flow, of being in a space and in a moment. Now, images are out of sequence. Old news and ads also break my sense of being "among friends."

In conclusion, to understand practices of social media photography, it may be helpful to abandon oppositions between passive subjects and lively algorithms, or between feeling individuals and rational machines, and to question assumptions that abundance is threatening or that a lightness of interest is morally or politically suspect. Our engagements with contemporary mass photography may be fodder for markets in behavior predictions, but they exceed what can be captured as behavior and need to be understood, as Frosh has suggested, in terms of the ways we live with and alongside media, and as aesthetic practices, that mobilize affects into emotion-as-cognition (not just "emoting" and "expressing") (Frosh, 2019: 5). The sentiments and moods conjured via social media are the sudden gusts and passing storms that drive performances of sociability.[12] In turn, these performances are cultural practices, and culture does not merely express emotions or feelings but structures, translates, encodes, and transforms them.

Notes

1. My approach may be linked to my Englishness: Daniel Miller writes that, for his English participants, "social media was always going to be as important for keeping people at a distance as it was for coming closer to them," aiding English people in keeping relationships not "too hot" and not "too cold"—something he calls "the Goldilocks strategy." (Miller, 2016: 99–100)

2. As well as the examples discussed by Huyssen, see, for example, Malraux, 1951 and the discussion of Malraux in Didi-Huberman, 2013.

3. Instagram in particular is associated with a certain kind of positive and light affect (in contrast to Twitter and Facebook), rooted in the notion that good feelings produce high returns. On how this plays out for certain Instagram users, see Miller, 2016: 85.

4. Leys rejects both affect theory and behaviorism in favor of a theory of emotion that centers around intention or volition and allows for "a degree of complexity and uncertainty." (Leys, 2010: 89) For Leys's critique of affect theory, see Leys, 2017.

5. Similarly, Jonathan Flatley discusses mood as "fundamentally historical and social," arguing against the assumption (by critics of the so-called "affective turn") that affect is to do with individual identity and subjective experience (Flatley, 2017: 140).

6. Sianne Ngai points to the role gender plays in ideas about contagious and transmittable emotions, through the linking of femininity with imitation (Ngai, 2005: 149–151).

7. This simplistic assumption also seems to be shared by Jurgenson, who sees social photos as unproblematically expressive at the same time as he compares them to emojis, icons, and comics, all highly coded means of communication (Jurgenson, 2019).

8. To demonstrate that social photos are expressive of feelings, Jurgenson gives the example of a palm tree as something "which can convey that the weather is warm, or that you are on vacation, or that you are having a relaxing time, or whatever a palm tree conveys to you and the people you expect to see the image," an explanation that inadvertently exemplifies the difficulties in isolating the expressive content in photographs (Jurgenson, 2019: 18–19).

9. Correlating images to emotions except via words seems particularly difficult (Poria et al., 2018).

10. Geertz, who took the term "thick description" from Gilbert Ryle, is clear: his concept of culture is "essentially a semiotic one," since he believes "that man is an animal suspended in webs of significance that he himself has spun"—the task of studying culture is "an interpretative one in search of meaning." (Geertz, 1973: 5–6)

11. See Karen Barad on "mattering." (Barad, 2012: 69) The "grip" of images on bodies is discussed in Coleman, 2014: 35–37.

12. Stark writes that the ideal subject of sentiment analysis will be "fluent in the emotional expressions, behaviors and gestures aligned with a platform's models—conforming to classificatory schemes." (Stark, 2018: 214)

Bibliography

Sara Ahmed, "Happy Objects," in *The Affect Theory Reader*, eds Melissa Gregg and Gregory J. Seigworth (Durham, NC: Duke University Press, 2010), 29–51.

Mark Andrejevic, *Infoglut: How Too Much Information Is Changing the Way We Think and Know* (London: Routledge, 2013).

Interview with Karen Barad in *New Materialism: Interviews & Cartographies*, eds Rick Dolphijn and Iris van der Tuin (London: Open Humanities Press, 2012), 48–71.

Lauren Berlant, *Cruel Optimism* (Durham, NC: Duke University Press, 2011).

Eric P. Charles, Michael D. Bybee, and Nicholas S. Thompson, "A Behaviorist Account of Emotions and Feelings: Making Sense of James D. Laird's Feelings: The Perception of Self," *Behaviour and Philosophy*, 39, 40 (2011): 1–16.

Patricia Ticineto Clough, Karen Gregory, Benjamin Haber, and Joshua R. Scannell, "The Datalogical Turn," in *Non-Representational Research Methodologies: An Introduction*, ed. Phillip Vannini (New York: Routledge, 2015), 146–164.

Rebecca Coleman, "Inventive Feminist Theory: Representation, Materiality and Intensive Time," *Women: A Cultural Review*, 25, 1 (2014): 27–45.

Richard Coyne, *Mood and Mobility: Navigating the Emotional Spaces of Digital Social Networks* (Cambridge, MA: MIT Press, 2016).

Ricky Crano, "The Real Terror of Instagram: Death and Disindividuation in the Social Media Scopic Field," *Convergence*, 25, 5–6 (2018): 1123–1139.

Sean Cubitt, "The Mass Image," in *Photography Off the Scale*, eds Tomáš Dvořák and Jussi Parikka (Edinburgh: Edinburgh University Press, 2021).

William Davies, "How Are We Now? Real-Time Mood-Monitoring as Valuation," *Journal of Cultural Economy*, 10, 1 (2017): 34–48.

Georges Didi-Huberman, *L'album de L'art à L'époque du "Musée Imaginaire"* (Paris: Hazan and Musée du Louvre, 2013).

Jonathan Flatley, "Reading for Mood," *Representations*, 140 (Fall 2017): 137–158.

Vilém Flusser, *Towards a Philosophy of Photography* (London: Reaktion Books, 2000).

Paul Frosh, *The Poetics of Digital Media* (Cambridge: Polity Press, 2019).

Paul Frosh, "The Showing of Sharedness: Monstration, Media and Social Life," *Divinatio*, 35 (2012): 123–138.

Clifford Geertz, *The Interpretation of Cultures* (New York: Basic Books, 1973).

Leslie Ernest Gill, *Advertising and Psychology* (London: Hutchinson, 1954).

Ernst Gombrich, "Expression and Communication," in *Meditations on a Hobby Horse and Other Essays on the Theory of Art* (London: Phaidon Press, 1963), 56–69.

Nelson Goodman, *Languages of Art: An Approach to the Theory of Symbols* (Indianapolis: Hackett, 1976).

Michelle Henning, "Feeling Photos: Photography, Picture Language and Mood Capture," in *Photography Off the Scale: Technologies and Theories of the Mass Image*, eds Jussi Parikka and Tomáš Dvořák (Edinburgh: Edinburgh University Press, 2021).

Michelle Henning, *Photography: The Unfettered Image* (London: Routledge, 2018a).

Michelle Henning, "Image Flow: Photography on Tap," *photographies*, 11, 2–3 (2018b): 133–148.

Barbara Herrnstein-Smith, "What Was 'Close Reading'? A Century of Method in Literary Studies," *Minnesota Review*, 87, 1 (2016): 57–75.

Ben Highmore, *Cultural Feelings: Mood, Mediation and Cultural Politics* (London: Routledge, 2017).

Andreas Huyssen, *After the Great Divide: Modernism, Mass Culture and Postmodernism* (London: Macmillan, 1986).

Nathan Jurgenson, *The Social Photo: On Photography and Social Media* (La Vergne: Verso, 2019).

Ruth Leys, *The Ascent of Affect: Genealogy and Critique* (Chicago: University of Chicago Press, 2017).

Ruth Leys, "How Did Fear Become a Scientific Object and What Kind of Object Is It?" *Representations*, 110, 1 (Spring 2010): 66–104.

Martin Lister, "Is the Camera an Extension of the Photographer?," in *Digital Photography and Everyday Life: Empirical Studies on Material Visual Culture*, eds Edgar Gómez Cruz and Asko Lehmuskallio (London: Routledge, 2016).

Martin Lister, "Overlooking, Rarely Looking and Not Looking," in *Digital Snaps: The New Face of Photography*, eds Jonas Larsen and Mette Sandbye (London: IB Taurus, 2013), 1–24.

Geert Lovink, *Networks without a Cause: A Critique of Social Media* (Cambridge: Polity Press, 2011).

André Malraux, *Les Voix De Silence* (Paris: Gallimard, 1951).

Daniel Miller, *Social Media in an English Village* (London: University College London Press, 2016).

Sianne Ngai, *Ugly Feelings* (Harvard: Harvard University Press, 2005).

Daniel Palmer, "Redundant Photographs: Cameras, Software and Human Obsolescence," in *On the Verge of Photography: Imaging Beyond Representation*, eds Daniel Rubinstein, Johnny Golding, and Andy Fisher (Birmingham: ARTicle Press, 2013), 49–67.

Luciana Parisi, *Contagious Architecture: Computation, Aesthetics and Space* (Cambridge, MA: MIT Press, 2013).

Rosalind W. Picard, *Affective Computing* (Cambridge, MA: MIT Press, 1997).

Annebella Pollen, "The Rising Tide of Photographs: Not Drowning but Waving," *Captures*, 1, (2016), revuecaptures.org/node/249 (accessed 4 June 2019).

Soujanya Poria, Amir Hussain, and Erik Cambria, *Multimodal Sentiment Analysis* (Cham: Springer Nature, 2018).

Daniel Rubinstein, "Cellphone Photography: The Death of the Camera and the Arrival of Visible speech," *Nerve: Issues in Contemporary Culture and Aesthetics*, 2, 1 (May 2005): 113–118.

Daniel Rubinstein and Katrina Sluis, "Notes on the Margins of Metadata: Concerning the Undecidability of the Digital Image," *photographies*, 6, 1 (2013): 151–158.

Daniel Rubinstein and Katrina Sluis, "The Digital Image in Photographic Culture: Algorithmic Photography and the Crisis of Representation," in *The Photographic Image in Digital Culture*, ed. Martin Lister (London: Routledge, 2013), 22–40.

Klaus R. Scherer, Tanja Banziger, and Etienne B. Roesch, *Blueprint for Affective Computing: A Sourcebook* (Oxford: Oxford University Press, 2010).

Stefan Schwartzkopf, "What Was Advertising? The Invention, Rise, Demise, and Disappearance of Advertising Concepts in Nineteenth- and Twentieth-Century Europe and America," *Business and Economic History On-Line*, 7 (2009).

Nick Srnicek, *Platform Capitalism* (London: Polity, 2016).

Eve Kokofsky Sedgwick and Adam Frank, "Shame in the Cybernetic Fold: Reading Silvan Tomkins," *Critical Inquiry*, 21, 2 (1995): 496–522.

Luke Stark, "Algorithmic Psychometrics and the Scalable Subject," *Social Studies of Science*, 48, 2 (April 2018): 204–231.

Klaus Theweleit, *Male Fantasies* (Cambridge: Polity Press, 1977/1987).

Ghislain Thibault, "Streaming: A Media Hydrography of Televisual Flows," *View: Journal of European Television History and Culture*, 4, 7 (2015): 110–119.

José Van Dijck, *The Culture of Connectivity: A Critical History of Social Media* (Oxford: Oxford University Press, 2013).

Raymond Williams, *Keywords: A Vocabulary of Culture and Society*, rev. ed. (Oxford: Oxford University Press, 1983).

Shoshana Zuboff, *The Age of Surveillance Capitalism: The Fight for a Human Future at the New Frontier of Power* (London: Profile Books, 2019).

Joanna Zylinska, *Nonhuman Photography* (Cambridge, MA: MIT Press, 2017).

13. "The Compass of Repair": An Interview with Ariella Aïsha Azoulay

Jacob W. Lewis & Kyle Parry

JACOB W. LEWIS & KYLE PARRY: When we were first thinking of keynote speakers for our symposium at the University of Rochester, we thought about work that directly addressed questions of photographic ubiquity, and what we *then* knew of your work—photography as a citizenry beyond the limits of the nation-state—was by far the most significant and suggestive in this respect.[1] Of course, by the time we reached out to you, you had dramatically shifted scales, from photography as an event to photography as a global imperial technology. Your premise of refusal, this idea that the beginnings of photography lie in 1492, struck us as yet another instance of a stirring and indeed demanding recasting of photography in your work—a forceful coordinate shift with enormous implications. We thought we would start with the question we posed back in Rochester in 2018. Are these coordinate shifts of a piece with each other, or are there certain respects in which the ever-expanding operations of the imperial shutter force us to rethink the notion of a citizenry of photography?

 ARIELLA AÏSHA AZOULAY: Thank you for your careful reading of the book and for inviting me to reflect on my engagement with photography in the last decade and a half. Did I "dramatically shift scales?" This is a challenging question. There is a shift in scale between *The Civil Contract of Photography* (Azoulay, 2008) and *Potential History* (Azoulay, 2019), but it happened through a consecutive series of shifts that were actually moments of unlearning. When I wrote *The Civil Contract of Photography*, I could not tell that it was imperialism that I was unlearning, but in retrospect, this is actually what I did. *Civil Contract* was an account of a process of unlearning a few imperial sovereign formations—the nation-state as a fait accompli (Israel), sovereign citizenship (inherent to the differential body politic, of which the persona of the modern citizen is part), and photography as a device-based technology with its own strata of experts (acting at the expense of other participants, who, though visible in the images, are often treated as if they are not party to the event of photography). In *Civil Contract*, I turned these sover-eign formations into contingent ones, rejecting them as transcendental forms of being together in an attempt to engage with political formations in which unrecognized actors (i.e., the noncitizen in politics and the photographed person in photography) participate. Accounting for such shadow formations was practicing potential history avant la lettre. I related to this potential history of photography and citizenship as a historical fiction. From this, I wrote it in situations that did or could take place, since I wanted this fiction of a civil contract between the participants in/of photography to be read by others as real and worldly. My assumption was simple: photography was institutionalized as a productive practice, whose products can be appropriated by sovereign subjects and institutions (state archives are emblematic) through violence. This violence resembles the violence used to institutionalize the body politic as if it consists only of sovereign citizens and not of the rest of the governed. Both formations are premised on the negation of the participation of those at the expense of whom such sovereign positions are formed. Through the process of unlearning what was institutionalized in the discourse of experts, and instead interacting with those whose worlds and lives were rendered extractable, exploitable, and disposable through them, the centrality of the photograph (as private property) to photography seemed in correlation with and serviceable for/benefiting the differential political regimes that invented citizenship as an asset given to some and denied to others.

The fabulation of a *Civil Contract* was written based on several examples, yet it still felt somehow speculative. That is, until I created the two photographic archives for exhibition—*Act of State: A Photographed History of the Occupation 1967–2007*, and *From Palestine to Israel: A Photographic Record of Destruction and State Formation, 1947–1950* (Azoulay, 2011).[2] Through the imaginative space created through these archives committed to the presence of those disregarded by formations of sovereignty, the active participation of the photographed persons no longer required any speculation. Photography was never actually only what photographers produce; rather, it is an arena wherein many participate even as these participants are exposed to or targeted by violence. This is, in a nutshell, the political ontology of photography. The latter archive (*From Palestine to Israel*) was composed of photographs in which one could see the simultaneity of the destruction of Palestine and at once the establishment of the state of Israel. Rather than two consecutive narratives, that archive is already committed to a potential history of Palestine.

The ontological account of the event of photography that I offered in a more systematic way in the *Civil Imagination: A Political Ontology of Photography* (Azoulay, 2012) rejected the institutionalized temporality of photography that associated the photograph with *what had happened*—a temporality that was constructed by and that served the formation of imperial sovereignty. The political ontology that I drafted went against what I learned from white male theoreticians of photography, many of whom inadvertently acted as spokespersons for imperial temporality and taught us that what was taken (in the photograph) was seized in it forever. The political ontology of photography rejected the centrality of the photograph and its conflation with photography. Different languages reflect this conflation and lure us to relate to photography as a productive practice—"a photographer took a photograph"—in a way that identifies the photographer's work and the outcome of an encounter with the photograph. This is as if the photographer's work was not dependent on and made possible by others, whose photographs are *being taken*. Already in *Civil Contract*, I argued against the ubiquity of this capitalist assumption that assigns ownership and authorship over wealth extracted from a situation of encounter to those who hold the means of production or circulation. The aim was to undermine the norm that equated the person who holds or owns the means of production (the camera) with the right to own the photograph.

What I didn't understand before working on *Potential History* is that, as radical as my account of photography was, as long as I continued to relate to photography as a sui generis practice, I was actually trapped in the imperial temporality of the new (a singular moment of beginning) that inaugurates separate histories of things that are actually entangled. This is a common trap in the conception of imperial technologies as device-based. With *Potential History*, the understanding that photography should be accounted for in continuity with and in connection to other imperial technologies became explicit. While in *Civil Contract*, I unsettled the imperial temporality of the photograph (what already happened) with the temporality of the event, in *Potential History*, I expanded this intervention by conceiving the shutter as an onto-epistemological mechanism. The shutter, I argue in this book, was not invented with the camera but rather with earlier imperial technologies that are not device-based and whose operation is ubiquitous. These imperial technologies are programmed to destroy existing worlds and organize them anew around a set of racial capitalist principles. Photography, as I show in *Potential History*, is not *about* the imperial world but rather part of it. For that, we have to refuse to study photographs independently of the event of photography.

It seems to me that, throughout my work, I sought ways to question the common understanding of photography as a productive practice that produces photographs, to reject the status of this product as a private property, and to refuse to ignore the conditions under which photography was made ubiquitous. Suggesting that photography is an event that takes place among different people, I asked what is the condition under which it operates, what is taken and from whom when a photograph is *being taken*. Furthermore, I asked what happens when a camera operates and there are no (accessible) photographs, especially for the people from or of whom they were taken, who were never meant to receive anything in return.

JWL & KP: Among the most bracing and thought-provoking aspects of your recent work is your contention that it isn't so much something seemingly innocent, like the camera or the photograph that has come to pervade this planet, but *destruction*. At the same time, in your book and in your recent open letters, you consistently refer to pernicious *constructions* that manage to achieve widespread presence and obviousness, whether this is what you call the "fabricated phenomenal field" of imperial violence or the untroubled notion of the "Judeo-Christian" you address in the open letter to Sylvia Wynter (Azoulay, "Open Letter," 2020). How do we best think through the interrelations and interconnections of pervasive imperial destruction and mass-distributed imperial constructions, and how does the omnipresence of photography figure in these operations? Does potential history seek to redistribute alternative constructions at a world scale, or does it refuse projects of ubiquity altogether?

AAA: *Potential History* is also a manifesto against history. The past, I argue in the book, is an imperial invention that provides impunity to the different operators of the different imperial violent technologies that destroy the world. Photography, like archives and museums (that I also study as technologies), render the past palpable, in a way that scholars and laypersons alike are trained to recognize "it" as if it truly exists, and to recognize in it the time before "we were as we are, modern." In addition, scholars and other experts are trained to recognize each of these technologies as having its own history, and, thus, you can see scholars motivated by a revisionist impulse setting off inadvertently to write the history of photography in different "forgotten" or "less-central" places, proving that different people, whose worlds were destroyed and their wealth was plundered, were also modern and progressive, meaning that they embraced modern technologies as early as their colonizers. It's true that once different places were exposed to military violence and photography could impose itself, local people also used the technology with inventiveness, creativity, or playfulness, though often in substantially smaller proportions to the imperial enterprise of producing of them orientalist or stereotypical images. What is often forgotten in these narratives is that it was not the dissemination of a device, invented in 1839, but the intrusion of a technology that normalizes the violent outcome of military invasions and colonization. Anticolonial resistance had to be violently repressed so that military forces and operations would be able to "open up" places for the penetration of "modernity" (i.e., destruction) and these crimes relegated to the past so that history of photography could be written independently of them. As part of this process, different kinds of experts (photographers among them) installed their firms (studios, in photography's case) to extract local wealth and engage part of the local population in their activity. For the past to exist as a separate tense everywhere, and for modernity to be "its" future, and for the transition from the one to the other to be experienced as unavoidable and organic—many different temporal formations and diverse worlds in which they made sense had to be destroyed. The challenge of *Potential History* is how not to lose sight of this ubiquitous destruction and, at the same time, how to reconfigure the ontology of photography in a way that allows us to continue both to engage with it in order not to forget this mass destruction, and to transform it into the compass of repair.

JWL & KP: For the book, we approach the notion of photographic ubiquity not as a given but as a kind of orthodoxy from the technical beginnings of what you identify as device-based photography in 1839, through the era of Kodak to the age of the internet; that is, an idea with a history. This is akin to a term you deploy in your own work, *omnipresence*, as appearing everywhere, either in actuality or virtually so. In your approach to photography using political ontology, where does the notion of photography's universal presence belong? Would you say that the camera's ubiquity functions as a necessary condition for many of your interventions, or are there other ways to think through the problem of photography's seeming everywhereness? As an example, in researching the history of the term "ubiquity," we came across something we hadn't expected: the term "ubiquity" once named a quality of the sovereign. On the one hand, the sovereign monarch can possess a kind of fictive ubiquity, as though they were "in a manner everywhere" (1708), present and effective in all courts of justice even when not physically present. On the other hand, as an 1841 Supreme Court decision puts it, the United States has "no particular place" but instead can be seen to possess "an ubiquity throughout the Union." ("Ubiquity," 2021) It seemed to us that these now historical uses of ubiquity very much speak to your notion of imperial rights and that they also speak to forces at odds with what you call "worldly sovereignty." We found ourselves wondering what you might make of this notion of presence and power unbound, both in connection to photography and beyond. Is it possible, for instance, for freedom to be "in a manner everywhere"?

AAA: There is something troubling about this kind of common chronology of photography as a realm apart—as if there are given points on the timeline—the invention of the device, the Kodak, digital, etc.—and scholars are expected to turn the transition between them into a smooth one. The organized crime of plundering the visual wealth of non-white and non-Christian cultures was already in motion when the

French announced the birth of photography in 1839. The Napoleonic invasion of Egypt at the turn of the 19th century, as well as the colonization of Algeria in 1830, consisted of the destruction of existing forms of sharing the world and their forced replacement with an infrastructure of extraction that facilitated the implementation of a regime of plunder that targeted natural and cultural treasures and with the help of battalions of French draftsmen, engineers, linguists, and other experts produced a visual wealth based on local resources and labor. Photography was praised and advocated in the French Academy of Science as an instrument that could improve and extend this robbery (Arago, in Siegel, 2017: 235; Azoulay, 2019, 2–5). What was achieved—with much violence—through previous expeditions is that everything of the invaded cultures could be taken and *taken in a photograph*, and the imperial ontology of photographs indoctrinated people with the idea that photographs carry an innate archival value that records and testifies to a past; this is the demiurgic power of an *imperial shutter* to relegate the now into a past. So while it is true that from 1839 on, the propagation of photographic devices had increased constantly (as it is often reflected in this kind of timeline that consists of such different milestones in the development of the device and its features), we have to put at the center the fact that this ubiquity of the device is the outcome of a campaign of destruction in which racial capitalism has invested since its inception and of a violent proclamation that all local and previous taxonomies, prohibitions, and rights are obsolete. *Potential History* rejects this normative dissociation of photography from its entanglement with other imperial and racial capitalist technologies and its fabrication as a sui generis idea and practice.

JWL & KP: The imagined origins of photography in 1492 is one of the more provocative claims that presents a demonstration of the practice of unlearning imperialism. Relatedly, we're struck by the centrality of the camera shutter as a tool of imperial violence that pierces space, time, and the body politic; it is "a synecdoche for the operation of the imperial enterprise altogether, on which the invention of photography, as well as other technological media, was modeled." (Azoulay, 2019: 2) Your demand becomes all the more apparent toward the end of the book, where you write "To call for reparations is to hold the shutters open." (580) We're struck by how *anachronism* is central to these claims, and how these claims might provoke the ire of conventional historians who posit that the world's first cameras were introduced to the public in 1839, and who might counter that, for the first forty years of camera technology, photographers commonly operated cameras without shutters. How do you see anachronism figuring into the project of potentializing photography's history, challenging the persistence of revisionist histories that don't go far enough?

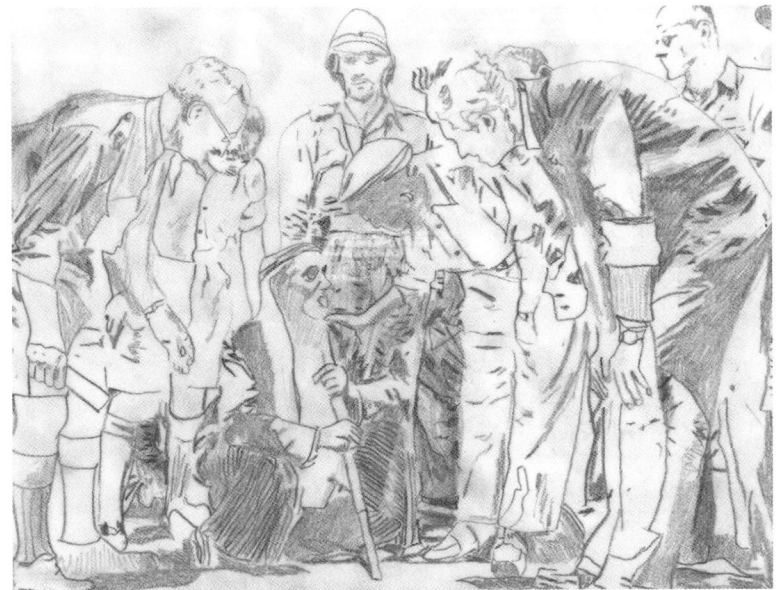

Figure 13.1

Unshowable photograph: a Palestinian refusing to be expelled. "He is neither a prisoner of war nor a refugee as he is depicted in the archive but was my companion in writing *Potential History*" (AAA).

AAA: That in the first decades since their invention, cameras operated without the mechanical device of the shutter, doesn't mean that cameras were not premised on the operation of what I describe in the book as the imperial shutter. As I have explained in my previous reply, *Potential History* is also a kind of manifesto against the discipline of history, whose raison d'être is the existence of a past of which historians become experts. Becoming experts of "the past" means operating in a different time frame than that in which those studied by the historians exist and act. Hence, historians can write about imperial violence without being motivated by or committed to join those about whom they write in opposing the normalization of its consequences and in calling for the repair of the wounds that it creates. *Potential History* is invested in studying the roots of violence in order to join the many struggles against its naturalization, based on the assumption that none of these struggles is over. Here is an example of a deliberate "anachronistic" gesture: a refusal to study photographs of the expulsion of Palestinians in 1948 as if what I'm looking at happened in the past; a refusal to inhabit the position of the historian authorized to study a person who is being expelled from his homeland as if he is a subject of research rather than a political actor; a refusal to participate in relegating his struggle to the past, as if the declaration of the state of Israel turned this struggle against its creation irrelevant. (fig. 13.1) This also means that *all* photographs taken in the settler colonial state that was imposed on Palestine should be read in continuity with this photograph, in the span of seventy-something years during which he struggled not to be expelled from Palestine.

JWL & KP: You have a vivid sense of what form a general strike in photography might take, particularly with regard to photojournalism. You also demonstrate certain kinds of tactics of refusal throughout *Potential History*, both in your writing and in your use of illustrations, many of which are drawn from photographs rather than standard reproductions of photographs that come with image rights. Recently, you've written about Tamara Lanier's legal challenge against the Peabody Museum, which holds in its possession a 170-year-old daguerreotype depicting Lanier's enslaved ancestor Renty Taylor (Azoulay, "Free Renty," 2020). This person was photographed against his will by J. T. Zealy and under the direction of Harvard professor Louis Agassiz, a scientist seeking to visually demonstrate his belief in white supremacy. In this sense, historical photographs have a major role to play in defining and redefining reparations. How might those who study photography and related visual cultures contribute to a general strike and take part in establishing anti-imperial conditions for photography? We're wondering, for instance, whether the enactment of a strike might look very different for scholars who use historical photographs and archives, and for those who write on (and might themselves work in) social media and internet culture, particularly in an era of widespread surveillance and public protest.

AAA: Every strike is somehow different, and I would especially refrain from reifying such differences along the lines of the differences between historical or current images. The question is how to depart from the imperial organization of knowledge that anchors our activities on the specificity of genres or media and rather anchor them in principles of overdue justice, and cultivate a commitment to undoing imperial and racial regimes of violence while replacing the principles on which different technologies operate. The example of Tamara Lanier's lawsuit is extremely relevant here. (fig. 13.2) Allegedly, it is about a historical image taken during the time of slavery. As is well known and as Lanier's lawsuit emphasizes explicitly, slavery's institutions were never abolished. The proof is in how Harvard University and the Peabody Museum continue to hold an image that was seized from Taylor, and in the arguments that they provide to justify why they should continue to hold it, arguments that, for many ears, sound convincing. This is the direct effect of the policing logic of tools such as "anachronism" that seek to introduce binding distinctions through timelines,

Figure 13.2

Shonrael Lanier, #FreeRenty, 2020.

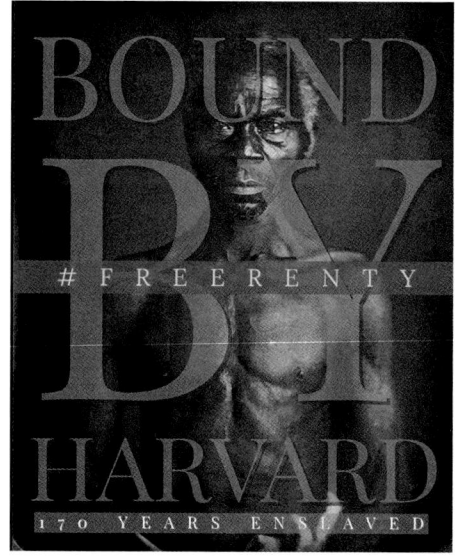

　　　Ubiquity: Photography's Multitudes

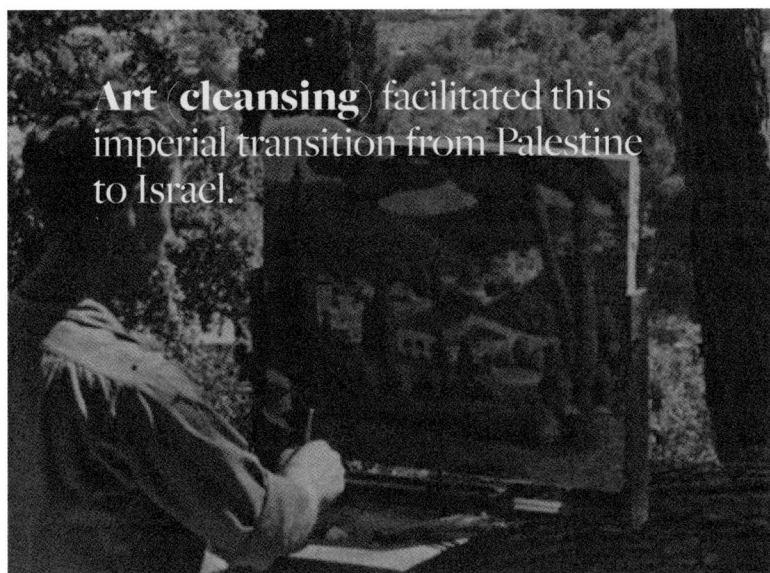

Art (cleansing) facilitated this imperial transition from Palestine to Israel.

Figure 13.3

Ariella Aïsha Azoulay, "Modernity is an Imperial Crime" (still), Strike MoMA, 2021, https://www.strikemoma.org/week-3

media specificity, or geographies, and in so doing prevent us from maintaining our commitment in its right place where repair, redress, and abolition of structures that obfuscate emerge as urgent and necessary. However, what is at stake with this lawsuit, beyond the explicit desired outcome—restitution—could have far more substantial implications on the existing infrastructures that enabled the accumulation of visual wealth and its use against people from whom it was expropriated. Hypothetically, if Lanier wins, it means not only the restitution of the object to Taylor's descendants but also its expropriation from the institution in which slavery still survives, alongside the refusal of institutional authority and standing to continue to possess what they seized through the institutionalized violence of private property. Strike MoMA is one of the important movements that strikes against the entanglement of art institutions with military and carceral technologies, and broadly speaking, with the genocidal campaigns of violence in different places in the world. This movement holds the space for "interconnected struggles" to come together and to understand that, from Puerto Rico to Palestine, this is a shared struggle that goes through institutions that were created to protect private property over people and to do so in the name of the public. I contributed two video lectures to the activity of Strike MoMA. The first, in collaboration with the artist AGF aka poemproducer, is titled "Modernity is an Imperial Crime." (fig. 13.3) The second, with Jina Alhenawi, is titled "Abolish MoMA: The Case of Palestine." It targets the role of art in the ethnic cleansing of Palestine. Both are available on the Strike MoMA website (weeks 3 and 10).[3]

Notes

1. Ariella Aïsha Azoulay, "Imperial Rights and the Origins of Photography," keynote lecture for Ubiquity: Photography's Multitudes, a two-day symposium at the Humanities Center, University of Rochester (April 26, 2018).

2. See the exhibitions *Act of State: 1967–2007* (Minshar Gallery, Tel Aviv, 2007; Internazionale, Ferrara, 2008; Constitution Hill, Johannesburg, 2009; Centre de la Photographie, Geneva, 2010; La Vareina, Barcelona, 2010; Mediations Biennale, Poznan, 2010; Foam, Amsterdam, 2010) and *From Palestine to Israel: A Photographic Record of Destruction and State Formation, 1947–1950* (The Mosaic Rooms, A.M. Qattan Foundation, London, 2011). The *Act of State* archive is now held in the Centre Pompidou, Paris.

3. See "Modernity is an Imperial Crime," http://www.strikemoma.org/week-3, and "Abolish MoMA: The Case of Palestine," http://www.strikemoma.org/week-10.

Bibliography

Dominique François Arago, "The Report (1839)," in *First Exposures: Writings from the Beginning of Photography*, ed. Steffen Siegel (Los Angeles: The J. Paul Getty Museum, 2017), 230–240.

Ariella Aïsha Azoulay, "Open Letter to Sylvia Wynter: Unlearning the Disappearance of Jews from Africa," *The Funambulist*, 30 (July–August 2020), https://thefunambulist.net/magazine/reparations/open-letter-to-sylvia-wynter-unlearning-the-disappearance-of-jews-from-africa-by-ariella-aisha-azoulay (accessed June 9, 2021).

Ariella Aïsha Azoulay, "Free Renty! Reparations, Photography, and the Imperial Premise of Scholarship," *Hyperallergic* (March 2, 2020), https://hyperallergic.com/545667/free-renty (accessed June 9, 2021).

Ariella Aïsha Azoulay, *Potential History: Unlearning Imperialism* (London: Verso, 2019).

Ariella Azoulay, *Civil Imagination: The Political Ontology of Photography* (London: Verso, 2012).

Ariella Azoulay, *From Palestine to Israel: A Photographic Record of Destruction and State Formation, 1947–1950* (London: Pluto Press, 2011).

Ariella Azoulay, *The Civil Contract of Photography* (New York: Zone Books, 2008).

"Ubiquity," *Oxford English Dictionary*, September 2021, Oxford University Press, https://www.oed.com/view/Entry/208517 (accessed September 9, 2021).

Plates

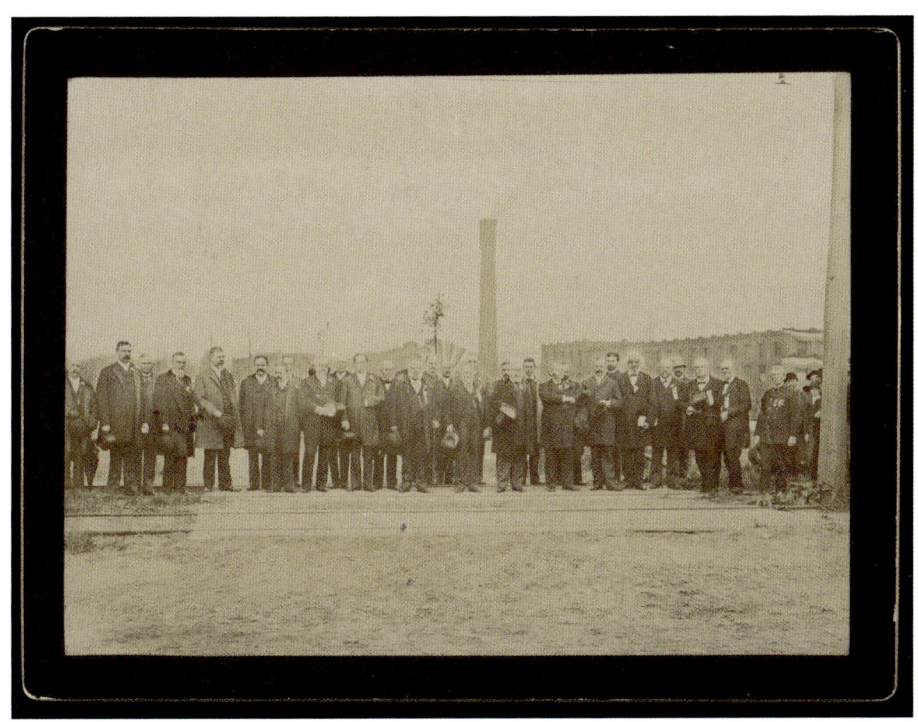

Plate 1

Souvenir photograph of guests, including Frederick Douglass, at President Harrison's visit to Kodak Park, Memorial Day, 1892, Frederick Douglass papers, A.D74, Rare Books, Special Collections, and Preservation, River Campus Libraries, University of Rochester. Courtesy of Rare Books, Special Collections, and Preservation, River Campus Libraries, University of Rochester.

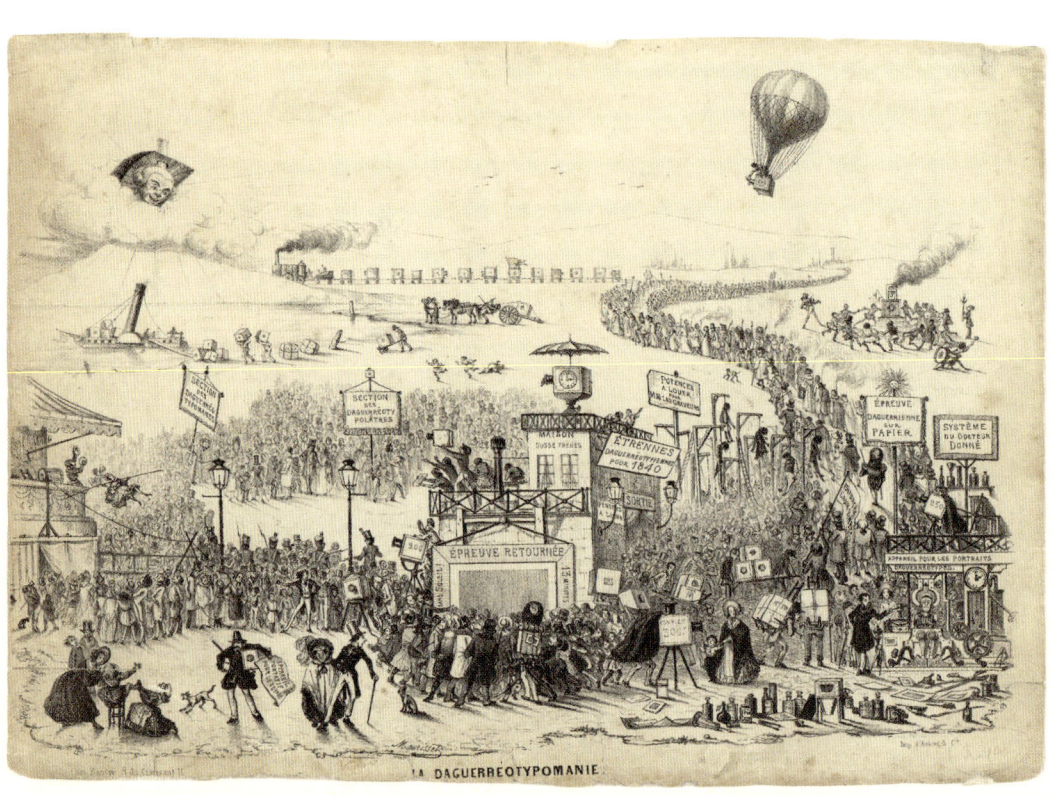

LA DAGUERRÉOTYPOMANIE.

Plate 2

Théodore Maurisset, *La Daguerreotypomanie (Daguerreotypomania)*, December 1839.
Lithograph, 26 × 35.7 cm, J. Paul Getty Museum.

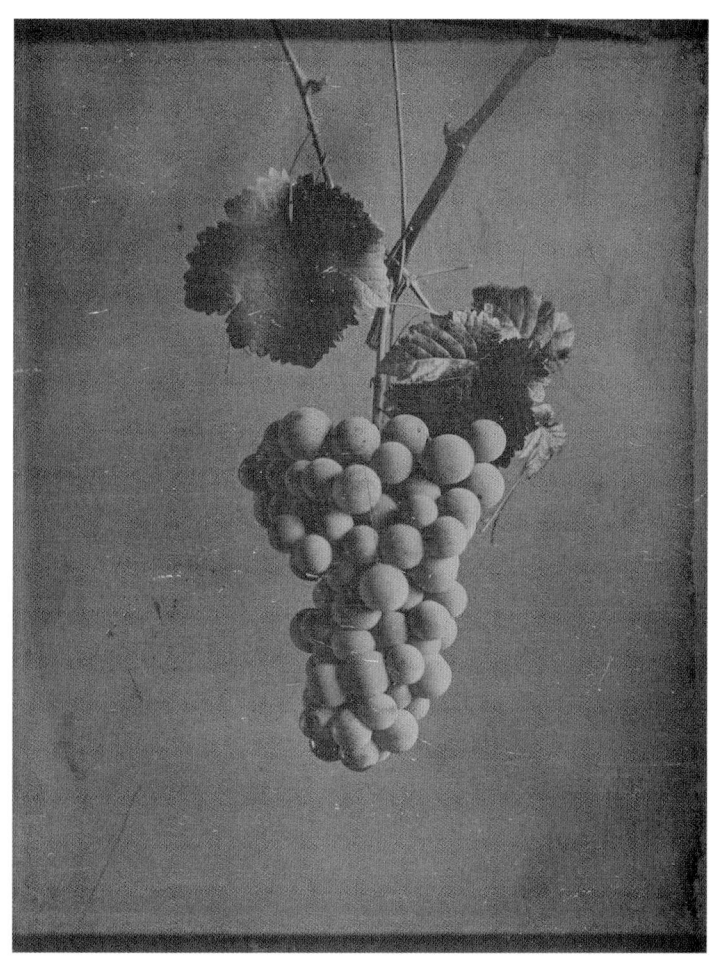

Plate 3

Léon Foucault, *Bunch of Grapes [Grappes de raisins]*, c. 1844. Daguerreotype, ¼ plate, 12×8.8 cm.
Collection Société Française de Photographie.

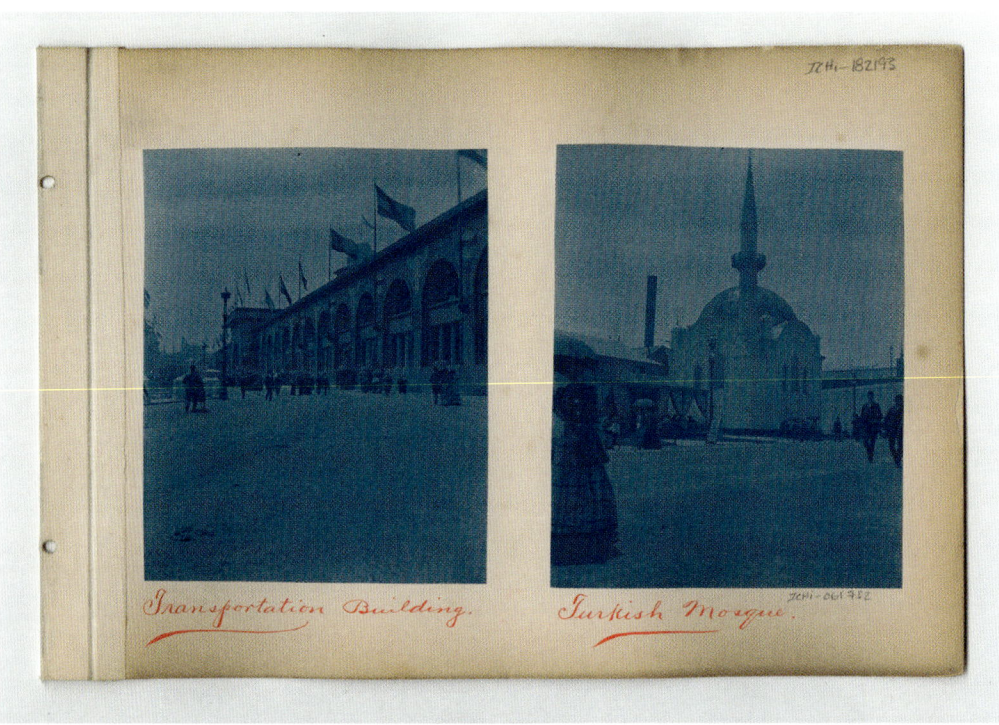

Plate 4

Page from an album of photographs, mostly cyanotypes, taken by Jos. E. Hartman at the Chicago World's Fair on June 15, 1893. Chicago History Museum.

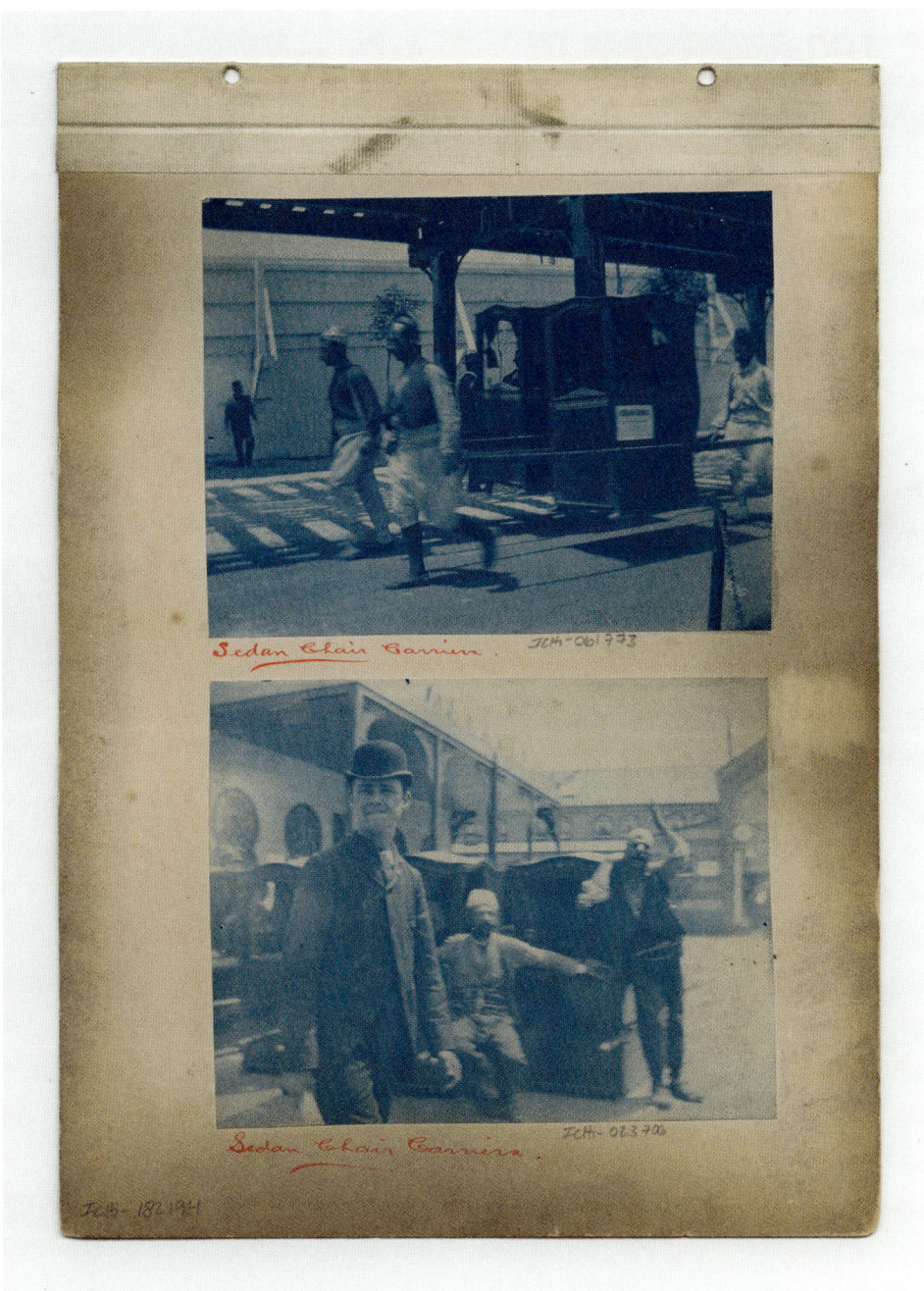

Plate 5
Page from an album of photographs, mostly cyanotypes, taken by Jos. E. Hartman at the Chicago World's Fair on June 15, 1893. Chicago History Museum.

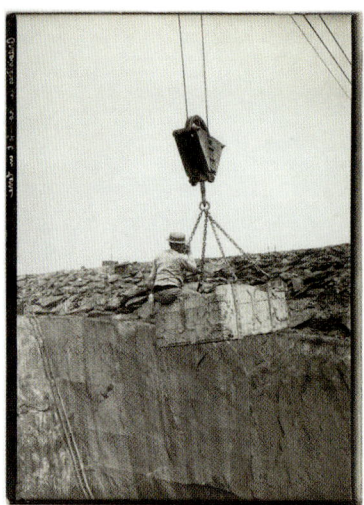

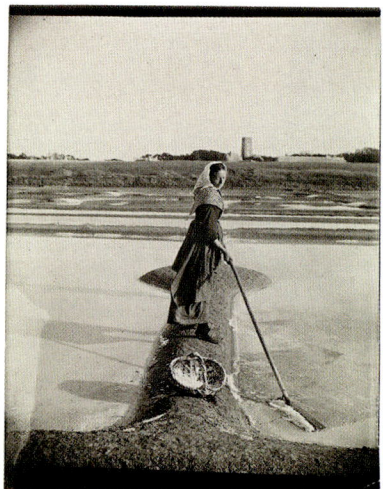

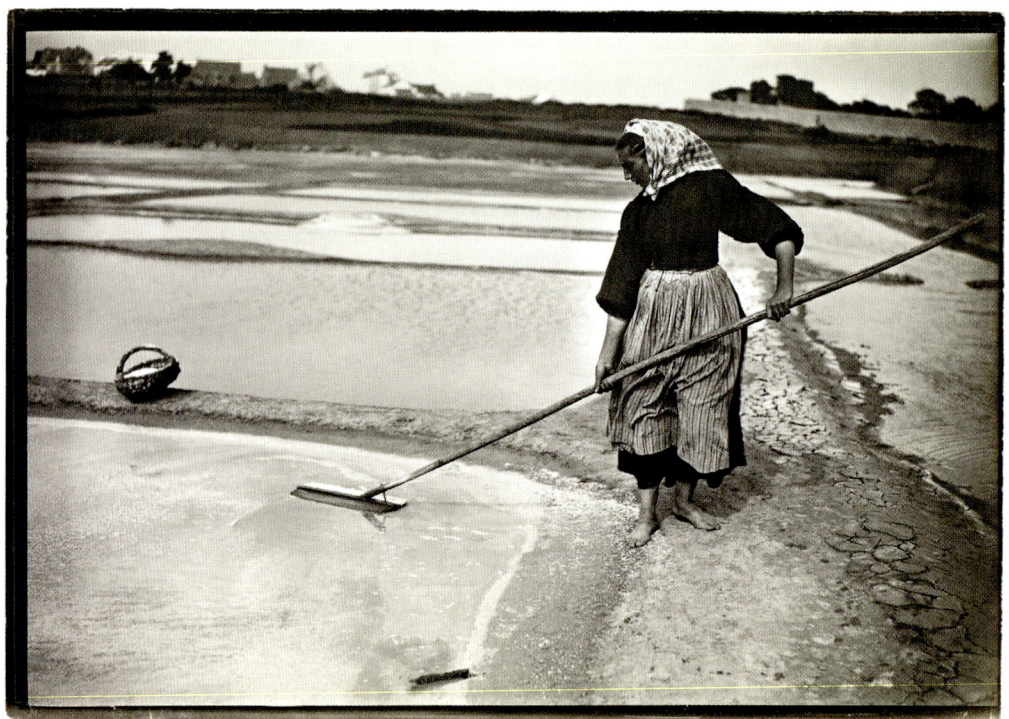

Plate 6.1 (Above left)

Paul Géniaux, *Ardoisières de Rochefort-en-Terre (Slate Quarries in Rochefort-sur-Terre)*, ca. 1910. Paper photograph, Musée de Bretagne, Rennes.

Plate 6.2, 6.3 (Above right; below)

Paul Géniaux, *Marais salants de Billiers prise de la fleur de sel (Salt marshes of Billiers, harvesting fleur de sel)*, ca. 1900. Gelatin silver print, Musée de Bretagne, Rennes.

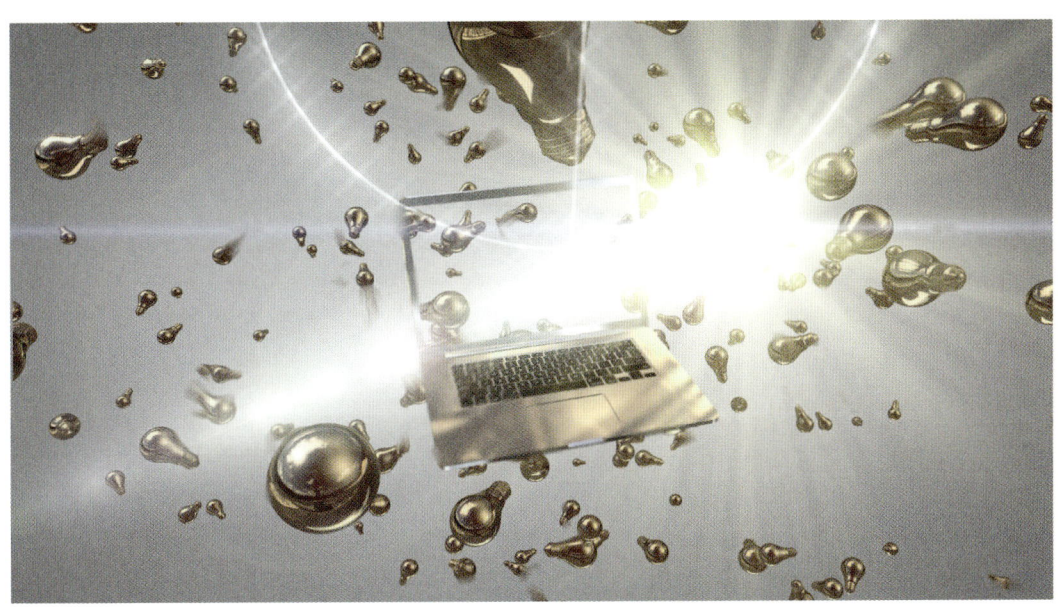

Plate 7

Hito Steyerl, *Factory of the Sun,* 2015. Single-channel high-definition video, environment, luminescent LED grid, beach chairs, 23 minutes. Image CC 4.0, Hito Steyerl. Courtesy of the artist; Andrew Kreps Gallery, New York; and Esther Schipper, Berlin.

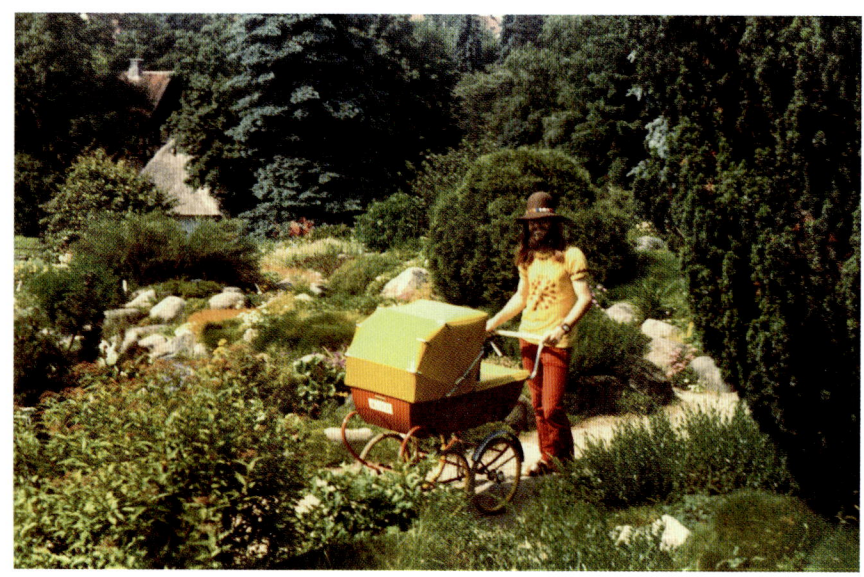

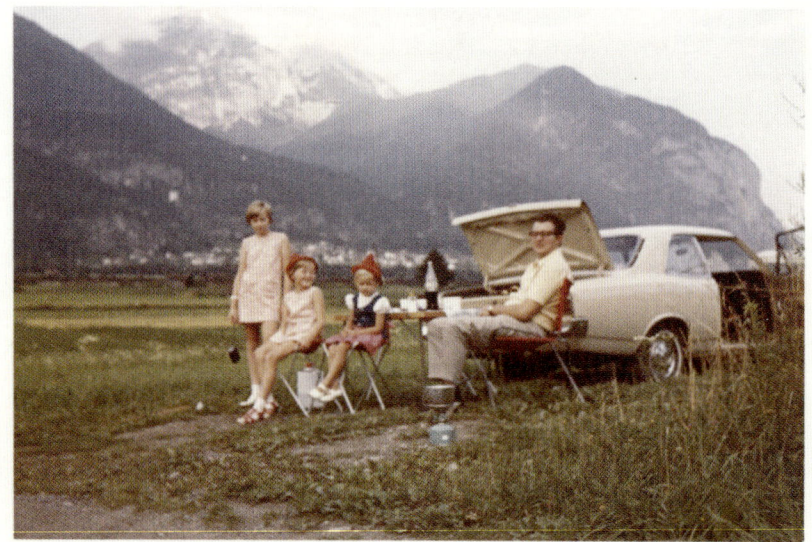

Plate 8.1 (Above)

Anonymous, Theme Family: "Father matching the baby carriage," Denmark, 1972.

Plate 8.2 (Below)

Anonymous, Theme Holiday: "Car trip to Austria," Denmark, 1972.

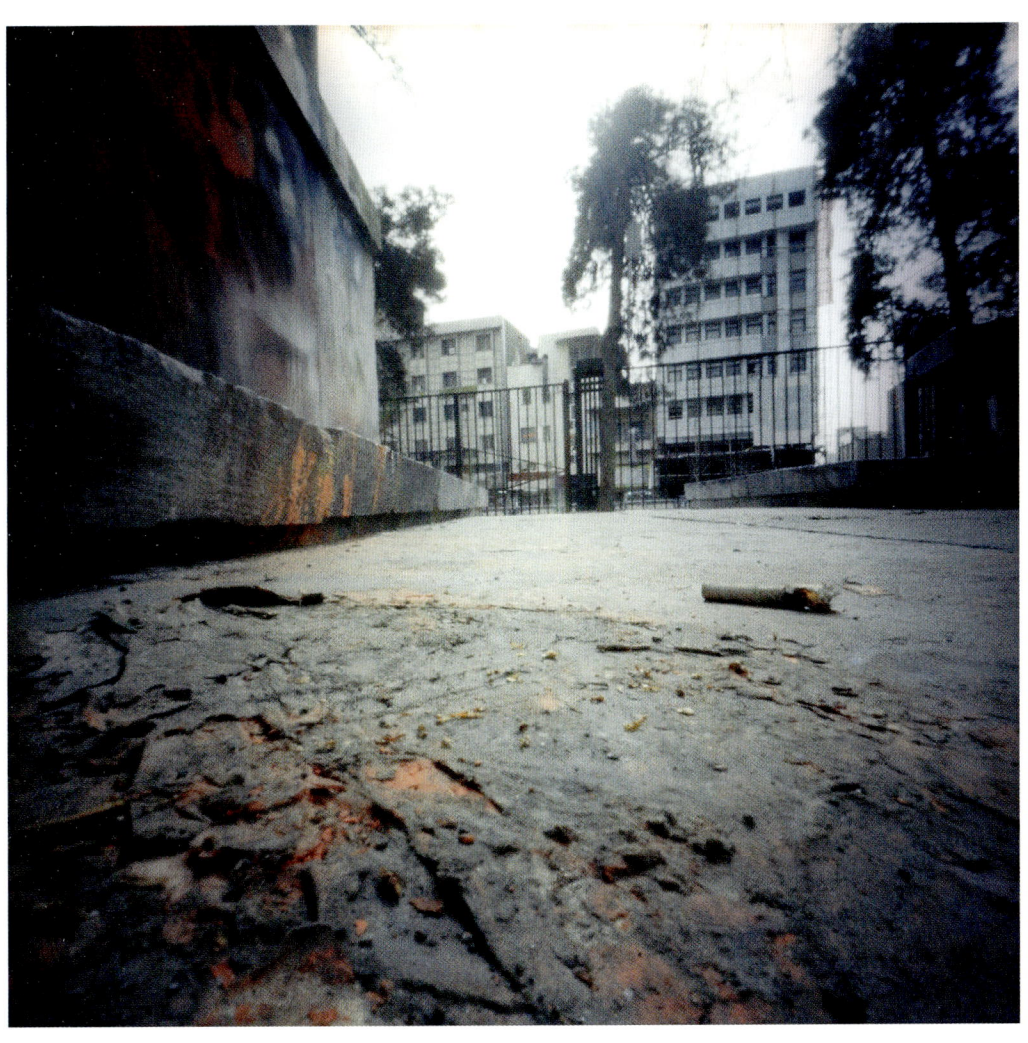

Plate 9

Mehran Mohajer, *Tehran, Undated*, 2008. Pigmented inkjet print on fine art paper, 76 cm×76 cm. Courtesy of the artist.

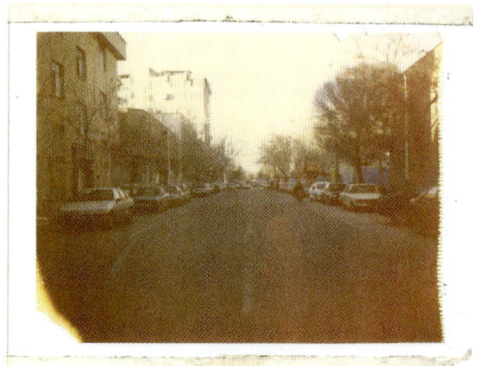
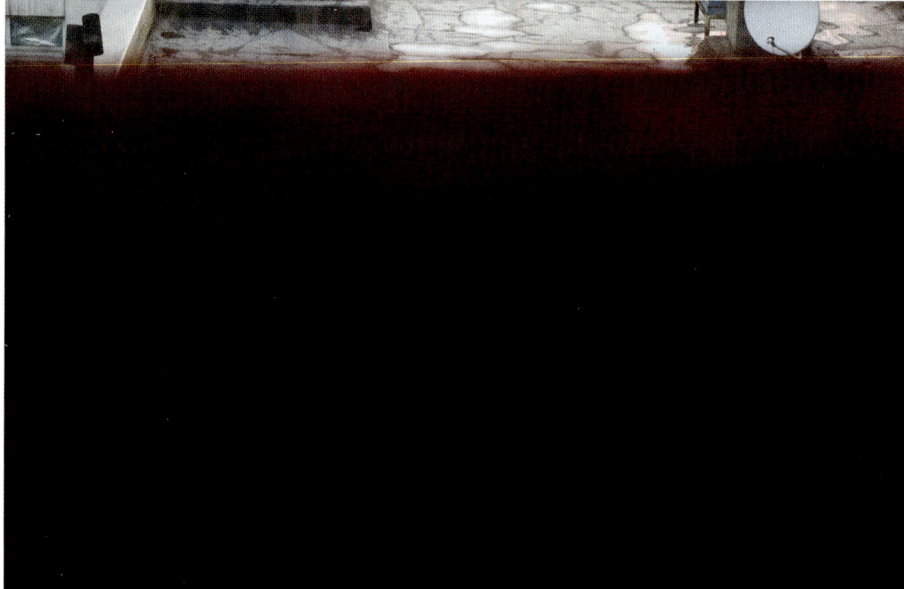

Plate 10.1 (Above left)

Sasan Abri, *Conjunctivitis*, 2012. Pigmented inkjet print, 86 cm×84 cm. Courtesy of the artist.

Plate 10.2 (Above right)

Mohammad Ghazali, *Tehran a Little to the Right*, 2010–2013. Expired Polaroid film, 8.5 cm×10.5 cm. Courtesy of the artist.

Plate 10.3 (Below)

Mehran Mohajer, *Closed*, 2013. Pigmented inkjet print on fine art paper, 60×90 cm. Courtesy of the artist.

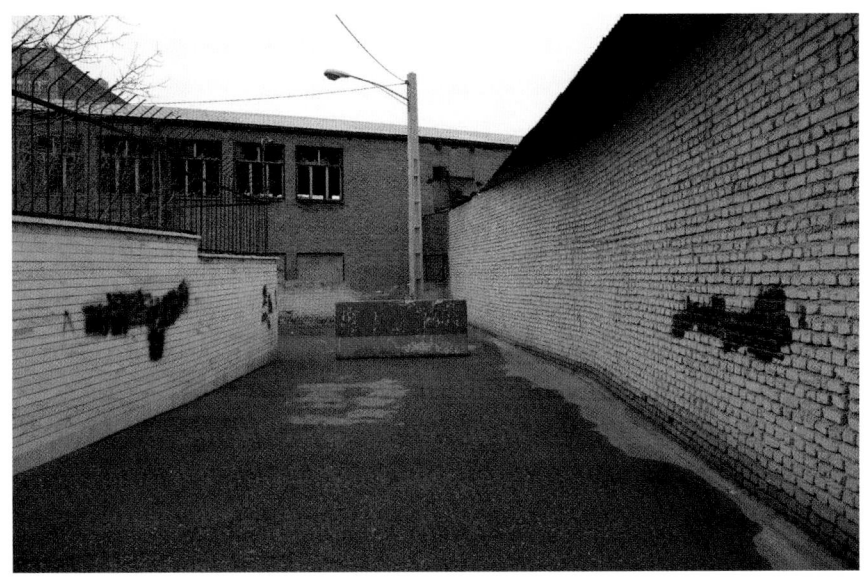

Plate 11

Ehsan Barati, *The Other City*, 2012–2013. Pigmented inkjet print on enhanced matte paper, 70 cm×100 cm. Courtesy of the artist.

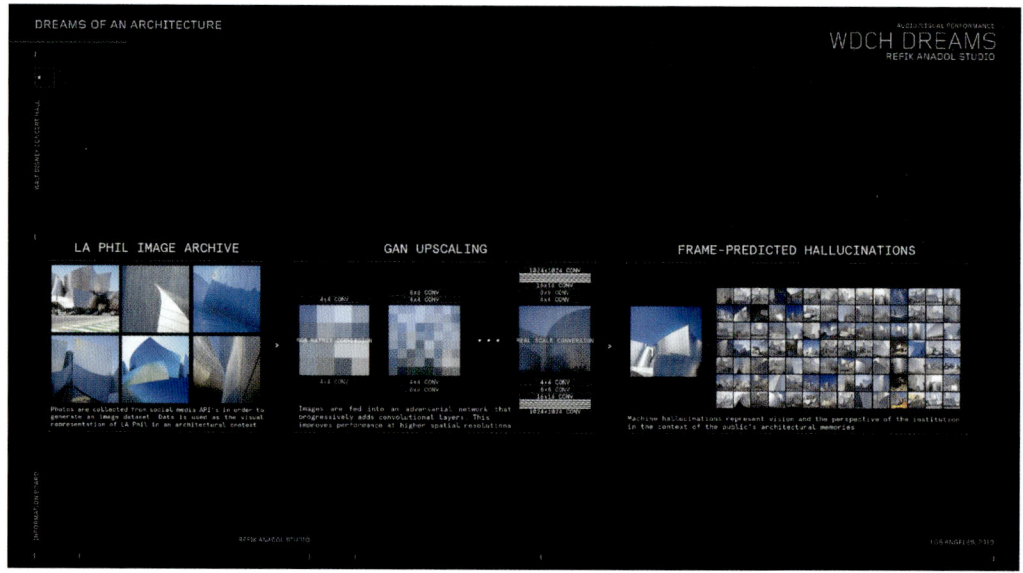

Plate 12

Refik Anadol, *WDCH Dreams* (presentation detail), 2018. Multi-projection site-specific video installation, 12-minute loop. Courtesy of the artist.

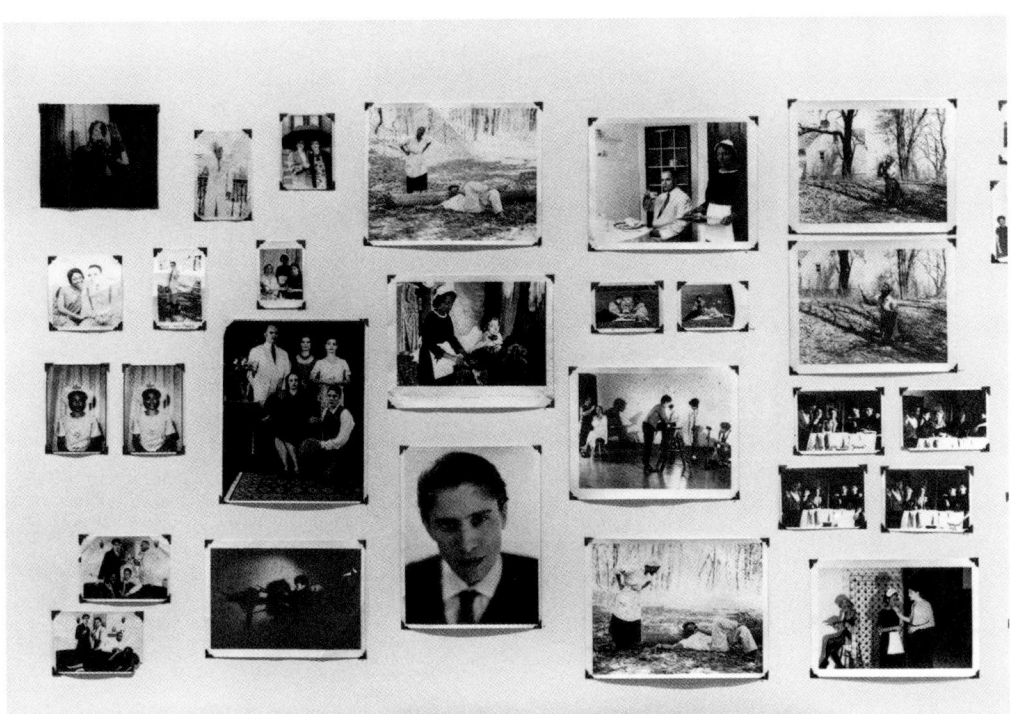

Plate 13

Zoe Leonard, *The Fae Richards Photo Archive* (detail), 1993–1996. 78 black-and-white photographs, 4 color photographs, 6 pages of typed text on typewriter paper, dimensions variable. Installation view, 1997 Whitney Biennial, Whitney Museum of American Art, New York. © Zoe Leonard. Courtesy of the artist; Galerie Gisela Capitain, Cologne; and Hauser & Wirth, New York.

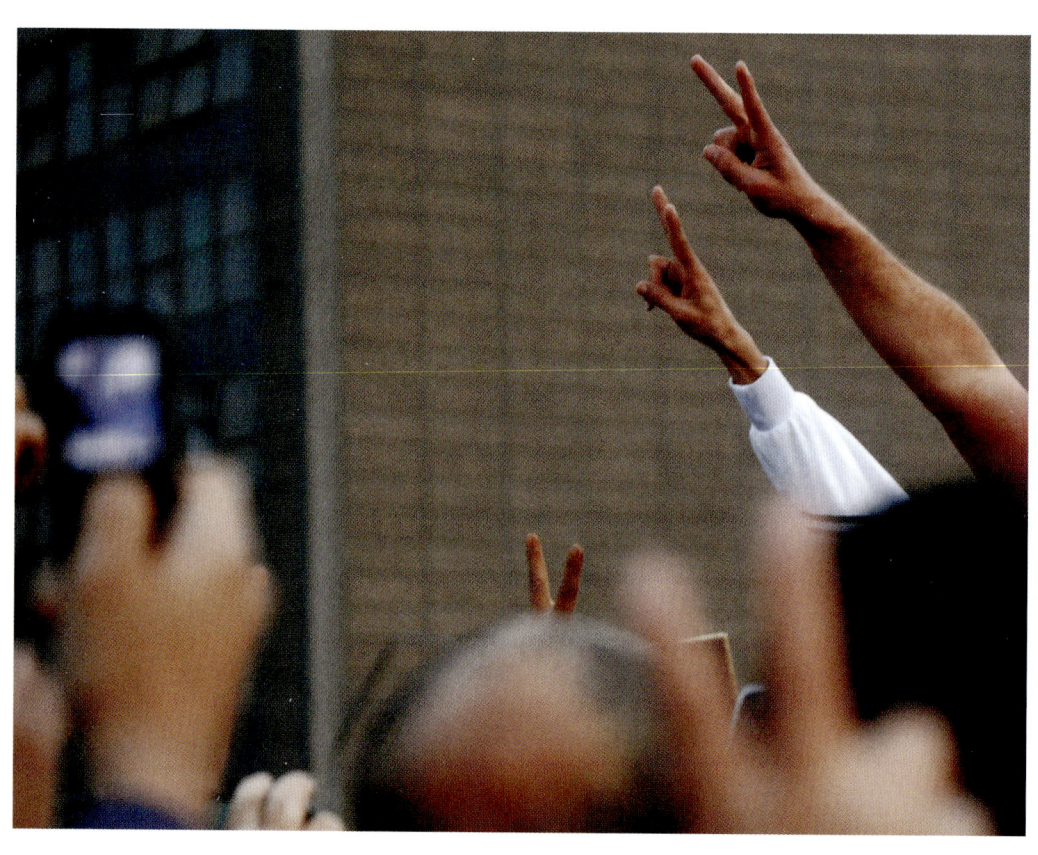

Plate 14
Mariam Soliman, "'We Want It Peaceful!'," February 9, 2011. Licensed under CC BY-SA 2.0.

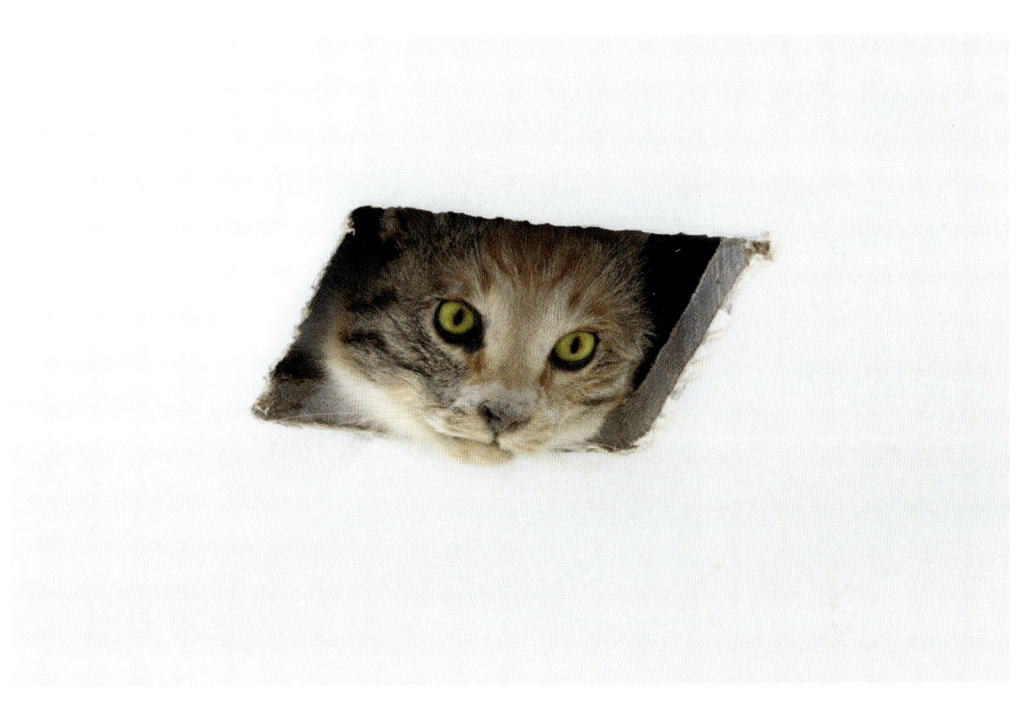

Plate 15

Eva Mattes and Franco Mattes, *Ceiling Cat*, 2016. Taxidermy cat, polyurethane resin, hole, San Francisco Museum of Modern Art, photograph by Katherine Du Tiel, CC0 1.0 Universal (CC0 1.0) Public Domain Dedication.

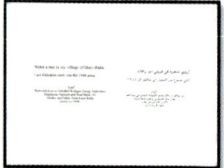

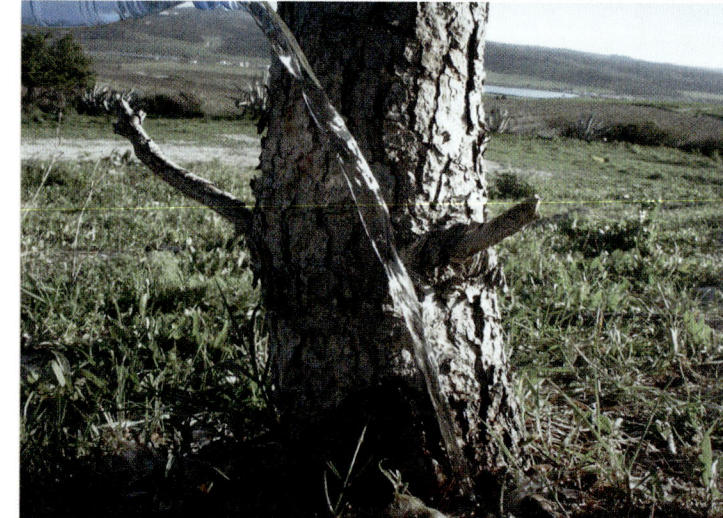

Plate 16

Emily Jacir, *Where We Come From (Iyad)* (detail), 2001–2003. American passport, 30 texts, 32 c-prints, and 1 video, dimensions variable. © Emily Jacir. Courtesy of San Francisco Museum of Modern Art.

Colophon

Every effort has been made to contact all holders of the copyright to the visual material contained in this publication. Any copyright-holders who believe that illustrations have been reproduced without their knowledge are asked to contact the Lieven Gevaert Research Centre for Photography, Art and Visual Culture.

Lieven Gevaert Research Centre for Photography, Art and Visual Culture
Arts Faculty KU Leuven
Blijde-Inkomststraat 21 box 3313
B-3000 Leuven
Belgium

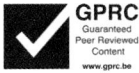

Published in 2021 by Leuven University Press / Presses Universitaires de Louvain / Universitaire Pers Leuven. Minderbroedersstraat 4, B-3000 Leuven (Belgium).

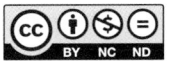
ISBN 978 94 6270 289 9 (Paperback)
ISBN 978 94 6166 402 0 (ePDF)
ISBN 978 94 6166 426 6 (ePUB)
https://doi.org/10.11116/9789461664020
D/2021/1869/49
NUR: 652
Lay-out and cover design: §DOGMA

Published with the support of the Arts Research Institute at the University of California, Santa Cruz; the KU Leuven Fund for Fair Open Access; and the Liz Warnock Publication Fund at Northwestern University.

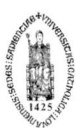 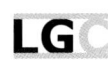

Previously published in the Lieven Gevaert Series